The Evolution of Agricultural Credit during China's Republican Era, 1912–1949

Hong Fu • Calum G. Turvey

The Evolution of Agricultural Credit during China's Republican Era, 1912–1949

palgrave
macmillan

Hong Fu
Shandong University of Finance
and Economics
Jinan, Shandong, China

Calum G. Turvey
Cornell University
Ithaca, NY, USA

ISBN 978-3-319-76800-7   ISBN 978-3-319-76801-4 (eBook)
https://doi.org/10.1007/978-3-319-76801-4

Library of Congress Control Number: 2018935191

© The Editor(s) (if applicable) and The Author(s) 2018
This work is subject to copyright. All rights are solely and exclusively licensed by the Publisher, whether the whole or part of the material is concerned, specifically the rights of translation, reprinting, reuse of illustrations, recitation, broadcasting, reproduction on microfilms or in any other physical way, and transmission or information storage and retrieval, electronic adaptation, computer software, or by similar or dissimilar methodology now known or hereafter developed.
The use of general descriptive names, registered names, trademarks, service marks, etc. in this publication does not imply, even in the absence of a specific statement, that such names are exempt from the relevant protective laws and regulations and therefore free for general use.
The publisher, the authors, and the editors are safe to assume that the advice and information in this book are believed to be true and accurate at the date of publication. Neither the publisher nor the authors or the editors give a warranty, express or implied, with respect to the material contained herein or for any errors or omissions that may have been made. The publisher remains neutral with regard to jurisdictional claims in published maps and institutional affiliations.

Cover image © Don Bartell / Alamy Stock Photo
Cover design by Ran Shauli

Printed on acid-free paper

This Palgrave Macmillan imprint is published by the registered company Springer International Publishing AG part of Springer Nature.
The registered company address is: Gewerbestrasse 11, 6330 Cham, Switzerland

Preface

For sure the modern student of agricultural finance and rural credit in China, and the thousands of Chinese engaged in rural and agricultural credit in the modern era, might well be puzzled about the dizzying pace of reform and wonder how China's system of rural credit evolved to its current state in the first place. Indeed, this is what has led us to prepare this book. The story of rural credit in China is evolutionary but few scholars in the modern era have paid attention to developments in agricultural credit before 1949. It is a story of poverty and inefficiency across China's agricultural economy, and the realization that for China to become a force in the world economy, it needed to strengthen its agricultural and industrial base and modernize its financial institutions. Throughout the Republican era, 1912–49 natural disasters, political tumult, warlords and banditry, the rise of communism, the Northern Expedition, and Japanese imperialism all conspired against China's agricultural, industrial and financial development. To even attempt to understand agricultural credit under these conditions was futile. There were simply too many moving parts with adversity after adversity springing up here and there in an endless pattern of economic subterfuge.

The authors of this book met in Zhejiang in 2015 at a conference of agricultural economists. Hong (Holly) Fu, an associate professor at Shandong University of Finance and Economics in Jinan, was interested in visiting Cornell University in 2016 to study agricultural credit and insurance with the second author Calum Turvey, who by then had written extensively on the subject. We decided to meet in Zhejiang to discuss research collaboration, where we discovered a mutual interest in Chinese agricultural credit history. Turvey had begun investigating credit history while working on an analysis of credit demand using newly discovered data that John Lossing Buck used in his famous 1937 book *Land Utilization in China*. That John Lossing Buck was the husband of Pearl S. Buck, the 1937 Nobel Laureate in Literature for her book *The Good Earth*, and that both Bucks were Cornell Alumni, made this story even more intriguing. Since at least 2014 Turvey had been pouring over history books and news reports from *China Weekly Review* to make sense of credit conditions during Buck's 1929–33 study period. To a foreigner, trained as an agricultural economist, and specializing in agricultural finance, this was a futile attempt at entering even the lowest rungs of sinology. But in a remarkable turn of events, our conversation in Zhejiang wandered away from modern day agricultural finance and insurance, to other matters, and it was then that Holly explained that her background was not in agricultural insurance or even modern day finance, but that her PhD dissertation at Nankai University department of finance was on the history of agricultural credit during the Republican era, and that she had published a book in Chinese on the subject. This was an astonishing coincidence, and it was decided that when Holly travelled to Ithaca we would dabble in history, while doing some work on finance and insurance. We did no work on finance and insurance. Instead, Holly was drawn into the research on agricultural credit demand using Buck's data, providing some translations from her book. We then expanded our scope to the document archives in the Asian Collection at Cornell University libraries and the National Archives at Beijing and Nanjing. Soon, simple questions became complex. Chapters 2 and 3 for example came about when Turvey rhetorically asked how conditions in 1921 agriculture could be so bad. Holly recalled a paper she once read on high-level equilibrium traps by Mark Elvin, so with no background in growth theory to start, we finished with a model describing fractional poverty traps. Likewise, with a rhetorical question about how agriculture survived in Japanese controlled areas, Holly pointed to the Luxi Bank in Shandong that issued its own currency in communist-held base areas. This gave us Chap. 11. And so it went until we decided that we should produce this book which Palgrave Macmillan decided to publish.

In preparing the book we should warn the reader, as one of the book reviewers warned us, that we are better economists than we are sinologists. This is correct. We are not trained as historians, nor can we be called sinologists. For example, why would we place such heavy reliance on Reverend DuHalde, or Malthus or Ricardo in Chaps. 2 and 3 when there might be much better descriptions of history prepared by modern historians? The reason was to note when these works were written; that these writers were describing contemporaneous conditions as they observed them at that time and we preferred the original source for effect. Nonetheless, we have adhered to the same documentation principles and style as many of the historians that we read, while also adhering to the documentation principles and style of agricultural economists. As we discuss below, we have opted for narrative rather than mathematics or economic theory with only a few departures.

As for form, we have used the modern terms for names and places, even though there are still many spellings used such as Sichuan versus Szechuan, Xi'an versus Xian and so on. Where we are not sure we italicize the name or place with its original spelling. On weights and measures we use modern units as best we can, but for traditional Chinese terms we use endnotes to describe the measures. Here and there we include the original Chinese characters when there is some dispute over their direct translation or when they might have multiple meanings. Hopefully, if we ever erred in translation, we are correct in context.

Our opening chapter discusses agricultural credit in the modern era and its developments since the end of the Mao era with the 1978 reforms. The history of agricultural credit between 1950 and 1978 has also not been told, but we do make a link between our story up to 1949 and the agricultural credit reforms of the past 40 years. Things are changing so quick that we could probably prepare a book entirely on this era, so what we provide is at best a synopsis of current conditions. This includes Rural Credit Cooperatives, the Agricultural Bank of China, the path to reforms after the turn of the century, agricultural credit conditions, the role of credit in inclusive rural transformation, and the expansion of Village Banks, joint stock banks, the conversion of Rural Credit Cooperatives to Rural Credit Banks, lending only companies and so on. We provide several appendices to Chap. 1 that include time series on agricultural credit from 1978 through 2016. We thank Hexian Wang, a MSc student at Cornell University for compiling this data from archival sources, gazetteers, and obscure statistical reports. We think this may be of use to modern students and scholars of agricultural credit as we are unaware of any data records of this sort published elsewhere.

As for the remainder of the book, understanding China's approach to rural credit in the Republican era requires an understanding of the conditions facing rural China over this period, and those times—as will be presented in detail—were very difficult with drought, floods, famine, bandits, communist insurgencies, KMT (Kuomintang) conflicts, Japanese expansionism, and other factors. Using primary data and papers written in contemporaneous time from both Chinese and English sources we piece together this story. We use the word 'story' with purpose. While our academic positions at Shandong University of Finance and Economics and Cornell University are rooted in agricultural and financial economics, we no doubt make economics as the focal point. But the economics makes little sense without fully understanding the conditions of rural credit prior to the end of the Qing in 1911, the disarray from the warlord period between 1912 and 1928, the era of reconstruction that followed the Northern expedition to unify China in 1928, Japanese aggression not only in Manchuria in 1930 and 1931, but the Sino-Japanese war from 1937 to 1945, and the war of independence between 1945 and 1949. Neither can we ignore the impacts of China's dynastic rule over the previous 4000 years. China, in 1921, may well have settled into a low-level equilibrium trap that bound the vast majority of Chinese farmers to conditions of poverty or sub-poverty. It is important to understand how China got to the state it was in 1921 when the International China Famine Relief Commission first proposed credit cooperatives as a means to extract farmers from persistent poverty. The alarm over rural conditions resulting from famine and floods requires some narrative on the frequency, intensity, and nature of the causes of famine and we include that as part of the story as well. Likewise, there are many personalities involved including Timothy Richards, an early advocate of international famine relief, and academics such as J.B. Tayler, John Lossing Buck, and Paul Hsu, and institutions such as Nanking University and Nankai University that were incredibly important in the push for rural credit, and deserve some space and discussion.

Although we wanted to present all this in story form, there are several places where we found no way around some mathematics to illustrate our point. We hope that our narrative is strong enough that this can be skipped by non-economists without losing the greater points made. In Chap. 2 we ask the question as to how China's agriculture got to the point it was in 1921. We elected to tell this story through the lens of equilibrium traps and take a Malthusian or neo-Malthusian approach relying on the early works of R. Nurkse, R.R. Nelson, M. Elvin, R. Sinha, and P. Huang among others. We incorporate Justin Y. Lin's ideas about the so-called 'Needham Trap' and extend the discussion even further to address the more recent attraction to the idea of poverty traps. In Chap. 2 we provide a softer discussion examining various aspects of dynastic rule and grading emperors on whether they were good for agriculture or bad for agriculture, and we examine the historical pattern in drought, flood, and famine, all with the same intent of trying to understand the state of agriculture and agricultural credit at the turn of the twentieth century. On examining the history in Chap. 2 and the economics of equilibrium and poverty traps in Chap. 3, we were not satisfied that we had enough of an explanation of how poverty traps happened. The equilibrium trap models are short-run models which might explain a state of poverty at a moment in time, but did not explain how such things could arise or persist. All the ingredients for an economic interpretation were in place except for the explicit consideration of risk as an exogenous force.

Thus, in Chap. 3 we tackled the problem of taking a classical model of population, land, productivity, and growth, and added to it certain stochastic processes, presenting a new, or at least modified, model of agricultural and population growth as an Ito process. Drawing on the limited data in Huang and Perkins we use Monte Carlo methods to simulate China's agricultural economy. Population growth, land limitations, and agricultural innovation all combine in a dynamic and uncertain way to affect the path of economic growth. For the most part we present the story graphically, and then explore, with some liberties, the effects of dynastic rule on agriculture and how calamities combined with dynastic rule might offer an explanation. From an economist point of view we felt that additional depth was required to merge our presentation with the modern stream of literature following from Malthus to equilibrium and poverty traps. So, we then went a step further and using certain properties of fractional Brownian motion, we provide measures of the Hurst coefficient and show that population growth and certain ratios such as output to population have fractional properties. There will never be enough real data to prove our assertion beyond the mathematical abstraction, but this is an important advance. Brent Swallow and Chris Barrett have argued recently that poverty traps are fractal. We illustrate this in a different, dynamic, and stochastic way. When measured as the expanse of time in which agricultural output falls below a certain level of subsistence, this is shown to be of a mean reverting form with periods of poverty so measured coming and going in Malthusian form as in a pattern of excursions. As stated, we did not intend when we started this book to end a chapter with a discourse on stochastic dynamic equations and fractional Brownian motion, but that is where the story led us, and we think this has advanced the discussions around population, land, and agricultural productivity in a meaningful way that might advance the study of low-level equilibrium and fractional poverty traps.

The only other chapter in which we use mathematics in a more than casual way is in Chap. 6 where we present some detailed econometric estimation of rural credit demand and supply using John Lossing Buck's individual household data which he used to compile his book *Land Use in China* in 1937. Around the year 2000 several cartons were discovered in Nanjing holding the original, handwritten, worksheets from Buck's study. Much credit goes to Professor Hua Hu and his students at Nanjing Agricultural University who spent hundreds of hours digitizing and collating the data before handing the spreadsheets to us for analysis, and meeting with Turvey and his Cornell students in Nanjing on several occasions. Dizi Chang and Ziang (June) Cheng, both Master of Science students at Cornell University, did a huge amount of the leg work and econometric estimation as part of their theses. This we believe is the first econometric analysis of credit demand during this period and represents original work. In order to investigate credit relationships between 1929 and 1933 we settled on a three-equation econometric model and for academic purposes felt we must present and discuss the model structure in economic and econometric terms. Again, we hope that we present to the casual reader without advanced understanding of demand elasticities and econometrics a readable narrative that gets to the points of historical significance without muddying the waters too much.

Leading up to this we discuss historical development in agricultural credit in Chap. 4 which we date back to 202 B.C. with the formation of granaries as a means of storage to smooth consumption and to make loans. This evolved into the Green Sprouts policy around 1058 A.D. which made loans to farmers at planting, to be repaid at harvest. We explore and present in detail a number of money-loan societies (*Qian Hui*), the ancient precursor to the modern day Rotating Savings and Credit Associations (ROSCA). These presented various forms of informal credit, including the beginnings of the pawn shop. We also present the origination of formal financial institutions in the form of Native Banks.

In Chap. 5 we explore the state of agricultural finance in the early Warlord period of the Republican era. We discuss there (and elsewhere in the book) the maddening currency and measures that described China at the time and the struggles to develop a modern financial system by the new governments. Notable in this period was the development of the Agricultural and Industrial Banks that were chartered not only to deal with agriculturally related businesses but also to promote credit associations and rural credit cooperatives. The Agricultural and Industrial Banks floundered in this goal, and had largely left the market by 1923, but by 1923 in the face of the 1921 famine a different economic force was pushing for agricultural credit.

In Chap. 7 we discuss the push for agricultural credit cooperatives by the International China Famine Relief Commission. This discussion includes a background to famine and a history of the International China Famine Relief Commission and its promotion of credit cooperatives. Based on the successful introduction of credit societies and cooperatives by the College of Agriculture at Nanking University, by the late 1920s and early 1930s cooperative credit societies were to be the backbone of agricultural finance in China. Chapters 8 and 9 discuss the formalization of credit cooperatives as promoted under Rural Reconstruction by the KMT and further development for a more centralized and national approach to agricultural credit via the so-called 'blueprint' which guided efforts, without too much success, between 1929 and 1933. Chapter 10 discusses more broadly the effects of these efforts on the growth of credit cooperatives, including the consequences and impacts of the Sino-Japanese war on cooperative development.

In terms of the war, we became curious as to how the communists in the border and base regions around and within Japanese-held territories provided credit access to farmers. In Chap. 14 we discuss the general impact of the war in greater detail, but early on we noted that many of the cooperative credit societies that were formed before the war had all but disappeared after the war started. Yet story after story appeared of robust agricultural economies within communist-held territories. In Chap. 11 we explore this issue. Using archival information and searching through gazetteers we were able to piece together an interesting story of currency and credit in base and border regions. Currency and credit worked hand in hand, but the idea that border currency could coexist with Chinese national currency and Japanese puppet currency provides an interesting backdrop to the credit story, and one perhaps not well known outside of Chinese academic circles.

China's efforts were not limited to cooperative credit. Central to the 'blueprint' was the formation of the Farmers Bank of China to which we dedicate Chap. 12. In Chap. 13 we discuss the 1936 initiative of *Nong Ben*

Ju which was implemented to consolidate the multi-thronged activities of the KMT towards agriculture including formalizing agricultural credit and integrating agricultural credit with the formal financial markets. The literal interpretation of *Nong Ben Ju* is 'Farm Credit Bureau' but we have opted to use the term in its programmatic sense of building institutions. We continue then with a discussion of the policies and debates that followed including discussions as to whether China should follow a system such as the cooperative Farm Credit System as developed in the United States.

Chapter 14 concludes the book. There we discuss in detail the effects of the war on agricultural credit. Here we rely on a study of Sichuan by Buck. But even despite the war, its effect on agriculture and agricultural productivity, hyperinflation and so on, the KMT continued to press forward with financial and credit reforms. These efforts were of course blunted by the ensuing civil war and collapse of the monetary system in 1948 and 1949, but the basic structure of agricultural credit cooperatives was retained as the embryo to the modern Rural Credit Cooperatives, and the basic design for policy banks such as the Agricultural Bank of China.

Finally, we have some acknowledgements. On the financial side we are grateful for the W.I. Myers Endowment fund assigned to Turvey's professorship. It is somewhat fitting that W.I. Myers was not only appointed by President Franklin D. Roosevelt as the first Governor of the Farm Credit System, but he was also the academic advisor to John Lossing Buck's Master of Science thesis from Cornell in 1923. We are also grateful for the receipt of a grant from Jeffrey Sean Lehman Fund for Scholarly Exchange with China, also awarded through Cornell University for providing the funds to travel and prepare this book and other upcoming works on this topic. We are also grateful to the Shandong Provincial Natural Science Foundation, China for giving us a chance to work together on rural credit and the International Cooperation Program for Excellent Scholars Grant from Shandong Provincial Education Department, which supported Hong's research at Cornell as a visiting scholar. Turvey also owes many Chinese colleagues a debt of gratitude. Professor Pei Guo at China Agricultural University introduced him to the world of rural credit in China in 2006. Pei, along with Professor Guangwen He from China Agricultural University and Jiujie Ma from Renmin University spent countless days traveling with him in rural areas. Professor Rong Kong of Northwest Agriculture and Forestry University has been indispensable in Turvey's research, organizing field research, providing graduate students, preparing and translating survey instruments, and coauthoring somewhere in the neighborhood of 20 scholarly journal articles together. Professor Xueping Xiong, Huazhong Agricultural University, worked with Turvey on understanding the problems of financial inclusion in China. Special thanks to Dr. Yanling Peng, who started working with us as a masters student, spent a year as a visiting student at Cornell University, and who is now an assistant professor at Sichuan Agricultural University. Also thanks to Tian (Katrina) Liu a doctoral student at China Agricultural University, who also visited Cornell as a student, provided some data, and provided very helpful comments on Chap. 1. Lastly we would like to thanks Allison Neuburger and Elizabeth Graber at Palgrave Macmillan for shepherding this book through the review and publication process.

Jinan, China
Ithaca, NY, USA

Hong Fu
Calum G. Turvey

Contents

1 Current Conditions of Rural Credit in China   1
  1.1 Introduction   1
      1.1.1 Financial Reform and Transition in China, 1978–2003   4
      1.1.2 Household Conditions and Credit in the Early Reform Era   8
  1.2 Joint Liability and Group Guarantees   11
  1.3 Administrative Independence of RCCs, 1996   12
  1.4 The Economic Rationale for Credit Policy   14
  1.5 The New Countryside Campaign of 2006   16
      1.5.1 Agricultural Development Bank of China (ADBC)   18
      1.5.2 Postal Savings Bank of China   22
      1.5.3 Rural Commercial and Rural Cooperative Banks   22
      1.5.4 Rural, Credit Only, Microcredit Companies   22
      1.5.5 County, and Township and Village Banks   23
      1.5.6 Mutual-Help Associations   24
  1.6 Private and Foreign Investment   25
  1.7 Outcomes of Credit Reforms 1978–2016   26
      1.7.1 RCC Loan Summary   27
      1.7.2 National Survey Results   29
      1.7.3 Credit Conditions of Farm Households   32
      1.7.4 Effects of Credit Policy on Credit Demand   34
  1.8 Macro Consequences of Credit Reforms 1978–2016   35
  1.9 Summary   37

2	**China's Sorrow**	**51**
2.1	Introduction	51
2.2	Affliction	52
2.3	Population Growth and Agricultural Productivity	55
2.4	The Malthusian Trap	61
2.5	Historical Weather Extremes and Agricultural Productivity in China	63
2.6	Agricultural Productivity	69
2.7	Political Economy and Dynastic Rule	70
2.8	Summary	77
3	**Low-Level Equilibrium and Fractional Poverty Traps**	**81**
3.1	Introduction	81
3.2	The Needham Puzzle	82
3.3	Low-Level Equilibrium Traps	87
3.4	High-level Equilibrium Traps	90
3.5	The Anthropological View	93
3.6	Equilibrium and Poverty Traps	95
3.7	Multiple Equilibria and Fractal Poverty Traps	98
3.8	A Stochastic-Dynamic Model for Low-Level/High-Level Equilibrium and Poverty Traps	99
	3.8.1 Population Dynamics	102
3.9	Agricultural Output	103
3.10	Technological Innovation and Output Uncertainty	104
3.11	Output Dynamics	104
3.12	Fractional Poverty Traps	108
3.13	Operationalizing the Simulation Model	109
3.14	Some Results from Monte Carlo Simulation	111
3.15	Fractional Poverty Traps	116
3.16	Summary	120
4	**Traditional Forms of Credit in Rural China**	**123**
4.1	Introduction	123
4.2	Granaries and Traditional Rural Credit	124
4.3	Ever-normal Granary (Chang Ping Cang) and Formal Credit	127
4.4	Charity Granaries (Yi Cang), Community Granaries, and Farmers' Mutual Aid System	128

4.5	Money-loan Society (Qian Hui) and Informal Traditional Rural Credit	131
	4.5.1 Green Sprouts Policy	132
	4.5.2 Money-loan Society (Qian Hui)	133
	4.5.3 Dice-throwing Society (Yao Hui)	135
	4.5.4 Amounts-increasing Society (Duiji Hui)	135
	4.5.5 Subscription-Decreasing Society (Suojin Hui)	138
	4.5.6 Rotating Society (Lun Hui)	139
	4.5.7 Bidding Society (Biao Hui)	141
	4.5.8 Pawn Shops (Dian Dang)	144
	4.5.9 Traditional Native Banks and Chinese Currencies: Piao Hao and Qian Zhuang	147
4.6	Mortgaging Land, Usufruct Rights and Merchant Credit	151
4.7	Lease Contracts	154
	4.7.1 The Manchurian Lease	155
	4.7.2 Changchun Lease Arrangements	158
	4.7.3 Between Landowners and CLCC	158
	4.7.4 Between Koreans and CLCC	159
4.8	Summary	160

5 Emergence of Modern Rural Financial Institutions in the Warlord Era: 1912–28 — 161

5.1	Introduction	161
5.2	Tariff Autonomy and the Likin Tax	162
5.3	Currency Chaos	164
5.4	The Beginnings of Financial Reform	166
5.5	The Warlord Era	168
5.6	Towards a Coherent System of Agricultural Credit	169
5.7	The Agricultural and Industrial Banks	170
5.8	Agricultural Credit Associations	172
5.9	Agricultural and Industrial Cooperative Loan Associations	174
5.10	The Chinese Postal Savings Bank	176
5.11	Summary	177

6 Estimating the Demand for Farm Credit in the Republican Era — 179

6.1	Introduction	179

6.2	Rediscovering Buck's Data	181
6.3	Summary of Buck's Rediscovered Data Used in Demand Analysis	183
6.4	Amount and Character of Farm Credit	187
6.5	Sources of Farm Credit	191
6.6	Uses of Credit and Special Expenditure	194
6.7	Livestock	196
6.8	Size of Farm Business	198
6.9	Agricultural Productivity	199
6.10	Yield Risk	202
6.11	Hired Labor and Subsidiary Labor	202
6.12	Time and Regional Variables	204
6.13	Estimation Method	210
6.14	Econometric Results: Who Is Borrowing?	213
6.15	Econometric Results: The Demand and Supply of Agricultural Credit	217
6.16	Econometric Results: The Demand and Supply of Non-productive or Consumption Credit	221
6.17	Results Analysis: Production Loan for Indebted Farmers with Time and Region Variables	226
6.18	Discussion on Credit Demand and Supply	230

7	**The China International Famine Relief Commission**	**233**
7.1	Introduction	233
7.2	The Raiffeisen Model for Rural Credit	234
7.3	Early Attempts at Cooperative Societies	237
7.4	The China International Famine Relief Commission	238
7.5	Famine and the Household Economy	243
7.6	Famine and Population	243
7.7	Conceptualizing Rural Credit Cooperatives	248
7.8	John B. Tayler, John Lossing Buck, and Rural Cooperation	250
7.9	Credit Relief and the Yangtze River Floods	252
7.10	Summary	255

8	**Rural Reconstruction**	**257**
8.1	Introduction	257
8.2	Communist Expansion	260
8.3	Rural Reconstruction and the Chinese Communist Party	264

	8.4	Rural Reconstruction and Price Volatility in Copper,	
		Silver, and Gold	266
	8.5	Japanese Aggression, Bonds, and Credit	266
	8.6	Lack of Currency Control Within China	268
	8.7	The Yangtze River Flood	269
	8.8	Canton Rebellion	271
	8.9	Institutional Development and the Rise of Credit	
		Cooperatives	273
9	A Blueprint for Credit Under Rural Reconstruction		275
	9.1	Introduction	275
	9.2	A Blueprint for Modern Rural Financial Institutions	
		by the Nanjing Government (KMT)	277
	9.3	The Rural Finance Discussing Committee	280
	9.4	Characteristics of Modern Rural Financial System	
		in Design	281
	9.5	Summary	283
10	Evolution of the Cooperative Financial System: 1927–49		285
	10.1	Introduction	285
	10.2	Administrative Structure of Cooperative Credit	286
	10.3	Rules and Law	287
	10.4	Funding Cooperatives	288
	10.5	Cooperative Credit Associations (Hezuoshe Lianshe)	291
	10.6	Expansion of Cooperatives	292
	10.7	Cooperative Treasury (Hezuo Jinku) System	298
	10.8	Differences Between the Credit Cooperative Association	
		and Cooperative Treasury	300
	10.9	Summary	300
11	Chinese Communists, Border Currency,		
	and Agricultural Credit during Wartime		303
	11.1	Introduction	303
	11.2	Border Regions and Base Areas	304
	11.3	Agriculture, the 'Fair Burden' Tax, and the Grain	
		Standard	307
	11.4	Monetary Control in CPC Base Regions	
		and Border Areas	310

11.5	Currency Formulation in the Base Areas: The Formation of the Luxi Bank	312
11.6	Border Currency and Regional Trade	313
11.7	Currency-induced Hoarding	316
11.8	Credit and Cooperation in the Shaanxi-Gansu-Ningxia Border Region	318
11.9	Mutual-aid and Group Guarantees	320
11.10	Economic Warfare	321
11.11	Summary	322

12 The Farmers Bank of China 327

12.1	Introduction	327
12.2	Rural Reconstruction and the Farmers Bank of Four Provinces	328
12.3	The Formation of the Farmers Bank of China	330
12.4	Joint Administration Office of the Four Policy Banks, Bank Specialization, and FBC's Monopoly and Banking Progress in War Time	336
12.5	Debates and Conflicts on the Rural Finance System	339
	12.5.1 Debates on Banks Specialization	339
12.6	Single or Ternary Agricultural Financial Structure?	340
	12.6.1 Conflicts Between Farmers' Bank of China and the Central Cooperative Treasury	342
	12.6.2 Conflicts Between County Banks and Other Rural Credit Institutions	344
12.7	Summary	346

13 Nong Ben Ju, the Farm Credit Bureau, and the KMT's Agrarian Policy 349

13.1	Introduction	349
13.2	Nong Ben Ju and the Farm Credit Bureau	350
13.3	The Farm Credit Bureau	351
	13.3.1 Agricultural Products Department	353
	13.3.2 Agricultural Loans Department	355
13.4	Agricultural Loans of Commercial Banks and the Chinese Rural Credit Syndicate	357
13.5	Developing a Cooperative Financial System Under Nong Ben Ju	359

13.6	Nong Ben Ju, *the Farm Credit Bureau, and the War Years*	360
	13.6.1 Impact of War on the Cotton Spinning and Weaving Industry	363
13.7	Reform and Dissolution of the Farm Credit Bureau	367

14 Successes and Failures of Agricultural Cooperatives and Credit Societies 369
14.1	Introduction	369
14.2	Overview of Credit Cooperatives	370
14.3	Pre-War Impacts of Credit Cooperatives	373
14.4	Cooperative Credit and the Sino-Japanese War	384
14.5	Impact of War on Farm Credit Demand	399
14.6	Summary	402

Index 403

List of Figures

Fig. 1.1	Household income and credit, Liaoning Province, 1987–2002	10
Fig. 1.2	The structure of rural credit. (Source: Guo and Jia 2010)	18
Fig. 1.3	RCC loans, aggregate, RMB/mou by region, 1978–2014	27
Fig. 1.4	RCC loans, aggregate differences from national average, 1978–2014	28
Fig. 1.5	Formal credit, by household and region, 1986–2009	30
Fig. 1.6	Formal and informal credit, 1993–2009. Upper left: formal, informal, and familial loans, RMB/mou, national, 1993–2009. Upper right: ratio of familial to formal loans, 1993–2009. Lower left: ratio of familial loans as a % of all informal loans. Lower right: ratio of all informal to formal loans, 1986–2009	31
Fig. 1.7	Macro impacts of credit reforms on China's agricultural economy	36
Fig. 2.1	Malthusian Trap	62
Fig. 2.2	Frequency distributions of rainfall-related risk events, China 1470–2000	65
Fig. 2.3	Frequency distribution for extreme flooding or extreme drought	66
Fig. 2.4	Extreme drought (% of locations available and 10-year moving average)	66
Fig. 2.5	Extreme flooding (% of locations available and 10-year moving average)	67
Fig. 2.6	Extreme flooding or drought (% of locations available and 10-year moving average)	67

Fig. 2.7	Potential aggregate output with rainfall sensitive exponential decay	70
Fig. 2.8	Patterns of effort on agriculture by dynasty and emperor	71
Fig. 2.9	The cumulative effects of dynasties and emperors on agricultural production cycles	72
Fig. 3.1	Water control projects from Perkins, 1969	83
Fig. 3.2	Fractional poverty trap dynamics showing possible path over 500 years with land and population, upper left; output to land on upper right; land per capita, lower left; and capacity to population ratio, lower right. Start and endpoints approximate China's observed growth. Poverty trap dynamics illustrated in lower right, where excursions below values of 1 indicate below subsistence living standards. In this scenario land reaches its maximum about 300 years in, or around the year 1700. Beyond that the combination of low innovation and high output risk causes periodic rises and falls in land cultivated. Output uncertainty, the continual rise in population, and the land constraint results in a poverty trap that extends for nearly 300 years with this simulation	113
Fig. 3.3	Fractional poverty trap dynamics showing possible path over 500 years with land and population, upper left; output to land on upper right; land per capita, lower left; and capacity to population ratio, lower right. Start and endpoints approximate China's observed growth. Poverty trap dynamics illustrated in lower right, where excursions below values of 1 indicate below subsistence living standards. Note that in this example land reaches its maximum in the mid-1800s which is when some experts conclude the maximum was reached. The combined rise and fall in output, together with the rise in population, ensures in this particular path that by the 1900s farmers were locked into a poverty trap	114
Fig. 3.4	Fractional poverty trap dynamics showing possible path over 500 years with land and population, upper left; output to land on upper right; land per capita, lower left; and capacity to population ratio, lower right. Start and endpoints differ from observed population and land use in China in 1900. In this scenario large gains in output due to technological innovation reduce the need to cultivate lower-quality land, while providing sufficient capacity for population growth. Poverty trap dynamics illustrated in lower right, where excursions below values of 1 indicate below subsistence living standards. Here we observe an excursion pattern that oscillates about the subsistence line	115

LIST OF FIGURES   xxv

Fig. 4.1	Bidding society, copper value of amounts of received and paid in	143
Fig. 4.2	Bidding society, silver value of amounts received and paid in	143
Fig. 7.1	Age distribution, 1921 male and female, North China	245
Fig. 7.2	Age distribution, 1921 male and female, South China	246
Fig. 9.1	Schematic of KMT blueprint for agricultural credit, circa 1933	282
Fig. 10.1	Structure of the cooperative system	299
Fig. 13.1	Total amounts of agricultural loans in the 1930s ($10,000). (Source: Yueping Bai, Yong Yu (2002), Study on the amounts of rural financial relief in 1930s, Journal of Inner Mongolia University, V.1)	358
Fig. 13.2	Cooperative treasuries established by *Nong Ben Ju*, 1937–41. (Source: Hong Fu (2009) *Op Cit*)	360
Fig. 14.1	Growth in number of cooperatives	370
Fig. 14.2	Growth of agricultural and credit cooperatives	371
Fig. 14.3	Distribution and growth of cooperatives in the reconstruction era, 1932–46	373
Fig. 14.4	Japanese occupation of China, circa 1940	387
Fig. 14.5	Japanese and communist zones of influence and occupation, circa 1945	388
Fig. 14.6	Growth of cooperative membership 1937–47	393
Fig. 14.7	Percentage change in money supply and capital contribution to cooperatives	395
Fig. 14.8	Cooperative capital stock: nominal vs real 1937–47	396
Fig. 14.9	Cooperative capital per member: nominal vs real 1937–47	397
Fig. 14.10	Agricultural indices, 1937-May 1941, Sichuan Province, 1937 = 100	401

LIST OF TABLES

Table 1.1	Household income, Gansu Province 1978 and 1984. (Gansu Province, Rural Social and Economics Survey (1985).)	9
Table 1.2	Household income and credit for three villages in Huangzhong County, Qinghai Province. (Qinghai Province, Rural social and economics survey (1985))	10
Table 1.3	Comparison of microcredit providers – clients and products	19
Table 1.4	Comparison of microcredit providers: performance	21
Table 3.1	Simulated Hurst exponents for population-land-output dynamics	119
Table 4.1	Types of *Qian Hui*	135
Table 4.2	Subscription of members in a single-stacked amounts-increasing society	136
Table 4.3	Subscription-decreasing society	139
Table 4.4	Subscription of each member at every meeting in seven-member rotating society	140
Table 4.5	A comparison of different types of pawn shops in the Republican era	145
Table 5.1	1882–1931 imports and exports in China, unit: thousand customs tael	163
Table 5.2	Agricultural and Industrial Banks before 1927	175
Table 6.1	Description of data tables in Buck's rediscovered data	182
Table 6.2	Descriptive statistics of Buck's data used in econometric credit demand analyses	184
Table 6.3	Amount and character of farm credit and interest rate	188
Table 6.4	Percentage of farms obtaining credit and percentage of credit for productive and non-productive purposes	189

Table 6.5	Loan amount summary	189
Table 6.6	Interest rate summary (%)	190
Table 6.7	Percentage of farms obtaining credit from the specified sources	192
Table 6.8	Rescaled borrowing sources of indebted farmers	194
Table 6.9	Special expenditure (in yuan) per farm family on all farms, by region	195
Table 6.10	Special expenditure of household sample	196
Table 6.11	Livestock holdings of sample farms ($N = 2,127$)	197
Table 6.12	Factors indicating the type of use of land—livestock and fertility maintenance	197
Table 6.13	Factors indicating the type of use of land—size of farm business	198
Table 6.14	Factors indicating the type of use of land—production	200
Table 6.15	Factors indicating the type of use of land—farm labor	203
Table 6.16	Summary of calamities facing Chinese farmers	205
Table 6.17	Factors indicating the type of use of land—crop production and crop risk	208
Table 6.18	Binary model of agricultural credit	214
Table 6.19	Total loan for indebted farmers with time and region variables	218
Table 6.20	Consumption credit	222
Table 6.21	Productive loan for indebted farmers with time and region variables	227
Table 7.1	Net income of famine-affected households	244
Table 7.2	Relationship between net income per local mou and land holdings	244
Table 7.3	Farm holdings in local mou	245
Table 10.1	Average subscribed capital per member	289
Table 10.2	Associations of cooperatives 1938–46	293
Table 10.3	Geographical distribution of cooperatives	294
Table 10.4	Summary of cooperative treasuries in various provinces over years	296
Table 12.1	Amounts of paid-up capital and reserves of the Farmers Bank of China, 1933–46	332
Table 12.2	Growth in branches and offices of Farmers Bank of China, 1933–47	333
Table 12.3	Loan dispersements by the Farmers' Bank of China, 1933–47 (unit: $1000)	334
Table 12.4	Major banks lending to agriculture, circa 1937	337
Table 12.5	County banks established each year: 1940–1948	345

Table 13.1	Amounts of jointly invested capital by participating banks (thousand dollars)	352
Table 13.2	Warehouses and cooperative banks maintained by the Farm Credit Bureau	354
Table 13.3	% Uses of loans made by cooperative banks maintained by the Farm Credit Bureau	356
Table 13.4	Amount of agricultural loans from four government banks and the Farm Credit Bureau (Unit: $1000)	359
Table 14.1	Geographical distribution of cooperatives	374
Table 14.2	Recognition of cooperative credit societies 1923–29	376
Table 14.3	Loan purposes, 1924–30	380
Table 14.4	Status of loans, December 1929	382
Table 14.5	Reasons for loan extension	383
Table 14.6	Changes in numbers of credit cooperatives 1937 to 1945 ranked by Japanese occupation	390

CHAPTER 1

Current Conditions of Rural Credit in China

1.1 Introduction

This book tells the story of major developments in the provision of agricultural credit in China with a particular emphasis on the Republican era between 1912 and 1949. We are motivated by the rapid expansion of agricultural credit and institutions in the post-1978 modern era to provide some semblance of understanding about agricultural credit in China more generally, and economic history provides a perspective for any student or practitioner in the agricultural finance space. This is particularly true since the reforms around 2003 that allowed the conversion of Rural Credit Cooperatives (RCCs) to Rural Credit Banks and Rural Cooperative Banks (RCBs) which may well see the era of the RCC soon coming to an end. The developments in RCCs in the modern era are usually attributed to reforms in the mid-1950s, but as our story tells, there was a thriving and growing industry of RCCs well before Chinese liberation. 1949 changed everything but the essential structure that was developed prior to liberation remained—that is, the heart of agricultural lending was to be based on cooperative principles, or at least some semblance of cooperative principles that was operational in the post-liberation economy.[1] The main

---

[1] For an overview of agricultural conditions in post-1949 China see Buck, J.L., O.L. Dawson and Yuan-li Wu. (1966). "Food and Agriculture in Communist China" Hoover Institute/Fredrick A. Praeger Publishers, Washington DC/NY NY.

© The Author(s) 2018
H. Fu, C. G. Turvey, *The Evolution of Agricultural Credit during China's Republican Era, 1912–1949*,
https://doi.org/10.1007/978-3-319-76801-4_1

difference, as far as we can tell given the historical record, is that between 1949 and 1950 rural credit societies remained intact in many locations in China but only in skeletal form. Rural credit societies promoted by the Kuomintang (KMT) disappeared at liberation, either dissolved or bankrupt as the Chinese national currency collapsed. But a few lingered on, reconstituting themselves by 1950 as pilots for the establishment of rural credit cooperation and Credit Unions and expanding thereafter.[2] The Communist Party of China (CPC) had experience in developing rural cooperation. During the early 1930s the communists formed credit societies in their soviets, and to a significant degree this provided encouragement to the KMT to follow suit under rural reconstruction. This in turn started the process of formalizing agricultural credit in China as a matter of policy, poverty alleviation, and agricultural productivity. In 1954 the CPC declared all private lenders as usurers and started pushing for Rural Credit Cooperatives. The 1958 formation consolidated and renamed these societies as Rural Credit Cooperatives and the RCCs were for many years the backbone of agricultural credit.

Of course the agricultural economies of 1912–49, 1950–77, and 1978 to the present are incomparable at so many levels. Even in the modern era the period between 1978 and 2003 differs remarkably from the period after 2003, and even more so after 2006. Nonetheless, to understand the current credit environment, where it stands currently, and how transformations in the financial sector affects agriculture, it is also important to understand its roots—the circumstances that brought about credit access in the Republican era, the evolution of institutions, and their impact on agriculture all have relevance in the modern era.

For example, of the many growth challenges facing the People's Republic of China one of the most critical is the urban-rural divide and an increasing income disparity between urban and rural households. For China to proceed in a sustainable growth pattern there must be an alignment between the rapidly growing industrial sector and agricultural production, productivity and urban-rural household income equality. Given the household responsibility system and the small allocations of land use rights (LUR) the opportunities for Chinese farmers to make a reasonable living from the land are few. However, one mechanism that can leverage

---

[2] Mingming Chang. (2006). Performance and Insufficiency: A Historical Investigation of Loan Activities of Rural Credit Cooperatives in the Early Years of New China – Taking Hubei, Hunan, Jiangxi Provinces as Center, in Chinese Agricultural History, No.3.

productivity growth is access to credit at a reasonable and affordable rate. On this there has been progress, especially since the implementation of microcredit loans through rural credit cooperatives and the Agricultural Bank of China since 2003. In Eastern provinces such as Shandong, Jiangxi, Guangxi and others, secondary processing of food has developed for domestic consumption and export. Forestry endowments have led to cottage industries and creditworthy villages are binding together to produce goods for export while horizontal and vertical relationships are developing in numerous provinces between fast-growing business entities and thousands of farm households. China's financial institutions and policies need to be adaptive to modern realities but in responding to these realities it is necessary that they address the institutional heritage that has led to the present; and when deemed inefficient, correct as much as is possible.

The current landscape of rural credit includes not only an expanded role for policy banks such as the Agricultural Development Bank of China, but also changes in regulations and oversight of existing banks such as the Agricultural Bank of China (ABC) and Rural Credit Cooperatives (RCCs). Since 2003 China has not only seen an initial public offering of shares in the ABC, opportunities for RCCs to convert to rural commercial banks (RCB) with joint-stock capital from other individual investors and financial institutions, but also a myriad of different financial institutions, with some accepting deposits and others being joint-stock companies that provide lending-only services.

The new era of institutional reform in China's credit markets is designed to increase capital flows into rural areas and improve financial deepening.[3,4] Of particular interest is the provision of credit to agriculture. However, an 'agricultural loan' in rural China does not necessarily mean that loans are being made to farm households, but rather to businesses and individuals in an agricultural region. Nonetheless, the expansionary policy has several modes of operation including centrally regulated interest rates and interest rate ceilings designed to induce demand at potentially lower rates than would otherwise be offered. This is a sensible policy. In credit demand studies we have found that as interest rates fall, demand for credit becomes

---

[3] Shaw, E.S. (1973). Financial Deepening in Economic Development, Oxford University Press, New York, NY.

Mckinnon, R.I. (1973). Money and Capital in Economic Development, Brookings Institution, Washington, DC.

[4] He, L. and C.G. Turvey. (2009). Financial Repression in China's agricultural economy. China Agricultural Economics Review. 1(3):260–274.

more elastic. Increased supply is encouraged by interest rate subsidies paid directly to lenders in direct proportion to increases in agricultural loans over the previous year. But it is also hoped that by expanding the number and types of financial institutions in rural areas there will be a degree of down-scaling in which increased supply will find its way to farm households. Additionally, provincial ministries of agriculture in partnership with counties and the Peoples Bank of China will establish specific funding arrangements with RCCs for targeted development. These include capital for the development of self-help cooperatives or direct interest rate subsidies for farmers' expansion into new areas of agriculture including fruit orchards (e.g. converting grain land to kiwi orchards) and greenhouses for vegetable production.

To provide at least some context, this chapter provides an overview of developments in agricultural credit from 1978 to the present. We start at 1978 and discuss the reforms through 2003. In 2003 rural credit reforms took on a sense of urgency and by 2006 they were the number one policy objective of the Chinese government. We then provide an overview of credit conditions by providing a review of some of our own field research and surveys in China, starting around 2007.

1.1.1 Financial Reform and Transition in China, 1978–2003

China's financial reforms in the years following the introduction of the household responsibility system in 1978 and its move towards a market-based agricultural economy were haphazard at best. If China's leaders were striving towards the creation of a modern financial sector reform it could not, by Western standards, be viewed as a success.[5] But, as Shen et al. (2010) explain a comparison to Western standards is not the relevant point: the relevant point is how it evolved given the state of the financial sector at the beginning of the reform period. Indeed, financial policy in the early reform period was haphazard and piecemeal responding mostly to contemporaneous policy initiatives which in the rural setting was the establishment and financing of township and village enterprises (TVEs). Overt policies directed towards financial sector development of the scale and scope of Western democracies did not come into force until about

---

[5] This section is abstracted largely from Shen, Minggao, Jikun Huang, Lingxiu Zhang and S. Rozelle. (2010). "Financial Reform and Transition in China: A Study of the Evolution of Banks in Rural China". Agricultural Finance Review 70(3):305–322.

1994 generally, 2003 more formally, and development of an inclusive financial system for agriculture in earnest after 2005/06.[6]

During the Mao era, the Peoples Bank of China (PBC) was the dominant financial institution. As a central bank, the PBC was engaged primarily as a cashier and accounting agency, with the Agricultural Bank of China (ABC) being a dominant division. As separate institutions, ostensibly independent Rural Credit Cooperatives were to serve the needs of farmers. But as a centrally planned economy without competition, neither the demand for lending or deposit-taking institutions, nor the ABC or RCCs, operated with efficiency and both were ultimately brought under PBC control by the late 1950s.

Thus, by 1978 when Deng Xiaopeng brought forward the responsibility system in a move towards a more market-based economy there was no formalized financial sector to really support the millions upon millions of small farms that emerged. Agricultural income and wages increased by 73.2% between 1978 and 1984; the output from the rural industrial sector increased by 1188%, while gross industrial output increased by 228%.[7] Financial sector development lagged behind this growth. Gains in output were derived from pent-up demand by Chinese consumers, and a new set of incentives to improve efficiencies of privatized state-run business. These were run by the entrepreneurial class and local leaders who could mobilize labor and resources. Town and Village enterprises began to flourish, and grow.

Eventually however, growth could not be sustained by gains in efficiency alone. Modernization required capital and eventually financial sector development was forced to address the increased demand for credit. The ABC and RCC were encouraged to make loans to TVEs, and loans to TVEs increased 12-fold between 1980 and 1994. The share of loans from the ABC and RCC made to TVEs increased from 13.8% to 33.2% over the same period.[8] In the early 1980s the PBC took on a more central banking role and developed the Bank of China, China Construction Bank, and Industrial and Commercial Bank of China. The ABC at the same time was elevated to a policy bank with the directive of satisfying the needs of farmers and rural firms, financing the state supply of farm inputs, and

---

[6] Shen et al., op cit is interesting since the data collected were 10 years prior to publication in 1998, with a focus on the 1994 to 1996 period when they believe fundamental reforms started to take place. Their intelligence and data gathering efforts were from a broad section of townships in Jiangsu and Zhejiang Province.

[7] Shen et al., op cit, page 310.

[8] Shen et al., op cit, page 311.

financing the procurement of agricultural output and products. No other bank was allowed to compete with the ABC and it was directed to supervise the network of RCCs across China. Around 1983 the RCCs were given some autonomy by forming county level associations now referred to as Rural Credit Cooperative Unions (RCCUs) or Rural Credit Cooperative Unions (RCC) Unions. But depending on location many RCCs were simply branches of the ABC with no material competition.

The directive that the ABC act as a policy bank created problems of its own. The most critical in the 1980s was the conflict between attaining the policy objectives and making loans to agriculture and TVEs. By 1983 the banks had moved towards a profit motive, but the amount of funds to be lent was secondary to making policy loans (for infrastructure development for example). Policy directives were unpredictable so whatever capital controls banks would impose on themselves internally would constantly require adjustments, challenging at times the liquidity of the banks and their ability to provide investment capital. By 1983 lenders were given incentives to generate profits and these profits were obtained more from the lending side than the policy side. This fell under the responsibility system, so that at some banks not only would lenders be rewarded for making profitable loans, but they would also face penalties if they made poor loans.[9]

---

[9] Around 2009 we were discussing bonus incentives with RCC lenders in Eastern China when one of the junior lenders remarked that in that office/county managers were held accountable for loan losses, and could face salary reductions if it was determined that the bad loans were due to poor judgement. Penalizing salaries was apparently permitted, but this was up to the discretion of the local manager and a review of circumstances. We raised this point at other RCCs and found that the policies varied. The more common was that bonuses from profitable loans would be reduced by some amount of loan losses for which the lender was deemed responsible. Curious about the adverse incentives of such a system we conducted a series of field experiments with front-line lenders (Cao et al. 2016) in Shandong province in 2014 and found that loan officers did ration credit by rejecting more loans when facing risks of personal income loss. However, providing risk information about the application pool boosted the approval rate and offset the behavioral responses by a roughly similar magnitude. Thus certain institutional settings, such as the responsibility system initiated around 1983 could have actually increased credit rationing, and reduced lending, via strategic loan misclassification. This suggests that lenders facing penalties might well be increasing Type II errors (rejecting loans that would otherwise be acceptable) in order to reduce Type I errors (accepting loans that are actually poor quality), which could become very costly to agricultural lenders as shown in Nayak and Turvey (1997).

While the policy loans created their own problems, bankers faced three critical obstacles in lending to TVEs and agriculture generally.[10] First, agricultural loans in China were highly risky. The spatially fragmented nature of markets led to significant price volatility. The unpredictability of government predation added to this uncertainty. Second, many of the TVEs were small firms and loans were costly to originate, monitor, and regularize. In addition, because of intense specialization the firms were largely undiversified. Since many firms had no credit history or long-term performance metrics, asymmetric information was significant, and adverse selection only made monitoring more demanding and expensive. Third, was the issue of security and collateralization of loans. Land was assigned to farmers based on the issuance of land use rights (LURs) which provided a means of production, but not a right of ownership. Ownership was retained by the state (collective or village). Likewise, TVEs had no right to offer land as security for loans, and with the degree of specialization, any secondary market for owned machinery or moveable assets had little resale value. As a point of comparison, the US Farm Credit System evolved as a national cooperative precisely because mortgages were secured by land, the mortgages were spatially diversified, and cooperative Farm Credit Associations were held jointly and severally liable for system loans, providing a last-resort guarantee. These features provided a framework similar to the German Raiffeisen system in which the system could issue bonds, collectively secured by owned land.[11] Without land title not only were conventional mortgages and loans difficult to secure on origination, but this also eliminated any possibility of developing secondary markets into which loans could be securitized to replenish liquidity and loanable reserves. Instead, Chinese agricultural banks and cooperatives had to rely on deposits to meet capital requirements. Shen et al. (2010) report from their lender surveys that even though the ABC started requesting collateral in 1985, as of 1993 only 15% of lenders actually required collateral.

Cao, Ying (Jessica), C.G. Turvey Jiujie Ma, Rong Kong Guangwen He Jubo Yan. (2016). "Incentive mechanisms, loan decisions and policy rationing", Agricultural Finance Review, 76(3):326–347.

Nayak, G.N., and C.G. Turvey. (1997). Credit risk assessment and the opportunity costs of loan misclassification. Canadian Journal of Agricultural Economics 45(3), 285–299.

[10] Shen et al., op cit.

[11] See Turvey, C.G. (2017). Historical developments in agricultural finance and the genesis of America's farm credit system. Agricultural Finance Review, 77(1), 4–21.

1.1.2 Household Conditions and Credit in the Early Reform Era

The early reform era, that is the transitional stage, had significant impacts on China's economy but microlevel details of impacts on household income and credit use are scant. In this sub-section we provide a glimpse of farm conditions at a few localities based on local gazetteers. For example in Suihua County of Heilongjiang Province in 1978–79 officials recorded that about 1949 of 20,700 farm households borrowed informally at interest of between 2% and 3% per month for weddings (52.9%), non-agricultural family business (29.3%), housing (14.3%), and illness (3.9%).[12] In Gannan County, 1982, 19 out of 30 families borrowed informally about 417 yuan, and 139 yuan in formal debt. In Yian and Keshan Counties, about 41.7% of 672 households borrowed informally 361 yuan in 1984 and 489 yuan in 1985. Other reports from Huachuan, Fujin, and Huanan Counties recorded informal interest rates at 3–4% for 55% of borrowing households; 5% for 29% of borrowing households; and 6–10% for 15.2% of households.[13] In Huaining County, Anhui Province about 13.5% of 11,951 yuan in total loans were formal loans, presumably from RCCs, 17.4% were familial (friends and relatives) loans at zero interest, and the remaining 69.1% were from other informal sources. Of the informal loans about 9.4% were at only 1% monthly and 12.9% had interest rates of 4% monthly. The remaining 77.7% of loans were at 2% monthly but could also be repaid in wheat equivalents.[14]

Table 1.1 summarizes information provided in the local gazetteers in Gansu Province for 1978 and 1984. We cannot speak for the statistical strength of these data except to say that the gazetteers are usually very precise, and the consistency across counties and villages is reasonably consistent. A fuller, aggregated, summary of credit use is provided in a later section of this chapter. With this caveat in place, the gazetteers for Qiutou village in Zhengning County reported per capita household income of 47 yuan and 96 yuan respectively, while Gongzhu village in Jingchuan County reported per capita household income of 100 yuan and 217 yuan. Formal loan per capita in 1984 was 104 yuan. Among 30 households surveyed in Qiutou village, six households had formal loans of 728 yuan per capita,

---

[12] Rural Agricultural Gazetteers of Heilongjiang Province (Published in 1992). Note slight rounding error of 0.4%.
[13] Ibid.
[14] Agricultural Finance Gazetteers of Anhui Province (1997).

Table 1.1 Household income, Gansu Province 1978 and 1984. (Gansu Province, Rural Social and Economics Survey (1985).)

	Zhengning County–Qiutou village	Jingchuan County–Gongzhu village	Qingshui County–Yaohuang village	Tongwei County–Wancai village	Wuwei County–Xiayuan village
Year	1978/84	1978/84	1978	1978/84	1984
Sample	2913 households across 8 villages in Zhengning county	165 families and 836 people	243 families and 1288 people	163 families and 872 people	273 families and 1371 people
Land base		2.3 mou/capita	3 mou/capita	7.4 mou/capita	2.4 mou/capita
Income	1978–47 yuan/capita 1984–96 yuan/capita	1978–100 yuan/capita 1984–217 yuan/capita	1978–60 yuan/capita 1984–118 yuan/capita	1978–62.6 yuan/capita 1984–142.9 yuan/capita	225 yuan/capita
Formal credit	1984–104 yuan/capita among 30 households: 1) 6 @ 728 2) 8 @ 175 3) 10 @ 45	1984–109.46 yuan/capita	1984–46.10 yuan/capita, informal credit 12.03 yuan/capita or 26% of formal credit	1984–65.37 yuan/capita	102 yuan/capita

eight had loans of 175 yuan per capita, and 10 had formal loans of 45 yuan per capita.

Surveys in 1978 and 1984 in three villages (Lijiangshan, Xiaping, and Xiakou) in Qinghai Province reported household incomes as provided in Table 1.2. With about 2.7 mou per capita (one mou equals one-sixth of an acre so that 2.7 mou is about one-third of an acre) household income grew from between 67 and 74 yuan/capita/year in 1978 to between 195 and 243 yuan/capita/year in 1984. These are still very small numbers, but represent mid-point gains of 310%, which correspond to the growth in TVEs discussed previously. Formal credit was about 56 yuan/capita in 1984. There were no loans recorded in 1978—likely because there were none—and the range of loans is in the neighborhood of those also recorded in Heilongjiang. Interestingly, informal credit in Xiaping village was only 33% of formal credit, but we are unclear as to whether this is informal in the sense of suppliers or money lenders, or informal in the sense of friends and relatives.

Table 1.2 Household income and credit for three villages in Huangzhong County, Qinghai Province. (Qinghai Province, Rural social and economics survey (1985))

	Lijiangshan	Xiaping	Xiakou
Year	1978/84	1978/84	1978/84
Sample		103 households and 593 people	70 households and 423 people
Land base	2.7 mou/capita		2.67 mou/capita
income	1978–74 yuan/capita	1978–67 yuan/capita	1978–70.64 yuan/capita
	1984–204 yuan/capita	1984–243 yuan/capita	1984–195 yuan/capita
Formal credit		Formal credit 1984–55.65 yuan/capita	1984–56.26 yuan/capita
		Informal credit 1984–18.55 yuan/capita	
		% informal to formal credit: 33%	

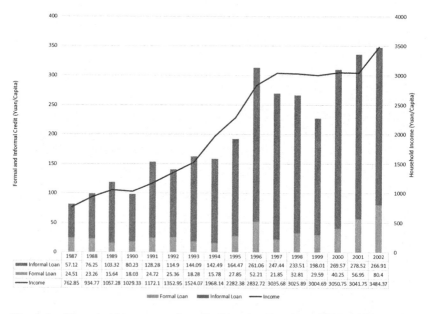

Fig. 1.1 Household income and credit, Liaoning Province, 1987–2002

Figure 1.1 shows summarized data for Liaoning Province between 1987 and 2002, matching gains in per capita income to changes in formal and informal credit. Per capita income increased from 762.85 yuan/capita to 3484.37 yuan/capita for a continuously compounded annual growth rate of 10.127%. Formal credit increased from 24.51 yuan/capita to 80.4 yuan/capita for a growth rate of 7.9%, while informal credit increased by 10.3% per year. To what extent these capture cause and effect is difficult to say: however the correlation between income growth and credit use is clearly evident.

1.2 JOINT LIABILITY AND GROUP GUARANTEES

To provide much needed security the banks implemented a program of joint liability. Under joint liability members of a group are held mutually responsible for repaying individual loans made to other group members. The idea of a group guarantee appears to have originated with the introduction of credit societies aligned with the Agricultural and Industrial Banks in 1915 but were more fully employed in CPC-controlled base areas during the Sino-Japanese war. To some effect, group guarantees were resurrected around 1983 for both farm loans and loans to TVEs. As a form of self-insurance the group guarantee was a satisfactory substitute for collateral, so long as group members did not conspire to default. Under joint liability a farmer or manager in need of credit would approach a number of related businesses to provide a guarantee for a loan. It was not necessarily a reciprocal arrangement since group members were not necessarily joint applicants but only guarantors, although no doubt member guarantors would expect reciprocity with a guarantee from the principal borrower at some future date. Nonetheless, the joint liability arrangement diversified firm-specific risks, reduced transaction costs, mitigated the effects from asymmetric information, and provided the means by which banks could lend more money.

By all accounts, the group guarantees were successful, especially those groups which included local governments as guarantors. Shen et al. found that in 1994, about two in three local governments provided local guarantees and 42% of group guarantees for TVEs included a local government guarantee.[15] This arrangement was desirable because the government had sufficient power to hold sway over businesses' intent on reneging on the loan or the guarantee obligation. Even for groups without a government partner, there would be little incentive to default on obligations, since doing so would negatively affect future opportunities for obtaining loans.

---

[15] Shen et al., op cit, page 316.

At least for TVEs the period of joint liability did not last as China's economy and financial sector development changed throughout the 1990s. There were several reasons for this. First, as China's economy grew the influence of the traditional collective diminished. Local cadres and leaders became less inclined to support businesses via guarantee as outside capital came into play, and new lending institutions—as few as they were—took on a more competitive role. As collateral assets grew, the mitigating benefits of joint liability weakened, and once local governments saw a decline in joint liability they were less inclined to support it. By 1997 meetings held by local leaders to support joint liability projects fell from to 2.6/year in 1994 to 1.6, while meetings to discuss loan repayment fell from 1.3/year to 0.6.[16] Meanwhile, group guarantees and joint liability for farm loans continued, and remain an important part of loan securitization to the present day.[17]

1.3 Administrative Independence of RCCs, 1996

With the structural changes in the credit market readily being observed, a new phase of financial development occurred in 1996 when Rural Credit Cooperatives (RCCs) were administratively untied from the Agricultural Bank of China and started to report to the Peoples Bank of China instead. At the same time, the so-called policy banks were encouraged to make loans across sectors and began to compete with each other. To push these changes the bonus system was improved considerably. Shen et al. (2010) found that the bonus share of 26.8% in 1994 increased to 41.9% by 1997. Cao et al. (2016) report that the bonus of lenders in Shandong Province in 2011 was even higher with a base salary than of a loan officers who on

---

[16] Shen et al., op cit, page 319.
[17] Kong, R., C.G. Turvey, H. Channa, and Y. Peng. (2015). Factors affecting farmers' participation in China's group guarantee lending program. *China Agricultural Economic Review*, 7(1), 45–64.

Here it was found that most farmers appear to be part of group guarantees only because they have to in order to get access to formal credit products. Some 87.21% of the people who belong to groups and utilize the formal credit products belong to this category because their lenders have made participation in groups compulsory for access to credit. This may ration farmers' willingness to even apply for credit. It also indicates a preference on the part of older and more risk-averse respondents to avoid participation in group guarantees. Furthermore the results indicate that informal and formal credit appear to be substitutable for farmers in the sense that farmers not participating in group guarantees, tended to borrow more from friends and relatives.

average get CNY2000–3000 per month as base salary and CNY4000–5000 as performance salary.[18]

One of the first reforms was to introduce a program of microcredit directed towards farmers. This was accomplished by opening an on-lending window for RCCs in 1977 that allowed RCCs to obtain loanable funds in addition to what was made available with deposits. These came at subsidized rates initially at 2–3% interest with legislated maximums. For most RCCs these rates were below the costs and this greatly imperiled an already fragile RCC system. On the other hand, guidance was given on several aspects of risk rating and determining credit worthiness. This was accomplished by a risk-rating task force with village leaders that would establish repayment capacity and creditworthiness of households, issuing credit certificates and eligible loan amounts.[19]

Starting in Jiangsu Province, the PBC initiated further reforms at centralization including the merging of RCCs within a county into a single RCCU (RCC Union) that became the legal entity for the county, piloting the conversion of RCCs into Rural Credit Banks, establishing a provincial RCC federation, and providing interest-free loans to RCCs from the PBC discount window.[20] These interest-free loans were also to be used to divest accumulated non-performing loans from previous lending regimes.[21] These structural changes to RCCs were ultimately expanded across China.

Starting in 2002, pilot projects were initiated to allow RCCs to make adjustments to both deposit and lending rates. RCCs could float deposit rates to 30% of the official base rate and 70% of the base lending rate in an attempt to encourage more deposits and recover more costs.[22]

---

[18] Cao et al., op cit, page 330.

[19] Xie, Ping. (2003). "Reforms of China's Rural Credit Cooperatives and Policy Options" China Economic Review 14:434–442.

[20] Xie. (2003). op cit.

[21] In 'true' cooperatives, loss burdens are typically spread amongst all members through reduced profit shares. Cooperative principles were widely applied before 1949, but during the Mao era, share ownership became muddied as cooperatives consolidated with collectivization and became less voluntary. This persisted well into later reforms particularly when it came to conversion to Rural Credit Banks newly structured as joint-stock companies. On one occasion we asked RCC managers seeking to convert to a RCB how new shares were to be allocated to farmer-members. Because members were not issued shares there was no mechanism for members to participate in the newly formed joint-stock RCB.

[22] Xie. (2003). op cit also states an objective to reduce high-interest money-lender rates. Over the years we have tried to determine the role of money-lending and usury but have found little background. We have reported some forms of money-lending for gambling and

The breakdown of joint liability forced the now decentralized banks and cooperatives to move towards greater collateral. This of course was good in theory, but in practice collateral must have liquidity value and for the very reasons that brought about joint liability in the first place, low-quality collateral, the collateral conditions had not changed. In addition lenders felt less inclined to obligate loans to policy initiatives and rapidly removed themselves from interacting with local officials and government. More money was placed in commercial loans than policy loans. As more commercial loans were made, the portfolio of low-quality collateral increased. Throughout the 1990s as more and more collateral substituted for group guarantees, loan performance deteriorated. As a consequence, banks were forced by market conditions to take more control over branch activities and decentralization reversed itself. A resurgent centralization did not mean a return to making policy loans a priority, but rather a greater focus on capital controls, oversight, and collateralization. Combined, lenders increased credit rationing activities and, following a lending peak in 1997, lending was reduced.

1.4 The Economic Rationale for Credit Policy

From an economic point of view credit reforms became necessary. The ambiguous nature of goals, objectives, and ownership and adherence to policy objectives over profit motives created a weak and vulnerable lending system. As the ABC moved towards more commercial lending, the bulk of local lending fell upon the RCCs. Xie (2003) argued that the policies provided soft constraints which created a managerial moral hazard signaled by bailouts of some troubled RCCs in order to maintain credit services. The hazards of soft constraints and subsidies have been criticized by many development economists for encouraging the inefficient use of resources away from their best alternative and competitive use.[23] By the late 1990s

---

vice but virtually no reporting of money-lending on a large scale. This was almost 10 years after these reforms so it is possible that the reforms worked on this objective, but the evidence is elusive.

[23] Besley, T. (1994). "How do Market Failures Justify Interventions in Credit Markets" The World Bank Research Observer 9(1):27–47.

Adams, D.W. and D.H. Graham. (1981). "A Critique of Traditional Agricultural Credit Projects and Policies" Journal of Development Economics 8:347–366.

Adams, D.W., D.H. Graham and J.D. Von Pischke. (1984). edts. Undermining Rural Development with Cheap Credit. Westview Press, Boulder and London.

and into the 2000s, financial and banking reforms across China were moving towards free market, laissez-fair economics, for example the Washington Consensus to encourage financial deepening.[24] The structural reforms initiated in 1995 represented a piecemeal approach to strengthening financial sector reforms to ensure that the institutional structures for agricultural credit were in place before full liberalization of credit can be realized.

With the focus on industrial growth rather than agricultural growth over the past 30 years, agricultural finance was much neglected, at least in the context of an inclusive financial system that would provide breadth and depth of credit, savings, and other financial services in agricultural and rural areas, including poverty zones. Up until 2003 when serious reforms were put in place, many local agricultural economies were suppressed through lack of credit. The purchase of production inputs were suboptimally constrained to savings or informal (or familial) borrowing amongst friends and relatives. Familial lending within villages is economically significant.[25] As a pro-poor policy it is in the public interest to substitute informal credit for formal credit which can increase not only agricultural productivity (an income leverage effect), but also consumption of non-agricultural goods and services by reducing the need for precautionary savings and freeing up capital tied up in familial loans.[26] History has shown that in the absence of direct government intervention no invisible hand will spontaneously emerge as a source of farm credit.[27] Even under current economic conditions, the credit demands from non-farm sources are so large that providing small, costly, and risky loans to

Gonzales-Vega, C. (1982). "Cheap Agricultural Credit: Redistribution in Reverse" Discussion Paper 10, Colloquium on Rural Finance, Sept 1–3, 1981. Economic Development Institute, World Bank, Washington DC (Revised January 11, 1982).

Adams, D.W. (1972). Agricultural Credit in Latin America: A Critical Review of External Funding Policy. American Journal of Agricultural Economics, Vol. 53, No. 2 (May, 1971), pp. 163–172.

[24] Williamson, J. (2004). The Washington Consensus as Policy Prescription for Development, World Bank Practitioners for Development lecture 2004 [http://www.iie.com/publications/papers/williamson0204.pdf]. Washington, DC: Institute for International Economics.

[25] Turvey, C.G. and R. Kong. (2010). "Informal lending amongst friends and relatives: Can microcredit compete in rural China?" *China Economic Review*, 21(4): 544–556.

[26] Dorward, A., J. Kydd and J.Morrison. (2004). "A Policy Agenda for Pro-Poor Agricultural Growth". *World Development*, 32(1), 73–89, 2004.

[27] Turvey, C.G. (2013). Policy rationing in rural credit markets. *Agricultural Finance Review*, 73(2), 209–232.

agriculture is not economically efficient. Instead, as in the United States, Canada, and elsewhere the hand of government will need to be visible to encourage the reallocation of resources to their socially optimum levels. Thus a policy of interest rate subsidization targeted towards lower income communities may be justifiable on the basis of repairing institutional flaws that have suppressed one group of individuals to the benefit of another. This view is clearly in line with Justin Y. Lin and Joseph Stiglitz.[28] Following the Washington Consensus, liberalization of financial markets works only in the context of perfect information and good behavior amongst all parties involved. That financial liberalization in China would miraculously find credit widely available to rural clients and farm households without government intervention would be somewhat naïve. The reality is that agriculture's plague has always been that capital will always flow to areas of highest demand with lowest risk and at lowest cost, and this does not characterize the demands and risks of the rural setting with small land holdings and tens of millions of relatively poor farm households facing a host of risks from markets and the environment. China needed to implement policy, governance, oversight, and a regulatory structure to address rural credit issues according to the institutions and conditions that are its reality. This was accomplished with the New Countryside Campaign of 2006.

1.5 THE NEW COUNTRYSIDE CAMPAIGN OF 2006

In 2006 rural economic development became a priority goal of the Chinese government, and with this explicit recognition of a more inclusive financial sector that addressed the needs of agriculture. These reforms were not new but were a continuation of the reforms started in 1995 and later in 2003. What was new was a focus on breadth and the encouragement of new-type financial institutions to expand financial and credit services to underserved areas in China, including poverty zones. On April 24, 2008, the China Banking Regulatory Commission (CBRC) issued the *Notice of Relevant Policies about Village and Township Banks (VTB), Lending Companies, RMCCs and Microloan Companies*, enabling pilot microloan

---

[28] Lin, J.Y. (2011). "New Structural Economics: A Framework for Rethinking Development" *The World Bank Research Observer* 26:193–221.

Stiglitz, J.E. (2008). China: Towards a new model of development, *China Economic Journal*, 1:1, 33–52.

Stiglitz, J.E. (2011). "Rethinking Development Economics" *The World Bank Research Observer* 26:230–236.

companies of the PBC to acquire a legal identity, and stipulating that natural persons, corporate legal entities, and other social organizations that meet the registration requirements can invest in the establishment of microloan companies, thus allowing eligible microloan companies to be transformed into Village and Township Banks or lending companies. Recently, the government has announced that there will be no cap on interest rates imposed by MFIs (compared to the previous cap of up to four times the benchmark interest rate).

The new reforms were bold, at least within the context of financial sector development in China, but after 10 years of reforms the rural sector still faced difficulties in balancing the outflow of capital from rural areas in search of higher profits and safer returns relative to deposits (redlining); unmet credit demand by farms and small and medium enterprises (SMEs); inefficient performance of rural policy-led finance (e.g. the burden of infrastructure and policy loans imposed on rural financial institutions); the ineffectiveness of inflexible hard constraints on rural enterprises; the continuing burden of non-performing loans incurred in the 1990s; the moral hazard of soft constraints and implicit guarantees on non-performing loans; and low operating efficiency of the rural banking industry.[29]

Figure 1.2 summarizes the structure of rural credit as it evolved throughout the 2000s, and categorized by formal, semi-formal, and informal rural finance institutions and organizations. This includes a number of new financial institutions and initiatives that were prohibited before the reform period. Tables 1.3 and 1.4 provide a partial list of financial institutions providing microcredit or other financial services that have emerged or evolved during the most recent reforms. A vast number of different types of microfinance operators have appeared within the Chinese market including: NGO MFIs,[30] the Agricultural Bank of China (ABC) and the Agricultural Development Bank of China (ADBC), RCCs, Urban Commercial Banks and Guarantee Companies (UCBs and GCs), Rural Financial Institutions (RFIs), the China Development Bank (CDB) and Harbin Commercial Bank (HCB), Microcredit Companies (MCCs),

---

[29] Guo, Pei and Xiangping Jia IA, "The Structure and Reform of Rural Finance in China", China Agricultural Economic Review, 1(2):212–236.

[30] Examples of Foreign NGO MFIs around 2010 are Wokai http://www.wokai.org/, Accion http://www.accion.org/, etc.; major domestic ones are Chifeng Zhaowuda Women's Sustainable Development Association (CZWSDA) in Inner Mongolia, and Association for Rural Development of Yilong County (ARDY) in Sichuan.

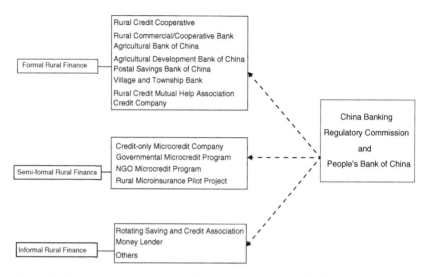

Fig. 1.2 The structure of rural credit. (Source: Guo and Jia 2010)

Village Banks (VBs), Rural Mutual Credit Cooperatives (RMCCs), Lending Companies (LCs), and Postal Savings Banks.

Of the different microfinance suppliers listed, only NGO MFIs (of which there are but a few) and MCCs are non-financial institutions and consequently not allowed to work with savings or receive funding from commercial banks, thus preventing them from enjoying economies of scale. In addition, the three newly created rural financial institution types (VBs, LCs, and RMCCs) as well as MCCs are subject to strict geographical restrictions.[31]

1.5.1 Agricultural Development Bank of China (ADBC)

The Agricultural Development Bank of China (ADBC) was formed as a formal policy bank to take over the grain procurement business of the ABC. The ADBC does not make direct loans to agriculture but ensures that sufficient liquidity is available for grain purchases.

---

[31] For example, RCCs are usually restricted to operate only within county borders. However, in recent years some RCCs have opened Village and Township Banks in different counties, or even provinces, in order to get around county and provincial RCCU restrictions and expand their lending activities in that way.

CURRENT CONDITIONS OF RURAL CREDIT IN CHINA 19

Table 1.3 Comparison of microcredit providers – clients and products[a]

	Type of institution	Since	Regions	Target clients	Traditional collateral	Average loan size	Annual interest rate	Savings	Remittances
1	NGO MFIs	1993	Country-wide	Mid/low income and poor clients	No	Several thousand	3–18%	No	No
2	ABC	1997	Country-wide	Mid/low income and poor clients	No	Several thousand[d]	3–5%	Yes	Yes
3	RCCs[b]	1997	Country-wide	All kinds of farm households and MSE	No, but yes for large loans	Originally several thousand to 10 thousand, but rapidly increasing	0.9–2.3 times basic rate	Yes	Yes
4	Urban Commer-cial Banks	2002	Urban areas	Microenterprise Laid-off workers	Yes, guarantee companies	Several thousand to several tens of thousand	Basic rate but subsidized by government	Yes	Yes
5	MCCs[c]	2005	Country-wide	Farmers and microenterprises	No, except for large loans	Several or tens of thousand to hundred thousand	0.9–4 times basic rate	No	No
6	Village Banks	2006	Country-wide	Farmers and microenterprises	No, except for large loans	Several thousand to hundred thousand	0.9–4 times basic rate	Yes	Yes
7	RMCCs	2006	Country-wide	Member farmers and enterprises	No, except for large loans	Several thousand	0.9–4 times basic rate	Yes	Yes

(continued)

Table 1.3 (continued)

Type of institution	Since	Regions	Target clients	Traditional collateral	Average loan size	Annual interest rate	Savings	Remittances
8 Lending companies	2006	Country-wide	Farmers and microenterprises	Yes	Several thousand to hundred thousand	0.9–4 times basic rate	No	No
9 Poverty Alleviation Loans	2004	Country-wide	Mid/low income and poor clients	No	Several thousand	Less than basic rate	Yes	Yes
10 Postal Savings Banks	2007	Country-wide	All kinds of farm households and MSE	No, except for large loans	Several thousand to hundred thousand	0.9–4 times basic rate	Yes	Yes
11 Microcredit Pilot Project of Commercial Banks	2005	More than 10 regions	Microenterprises and disadvantaged people	No	Several tens of thousand	Around 20%	Yes	Yes

[a]Notes: These rates are representative of conditions around 2013–2015, but frequently change as the regulatory environment changes

[b]RCC loans are generally microloans. For creditworthy borrowers, in our discussions with RCC lenders it would not be atypical to provide loans in the range of 30,000–50,000 RMB

[c]The loan amounts for MCCs are recently trending away from smaller microloans at the lower end, to millions of RMB on the upper end

[d]The Agricultural Bank of China since 1997 began to focus more on commercial and industrial loans, but still retained some activities in microloans for underserved areas. The loan amounts are for these loans, but have been much larger in recent years

Table 1.4 Comparison of microcredit providers: performance

	Type of institution	Number of active clients	Gender of clients	Value of loans disbursed in yuan	Portfolio quality	Ability to achieve sustainability
1	NGO MFIs	150 thousand	No gender limitation or mainly female clients	Billion	Uneven	A few can
2	ABC	No information	Mainly male clients	Several tens of billion	Poor in general	New loans can
3	RCCs[a]	70 million	Mainly male clients	Several hundred billion	Good	Uneven, but new loans can
4	Urban Commercial Banks	Several hundred thousand	Mainly male clients	Nearly ten billion	Good	Yes
5	MCCs[b]	Several thousand	Mainly male clients	Several hundred million	Good	Yes
6	Village Banks	Several thousand	Mainly male clients	Over one hundred million	Good	Good tendency
7	RMCCs	Several thousand	Mainly male clients	Several million	Good in general	Some can
8	Lending companies	Several thousand	Mainly male clients	Several million	Good	Yes
9	Poverty Alleviation Loans	Several ten thousand	Mainly male clients	No figure	Mostly good	Relying on subsidy
10	Postal Savings Banks	Several thousand	Mainly male clients	A hundred million	Good in general	Good tendency
11	Microcredit Pilot Project of Commercial Banks	No information	Mainly male clients	Billion	Good	Yes

[a] Notes: Several interpretations can be given to client numbers. Loans made are approximately 75 million but persons served is much larger. There are almost 80,000 branches throughout the villages and towns in China and approximate 800,000 staff servicing 800 million peasants and providing nearly 80% of the country's farmers loans, covering nearly 80% of township without financial institutions. (From a speech by the former chairman of China Banking Regulatory Commission (CBRC) at the National Financial Services Product Fair of RCCs. http://www.gov.cn/gzdt/2011-11/22/content_2000666.htm)

[b] The seasonal data from PBC about MCC is up to September 30, 2017 the amount of total outstanding loan of all the MCCs in China is 970 billion yuan. http://www.pbc.gov.cn/diaochatongjisi/116219/116225/3404729/index.html

1.5.2 Postal Savings Bank of China

The Postal Savings Bank of China was formed as a state-owned financial institution in 1986 as a savings-only bank. The Postal Savings Bank could offer higher savings rates on deposits than the RCCs which had regulated maximums on deposits due to the low rate of funds offered through the PBC discount window. In 2007 the prohibition on rural group lending, farmer microcredit, and microentrepreneurial loans were relaxed, providing a new source of agricultural credit.

1.5.3 Rural Commercial and Rural Cooperative Banks

The success of 2003 pilots on the conversion of RCC to Rural Credit Banks, Rural Cooperative Banks, or Rural Commercial Banks was extended, expanded, and encouraged. The conversion of cooperative banks to joint-stock companies also came with an allowance for private investment to bolster the capital base. While ostensibly profit-seeking banks, the new RCBs still retained a focus on rural lending, but perhaps with a greater emphasis on rural business rather than farming directly. As incorporated 'banks', these new institutions became regulated by the China Banking Regulatory Commission (CBRC).

1.5.4 Rural, Credit Only, Microcredit Companies

While RCCs, RCBs, and PSBCs were all deposit-taking institutions, the new reforms also made allowances for the formation of new types of lending-only companies. These are joint-stock lending institutions capitalized by private investors and other banks. Some would identify as Microfinance Institutions.[32] The institutions could lend within county boundaries (in fact most financial institutions were limited to lending within a county with very little cross-county competition)[33] and contrib-

---

[32] But these are not microfinance institutions of the group lending Grameen type. Rather the word 'micro' is relative to commercial/industrial credit demand not poor entrepreneurs. MFI loans could easily exceed 500,000 Yuan. In fact NGO sponsored MFIs of the Grameen type were not able to register (see Guo and Jia, op cit).

[33] Not much attention has been paid to these cross-county restrictions, but arose from the design of the RCCU. As an anectdote, around 2009 we visited two RCCs within a short drive of each other but across county boundaries in Eastern China. One RCC required not only group guarantees, but also personal guarantees and additional collateral. This RCC had a loan to deposit ratio around 50%. The second RCC took a different approach, and had a

uted to the financial deepening of rural credit markets and offered competition to traditional lenders. It is unclear as to whether lending-only institutions competed directly with the deposit-taking institutions or sought a less credit worthy clientele. It is also unclear as to whether they made direct loans to farmers or supported related agricultural and rural enterprises.

1.5.5 County, and Township and Village Banks

In early 2006 the China Banking Regulatory Commission released a document that described the permissible structure of County, and Township and Village Banks. These new-type banks served several monetary purposes, the most important being increased capital and deepening of rural financial markets. With a focus on villages and townships the idea was to increase credit supply with spillover effects to primary agriculture and related businesses. As the names suggest, the County Banks could operate within the boundaries of the county and would compete with RCCs although special consideration was given if the branch was to be set up in an underserved or poor region. Township and Village Banks were developed to operate within the boundaries of the township or village in which they were located. These banks could either purchase an existing bank, mostly RCCs, or establish new entities. As a new-type financial institution these banks had a different regulatory structure to RCCs and RCBs with the advantage of flexible interest rates and loan terms, and a streamlined approval process. Consequently, they were at times better able to support specialized cooperatives and agricultural products agents, each with varying and flexible needs in terms of loan cycles and interest rates. To encourage investment the rules permitted the establishment of bank branches in other counties or townships/villages with lowered registered capital (3 million yuan for county banks, and 1 million yuan for village/township banks) and lowered the minimum shareholder percentages for domestic partners. This meant that banks could capitalized or recapitalized using foreign capital as well as capital from existing Chinese financial

loan to deposit ratio of 80% (allowed at that time). The branch manager knew every farmer in his district and insisted that his lenders also made every effort to visit and get to know farmer-borrowers. This manager did not require group guarantees but loaned on trust. Non-performing loans were negligible. However, with cross-county restrictions farmers facing credit rationing in one county due to onerous guarantee requirements could not borrow from an RCC a short distance away because of county restrictions.

institutions. In December 2007, HSBC was the first foreign financial institution to open a branch office in rural China. Also in 2007, the central government requested that the ABC return to its rural roots to advance loans in support of farmers' production and consumption, SMEs in rural areas, and rural infrastructure construction.[34] Now a traded stock, the ABC could use its own capital, or attract new capital, to purchase township/village banks including RCCs. Deregulation also allowed the ABC and other institutions to purchase insurance companies, broaden financial activities to leasing, and so on.

1.5.6 Mutual-Help Associations

At the same time the CBRC established a new legal entity called the Mutual-help Association which could be registered at the county or township/village level with minimal capital of 300,000 yuan and 100,000 yuan respectively. Mutual-help Associations were most often linked to a local cooperative or mutual-help group. These were generally a group of farmers who wished to cooperate on some form of agricultural production or marketing enterprise. Members in the association were restricted to bonafide and creditworthy individuals in the same line of business. Each would purchase shares of membership (e.g. 1000 yuan per share) and each share would provide a right to borrow up to eight times the share value with a maximum imposed. The association used the share as capital to organize the nature of business and secure credit to farmers. In this sense it was like a mutual aid association. Each association would partner with a local financial institution, most likely an RCC, that would issue the loan using the association's capital and joint liability as security. For many Mutual-help Associations the PBC also provided a grant-in-kind as initial capital.

In other markets Mutual-help Associations organized as quasi-cooperatives for either marketing agricultural goods or supplying agricultural inputs. In these instances private individuals would put up their own capital and issue voting shares and then issue non-voting or lower-class shares to member farmers. Supplier cooperatives would then guarantee RCC loans to members who would use the proceeds to purchase supplies from the cooperative. Here there was not necessarily joint liability amongst all members since the cooperative's capital would be used as collateral for a loan guarantee.

---

[34] See Guo and Jia, op cit. This was in Suizhou village in Hubei.

1.6 Private and Foreign Investment

As previously mentioned the reforms also came about with relaxed rules for private investment and direct foreign investment in financial institutions. For example, in 2006 the PBC published its *Guidelines for MCCs* in 2006, which encouraged private investors, at home and abroad, to engage in credit-only lending activities, serving unbanked and underbanked regions. However, current foreign exchange control policy impeded the inflow of foreign capital in either equity or debt form. It is currently possible to receive foreign loans, as long as strict guidelines are adhered to and approved by the China Banking Regulatory Commission. Foreign investors could now make capital investments in NGO-MFIs, MCCs, RCCs, and Village/Township Banks and also by share issues on initial public offerings (IPOs) of Chinese banks. For example, the Chongqing Rural Commercial Bank Co. raised between $1.35 and $1.48 billion in its Hong Kong initial public offering between December 8 and December 16, 2010.[35] This was the first of the emerging rural commercial banks in China to raise capital in an IPO. This followed the IPO of the Agricultural Bank of China which raised about $22.1 billion in what was then then the largest recorded IPO.[36] Foreign investors were also allowed to establish strategic partners for Postal Savings Banks and Urban Commercial Banks. Rural Credit Cooperatives, converting to Rural Credit Banks or Rural Cooperative Banks, could do so with private equity or fixed-income investments with individual organizations unable to hold more than 20% of total capital, and shares of multiple investors should not exceed 25% in total. Conversion of an RCC to a joint-stock bank required approval from the provincial RCC Union as well as the provincial CBRC. The newly permitted Village and Township Banks, however, could actually be established by foreign banks registered in China as solo investors or as joint ventures. Non-banking foreign investors could also take an equity share so long as the shareholdings individually did not exceed 10%. In August 2007, HSBC was the first global lender to launch a village bank in China—the

---

[35] Chongqing Rural raises $1.35 billion in HK IPO: sources. Reuters. December 9, 2010. https://www.reuters.com/article/us-chongqing-pricing/chongqing-rural-raises-1-35-billion-in-hk-ipo-sources-idUSTRE6B81F720101209

[36] AgBank IPO officially the world's biggest. Financial Times, August 13, 2010 https://www.ft.com/content/ff7d528c-a6bc-11df-8d1e-00144feabdc0

HSBC Zengdu Village Bank, in Suizhou, Hubei Province—after obtaining regulatory approval to commit to deepening rural credit.[37]

1.7 Outcomes of Credit Reforms 1978–2016

It is surprisingly difficult to find a complete series of data from 1978 to the present on formal credit in China, and thus difficult to precisely comment on the effect of policies and the particular timing of policies. In what follows we piece together a historical representation of credit use in the modern era from two separate data sources. The first is a parsing of RCC credit from various reports that provide at least the total loans made at the provincial level. This, when divided by the number of mou per province, provides a common scale that is useful to show the growth in RCC credit and the depth of credit in nominal terms, but it does not indicate the breadth of credit across farmers. These data are complete to 1979.

The second data set was sourced from the National Rural Social-Economic Survey Data which had been continuously applied to an unbalanced sample of farm households by geographic region (Eastern, Middle, Western) since 1986.[38] These data have the added advantage of parsing formal loans from the ABC and RCCs (at least since 2003) and informal credit. Informal credit is interesting because it can be broken down into informal loans at zero interest and informal loans with interest. The former we can safely attribute to familial borrowing amongst friends and relatives, and the latter through other sources of supplier credit, pawn shops, perhaps money lenders, and other informal sources.

Between the two data sources there is a clear and consistent trend, but when converted to a per mou basis the amounts are not so easily reconcilable. This is because the RCC loan data includes all loans including those

---

[37] HSBC Gets Approval for Rural Bank in China. August 9, 2007. Reuters. http://www.reuters.com/article/idUSL0930628220070809

[38] National Rural Social economic Survey Collection, 1985, 1986–1999, 2000–2009 Agricultural Bureau of China, Policy Research Office of CPC Central Committee, Rural Fixed Observation, Fixed observation office. Chinese Agricultural Press, Beijing.

Note: 1992 and 1994 were missing or not surveyed. We use the average of 1991 and 1993, and 1993 and 1995, respectively to impute these values.

Eastern Region: Heilongjiang, Jilin, Liaoning, Hebei, Beijing, Tianjin, Shandong, Jiangsu, Zhejiang, Fujian, Guangdong, Hainan, Taiwan, Guangxi.

Middle Region: Shanxi, Henan, Anhui, Jiangxi, Hunan, Hubei, Inner Mongolia.

Western Region: Xinjiang, Gansu, Shaanxi, Ningxia, Sichuan, Chongqing, Guizhou, Yunnan, Xizang, Qinghai.

to farm households, rural businesses, and individuals, and policy loans, whereas the survey data are aggregated only for farm households.

1.7.1 RCC Loan Summary

In this sub-section we detail the RCC data. The raw data, RMB/mou by geographic region are presented in Appendices 1, 2, and 3. These data are summarized to the average and provided in Figs. 1.3 and 1.4.

Figure 1.3 shows the trend in nominal loan amounts per mou from 1978 through 2014. The mobilization of credit has been significant, but with clear regional differences, between Eastern, Middle, and Western provinces. In 1979 the average loan/mou in the Eastern provinces was 3.45 RMB rising by a factor of nearly 1112 times by 2014 to 3846 RMB by 2014. Likewise the Middle and Western provinces saw RCC credit increase from 2.77 and 2.71 RMB/mou by 890 and 1243 times to 2464 and 3373 RMB/mou respectively. Nationwide, RCC credit in 1979 averaged 1.83 RMB/mou increasing 1097 times to an average of 3320 RMB/mou by 2014.

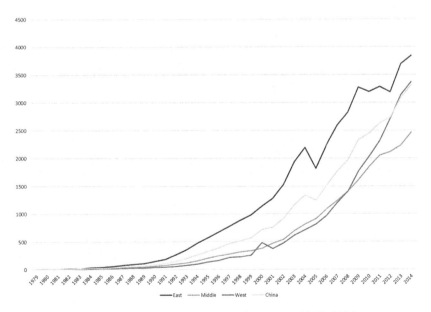

Fig. 1.3 RCC loans, aggregate, RMB/mou by region, 1978–2014

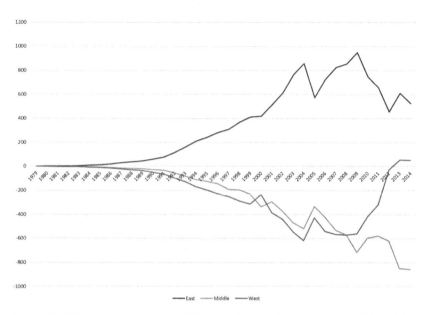

Fig. 1.4 RCC loans, aggregate differences from national average, 1978–2014

Figure 1.4 looks at the data in a different way by subtracting the national average loan/mou from each of the regional averages. This is a more telling graph in the sense that it shows that until around 2009, Eastern provinces received an increasing amount of credit/mou at the expense of Western provinces. But it also shows that efforts at a more inclusive financial system beyond 2009 reversed the trend, with increases in credit/mou being larger for Western provinces than Eastern provinces. This coincides with government efforts to increase development of the Western provinces, and by this account those progressive policies appear to have reversed the East-West imbalance. However, the middle provinces—while having a steady increase in RCC loans/mou—found an ever-decreasing share of national debt. The period of reversal, at least for the Western provinces in 2004, also coincides with the 2003 reforms and from 2006 and onwards, increasing numbers of Village/Township Banks, lending only companies, Chinese microfinance lending institutions, guarantee companies, and so on that would have increased the supply of credit with a spillover effect where surplus credit from Eastern RCCs was targeted more vigorously towards Western development.

1.7.2 National Survey Results

The second set of data we examine was compiled from an annual household survey of farm households. These data provide a somewhat different story in regards to the regional distribution of credit, but add greater depth by including familial (zero-interest loans from relatives and/or friends) and other informal loans, as well as a partial breakdown of RCC and other formal loans. In contrast to the RCC-only results above, the household survey results suggest that Western provinces held more formal debt per mou, followed by the Eastern provinces and then the Middle provinces. The difference with the survey is that it records the debts of borrowers, whereas the RCC data above simply divide total loans outstanding by number of mou under cultivation. As suggested above, the breadth of loans in the Western provinces, at least up to 2009, was deeper in the Eastern provinces than the Western provinces (i.e. more counties in the developed areas had financial lending institutions and functional RCCs). But penetration and usage also matters. It is entirely possible that although the aggregate supply of credit is lower in the Western provinces the penetration is also low, so that those households that borrow, while fewer, borrow more.

Figure 1.5 shows the formal loans (RCC and other financial institutions including the ABC) per mou for all respondents and the Eastern, Middle, and Western regions for the years 1993–2009. As with the RCC data above, greater loan amounts are found in the Eastern provinces, but the Middle provinces have smaller formal loans/mou than Western provinces. In all regions, nominal credit is increasing, with the greater increase over time accruing to the Eastern provinces. In fact in most years, formal loans/mou were higher in the Eastern and Western provinces than the Middle provinces.

How increasing access to formal credit affects other credit markets is also a very important aspect of financial reforms. The upper-left quadrant in Fig. 1.6, shows the national figures from the farm survey between 1993 and 2009 and possible impacts on informal credit from relatives and friends at zero interest—which we refer to as familial lending—and informal credit from other sources such as suppliers and pawn shops, etc. The lower-right quadrant shows the ratio of all informal loans to formal loans, suggesting a decrease in informal credit as access to formal credit increases.

There are a couple of interesting points here. First are familial loans. We have argued elsewhere that the bonds within families at the village level are

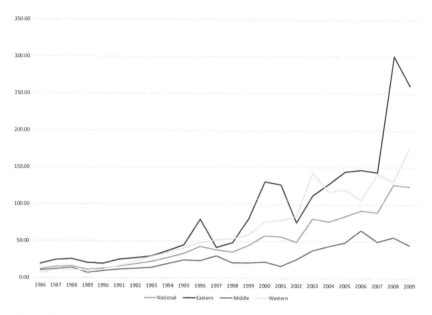

Fig. 1.5 Formal credit, by household and region, 1986–2009

incredibly strong in China. This is largely due to culture, but it also serves as a safety valve for future reciprocal arrangements. Familial borrowing is consistent with the existing literature in the sense that households tend to borrow more from family and friends than formal institutions. This story might be changing. Across China microcredit loans have increased substantially as RCCs working with village leaders identify farm households as being creditworthy, or even whole villages as being creditworthy. At the individual level, creditworthy borrowers are provided access to credit up to, if not greater than, 30,000 RMB. In some locations these loans are untied and can be used for any purpose, including non-productive expenditures on consumption, health, education, and housing which are traditional reasons for informal borrowing. Likewise, rather than borrowing from friends and relatives, farm households requiring capital to purchase materials and productive assets for artisan projects or secondary household businesses can access the funds through microcredit lines of credit.

By these numbers it appears that between 2007 and 2008 for the first time formal borrowing per mou exceeds familial lending nationally suggesting that substitutability between formal and familial lending is taking

CURRENT CONDITIONS OF RURAL CREDIT IN CHINA   31

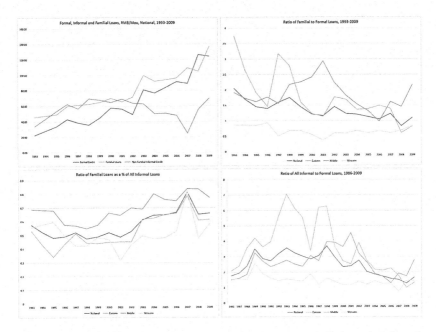

Fig. 1.6 Formal and informal credit, 1993–2009. Upper left: formal, informal, and familial loans, RMB/mou, national, 1993–2009. Upper right: ratio of familial to formal loans, 1993–2009. Lower left: ratio of familial loans as a % of all informal loans. Lower right: ratio of all informal to formal loans, 1986–2009

hold. The upper-right quadrant in Fig. 1.6 breaks out this effect by region by plotting the ratio of familial to formal loans. The greatest effect appears to be in the Eastern provinces, with more volatile ratios in the Middle provinces. The swings represented in the Eastern and Middle provinces suggest that familial lending may be used as a buffer, or hedge, against adverse events such as droughts, floods, or earthquakes. These results also suggest that the Western provinces generally borrowed less from friends and relatives than formal loans (ratio < 1.0). Nationally the general trend was reversed by 2008–09, perhaps due to tightening credit conditions following the US financial crisis, but it is a remarkable turn of events nonetheless.

The second interesting observation is the amount of non-familial informal borrowing which rose between 1993 and 2001, declining through 2007, and then recovering thereafter, perhaps again due to the tightening credit conditions following the financial crisis (upper-left quadrant, and regionally, lower-left). But another explanation is also at play. Since 2006 quasi-cooperatives were allowed to operate within China. These cooperatives could be supplier or marketing cooperatives, and would not be capitalized entirely by member capital. Investors might use their own capital, issuing a particular class of voting shares, while a second class of shares (perhaps non-voting) would be issued to members. As a member, the farmer could borrow on credit with funds flowing through the cooperative and secured by the cooperative's capital. To what degree this explains the upturn starting in 2007 we cannot say with certainty, but it does suggest that the 2006 reforms that expanded the number of regulated and unregulated financial institutions appeared to be effective in driving money supply to meet a clear demand.

1.7.3 Credit Conditions of Farm Households

Up until recently, nearly 30% of Chinese farmers had no access to formal credit and in many areas credit access is of rudimentary form and supply is limited. The role of production credit goes far beyond the objectives of lifting agricultural productivity. Kumar and Turvey (2011) using data collected in Shaanxi in 2008 find that when farmers faced increased credit constraints 74% would have to reduce inputs, 90% would have to seek off-farm wage labor employment, 50% would have to reduce expenditure on healthcare and education, and 21% would reduce food expenditure. Furthermore there are observable differences across asset quintiles with the greater negative impacts disproportionately affecting the poor.[39]

The perspective on rural credit in China presented in this chapter comes from a series of surveys conducted in China between 2007 and 2010 in the Western and Central provinces of Gansu, Shaanxi, and Henan on which we have a chronology of survey results. In Turvey and Kong (2009),[40] a 2007 farm household survey ($N = 400$) in Shaanxi indicated household income of CNY13,147 with 70% of income from farming, RCC debt of CNY6,973, and an average farm size of 5 mou. In surveys of

---

[39] Kumar, C. and C.G. Turvey. (2011). "Credit Constraint Impacts on Farm Households: Survey Results from India and China" Cornell University, Applied Economics and Management, unpublished paper, August.

[40] Turvey, C.G. and Rong Kong. (2009). "Business and financial risks of small farm households in China", China Agricultural Economic Review, Vol. 1 Iss: 2, pp.155–172.

1565 farm households conducted across Gansu, Shaanxi, and Henan in 2007 and 2008 (Turvey and Kong 2010)[41] we found average household income of CNY11,477 across an average of 5.52 mou with 58.71% of income from farming. On average, informal loans between friends and relatives were CNY10,395 and formal loans were CNY22,003. In Turvey et al. (2011) and Turvey and Kong (2010) we report on a survey conducted in 2009 ($N = 897$) that found 16% of Shaanxi and Gansu farmers borrowed on average CNY8452 from friends; 39% borrowed CNY11,642 from relatives, and 34% borrowed CNY21,611 from RCCs. Average household incomes were CNY21,422 on 6.50 mou. In a survey of 730 farm households in Shaanxi conducted in 2010 we found that a typical farm household had CNY23,796 in household income, CNY29,329 in debt, and a farm size of 4.9 mou. In that study we explicitly set out to measure the degrees of risk rationing, quantity rationing, and price rationing (see Boucher et al. 2008)[42] and found that of farm households that indicated a demand for credit, risk-rationed households comprised 6.5% of farm households, 14% were quantity rationed and the remaining 80% were price rationed.[43] These results indicate that in general farm incomes are low. A household income of CNY23,796 translates into about $3761 and household debt of CNY 29,329 translates into about $4635. While low by Western standards the role of credit is critically important for not only production but also consumption. In Turvey et al. (2011)[44] we find that an additional RMB of debt increases household income by 0.073 RMB, or 7.3% from debt use.

There is much heterogeneity in credit demand and we would argue that a full spectrum of targeted credit policies can be used to address differences across farms. Credit demand is highly variable in terms of the amount required and the sensitivity of borrowing that amount to changes in inter-

---

[41] Turvey, C.G. and R. Kong. (2010). Informal Lending Amongst Friends and Relatives: Can Microcredit Compete in Rural China? China Economic Review 21(4):544–556.

[42] Boucher, S., M. Carter, and C. Guirkinger, 2008. Risk rationing and wealth effects in credit markets: Theory and implications for agricultural development, American Journal of Agricultural Economics 90, 409–423.

[43] Verteramo Chiu, L., V.S. Khantachavana, and C.G. Turvey. (2014). Risk rationing and the demand for agricultural credit: a comparative investigation of Mexico and China. *Agricultural Finance Review*, 74(2), 248–270.

[44] Turvey C.G., Guangwen He, Rong Kong, Jiujie Ma, Patrick Meagher (2011). "The 7 Cs of rural credit in China", *Journal of Agribusiness in Developing and Emerging Economies*, Vol. 1 Iss: 2, pp. 100–133.

est rate. The amount depends on size of farm, what is actually grown, what investments are required to sustain or grow production, and what technological improvements are necessary for sustained production or growth. Not all farmers are interest-rate insensitive. Non-borrowers may mobilize savings or curtail consumption in order to avoid debt use. They may not need credit at all, or may have a demand for credit but fail to borrow it because of a risk of collateral loss (risk rationed). Others might have a demand for credit but do not borrow because of guarantee requirements (policy rationed). Others may appear to be non-responsive to interest rates but cannot obtain all of the credit desired at the prevailing rates because of restraints placed upon the farm by the lender (credit rationing), and others reveal a range of demands that are highly unresponsive to changes in interest rates (inelastic demand for credit) while others are very responsive to changes in interest rates (elastic demand for credit). There is no such thing as an average or typical borrower!

1.7.4 Effects of Credit Policy on Credit Demand

The artificial ceiling on interest rates is often viewed as an implicit subsidy for farmers, but care must be taken with this interpretation. In our 2009 surveys of 897 farm households in Shaanxi and Gansu, and our investigation of credit demand, we used survey-based experimental techniques to extract individual household credit demand functions from which we estimated point demand elasticities.[45] From a theoretical point of view, we proposed that as interest rates fell the demand for credit increased in elasticity, and this appears to hold in our data. We found a range of elasticities with mean point estimates of about −0.6, but also that nearly 20% of farm households had nearly perfectly inelastic demands for credit while nearly 20% had elasticities above −0.75 including some 15% having elasticities greater than −1.0. Previous studies that have argued against credit policies because of the low inelasticity of demand do not generally hold since there is much heterogeneity in credit demand that justifies a full spectrum of targeted credit policies to address differences across farms. To place this in context, RCC loans at the time had an interest rate ceiling of 15.088%. Based on standard rates and the elasticity of demand it is highly unlikely that farmers would borrow significant amounts at the ceiling. In this sense,

---

[45] Turvey, C.G., G. He, M. Jiujie, R. Kong., and P. Meagher. (2012). Farm credit and credit demand elasticities in Shaanxi and Gansu. *China Economic Review*, 23(4), 1020–1035.

and with the exception of the minority of farmers who would borrow at this rate, most banking institutions can compete for the majority of farm loans below the RCC ceiling. But it is unlikely that any increases to the ceiling on RCC loans rates would have an impact on either the demand for loans by farmers or the amount of loans supplied to farmers.

On the other hand, there are several justifiable reasons for supporting lowered ceilings on agricultural loans. First is the principle of food security and second is the principle of income equality. On the first measure the policy objective is to encourage farm households to borrow in order to purchase inputs to increase outputs. Assuming that this can be done profitably, the principal benefit would be an increased supply of domestically produced foods, which would reduce food prices, lead to a reduction in food imports, and perhaps increase food or processed food exports. The secondary benefits would be to increase livelihoods of farm households, lift them out of poverty, and reduce urban-rural income inequality and rural unrest.

1.8 Macro Consequences of Credit Reforms 1978–2016

A final consideration of China's credit policies and reforms since 1978 should examine the broader impacts on China's agricultural economy in terms of three metrics: technology adoption, gains in agricultural productivity, and poverty reduction. Assessing these in detail would require a book on its own, so here we can only provide a synopsis of observable metrics drawn from China's Agricultural Yearbook for 1978–2015. We provide a simplified view of the impacts in Fig. 1.7 which includes six sextants: Top Left: Technology and Rural Population, Top Right: Land per Capita and Rural Population, Middle Right: Rural Population and Agricultural Productivity, Middle Left: Technology and Agricultural Productivity, Lower Left: Technology and Engel Coefficient, and Lower Right: Engel Coefficient.

We are fortunate that the horizontal scales are either increasing or decreasing in a way that is more or less consistent with a time scale starting in 1978. In the top-left sextant we include technology adoption—measured here by the power of agricultural machinery (10,000 kw)—as a consequence of capital invested including credit. Contemporaneously occurring over the time period was a decrease in the rural population and

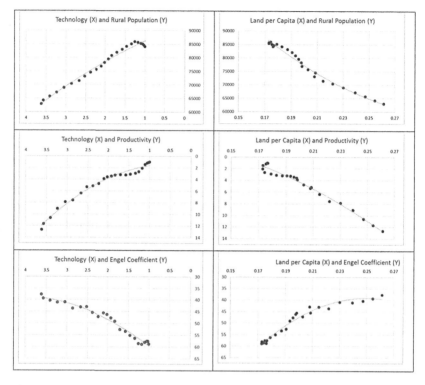

Fig. 1.7 Macro impacts of credit reforms on China's agricultural economy

therefore an increase in agricultural land per capita (top right) also following closely in time. Technology-labor substitution is evident in that as the farming population decreases, technology adoption increases, which in turn supports the higher per capita allocation of land. In the middle sextants the partial effects of technology on productivity is coincident with increased labor productivity as land per capita increases. As farm sizes increase, technology adopted and production increases, so the period has seen a nearly continuous decline in the rates of poverty, here measured by the Engel coefficient which measures the percentage of farm income used for food consumption. As the Engel measure decreases farmers are better able to save and accumulate wealth, or make follow-on investments in productive or non-productive assets. As capital is invested in agriculture the partial impact trickles down to poverty reduction and income enhancement—major policy goals.

This is of course simplified. There are temporal and endogenous factors that need to be considered and the marginal effects or economic multipliers that are causal likely need more evidence than provided here. With this caveat, what is observed in China is classic textbook development economics: reforms lead to financial sector development and a pathway towards financial deepening and spillover effects that encourage investment in technology. With investment in technology, capital substitutes for labor, which provides a pathway for the vast rural population to exit agriculture, increasing land and potentially economies of size. Productivity effects here are notable, and so is the impact on poverty reduction with the concomitant effects on increased savings and household wealth.

1.9 Summary

In October 2017, a proposal on rural development for the 13th Five-Year Plan (2016–20) was unveiled at a Central Committee plenum of the Communist Party of China in 2015 with a goal to rid all Chinese of poverty—including some 600 state poverty counties—by 2020. Poverty reduction in rural areas is to be accomplished by promoting, on the one hand, entrepreneurship, and on the other by promoting commercial agriculture through land transfers of land use rights, increased access to farm mortgages for longer-term investments, and increased access to operating credit. In 2015 the China Banking Regulatory Commission opened an Office for Financial Inclusion with the specific purpose to supervise and promote financial inclusion across China. At the beginning of 2016, the state council of China issued *The Plan for Promoting the Development of Financial Inclusion (2016–2020)* with the final goal that by 2020 China's financial inclusion can at least achieve levels observed in the upper echelons of developing economies. The key objectives and goals of both the office and the plan are to effectively improve accessibility of financial services, satisfy increasing financial demand from the public, and make affordable, easy, and secured financial services available for farmers, small and microenterprises, low-income urban populations, poverty-stricken populations, and the disabled and the elderly.

The goals and objectives of policies and programs in the modern era cap nearly 100 years of credit promotion and development in China. The goal then, as now, was to reduce poverty and promote agricultural development at the commercial and industrial levels. The tumult of the Republican era, which is the central focus of this book, moved credit for agriculture to a central policy position. Debate and progress was nearly continuous with the foundations of the Agricultural and Industrial Banks in 1915, the initiatives and push towards cooperative credit in 1928, the development of a blueprint for agricultural credit in 1930, rural reconstruction in the 1930s, providing critical financing during the Sino-Japanese war between 1937 and 1945, and with debates continuing through the end of the war on liberation.

Whatever progress was made then was largely lost during the collectivization period, but what remained eventually morphed into the Agricultural Bank of China and the development of Rural Credit Cooperatives as the primary arteries for agricultural credit. When reforms started in 1978 the Chinese government attempted many, first with the Agricultural Bank of China overseeing RCCs, and then RCCs operating independently of the ABC, and finally expansive reforms starting around 2003 and a major drive for reforms starting in 2006 bring us to the present.

Growth in agricultural credit has not been ineffective, although it can be argued for a number of reasons that the slow pace of credit access has likely contributed to the growing disparity and inequality between rural and urban incomes. This changed in 2006. Since then reforms have led to increased deepening in rural financial markets with an array of new types of financial institutions and conversion of the historic RCCs to joint-stock banks. County and Village/Township banks have added to the flow of capital into rural areas and at least some of this is finding its way into primary agriculture. But in the modern era, as in the Republican era, the high costs and risks in agriculture hampered progress and new banks find it more convenient to lend to non-farm households. Nonetheless, we draw a link between increased access to credit, technology adoption, rural depopulation, increased productivity, and decreased poverty. It is not lost on us that these outcomes were precisely the outcomes sought by the efforts at agricultural finance in the Republican era.

Appendices

Appendix 1: Average RCC Loans, Billion RMB, 1979–2014, Eastern Provinces

Year	Guangdong	Shandong	Zhejiang	Jiangsu	Hebei	Liaoning	Guangxi	Fujian	Heilongjiang	Jilin
1979	4.22	4.74	2.06	3.45	2.81	1.04	1.53	1.15	0.93	0.55
1980	11.98	6.82	5.15	3.41	3.84	2.28	2.07	1.71	1.00	1.66
1981	16.20	10.03	5.24	4.13	4.83	2.71	2.74	2.47	1.93	1.46
1982	20.11	11.75	5.86	5.32	5.91	3.81	4.56	3.18	3.09	2.07
1983	24.19	15.18	7.67	13.56	7.95	5.76	5.50	4.07	3.36	2.61
1984	50.32	37.57	17.12	31.37	23.95	12.99	8.29	7.97	5.97	7.78
1985	60.71	41.82	20.16	33.81	27.45	14.91	10.05	8.88	6.74	8.04
1986	83.18	65.14	35.43	48.63	43.44	22.45	12.88	12.40	9.87	10.01
1987	116.38	85.60	43.09	63.84	65.21	32.23	17.96	15.61	13.12	13.35
1988	142.98	103.71	47.51	72.11	84.13	41.38	19.87	16.14	15.42	14.56
1989	175.13	127.92	57.09	86.37	102.56	50.88	21.34	19.38	17.82	16.36
1990	245.48	162.18	79.86	110.04	135.32	70.13	28.44	26.65	24.38	21.16
1991	315.83	196.44	102.62	133.71	168.08	89.39	35.54	33.93	30.93	25.96
1992	495.57	243.31	150.64	171.62	207.63	125.89	50.13	51.80	40.31	33.44
1993	670.14	285.18	208.26	217.37	248.59	158.44	73.58	66.12	46.27	40.51
1994	875.05	350.69	301.26	299.26	304.47	205.31	112.40	84.74	59.39	50.02
1995	1050.19	417.05	386.68	368.25	367.56	250.28	127.71	97.28	72.55	61.53
1996	1237.61	531.82	461.24	455.61	463.14	295.94	140.63	115.98	86.81	69.91
1997	1389.11	616.46	611.57	510.40	514.94	328.44	149.76	134.71	97.18	92.00
1998	1607.45	678.85	694.52	554.82	669.99	362.52	155.15	154.75	105.99	94.39
1999	1743.02	739.03	788.78	607.47	738.77	374.13	160.35	174.19	111.96	103.66

(*continued*)

(continued)

Year	Guangdong	Shandong	Zhejiang	Jiangsu	Hebei	Liaoning	Guangxi	Fujian	Heilongjiang	Jilin
2000	1781.23	951.02	940.61	745.68	895.70	403.43	173.68	201.22	114.61	113.85
2001	1862.07	1170.71	1084.05	854.86	996.75	427.20	194.71	217.05	129.72	130.88
2002	1998.47	1402.01	1338.86	1070.21	1077.09	460.07	227.62	252.15	156.92	160.18
2003	2250.16	1739.97	1802.87	1244.54	1207.89	523.19	263.54	328.45	186.67	194.09
2004	2536.36	1947.94	1998.31	1318.46	1353.51	604.50	326.85	379.18	240.23	219.47
2005	2431.82	2001.71	999.71	1110.95	1362.00	599.70	389.08	436.34	278.03	250.80
2006	2861.10	2155.56	1063.33	1165.05	1623.99	685.13	498.54	499.31	325.64	426.94
2007	3330.86	2524.42	1209.65	1265.72	1893.13	805.70	621.88	532.36	405.69	536.82
2008	3791.14	2925.39	1099.80	1406.47	2084.29	943.19	694.67	630.07	526.98	614.27
2009	4586.32	3356.18	1094.57	1615.00	2541.76	1208.81	904.29	764.65	715.21	696.51
2010	3116.59	3802.91	1155.13	1458.14	3033.53	1411.01	1129.96	911.77	860.59	726.29
2011	2816.73	3816.82	1379.94	974.75	3535.19	1623.30	1272.39	927.27	974.69	732.14
2012	2455.16	3628.37	1495.33	387.66	3972.28	1360.66	1498.16	855.19	1107.56	764.25
2013	2412.68	3582.87	1699.30		4042.53	1330.50	1727.93	1034.19	1233.01	750.84
2014	2699.03	3176.17	1592.60		4361.03	1308.55	2058.29	1196.04	1378.98	621.00

Appendix 2: Average RCC Loans, Billion RMB, 1979–2014, Middle Provinces

Year	Henan	Hunan	Shanxi	Hubei	Anhui	Jiangxi	Inner Mongolia
1979	4.76	2.00	2.46	2.10	1.10	0.65	0.83
1980	6.87	3.01	3.39	2.65	1.92	0.95	0.96
1981	9.29	3.91	4.41	2.83	2.76	1.23	1.04
1982	11.07	4.79	4.99	3.42	4.02	1.86	1.27
1983	13.10	5.41	6.98	4.74	4.95	2.81	1.60
1984	25.58	9.43	15.68	12.98	10.10	5.36	2.98
1985	28.14	10.97	15.93	13.05	11.69	6.42	3.18
1986	39.15	16.99	19.71	16.03	16.99	8.41	3.74
1987	54.73	24.51	25.01	21.72	21.49	10.43	4.77
1988	62.71	25.72	33.42	25.50	23.24	12.19	6.17
1989	74.04	29.98	43.91	29.87	24.85	14.20	7.80
1990	97.13	42.39	57.93	38.78	32.91	20.11	10.15
1991	120.23	54.81	71.95	47.68	40.98	26.02	12.51
1992	146.59	73.77	89.15	61.11	48.74	35.28	16.90
1993	172.50	98.55	104.15	76.41	61.70	46.22	22.32
1994	233.57	151.76	128.91	91.41	84.74	62.86	30.58
1995	294.76	210.93	156.69	117.52	112.74	83.73	41.79
1996	369.73	254.61	187.18	146.57	141.05	107.18	47.51
1997	441.97	262.91	208.17	177.58	170.76	117.12	55.31
1998	512.64	301.72	246.18	205.34	196.90	130.06	64.30
1999	568.11	326.17	255.50	197.85	223.09	140.94	74.27
2000	670.75	372.04	281.92	213.01	246.08	169.21	91.62
2001	766.63	414.45	347.40	247.15	295.32	195.47	124.62
2002	875.64	459.97	423.30	283.36	354.25	237.29	146.35
2003	1009.24	534.04	581.86	341.39	428.68	310.17	174.11
2004	1167.64	626.13	706.51	404.69	513.35	353.58	211.15
2005	1274.92	674.24	818.08	449.74	589.01	423.62	245.99
2006	1521.38	728.20	931.45	519.98	670.60	459.46	315.96
2007	1720.87	772.37	1098.97	630.06	790.46	538.52	378.46
2008	1951.58	911.03	1227.50	744.83	855.92	665.06	490.34
2009	2366.85	1132.11	1464.24	683.85	839.70	837.10	590.02
2010	2703.01	1319.88	1776.83	830.99	776.22	980.28	720.58
2011	2833.54	1417.51	2017.01	931.26	861.74	1133.59	846.14
2012	2951.17	1542.97	2084.46	838.10	713.66	1236.28	985.10
2013	3331.45	1641.26	2269.54	656.30	684.39	1275.25	1120.31
2014	3507.66	1606.46	2280.87	414.94		1354.18	1132.09

Appendix 3: Average RCC Loans, Billion RMB, 1979–2014, Western Provinces

Year	Sichuan	Shaanxi	Yunnan	Gansu	Guizhou	Xinjiang	Ningxia	Qinghai
1979	3.87	1.79	1.26	0.68	1.14	0.30	0.15	0.18
1980	8.25	2.47	1.63	0.85	1.60	0.30	0.18	0.21
1981	7.92	2.85	2.09	1.05	2.04	0.30	0.17	0.22
1982	10.00	3.42	3.04	1.30	2.70	0.32	0.21	0.28
1983	14.52	4.65	5.06	1.43	3.55	0.50	0.32	0.35
1984	26.18	9.49	9.35	2.82	4.64	1.73	0.62	0.59
1985	27.14	10.47	10.32	3.55	5.09	1.85	0.83	0.83
1986	36.97	14.68	12.52	4.60	6.10	2.11	0.85	0.85
1987	47.47	19.66	15.68	5.70	7.29	3.05	1.02	0.81
1988	47.35	22.89	16.67	6.35	7.93	3.79	1.54	0.92
1989	59.64	27.68	17.45	7.51	7.95	4.84	2.05	1.01
1990	78.16	35.62	20.20	9.60	9.33	5.64	2.48	1.12
1991	96.69	43.56	22.95	11.68	10.70	6.45	2.91	1.22
1992	132.22	55.99	30.70	15.17	14.29	7.97	3.53	1.43
1993	175.14	70.62	41.16	21.66	17.41	9.95	4.94	1.81
1994	242.46	91.77	55.05	29.18	21.87	16.82	6.85	2.50
1995	322.93	117.88	72.25	38.73	27.94	24.32	9.48	3.67
1996	405.08	146.67	105.53	50.10	32.84	24.01	11.72	4.15
1997	370.92	179.55	137.99	59.53		29.23	13.79	4.64
1998	427.58	208.63	145.87	69.26	46.85	31.97	15.12	6.18
1999	527.95	228.50	162.70	81.35	56.98	35.98	16.15	7.33
2000	568.35	261.54	186.05	103.38	71.17	41.42	19.11	91.40
2001	659.87	308.47	218.38	124.44	92.18	56.92	28.10	14.38
2002	728.71	358.48	260.29	157.50	125.50	77.75	50.20	19.27
2003	832.37	416.64	323.48	189.03	148.59	112.07	83.37	27.07
2004	921.78	472.57	382.96	216.18	196.69	134.67	106.67	29.16
2005	969.48	537.22	517.09	242.80	248.99	149.81	131.25	29.28
2006	1142.59	632.92	563.47	288.24	333.86	156.26	154.34	34.77
2007	1383.01	740.64	711.20	344.19	418.56	224.80	173.52	62.79
2008	1677.32	823.89	897.39	358.02	517.79	301.62	204.73	80.84
2009	2277.01	1026.36	1167.28	504.16	726.58	425.57	211.24	101.75
2010	1930.56	1178.46	1439.90	591.64	925.38	621.93	266.67	126.97
2011	2225.01	1328.77	1745.00	684.00	1051.16	862.31	321.74	127.73
2012	2651.12	1560.49	2081.72	912.01	1315.35	1147.11	281.75	163.87
2013	2963.01	1804.51	2498.14	1149.11	1637.51	1142.03	348.36	199.14
2014	3337.42	1923.90	2984.36	1369.27	1612.72	1215.43	293.44	229.46

Appendix 4: Average RCC Loans, RMB/Mou, 1979–2014, Eastern Provinces

	Fujian	Guangdong	Guangxi	Hebei	Heilongjiang	Jiangsu	Jilin	Liaoning	Shandong	Zhejiang
1979	4.35	6.03	3.00	3.04	1.10	4.07	1.35	2.63	4.44	4.56
1980	6.65	18.11	4.25	4.25	1.14	3.90	4.08	5.81	6.45	11.16
1981	9.76	25.33	5.67	5.47	2.21	4.86	3.59	7.04	9.62	11.29
1982	12.90	31.42	9.49	6.87	3.65	6.17	5.10	10.06	11.39	12.66
1983	16.77	38.47	11.89	9.17	3.90	15.87	6.42	15.41	14.46	16.75
1984	33.39	80.41	18.38	27.51	6.92	36.54	19.06	34.75	34.88	37.81
1985	38.01	99.55	22.61	31.71	7.86	39.50	19.77	40.25	38.51	45.27
1986	51.65	136.11	28.31	49.51	11.66	57.12	24.79	61.28	58.98	81.23
1987	61.38	214.18	38.95	75.04	15.41	75.11	33.06	89.02	78.62	98.52
1988	62.32	265.95	41.96	95.74	18.73	86.00	36.09	114.85	94.64	110.54
1989	72.96	315.66	43.11	117.01	21.08	103.01	40.68	141.56	118.46	132.38
1990	97.06	432.79	55.32	154.00	28.48	133.24	52.38	193.79	149.02	182.11
1991	120.02	558.11	66.71	190.68	35.90	165.24	63.85	245.71	178.63	234.28
1992	179.80	903.17	93.28	242.25	47.54	208.40	82.59	346.52	224.50	352.37
1993	241.93	1302.25	136.64	286.49	53.51	270.63	100.00	436.47	265.43	530.46
1994	302.53	1681.17	203.77	352.03	68.50	380.93	123.20	566.53	322.44	792.37
1995	343.14	1980.00	222.26	421.51	83.90	465.61	151.55	690.62	384.84	985.67
1996	399.82	2276.06	233.97	522.02	97.72	575.69	172.06	815.76	484.53	1163.63
1997	457.62	2520.38	241.43	581.39	107.61	640.66	226.19	905.54	561.28	1550.59
1998	530.18	2901.45	246.53	736.44	115.28	688.51	232.40	998.61	609.49	1771.92
1999	597.48	3311.94	254.95	815.85	120.89	757.12	255.05	1027.81	657.70	2022.78

(*continued*)

(continued)

	Fujian	Guangdong	Guangxi	Hebei	Heilongjiang	Jiangsu	Jilin	Liaoning	Shandong	Zhejiang
2000	720.38	3454.07	277.41	992.53	122.85	938.57	250.65	1113.83	853.14	2646.38
2001	800.02	3585.68	309.65	1108.63	129.86	1099.16	267.64	1077.48	1039.14	3339.72
2002	947.48	4051.73	361.31	1205.46	159.17	1372.44	341.70	1207.79	1269.04	4368.89
2003	1303.93	4607.78	419.71	1398.26	190.43	1620.18	411.49	1406.75	1598.46	6360.70
2004	1505.09	5275.32	513.26	1556.59	242.94	1719.21	447.53	1623.54	1831.02	7192.28
2005	1758.53	5050.12	599.58	1550.29	275.72	1453.89	506.25	1579.53	1864.47	3522.66
2006	2232.70	6528.44	897.10	1863.67	278.84	1577.56	886.65	1888.86	2004.40	4234.06
2007	2429.56	7634.25	1111.61	2187.91	340.96	1708.65	1085.80	2175.29	2353.89	4911.65
2008	2837.28	8607.80	1219.67	2392.11	435.94	1872.73	1228.98	2538.08	2717.76	4430.34
2009	3386.39	10246.38	1552.03	2927.45	589.66	2136.77	1371.75	3084.38	3113.79	4369.91
2010	4015.28	6888.24	1916.21	3479.46	707.94	1913.68	1390.98	3463.60	3515.29	4649.07
2011	4056.65	6160.79	2121.89	4029.31	797.43	1271.98	1401.94	3915.64	3512.81	5603.34
2012	3778.81	5303.18	2463.02	4523.31	905.09	506.64	1437.87	3231.53	3338.89	6433.85
2013	4511.76	5135.46	2815.52	4620.45	1010.60		1387.09	3161.26	3264.15	7350.10
2014	5188.35	5688.22	3471.01	5005.15	1127.92		1105.91	3142.46	2877.51	7003.52

Appendix 5: Average RCC Loans, RMB/Mou, 1979–2014, Middle Provinces

	Anhui	Henan	Hubei	Hunan	Inner Mongolia	Jiangxi	Shanxi
1979	1.37	4.36	2.69	2.40	1.69	1.14	5.72
1980	2.48	6.37	3.54	3.81	2.00	1.71	7.94
1981	3.51	8.44	3.90	4.88	2.23	2.21	10.64
1982	5.02	9.99	4.58	6.01	2.73	3.36	12.15
1983	6.29	11.56	6.41	6.98	3.46	5.14	16.91
1984	12.68	22.38	17.57	12.35	6.43	9.83	37.65
1985	14.28	24.08	17.80	14.67	6.98	11.86	40.06
1986	20.81	33.12	21.74	22.54	8.20	15.47	49.88
1987	25.67	45.79	29.60	32.79	10.66	19.02	62.65
1988	28.45	52.57	35.28	34.31	13.53	22.58	83.58
1989	30.16	61.70	41.14	38.68	17.05	25.56	109.65
1990	39.59	81.69	52.68	53.31	21.50	34.93	144.25
1991	50.00	100.18	64.23	68.17	26.23	44.64	181.18
1992	59.77	122.81	85.03	92.66	34.82	60.36	223.88
1993	74.65	142.94	107.23	128.76	45.85	80.79	260.44
1994	102.54	193.22	127.29	196.30	62.09	109.26	321.71
1995	134.95	242.86	158.51	269.04	82.28	140.70	402.18
1996	168.69	301.64	193.39	321.18	89.79	178.18	474.29
1997	201.16	360.01	229.46	328.27	94.74	193.98	544.25
1998	229.91	407.92	266.81	380.18	106.69	224.09	609.66
1999	259.95	448.75	254.02	406.30	122.21	240.06	643.46
2000	273.25	510.58	280.87	464.93	154.91	299.45	697.40
2001	338.16	583.98	330.02	522.52	218.35	353.17	946.01
2002	393.72	655.43	385.26	590.47	248.60	443.11	1085.24
2003	469.80	737.51	478.25	690.76	302.66	620.67	1569.22
2004	557.97	846.75	565.53	793.95	356.43	682.22	1888.32
2005	642.15	915.71	617.82	845.16	395.75	806.68	2155.48
2006	762.91	1087.05	753.53	998.94	479.45	870.04	2683.29
2007	892.78	1221.53	896.24	1045.06	559.73	1026.70	3008.28
2008	953.51	1379.46	1020.55	1205.86	714.69	1247.57	3293.98
2009	929.26	1668.98	908.47	1411.73	851.67	1557.00	3965.83
2010	857.38	1897.02	1039.05	1606.45	1029.03	1796.14	4720.69
2011	955.05	1987.25	1162.68	1687.12	1190.09	2066.03	5311.53
2012	795.64	2069.23	1037.39	1812.73	1377.00	2237.65	5473.70
2013	765.05	2325.86	809.63	1897.41	1553.57	2296.68	6000.20
2014		2439.55	511.50	1832.92	1539.01	2430.96	6028.58

Appendix 6: Average RCC Loans, RMB/Mou, 1979–2014, Eastern Provinces

	Gansu	Guizhou	Ningxia	Qinghai	Shaanxi	Sichuan	Xinjiang	Yunnan
1979	1.96	3.79	1.65	3.49	3.50	3.27	1.01	3.05
1980	2.46	5.64	2.01	4.15	4.88	6.87	0.99	4.07
1981	3.09	7.15	2.01	4.40	5.90	6.51	0.99	5.27
1982	3.80	9.21	2.62	5.63	7.21	8.20	1.08	7.66
1983	4.12	12.23	3.77	7.02	9.76	12.30	1.71	12.75
1984	8.14	15.51	7.45	11.68	20.17	22.25	6.02	23.40
1985	10.18	16.84	10.01	16.57	22.45	23.06	6.50	25.77
1986	13.13	19.46	10.32	16.72	31.39	31.19	7.39	31.12
1987	15.93	22.46	12.21	15.95	41.00	39.73	10.43	38.46
1988	17.81	23.81	17.62	17.90	47.92	39.14	12.90	39.45
1989	21.01	22.89	23.32	18.96	57.26	48.50	16.49	40.03
1990	26.57	26.06	27.88	20.48	73.29	62.66	18.94	44.97
1991	32.55	28.11	32.31	22.52	89.22	75.89	21.25	49.89
1992	41.43	36.58	39.44	26.14	114.64	103.69	25.98	65.21
1993	59.52	43.83	54.59	33.03	147.43	138.30	33.24	86.29
1994	78.67	53.92	74.62	44.48	190.95	191.88	56.18	113.55
1995	102.65	66.48	99.16	64.50	262.13	251.52	79.74	145.69
1996	133.11	75.95	119.85	73.53	307.01	311.92	77.92	206.71
1997	158.41		141.06	81.69	398.64	390.54	91.59	264.08
1998	183.82	103.78	150.40	109.01	444.16	440.15	97.51	279.13
1999	213.60	123.53	156.63	128.37	483.46	543.29	106.45	296.67
2000	276.40	151.53	188.00	1,650.77	574.13	591.47	122.13	321.55
2001	337.34	198.21	278.88	271.82	712.10	689.41	167.21	368.29
2002	431.52	270.16	437.32	389.83	853.87	761.89	223.53	447.76
2003	522.05	320.64	738.13	579.91	1027.27	886.97	317.03	561.99
2004	589.22	418.94	920.91	616.10	1152.66	981.92	374.89	650.19
2005	651.64	518.29	1193.91	614.18	1278.54	1022.64	401.51	854.16
2006	787.81	750.34	1391.33	672.25	1588.87	1223.08	374.13	975.51
2007	915.64	937.52	1458.36	1215.26	1831.12	1490.60	534.90	1225.81
2008	925.45	1120.90	1692.47	1573.90	1977.77	1777.03	672.26	1481.77
2009	1280.04	1519.82	1722.06	1979.38	2470.72	2402.78	912.49	1840.02
2010	1480.88	1892.73	2137.02	2321.50	2815.52	2036.72	1306.95	2236.80
2011	1670.43	2093.44	2552.70	2331.99	3178.08	2326.07	1730.34	2617.18
2012	2224.50	2537.88	2270.02	2956.82	3681.87	2745.28	2238.74	3008.09
2013	2764.98	3037.99	2754.60	3583.14	4226.99	3060.27	2191.05	3494.80
2014	3262.10	2923.47	2341.60	4144.12	4513.93	3451.81	2202.81	4148.15

Appendix 7: *National Rural Household Loans Per Mou*

Year	Total loan	Formal loan			Informal loan			
	RMB/mou	Total	Bank loan	RCC	Total	Rural Cooperative Fund	Informal lending	Zero-interest informal lending
1986	32.84	11.85	11.85		20.99			
1987	45.38	15.39	15.39		29.99			
1988	54.38	15.96	15.96		38.42			
1989	50.04	11.09	11.09		38.95			
1990	51.22	13.20	13.20		38.02			
1991	60.44	16.15	16.15		44.29			
1992	80.82	19.20	19.20		61.62			
1993	102.22	22.40	22.40		79.82	4.58	75.24	45.81
1994	118.76	27.92	27.92		90.84	6.10	84.75	47.40
1995	135.82	33.62	33.62		102.20	7.66	94.54	49.03
1996	164.94	42.78	42.78		122.17	6.22	115.94	59.79
1997	156.33	38.42	38.42		117.91	4.67	113.24	61.32
1998	167.26	35.63	35.63		131.63	5.87	125.76	62.32
1999	177.27	44.69	44.69		132.58	6.27	126.31	64.81
2000	192.27	57.56	57.56		134.70	0.89	133.81	69.90
2001	190.81	56.24	56.24		134.57	1.52	133.05	65.46
2002	184.40	49.08	49.08		135.32	0.94	134.39	71.56
2003	243.60	80.88	38.45	42.43	162.71		162.71	99.91
2004	219.32	76.82	32.80	44.02	142.50		142.50	92.19
2005	228.74	83.91	34.43	49.48	144.84		144.84	94.03
2006	236.13	91.63	36.00	55.63	144.51		144.51	96.46
2007	223.61	89.17	27.13	62.04	134.45		134.45	109.47
2008	287.38	126.49	40.06	86.43	160.88		160.88	105.07
2009	330.76	124.21	55.68	68.53	206.55		206.55	136.57

Appendix 8: Eastern Rural Household Loans Per Mou

Year	Total loan	Formal loan			Informal loan			
	RMB/ mou	Total	Bank loan	RCC	Total	Rural Cooperative Fund	Informal lending	Zero-interest informal lending
1986	59.32	19.21	19.21		40.11		40.11	
1987	83.26	24.47	24.47		58.79		58.79	
1988	118.19	25.83	25.83		92.36		92.36	
1989	107.14	20.58	20.58		86.56		86.56	
1990	91.24	19.65	19.65		71.59		71.59	
1991	125.95	25.33	25.33		100.62		100.62	
1992	181.91	27.41	27.41		154.51		146.94	
1993	239.44	29.70	29.70		209.74	11.47	198.27	111.44
1994	267.48	37.32	37.32		230.16	17.41	212.75	98.67
1995	295.58	44.96	44.96		250.62	23.35	227.27	85.87
1996	349.32	79.77	79.77		269.54	10.18	259.37	117.09
1997	300.90	41.78	41.78		259.12	5.82	253.29	132.62
1998	350.51	48.11	48.11		302.40	4.74	297.66	134.01
1999	375.36	80.66	80.66		294.70	14.47	280.23	129.66
2000	486.99	130.60	130.60		356.39	0.96	355.43	160.30
2001	445.70	126.44	126.44		319.25	0.15	319.10	144.31
2002	368.82	75.28	75.28		293.54	0.97	292.57	132.89
2003	418.21	112.11	82.67	29.44	306.10		306.10	189.40
2004	404.96	127.63	70.59	57.04	277.34		277.34	173.54
2005	449.42	144.17	60.35	83.82	305.25		305.25	199.12
2006	477.64	146.48	51.47	95.01	331.16		331.16	218.94
2007	397.03	143.46	41.46	102.00	253.57		253.57	199.76
2008	599.30	300.69	104.83	195.87	298.60		298.60	182.17
2009	610.13	260.76	161.42	99.33	349.38		349.38	215.13

Appendix 9: Middle Rural Household Loans Per Mou

Year	Total loan	Formal loan			Informal loan			
		Total	Bank loan	RCC	Total	Rural Cooperative Fund	Informal lending	Zero-interest informal loan
1986	25.77	10.24	10.24		15.52		15.52	
1987	33.01	12.60	12.60		20.41		20.41	
1988	40.61	14.18	14.18		26.43		26.43	
1989	30.65	7.19	7.19		23.46		23.46	
1990	36.98	9.95	9.95		27.03		27.03	
1991	39.90	11.88	11.88		28.02		28.02	
1992	46.79	13.17	13.17		33.63		33.63	
1993	55.91	14.55	14.55		40.45	0.80	39.65	27.88
1994	70.03	19.62	19.62		49.61	1.42	48.19	33.95
1995	84.17	24.70	24.70		58.78	2.03	56.75	40.03
1996	97.60	23.78	23.78		73.10	3.18	69.92	41.98
1997	113.66	30.23	30.23		82.81	4.03	78.78	47.14
1998	104.33	20.86	20.86		82.69	2.65	80.04	45.29
1999	104.15	20.81	20.81		81.84	2.09	79.75	46.99
2000	104.01	22.10	22.10		80.56	0.42	80.14	53.46
2001	92.18	16.53	16.53		75.05	0.14	74.91	48.54
2002	106.57	25.24	25.24		80.70	0.31	80.38	56.51
2003	139.61	37.55	7.62	29.93	99.04		99.04	68.42
2004	129.51	43.22	18.56	24.65	82.59		82.59	66.37
2005	134.25	48.09	17.98	30.11	82.86		82.86	63.02
2006	155.96	64.94	23.94	41.00	84.77		84.77	63.71
2007	147.42	49.29	10.41	38.88	94.89		94.89	79.66
2008	154.84	55.35	15.40	39.96	96.16		96.16	80.42
2009	171.06	45.13	10.34	34.79	125.90		125.90	97.61

Appendix 10: Middle Rural Household Loans Per Mou

Year	Total loan	Formal loan			Informal loan			
	Total	Total	Bank loan	RCC	Total	Rural Cooperative Fund	Informal loan	Zero-interest informal loan
1986	17.63	6.94	6.94		10.69		10.69	
1987	27.65	10.68	10.68		16.97		16.97	
1988	28.60	11.32	11.32		17.28		17.28	
1989	35.93	10.04	10.04		25.88		25.88	
1990	35.13	12.17	12.17		22.96		22.96	
1991	44.19	16.87	16.87		27.32		27.32	
1992	57.77	23.47	23.47		34.31		34.31	
1993	75.74	29.53	29.53		46.21	5.49	40.72	25.71
1994	86.78	34.85	34.85		51.94	5.26	46.68	29.98
1995	99.15	40.80	40.80		58.35	4.99	53.35	34.76
1996	139.52	48.27	48.27		91.25	8.82	82.43	45.24
1997	114.53	51.81	51.81		62.72	4.93	57.79	26.48
1998	140.15	53.64	53.64		86.51	12.92	73.59	36.71
1999	141.98	59.00	59.00		82.97	7.00	75.98	40.01
2000	167.07	76.38	76.38		90.69	1.87	88.82	42.50
2001	171.63	78.76	78.76		92.87	6.02	86.85	29.42
2002	201.83	83.85	83.85		117.98	2.51	115.47	50.99
2003	314.72	143.00	55.24	87.76	171.72		171.72	85.40
2004	284.05	117.00	32.44	84.56	167.05		167.05	79.10
2005	271.72	120.28	52.75	67.53	151.43		151.43	73.10
2006	240.66	105.87	46.50	59.37	134.79		134.79	71.15
2007	244.74	141.00	59.55	81.44	103.75		103.75	85.60
2008	321.48	131.27	36.71	94.56	190.21		190.21	90.78
2009	433.26	176.46	53.02	123.44	256.81		256.81	149.76

CHAPTER 2

China's Sorrow

2.1 Introduction

In this chapter and the next we ask: how did China's agricultural economy get to the state of dismal subsistence found in the Republican era? This is not a trivial question, nor is it easy to answer. As Edgar Snow once remarked: "*In China, the blow falls as the culmination of a long series of afflictions*".[1] These afflictions arise from calamities and conflicts, from nature and from man, and with path dependencies that cause friction against any static depiction of China's condition at any moment in time. In our context, the Republican era is a moment in time—dynamic within itself, yes—but an endpoint to some 4000 years of geopolitical and natural history. How this history evolved is important to understand so as to place follow-on topics of agricultural finance and credit within a proper context. The context is not only agricultural credit in its current state as presented in Chap. 1, but the need over 2000 years before the Republican era to make multiple attempts at bringing credit in one form or another to farmers; and then to recognize that public—or governmental—involvement in agricultural credit was largely as a consequence of this history.

---

[1] Snow, Edgar "In the Wake of China's Flood" China Weekly Review, January 23, 1932, page 243 (originally published in New York Herald Tribune magazine, December 6, 1931.

2.2 Affliction

Consider then the afflictions of 1932 and through the middle of 1933. In the period between January 1 and July 10, 1933 the National Flood Relief Commission in China itemized the following natural catastrophes: Zhejiang with flood in six districts; Jiangxi with flood in 14 districts; Hunan with flood in 32 districts; Henan with flood in 11 districts, drought in seven districts, frost in four districts, hailstones in 11 districts, locusts in three districts, and windstorm in six districts; Shaanxi with drought in 13 districts, frost in 31 districts, hail in seven districts, wind in 37 districts, and flood in three districts; Gansu with earthquake in seven districts, drought in four districts, famine in 30 districts, and plague in one district; Anhui with wind in two districts, flood in four districts, and hail in two districts; Guizhou with drought in 13 districts, hail in three districts, flood in four districts, and wind in three districts; Jiangsu with flood in one district.[2] A week after releasing this report the Yellow River, often named as 'China's Sorrow', 'The Ungovernable', and 'Scourge of the Sons of Han' began to rise. In Sanyuan, Shaanxi Province, the river rose rapidly drowning some 5,000 peasants from both farmlands and mountain areas. Flooding spread to Henan, Hebei, and Shandong.[3] By the time the Yellow River subsided, approximately 50,000 Chinese in total had perished, 2 million were rendered homeless and 1 million starving. In Changyuan district of Hebei alone, losses were evaluated at $37,210,000 (Mexican silver), with 2223 villages flooded, 619,000 Chinese homeless and 475,000 mou (1 acre = 6 mou) under water.[4]

Meanwhile China was embattled. As the Yellow River began to rise an Armistice was signed by Japan and China halting further militarism in

---

[2] Editorial, "Details of Recent Floods, Famines and Droughts" China Weekly Review July 29, 1933, page 373.

Buck, J.L., S.Warren, Y.C, Yieh, H.Y. Shen and L.S.C. Smythe (1932). "The 1931 Flood in China: An Economic Survey" Dept. of Agricultural Economics, College of Agriculture and Forestry, University of Nanjing and the National Flood Relief Commission, Bulletin #1, April 1932.

[3] Editorial. "Yellow River Rises Rapidly" China Weekly Review. August 5, 1933, page 397.

Editorial, "Yellow River Threatens Return to Ancient Channel" China Weekly Review August 5, 1933, page 417.

[4] Editorial, "Yellow River has Subsided, But Losses are Great" China Weekly Review September 23, 1933, page 158.

Editorial, "Yellow River Floods Cost 50,000 lives" China Weekly Review, September 30 1933, page 182.

Manchuria and areas North of the Great Wall. Between 1931 and 1932 some 222,000 Chinese, including 54,000 civilians were killed or wounded in conflicts with Japan in Manchuria and Shanghai.[5] In Southern China, Sichuan was in the midst of a senseless civil war with casualties running into tens of thousands. Communist forces under Zhu De and Mao Zhedong were in constant battle with the Nationalist forces of Chiang Kai-shek in Henan, Hunan, Fujian, Hubei, Sichuang, Anhui, Jiangxi, and Guangdong with a horrible toll to the agricultural economy. Chiang Kai-shek ordered a reward for Zhu De or Mao Zhedong $100,000 alive or $80,000 dead with his head delivered to Nanchang.[6] In Western Hunan in 1932 it was reported that 50,000 people died in the strife and in Fujian the land was laid to waste and abandoned. In June of 1933 a burial detachment from the Shanghai Red Swastika (Red Cross) proceeded to Anhui to bury 18,000 uninterred bodies.[7]

Even in areas that were not vested in civil war or anti-communist campaigns or communist insurgency, roving warlords left over from the early republican period formed massive bandit gangs that laid havoc to rural regions. In some instances, warlord armies reached tens of thousands and they joined the formal government with provincial controls. But these were not truly governing forces and exploitation of farmers ensued through dues or common confiscation of crops. To maintain the warlord army farmers were taxed to the extreme. For example, Shaanxi Province wrecked in recent years by drought and famine was one of the poorest in China. But poverty in China was not always driven by natural calamities, with the remnants of the warlord period playing havoc on farm income and consumption. Shaanxi had been under the control of the 'Christian General' Feng Yu-xiang since 1920 and it was he who ordered the paying of a land tax through 1934. The nationalist government had outlawed Likin—a transit tax—in 1930 but this was simply replaced by taxes in disguise. The central government had ordered production and consumption taxes, but at the local level there was also a host of taxes and duties which farmers had to pay including land tax, poll tax, bandit-suppression duties, military dues, commissary dues, *ming-tuan* or militia dues, land registration fees, opium

[5] Editorial, "Japanese Losses 11,380: Chinese losses 222,000 in Undeclared War" China Weekly Review, June 17, 1933, page 94.
[6] Editorial, "Chiang Kai-shek Increases Price on Communists Heads" China Weekly Review, October 21, 1933, page 311.
[7] Editorial, "Shanghai Red Swastika Society Burial Corp will Proceed to *Anhuei*" China Weekly Review, June 10, 1933, page 80.

land duty, shares of provincial bank, provincial treasury note, village pacification fee, rice duty, trade tax, special tax, land deed examination fee, stamp tax, and other duties and surcharges levied by local (rather than provincial) governments. Some of these taxes were extraordinarily extortionary. If the farm registration fee was not paid the land could be confiscated; the bank shares were never issued to farmers; the stamp tax was paid whether or not a shop was in the village; provincial treasury notes were apportioned and issued to farmers whether they wanted them or not; the lands planted to opium were decided by the province, but when yield was not sufficient the $10/mou duty had to be paid by those farmers who had not yet planted opium. And when the provincial government sent its agents to press farmers for these taxes, the agents had to be fully, and generously, accommodated and entertained at the expense of farmers. In the region of *Hanzhong*, fertile with irrigation, the net proceeds from double-cropped grain, wheat, and beans netted the farmer about $8/mou. The land tax on this was $3.50/mou with $12/mou required to pay for other taxes and duties, meaning the farmer had to come up with $8.50/mou. In the mountainous region of *Liupan* the cost of production per mou was about $3 but the levies and taxes were over $11/mou. When these could not be paid the farmer sold or pawned whatever possessions he had (clothes, furniture etc.) and when that did not satisfy the demand, he simply moved off the land, risking torture or even death if caught.[8]

Taxes, of course had to be paid in cash, with no facility for credit and when pressed at harvest, farmers could not afford to store grain for future sale. Hence, with all farmers selling at the same time, abundance lowered the price, so that any possible benefit to store post-harvest was lost to taxes while benefits of storage accrued to the marketers and wholesalers. And in times of scarcity, due perhaps to drought, the farmer had no crop to sell and could not afford the steep rise in prices that accompanied famine. And even if the farmer had surplus worth selling, often the commodities could not be moved. For example, the local price of rice in Xi'an was $20/picul (a picul being about 60kg) while the local price in South Shaanxi was $3/picul. A merchant could profit by transporting from South to North. But the exactions and extortions along the way by 'special' tax collections,

---

[8] Henry S.T. Liu "The Poverty of Shensi" China Weekly Review, January 7, 1933, page 276.

extortion by agents and city gate keepers, bandits, and lack of communication with potential buyers made the venture perilous if not unprofitable.[9]

2.3 Population Growth and Agricultural Productivity

China's growth path has puzzled many Chinese scholars for decades and what is clear is that to understand the state of agriculture is a consequence of centuries of dynamic adjustments in land, labor, innovation, politics, and culture. Data limitations prohibit robust econometric or statistical means to map out with exactness the dynamic adjustments in agricultural productivity, but certain frameworks in economics provide a convenient means to provide reasonable conjectures and a story line that we believe to be reasonable. That we use the word 'conjecture' signifies that our story line is open to debate and question, but our framework does not depart too much from the conventional wisdom of many development economists and China scholars.

The notion of subsistence plays a critical role in any study of economic growth and development. Subsistence, as we shall define it, is the barrier between economic surplus and poverty. For the laborer it is the wage rate that can purchase food, shelter, and clothing to survive a minimal nutritional state of survival. The wage earner has no surplus and cannot save to any extent that would contribute in the present or in the future to capital. Poverty is a state of deficit where capital, if it was ever present, is de-accumulated to meet the most basic nutritional requirements or less. The further removed these people are from subsistence the more they are confined to a poverty trap, with fewer and fewer opportunities to save even to the point of smoothing consumption, let alone accumulating capital. Surplus is the main economic driver of an economy and this would accrue to the lucky wage earner who can save beyond subsistence with the opportunity to invest in capital of one form or another.

For the farmer who owns land the wage equivalent is economic rent, and by rent we refer to the Ricardian concept in which rent captures the incremental gain in surplus from the next unit of capital added to the production process. To the farmer, the total surplus is the accumulation of these marginal rents across all units of capital employed. Surplus is equivalent to profit. So it may be the case that the farmer gains nothing from the

---

[9] Henry S.T. Liu, op cit.

last unit of capital employed, but profits on margin from all units of capital previously employed.

Malthus[10] and Ricardo,[11] writing in 1815, were the first to lay out the relationships between land and labor, and land and output, and labor and output, ideas which have taken on fundamental importance in modern day development economics. Malthus in particular noted the relationship between the abundance of land, and the relationship between this abundance and a growing population. From the standpoint of economic utility the agricultural economy represented a zero sum game. The farmer (or landlord) who achieved surplus of price minus cost on the last and all previous units of output could only do so at a cost to the consumer who faced the high prices and thus a general reduction in welfare. As prices rise then so too will the demand for wages, so that a level of subsistence could at least be maintained. As wages (and other forms of input, each ultimately driven by wages) rise then rents and profits must fall accordingly to the disadvantage of the farmer. Thus, in the commodity world of agriculture, with little room for monopoly profits on land, any gain in producer surplus can only be achieved at the expense of consumers, and any gain in welfare to consumers (generally referred to by economists as consumer surplus) is achieved only at the expense of the reduced surplus of the farmer. Such is the nature of supply and demand.

But Malthus went further than any other economists of the time to link land to population "*It is, therefore strictly true, that land produces the necessaries of life, – produces food, materials, and labor, – produces the means by which, and by which alone, an increase in people may be brought into being, and supported. In this respect it is fundamentally different from every kind of machine known to man; and it is natural to suppose that it should be attended with some peculiar effects*".[12] And then… "*There is nothing so absolutely unavoidable in the progress of society as the fall of wages, that is such a*

---

[10] Malthus, T. R. (1888). An essay on the principle of population: or, A view of its past and present effects on human happiness. Reeves & Turner.

Malthus, T. R. (1815). An inquiry into the nature and progress of rent, and the principles by which it is regulated. for J. Murray, and J. Johnson and Company.

[11] Ricardo, D. (1815). An Essay on the Influence of a Low Price of Corn on the Profits of Stock: Shewing the Inexpediency of Restrictions on Importation, with Remarks on Mr. Malthus' Two Last Publications: "An Inquiry Into the Nature and Progress of Rent," and "The Grounds of an Opinion on the Policy of Restricting the Importation of Foreign Corn," John Murray.

[12] Malthus, T. R. (1815), Op Cit, page 11.

fall as, combined with the habits of the laboring classes, will regulate the progress of population according to the means of subsistence. And when, from the want of an increase in capital, the increase in produce is checked, and the means of subsistence come to a stand, the wages of labor must necessarily fall so low, as only just to maintain the existing population, and to prevent any increase".[13] Malthus then contends further that the economy of subsistence, and really the perpetuation of subsistence, as a steady state or economic attractor is tied inevitably to the land. As the most fertile land becomes more fully utilized it is worth the farmer's while to expand to less-fertile land, which uncultivated would have a considerably lower market value, and could ultimately achieve rents or surplus, even at a lower yield, and that for incremental profits to be the same on the new land as the old, real wages must fall. Inevitably, as populations rise more land must be brought into production, but with the most fertile land already under cultivation, new cultivation must be on lower-quality or less-fertile land. Since this land produces less output, the production per capita must fall even if the rate that new land is brought into production keeps pace with the increase in population. Prices must rise with demand, but so also must wage rates rise so labor can afford the same nutrition bundle as the previous generation. If this is not the case then even more of the population is driven below the subsistence level into persistent poverty. If wages do rise, then farms employing labor will see diminished profit, and will hire only so much labor and provide so much product that the surplus available to it provides at least the subsistence level. If wages are sticky and do not rise with the cost of food, then food demand will fall, and with this so must prices to clear supply, and again the farmer will stop producing when all surplus is exhausted at the level of subsistence. Once again, the economy falls into a Malthusian trap[14] of sustained subsistence, and this pattern continues as each generation of a rising population is followed by ever-increasing cultivation of poorer and poorer land quality and fertility.

This Malthusian trap is driven by two factors. The first is the dynamic relationship between land cultivation and population growth and the second determined by agricultural output and population growth. These,

---

[13] Malthus, T. R. (1815). Op Cit, page 19.

[14] The earliest paper to discuss the Malthusian Trap are
Boulding, K. E. (1955). The Malthusian model as a general system. Social and Economic Studies, 4(3):195–205.
Hagen, E. E. (1959). Population and economic growth. The American Economic Review, 49(3):310–327.

combined, lead to the economic relationship between agricultural production and land under cultivation. Now, to distinguish between developed and underdeveloped economies we can start at the same place of abundant arable land of good quality brought under cultivation, with land—initially being free—gaining value as it is tamed and brought under cultivation. There would exist in this primitive economy two classes of people; those that cultivate land and create wealth in doing so, and those that provide the labor for cultivation. Of the land class living at least for the time being with a surplus, that surplus can be invested or consumed. But consumed on what? Clothes and shelter would be a start and so it might be that the demand for these things increase and some farmers put some of their capital, not into new lands but into garments and manufacturing. Raw materials would have to be extracted and so again new industries would build up until the economy becomes diversified. With free and open trade any excess in inventory could be sold and traded for other goods, giving rise to a permanent merchant class, and as the industrial base grows as such, the agricultural share of the economy diminishes.

As for the largely agricultural economies Malthus identifies four drivers of economic surplus to agricultural production.[15]

1. An accumulation of capital that will lower the profits of stock (meaning that the next bundle of surplus invested in newer uncultivated lands or improvements to existing lands may reduce profits at the margin, but increase profits to the whole.),
2. An increase in population that will lower the wages of labor,
3. Such agricultural improvements, or such increase of exertion, as will diminish the number of laborers necessary to produce a given effect (output).
4. An increase in the price of agricultural produce, from increased demand, without nominally lowering the expense of production.

Both Malthus and Ricardo focused their ideas on the value of rents. Rent in this context has two meanings. In the first case, rent can be viewed in the non-economist way as an amount paid by a tenant to the landlord and this would be set equal to the amount of surplus the landlord could have earned had he cultivated the land himself after the employment of labor. This is the amount charged to a tenant who using his own labor and

[15] Malthus, T. R. (1815). Op Cit, page 22.

whatever tools and capital available could extract a profit of at least the prevailing wage plus perhaps a return on capital employed. The landlord would be indifferent to receiving the rent in payment or cultivation since the two flows of capital are (theoretically) equivalent. The economists' view of rent is quite similar, but does not require a comparable transaction or negotiation between landlord and tenant. The economists' use of the term 'rent' applies to the amount of profit that can be earned on the next unit of land put under cultivation. On this latter point, Malthus points out (as does Ricardo) that across time, a farmer will not willingly invest in arable, uncultivated land unless the last unit of land also showed positive economic rents from either the market or a tenant. If the last unit of land was not providing a profit, and the next unit of land was of lower quality and fertility, then under those present conditions the next unit of land would surely be unprofitable.

Seventeen years earlier in 1798, Malthus had published his "Essay on the Principle of Population". No doubt his views on population set the foundations for the views expressed in the 1815 essay on the theory of rents. Malthus took an ecological view to economics. He could not easily settle with static assumptions about populations and economic growth: "*But as, by the law of our nature which makes food necessary to the life of man, population can never actually increase beyond the lowest nourishment capable of supporting it, a strong check on population, from the difficulty of acquiring food, must be constantly in operation. This difficulty must fall somewhere, and must necessarily be severely felt in some or other of the various forms of misery, or the fear of misery, by a large portion of mankind*".[16] It was from this that Malthus imagined a relation defined by the ratio of the rate of growth in agricultural productivity and the rate of growth in population and illustrated how this ratio depreciated as the rate of population outstripped the rate of agricultural production. Every unit of depreciation represented an unbounded increase in the proportion of population shifting from bountiful food consumption to subsistence, or worse. With Darwinian insight, which we can say because Darwin was heavily influenced by Malthus, Malthus wrote: "*Yet still the power of population being in every period so much superior, the increase of the human species can only be kept down to the level of the means of subsistence by the constant operation of the strong law of necessity acting as a check upon the greater power*".[17]

---

[16] Malthus, T. R. (1798). Op Cit, page 2.
[17] Malthus, T. R. (1798). Op Cit, page 7–8.

Considering only the population dynamic, Malthus saw the inevitability of nature's course in reducing populations so that individuals caught in the poverty trap—as we define it those individuals whose best hope of livelihood from any sources is sustained for some period of time always below the rate of subsistence—would ultimately perish from nature, vice, or man so that an equilibrium at the subsistence level is returned to balance. Sadly, the burden of death would almost always fall on the poor, with those farmers in surplus for whatever reason perishing in only the direst of circumstances.

Interestingly, Malthus mused over population control by policy and weighed the evils of human intervention versus nature. Malthus was a reverend, a man of religion, so it is not unreasonable that he would blame human sexual nature—vice—in keeping the population in check. He argued that man's (sexual) inclination is voluntary and does not often come about with mathematical calculations of the reduced food share should such inclinations result in procreation, and he believed that this was unique to humans. Other animals, and indeed vegetation, keep this in check so that a natural balance is always in place: "*Considered as a restraint on a strong natural inclination, it must be allowed to produce a certain degree of temporary unhappiness; but evidently slight, compared with the evils which result from any other checks to population; and merely of the same nature as many other sacrifices of temporary to permanent gratification, which it is the business of a moral agent continually to make*" and then, "*When a general corruption of morals, with regard to the sex, pervades all the classes of society, its effects must necessarily be to poison the springs of domestic happiness, to weaken conjugal and parental affection, and to lessen the united exertions and ardour of parents in the care and education of their children; – effects which cannot take place without a decided diminution of the general happiness and virtue of society...*" and then again, "*Promiscuous intercourse, unnatural passions, violations of the marriage bed, and improper arts to conceal the consequences of irregular connections are preventive checks that clearly come under the head of vice*". Societies that rest on the frequent precipice of subsistence when compared to those societies of greater prosperity are more inclined to sex, vice, and the abuse of women, and in many of the examples provided Malthus seems to correlate this with the most primitive forms of agriculture and rudimentary hunter/gatherer societies.

Moralizing notwithstanding, Malthus' point was (is) unmistakable. That the conflict between population and food security was paramount to resolving persistent poverty. So there are two forces at play and this is critically important. The first is the natural balance between population and food and the human and natural competition for food. Famine is one outcome, but so too is war and bandits as one group in need of food raiding those with food. The constant sub-dividing of land across generations only added to the plight of poverty, sustainability, and subsistence. Malthus did not avoid discussing all of these issues as part of the natural and human consequences of food shortages. The second is economics as previously described and the oscillation between food prices and real wages. These two effects confound each other to deliver a dynamic oscillation around a level of subsistence that is economically relevant not only in the Republican era of China with which were are interested, but also in explaining the main question of this chapter as to how China's agricultural economy got to where it was at that time.

2.4 The Malthusian Trap

The dynamic oscillations so described and the tendency (and by Malthus, the inevitability) of agricultural output to trend always towards subsistence is referred to as the Malthusian Trap. In Malthus' view, even if there is a resurgence in productivity due to a technological innovation of one sort or another, the gains in productivity will be short lived (years or even generations) if populations keep on rising.

We assume that labor is in proportion to population and that land is finite. In the upper-right quadrant of Fig. 2.1 the amount of land put under cultivation increases but at a diminishing rate. This captures the natural effects discussed by Malthus and Ricardo on diminishing marginal productivity. The two-dimensional elements of the Malthusian Trap are captured in the lower-left quadrant. Here is illustrated the productivity oscillations as described by Malthus. These oscillations can rise based along the x-axis to capture technological innovations in cultivation, irrigation, fertilization, seed selection, and so on, which even without exogenous factors such as drought, flood, hurricanes, or locusts would ultimately diminish as population increases down the y-axis. In actuality the oscillations come from both economics and natural calamities, and we can add to this war, civil or otherwise. But ultimately, no matter whether the recent history is one of surplus or one of deficit, one way or another the productivity-population curve will return to the subsistence level. The lower-right quadrant is simply a labor/population transfer quadrant to

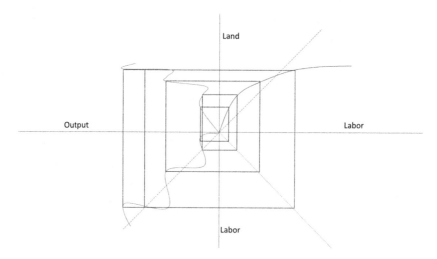

Fig. 2.1 Malthusian Trap

ensure a proper mapping of labor across the upper-right and lower-left quadrants. The unknown, but very interesting upper-left quadrant illustrates the consequence of the two effects. The x-axis is output and the y-axis is land and the result shows periodic rises and falls in agricultural output, even as land put into cultivation increases. Aggregate output is rising on trend as more land is put into production, but with the consequences of rising populations, and diminishing returns to land and the output/population oscillations assigned it is expected that the agricultural economy would see periods of plentiful above trend and periods of misery below trend. Because the rate of agricultural adaptation is so slow, especially in a world with negligible communication, these highs and lows could persist for many years at a time, a sort of Joseph effect with years of plenty followed, inevitably, by years of famine.

How believable is this story? There is no rich data source that would permit this version of the Malthusian model to be tested to proof, but we can rely on historical fact, observations, and anecdote to justify within reasonably logical bounds that the model should not be discarded. Few economists would doubt the long-run appropriateness of the log function in the top-right quadrant. This is the basis of the Malthusian Trap, that as populations increase and more land is brought into production, the per capita quantity of land diminishes and will eventually remain unchanged.

If there were direct empirical evidence that either the lower or upper left figures hold true, then that would provide a strong indication that its opposite would also hold true.

But in the absence of long-term historical population, production and/or land data we must take a back-door approach to using available historical data that would be supportive of the proposed relationships. We can rely on the land to labor ratio diminishing in China (but at an undetermined rate), that China's population has continually increased in time (but with unobserved or immeasurable variance), and that in the absence of labor unions and other wage-setting organizations, the wage-price-labor configuration suggested by Malthus and Ricardo in 1815 hold to be true enough that there are real economic effects that continually push an oscillating wage-price-labor market towards the prevailing level of subsistence. If we can rely on these factors as being more or less true, then we can gain some insights into the lower- and upper-left figures by examining historical patterns in rainfall data.

2.5 Historical Weather Extremes and Agricultural Productivity in China

Historical climate data are rare, but in the case of China records have been reconstituted from local gazetteers and government records on drought and flooding for 120 locations throughout China, but with the most reliable (fewest missing) in East China.[18]

The rainfall data have annual indicators for 120 locations throughout China from 1470 to 2000, covering 531 years of history. The coded identifiers are extreme rainfall (flooding), above average rainfall (moderate

---

[18] CNMA (Chinese National Meteorological Administration) (1981). Yearly charts of dryness/wetness in China for the last 500-year period. Chinese Cartographic Publishing House, Beijing.

Shen et al. (2007). provide a nice description of this data which is sourced from Chinese National Meteorological Administration (CNMA 1981) with updates from Zhang et al. (2003)

Shen, C., Wang, W. C., Hao, Z., & Gong, W. (2007). Exceptional drought events over eastern China during the last five centuries. *Climatic Change*, 85(3-4), 453-471.

Tan, X. (2003). The study of major droughts in China during the past 500 years. *J Disaster Prev Mitig Eng*, 23:77-83.

Zhang D., Li X, and Liang, Y. (2003). Supplement of yearly charts of dryness/wetness in China for the last 500-year period, 1993-2000. *J Appl Meteorol Sci* 14:379-389.

flooding), normal precipitation, below average rainfall (modest drought), and extremely low rainfall (severe drought). Since not all locations had records in each year the best that can be done is to take the percentage of each category for those locations that had an available record. Across all years the average number of missing records was about 43 but prior to 1800 the number of missing records was higher at 53. Nonetheless, the records available probably reflect the important locations at the time, with many simply not existing 300 or 400 years ago, and our presentation is very close to the more in-depth calculations provided in Shen et al. (2007).

The frequency distributions of the four non-normal states are provided in Fig. 2.2 with extreme upper and lower 5% bands provided. These bands can be viewed to capture one in 20 year outcomes, and our main interest is in the right-hand side frequencies. There we find that at least once in every 20 years or five times in a century, at least 36.99% of locations faced extreme floods, 24.10% moderate floods, 37.7% moderate drought, and 25.8% extreme drought. On average 23.2%, 9.78%, 21.01%, and 8.98% of locations faced extreme flooding, moderate flooding, moderate drought, or extreme drought respectively. It is rather astonishing that in any given year nearly one in four locations faced extreme flooding, and one in 10 faced extreme drought.

In Fig. 2.3 we combine the two extreme events of extreme rainfall or extreme drought and find that the distribution is approximately normal with a mean of 32.22% and standard deviation of 7.99%. We find that in one of every 20 years at least 45% of all locations face drought or flooding, and astonishingly in any given year nearly one in three locations faced either extreme drought or flooding. The maximum was 68.18% recorded in the 1640 drought year, and the minimum was 9.26% recorded in 1580.

In Figs. 2.4, 2.5, and 2.6 we plot the extreme drought, flooding, and combined results along with the 10-year moving average. It is observable in each case that over time these events hit certain locations in a seemingly random fashion. But this also provides strong evidence for at least one important aspect of Fig. 2.1, and that is the cyclicality with which these events occur.

The historical record on drought and flooding events are sketchy. As to flooding, the worst year in terms of frequency of floods, Fig. 2.5, was around 1635. To get some perspective on how tragic this flooding might have been, consider this description of the 1930 flood, which may have killed as many as 900,000 Chinese, as described by Edgar Snow: "*Try to visualize in terms of the United States what this colossal misfortune means to*

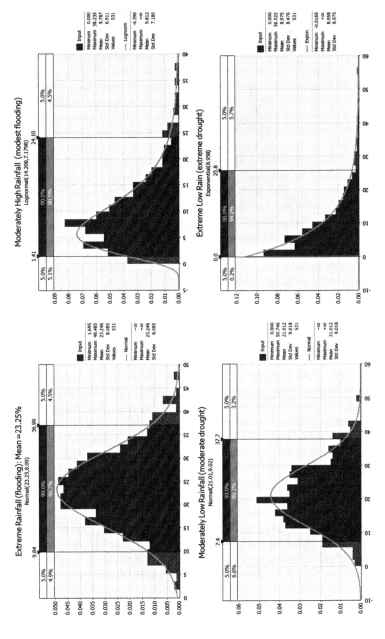

Fig. 2.2 Frequency distributions of rainfall-related risk events, China 1470–2000

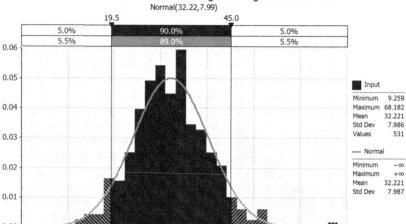

Fig. 2.3 Frequency distribution for extreme flooding or extreme drought

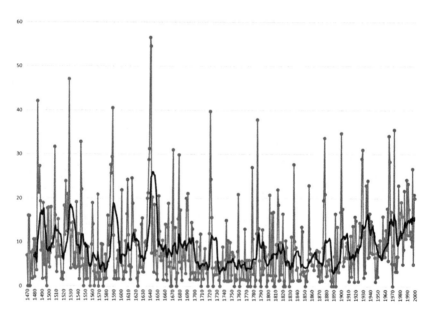

Fig. 2.4 Extreme drought (% of locations available and 10-year moving average)

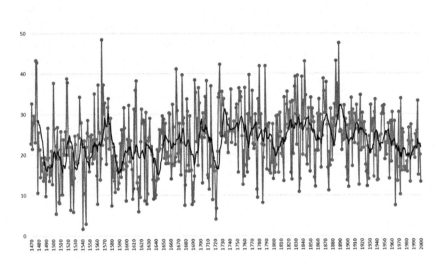

Fig. 2.5 Extreme flooding (% of locations available and 10-year moving average)

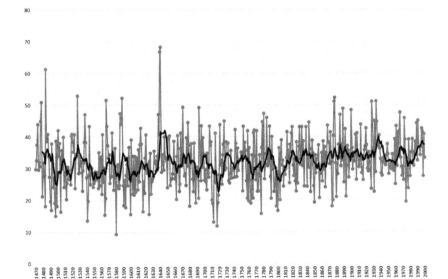

Fig. 2.6 Extreme flooding or drought (% of locations available and 10-year moving average)

China. Imagine that the great lakes were to swell over their shores, cut a wide pathway from Chicago to New York, bury whole cities, completely destroy all crops, wash out railway embankments, cripple light and power facilities, millions of head of cattle, and in the space of a few days change the whole physical appearance from one of thousands of miles of fertile, populated farmlands and prosperous towns to that of a tideless sea, spreading limitless and hiding beneath its calm the wreckage of men and the fruit of their toil. That is what happened in China".[19]

Shen et al. (2007) citing Tan (2003) gives an idea of just how significant the major drought events were.[20] The 1586–89 event affected 47% of locations. This was significant because it was not necessarily a one-year event but an accumulation as indicated by the three-year moving average. Again the three-year moving average is a significant measure because as the drought spread between 1586 and 1587 the number of affected regions was increasing, and because of the duration the amount of groundwater would have been greatly diminished. By 1589, more than 906,000 km² were affected by drought mostly in the Yellow River delta. The effects were devastating with thousands of square kilometers of barren land, no water flowing in rivers, and lakes and dried up springs. One of the lakes was *Taihu* Lake, the third largest freshwater lake in China, which was also a catchment area for any irrigation in the South. The next driest year in the *Taihu* Lake area was the 1934 drought but as severe as that was, the lake did not dry up. So severe was the resulting famine that cannibalism was widely reported.

The most extensive drought on record culminated in 1640 and 1641 which was the culmination of a three-year period with more and more locations falling under drought conditions. Again, any hope of cultivation by groundwater was long lost to much of the affected 1,100,000 km² affected with over 50% of locations under severe drought conditions. The Yellow River dried up as did its expansive catchment area. As a point of comparison, Shen et al. (2007) indicate that the most severe drought since then in the same locality occurred in 1997 when there was no outflow to the sea for more than 300 days and about 700 km or the lower Yellow River completely dried up. No period since has seen such an expansive drought of such intensity and duration and the human cost, for which we

---

[19] Snow, Edgar "In the Wake of China's Flood" *China Weekly Review*, January 23, 1932, page 243 (originally published in *New York Herald Tribune* magazine, December 6, 1931.
[20] Shen et al. (2007). Op Cit, Tan (2003). Op Cit.

can find no specific records, must have been horrendous. Some indications suggest that between 1585 and 1645 (after the demise of the Ming Dynasty in 1644) China's population declined by 40%, but how much was due to the wars of the Ming or a consequence of the famine is not clear.[21] Because famine was a key motivator in the path to developing credit institutions in the Republican era we will devote a later chapter to the economics of famine and the International China Famine Relief Commission.

2.6 Agricultural Productivity

While few would argue that in the extreme years output would be affected, there is no historical record, except anecdotal, of how extreme the events would be. To provide an illustration of output we present in Fig. 2.7 a possible (but by no means verified) history of aggregate output. We assume that in at least one state of nature conditions are perfect so that output is indexed to 100% of potential output. This occurred in 1580 with only 9.259% of locations so affected. The worst outcome we assume occurred in 1640, and by proration assume that in 1640 only 35% of aggregate output was obtained. We next assume that aggregate output decays from the maximum of 100–35% exponentially so that

$$Y_t = 100 e^{\left(-0.017788^* (W_t - 9.259)\right)}$$

and W_t is the recorded percentage of affected locations in year, t.

The result in Fig. 2.7 shows the estimated values across time as well as the 10-year moving average. While by no means representing known aggregate outputs, if it can be believed that the percentage of output decays exponentially with the frequency of locations capturing intensity and duration, the figure may not be far off what China actually suffered in a relative sense. Nonetheless, the important point of consideration is that over history, China has faced considerable challenges to productivity. These exogenous factors only exacerbate the Malthus-Ricardo model of

---

[21] Shen et al. (2007). citing Wakeman (1985) and Temple (2002): Temple R. (2002) The modern world: a joint creation of China and the West. In: Proceedings of the international conference on the review and forecast of Chinese science and technology, Chinese Academy of Engineering and the Chinese Academy of Science, Science Press, Beijing, pp 111–119.

Wakeman F.E. Jr. (1985). The great enterprise: the Manchu reconstruction of imperial order in seventeenth century China, vol. 1. University of California Press, Berkeley, CA.

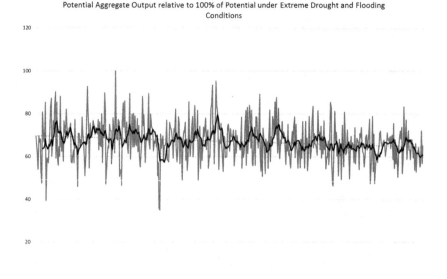

Fig. 2.7 Potential aggregate output with rainfall sensitive exponential decay

wage-price-labor in the sense that in high impact years with diminished agricultural productivity, prices would rise to reduced supply, pushing wage earners into despair. With the rise in prices, real wages fall and households are forced to demand less, and will also demand higher wages if a job can be found. Households unable to access or afford food would perish from starvation affecting further the labor supply. As labor supply declines, real wages would increase, but so too would the cost to those farmers who could raise a crop, reducing profitability, so that eventually between rising wages and decreased profits, both farmer and laborer find an equilibrium at the level of subsistence.

2.7 Political Economy and Dynastic Rule

While economics and natural calamities are very much in line with the oscillations described by Malthus, we cannot ignore the dynastic growth of China's development. Our challenge is in attempting to reduce 2000 years of dynastic rule into a simple two-dimensional figure. This is repre-

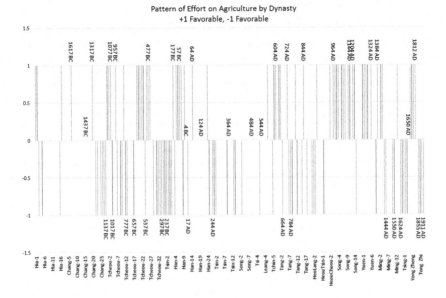

Fig. 2.8 Patterns of effort on agriculture by dynasty and emperor

sented in Figs. 2.8 and 2.9. The representation comes from a 1741 history of China prepared by P. DuHalde, a Jesuit missionary who resided in China for 32 years, documenting from whatever sources the evolution of the Chinese monarchy prior to the first dynasty, and each emperor from the first dynasty of Xia to the Qing dynasty in power at the time of writing.[22]

In the earliest days of China as a nation, it was an agricultural economy that evolved from a hunter-gatherer society. The taming of the land is attributed to China's first emperor Fo Hi, who was so gifted that the people called him *Tien Tse* (Son of Heaven). Fu Xi transformed the hunter-gatherer China into an agrarian economy by teaching the people how to make nets for fishing, and to raise domestic animals and other foods for sacrifice. He also introduced the Chinese character in the form of eight symbols, each made up of lines, that when combined made up 64 charac-

---

[22] DuHalde, P. (1742). The General History of China; Containing a Geographical, Historical, Chronological, Political and Physical Description of the Empire of China, Chinese Tartary and Tibet, Volume 1. 3rd edition. J. Watts, London.

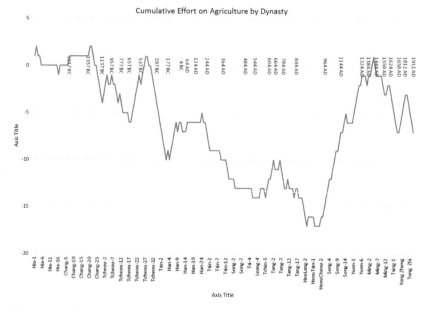

Fig. 2.9 The cumulative effects of dynasties and emperors on agricultural production cycles

ters which were sufficient to get his messages across to the people. He created the Mandarin class by establishing six ministries including Flying Dragon to compose books, Hidden Dragon to establish a calendar, Resident Dragon to design buildings, Protecting Dragon to obviate and relieve the miseries of the people, Terrestrial Dragon to care for the lands, and Water Dragon to look after woods and plants, and manage the water.[23]

With the rising population from domestication (and the implementation of conjugal laws) the second emperor Shen Nong promoted increased productivity and production of food. He invented basic implements for cultivation and established the idea of a central marketplace for trade. He explored biology and sought out plants with certain poisonous qualities that could be used for medicines and the cures for many ailments of the day.[24]

The third emperor Huang Di was only 12 when he inherited the throne but was gifted nonetheless and leveled mountains and built highways to

[23] DuHalde (1742), pages 270–271.
[24] DuHalde (1742), pages 271–273.

promote trade. To foster trade he invented wheel carriages and the use of domesticated oxen and horses to pull them. To promote trade further he was the first emperor to coin money and develop weights and measures. This included the area measure of the mou as 240 paces in length and one in breadth. With each pace being 5 ft a mou measured 6000 ft^2. (The measure of mou used in the present day is one-sixth of an acre or 7260 ft^2 but as early as the Republican era local mou differed considerably.) He ordered physicians to examine the structure of blood-vessels and to develop medicines to prolong life. He discovered the art of dyeing and promoted crafts and instruments including the machines for bruising rice, kitchen furnaces, and kettles which then encouraged not only the production of rice but also its consumption as a Chinese staple. He had the people instructed on the breeding of silk worms, developed techniques to spin off the webs, and then taught them how to use the resulting silk to make clothing.[25] By the time the eight emperor Yao took the throne China was facing immense population pressures, largely because the low lands were subject to such severe flooding that the land could not be populated or cultivated. Emperor Yao undertook the first water management programs by leveling mountains, draining lakes and marshes, enclosing torrential lengths of rivers with high banks or dykes, dividing rivers into several canals expanding the land base considerably, and relieving population pressures while increasing the amount of cultivated land to feed them.[26] So important was cultivation to China's development that the last emperor, Chun, before dynastic rule began, forbade any governor under threat of severe penalties to do anything to discourage husbandry.[27]

Our two-dimensional representation starts at this point—around 2217 B.C.—and is based upon a reading of the many emperors and dynasties, with particular attention as to whether the emperor was enlightened towards agriculture and agricultural development, neutral or unsupportive, unenlightened or destructive. The obvious flaw to the reader is that this is highly subjective. For example, the first emperor of the Xia dynasty, Yu, wrote perhaps the first treaties on agriculture and it was under his reign that the art and science of leveling and contouring mountain lands began, suggesting even at that time that the amount of cultivated lowland was insufficient. In his treaties he taught people how to cultivate, sow, and

---

[25] DuHalde (1742), pages 275–276.
[26] DuHalde (1742), pages 282–283.
[27] DuHalde (1742), pages 284–285.

manure crop lands and modified mountain streams so that the water would flow to agricultural lands.[28] Most readers would agree that such an emperor might be graded as +1, as was emperor Kang Wang around 1077 BC in the early Zhou dynasty who for 26 years had a reign free of war in which his entire time was spent on perfecting agriculture.[29] In comparison, Tai Kan, the third emperor was so absorbed with horses and women that he gave no concern to agricultural land and would without concern trample harvests for the hunt.[30] We assigned Tai Kang a −1. Likewise, the seventh emperor of the Xia dynasty married a woman so cruel and uncaring that (as legend has it) she built a large lake out of agricultural lands, filled it with wine and ordered 3000 people to throw themselves in it.[31] Few would disagree that this rule failed agriculture and so was awarded a score of −1. Many other emperors who survived only a few years (many were poisoned and murdered) and so had not long enough to materially affect agriculture one way or another, or the narrative failed to mention some form of benevolence or agricultural or scientific enlightenment at all, received scores of 0. A benevolent ruler would be like Sui Wen Di, the first ruler of the Sui dynasty around 604 A.D. who built granaries in all towns and ordered that each family, according to their level of subsistence, contribute to the granaries so that rice and corn could be distributed in years of famine.[32] Enlightenment referred to emperors such as Xiao Ming Di, around 64 A.D. who established the first Academy of Science and employed 100,000 men to shore up the walls of the Yellow River for a distance of 55 km.[33] Emperors who undertook warring with the Tartars or other groups, would likely have taxed farmers for grain and paid more attention to geopolitical power, so received a score of −1. On the other hand, emperors who embraced science, literature, and the arts, or who were identified as being specifically kind to farmers, caring in times of calamities, building granaries, expanding canals, building dykes, and so on were given a score of +1.

Figure 2.8 records the raw subjective score. It has certain patterns confined largely to the activities within dynasties through the end of the Qing dynasty in 1911. Perhaps more telling is the cumulative effect in Fig. 2.9.

---

[28] DuHalde (1742), pages 287.
[29] DuHalde (1742), pages 316.
[30] DuHalde (1742), pages 289.
[31] DuHalde (1742), page 296.
[32] DuHalde (1742), page 387.
[33] DuHalde (1742), page 360.

The *x*-axis is by emperor and not time so this does not follow a conventional time scale although we do label years identified in DuHalde's text and from other sources. The *y*-axis should not be interpreted as an absolute scale of productivity but rather as a count measure of the number of consecutive emperors across the dynasties who might have had a positive or negative impact on agriculture. For example, a consecutive decline over 5 or 10 or more emperors is not evidence of a decline in agricultural productivity for it could just be that growth and innovation in agriculture were stagnant. On the rise, we are more comfortable suggesting that those periods are likely correlated with gains in agricultural productivity and technologies. Nonetheless, Fig. 2.9 illustrates the fractional and chaotic evolution of agriculture in China across some 4000 years of history showing periods of great and accumulated neglect and other periods of agricultural enlightenment. Advances, as rudimentary as they might have been in real time, would decline across decades or centuries, only to be countered by periods of enlightenment covering decades or centuries.

In understanding agriculture in the Republican era this history cannot easily be ignored. It is relevant on a number of different levels that Malthus referred to. The fluctuations in economics, nature, and social governance all contribute independently or collectively to challenge population pressures. Malthus viewed these three as conspiring towards balancing population with the real subsistence economy, and the way out of the Malthusian Trap was through mitigation of calamitous forces, and stable governance. From there the economics would take care of itself.

The pitfalls of ecological neglect and political myopia were not lost on the Chinese. Tai Zong, the second emperor of the Tang dynasty around 630 A.D. wrote on the avarice witnessed at times of the Chinese emperors: "*...the welfare of the Empire depends upon the people: An emperor who fleeces his people to enrich himself, is like a man who cuts off his own flesh to supply his stomach, which is filled, t'is true, but in short time his whole body must perish. How many emperors have owed their ruin to their ambition? What expenses were they at to maintain it? and what heavy taxes were charged upon the poor people to supply those expenses? When the people are racked or oppressed what becomes of the empire? Is it not upon the brink of destruction? And what is the emperor if the empire perish?*"[34]

---

[34] DuHalde (1742), page 391.

Here, much like Malthus, Tai Zong is presenting a realization of the inevitability of decline under such circumstances and Chinese history is replete with such examples which are reflected in the strange dynamics of Fig. 2.9. For example, around 1557 B.C. the Emperor Zhong Ding in the Shang dynasty was forced to move the court from *Chensi* to *Honan* and then *Pe tcheli* (sic) from the constant flooding of the Yellow River. But there, they found that they were under continuous pressure from inhabitants below the Yangtze River and were forced to go to war. The Yangtze River is the segregating barrier of what is now referred to as North and South China, with distinctive cultures and anthropology that persisted even beyond the Qing dynasty. Around 17 A.D. an infestation of locusts devoured the harvest and a great famine ensued, occasioning an abundance of riots and robberies leading ultimately to the defeat of the emperor Wang Mang who was so despised that his head was placed on a pitchfork and publicly exposed.[35] Xi Zong, the eighteenth emperor of the Tang dynasty around 871 A.D. was placed on the throne at 12 years of age, under the tutelage and control of the eunuchs of the court. While he played and hunted, outside the court there was nothing but tumult and revolt resulting from excessive taxation, famine from flooding, and locusts destroying the corn, only exacerbating the revolt with a constant influx of rebels.[36] We believe from Fig. 2.6 that a great famine occurred in 1478, but at that time the emperor was so engaged in war that no mention of the famine is recorded. Another famine in 1484 was so horrendous that it was said that fathers were forced to eat their own children, but there was no mention of famine aid. A famine in 1508/09 in which 40% of localities faced severe droughts resulted in such bad conditions in Shandong and Henan that the people left and ignored by the Imperial Court moved en masse towards Beijing, spreading across the province and destroying all before them.[37] Likewise, we believe a great famine in 1528 during the Ming dynasty went ignored by emperor Shi Zong who was self-absorbed in poetry, superstition, and foreign alcohol.[38] In 1583, about the same time the Tartars were defeated by the Ming, another famine, localized in

---

[35] DuHalde (1742), page 359.
[36] DuHalde (1742), page 411.
[37] DuHalde (1742), page 462.
[38] DuHalde (1742), page 463.

Shaanxi Province (with only about 9% of locations reporting severe drought), occurred and it was reported that 60 burial pits were dug, each holding 1000 bodies.

As previously indicated, we believe from the historical climate data that the conditions of 1640 and 1641 suggest the worst famines ever to affect China, and that between 1585 and 1645 China's population declined by 40% according to at least one estimate. Yet in DuHalde's report there is not a whisper of famine for these years. However, he did report a huge series of murders, robberies, and intestine war, with a vast number of malcontents forming themselves into eight armies. These armies laid siege to Sichuan, Hu Guang (sic), Shaanxi, and Henan. At *Kai Feng* the siege lasted six months with the city members starving. By the time the Imperial forces arrived the rebels had escaped to the mountains, but the Imperial army unaware of this blew the dykes of the Yellow River drowning 300,000 in *Kai Feng*. As happened so often in China's history the combination of imperial neglect and arrogance, along with some sort of natural calamity, led to the deaths of millions of souls. In this particular example, the drought and inaction by the Imperial court ultimately led to the end of the Ming dynasty in 1644.

2.8 Summary

In the introduction to this chapter we asked how it was that China's dire conditions in 1921 came about. This is, we feel, not a trivial question and while seemingly distant from the central story of agricultural credit in the Republican era, it provides important context to the agricultural economy in general. Our arguments are Malthusian and Ricardian, which are based on primitive notions of life and death, population growth, land dynamics, and productivity. The conditions in the early Republican era were not simply points in history but the end result of an accumulation of seemingly random events over thousands of years that were very much beyond the farmer's control.

Tayler and Zung writing in 1923 observe that: "*The joint family has suffered from the subdivision of the land into holdings incapable, in many cases, of supporting more than four or five people, even at a bare subsistence level. The pressure of population is creating very serious difficulties in connection with the standard of living for unskilled labour*".[39] It appears evident that around 1921 labor markets were vastly Malthusian with labor being commoditized across a vast range of industries, leaving little opportunity for farmers to improve their lot by seeking wage labor. This was at its cruelest during time of stress (drought, flood, locusts) which forced entry into the wage economy, although in some instances entry into the wage market was for many individuals necessary to keep relieving pressures on meagre incomes at the farm level. For example, Buck's (1923) study of 102 Anhui farms finds family income (for a family size of about five persons) was $160/year with another $199/year of produce grown but consumed by the farm, giving a total of about $359/year or $71.8/person/year.[40] Compare this to a daily wage for unskilled workers of between 15 to 20 cents/day so about $45 to $60 per 300-day work year. Buck argues that a family living on the farm could get by on about $100/year with a minimalist diet and wardrobe, and meat only on festival days. But Tayler and Zung report that the standard of living in Shanghai in 1922 for a single laborer was about $11.85/month, far higher than could be satisfied with the unskilled wage rate. Women earned about 81% of this wage and children, about 75% of women's wage. (Children would start work at eight years of age or younger: as Tayler and Zung state when "they are more use than nuisance".) The point here is that the migration for seasonal work was at best a stop-gap measure to stave of starvation when food stocks declined or food prices rose, but was not at least through 1923 a mechanism for savings that could be converted into investment. Indeed, so far as the historical record is concerned, the commoditization of labor was not much improved in the early 1920s than it was in DuHalde's time.

As to the point of agricultural credit, throughout this book there are constant references to the poor conditions of farmers and peasants, the uncertainties they face, the scale of operations, and persistent poverty. It was the conditions of 1921 that led the China International Famine Relief Commission to consider and pour resources into agricultural

---

[39] Tayler, J.B. and W.T. Zung (1923). "Labour and Industry in China" International Labour Review 8(1):1–20, page 2.

[40] Buck, J.L. (1923). "An Economic and Social Survey of 102 Farms Near Wuhu, Anhwei, China" University of Nanjing, Agriculture and Forestry Series, Volume 1, #7, College of Agriculture and Forestry.

credit as a means to escaping the low-level equilibrium or poverty trap in which China's farmers found themselves. Low-level equilibrium and poverty traps are discussed in the following chapter, with an unmistakable conclusion that to escape the traps requires public investment in institutions that provide credit to farmers. How those institutions came about, and what their outcomes were, is discussed in the remaining chapters of this book.

CHAPTER 3

Low-Level Equilibrium and Fractional Poverty Traps

3.1 Introduction

In the previous chapter we discussed in detail some of the historical conditions that might have led to the conditions observed in 1921 agriculture in China. At the risk of straying too far from the historical considerations of the previous chapter, and indeed the focus of agricultural credit as the subject matter of this book, this chapter delves further into the problem of growth theory and what has previously been referred to as low- or high-level equilibrium traps. It is a technical chapter in the sense that we develop a conceptual model that links population, land, output, innovation, and uncertainty in a dynamic and stochastic way. We then establish some initial conditions and calibrations based on data available for Shandong and Hebei, and use Monte Carlo methods to run the model over a 500-year period intended to mimic the years 1400 through 1900. Although we do this calibration, Monte Carlo simulations do not actually explain the actual economic pathway that led to conditions in 1900 from a 1400 starting point. Instead we can simulate thousands of possible paths, each of which is feasible given the initial conditions and model assumptions and structure, but only one of which actually happened. The problem is that with data too scant no one knows with any certainty what the true path actually was, although we can connect a few dots along the way to eliminate some possibilities. Instead it is best to look at the Monte Carlo model as a form of experimental mathematics from which the influence of risk on economic systems can be observed.

3.2 The Needham Puzzle

In terms of economic growth, China's agricultural economy might best be characterized as being historically perplexing. With the exception of minor adaptations to agricultural practices, it appears that China progressed little in terms of agriculture between the fourteenth century and the era of rural reconstruction which started about 1921 during the Republican era. Perhaps the most intriguing aspect of China's growth has been labeled the 'Needham Puzzle'.[1]

The Needham Puzzle refers to a question posed by Joseph Needham as to why up until the past three or four centuries, China led the Europeans in so many aspects of science and technology yet failed to lead in the industrial revolution. Needham put this paradox in the form of two challenging questions: first, why had China been so far in advance of other civilizations; and second, why is China not now ahead of the rest of the world?[2] By the fourteenth century China was cosmopolitan, technologically advanced, and economically powerful, so much so that in relation the West was essentially agrarian, poor, and underdeveloped.[3] The Needham Puzzle suggests that somewhere around the fourteenth century China stopped innovating in agriculture, allowing the greater progress to be made in Europe several centuries later. The marvels of agricultural innovation at the turn of the fourteenth century are not in dispute, nor is the observable decline in agricultural and related innovations. Perkins, for

---

[1] Lin, J. Y. (1995). The Needham puzzle: Why the industrial revolution did not originate in China. *Economic Development and Cultural Change*, 43(2), 269–292.

Lin, J. Y. (2008). The Needham puzzle, the Weber question, and China's miracle: Long-term performance since the Sung dynasty. *China Economic Journal*, 1(1), 63–95.

Reference is to British sinologist Joseph Needham who published Needham, Joseph. Science and Civilization in China. Volume 1. Cambridge: Cambridge University Press, 1954 and multiple volumes thereafter. Posing the paradox established by Needham as a puzzle appears to have been asked by Needham in Joseph Needham, "Introduction," in China: Land of Discovery and Invention, by Robert K. G. Temple. (Wellingborough: Patrick Stephens, 1986), page 6.

Boulding, Kenneth. "The Great Laws of Change." in Anthony M. Tang, Fred M. Westfield and James S. Worley, eds. Evolution, Welfare and Time in Economics. (Lexington: S.C. Heath Lexington Books, 1976).

Simon Winchester's biography on Needham explains Needham's exploits: Winchester, S. (2008). The man who loved China. Harper, NY.

[2] Lin, J.Y. (1995). *Op Cit*, page 271.

[3] Lin, J.Y. (1995). *Op Cit*, page 270. Cf. Mark, page 177, Elvin, Mark. (1973). The Pattern of the Chinese Past. Stanford, Calif.: Stanford University Press.

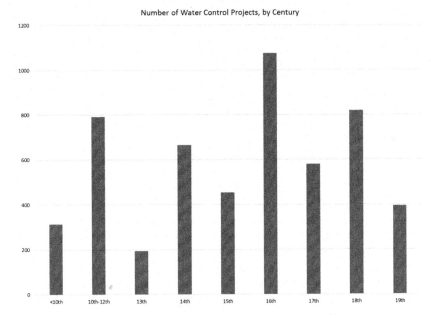

Fig. 3.1 Water control projects from Perkins, 1969

example notes that starting around the fourteenth century there were no dramatic changes in farming techniques or in rural institutions. As evidence, he notes that three separate handbooks dated 1313, 1628, and 1742 included virtually the same list of 77 implements. But Perkins also provides some data on water-control projects from the tenth century through the nineteenth century which include the construction of dykes, canals, and irrigation systems which we replicate in Fig. 3.1.[4] To some extent this vindicates our argument in Chap. 2 that the variability in agricultural development had some dependence on the benevolence of emperors and dynasties. Perkins seems to agree: "*because these construction activities were in part the responsibility of the government, the pace of construction activities were also related to the political vigor of the reigning emperor and his bureaucracy*".[5] But the expansiveness of these projects as

---

[4] Perkins, D. (1969). Agricultural Development in China, 1368–1968. Aldine Publishers, Chicago Illinois, Chapter 4 and Table IV.1.
[5] Perkins, D. (1969). *Op Cit*, page 63.

distributed throughout China also explains how aggregate production can increase even though other technologies and implements changed little, and also how unevenly growth could occur. Irrigation, for example, would have greatly enhanced rice production in South China, while dykes and canals could preserve production from flooding, while enhancing distribution channels and opening up markets. So at one scale it is entirely possible to observe what Huang defines as 'involution' and a diminishing marginal productivity of labor,[6] while on another scale observing gains in aggregate output to keep up with population increases, even at the level of subsistence. Nonetheless, Justin Y. Lin divides the many explanations into two categories, those which hypothesize that the explanation is due to a failure of demand for technology and those based on a failure of supply of technology. Of course these do not have to be mutually exclusive and may from time to time occur simultaneously, while at other moments in time one might dominate another, and yet in other moments of time bursts of demand might be met with bursts of supply.

However, the notion that no innovation took place beyond the fourteenth century is economically implausible, if not impossible. The problem lies with the production elasticity of land itself. As new, lower-quality land is put to the till the percentage change in output per unit of land will decrease. Without any innovation in production practices, this could only lead to lower per capita output, or involution, as a permanent state. In order for a growing population to be sustained—and of course it is population pressure that brings new land into production in the first place—there must be some form of human learning or buildup in human capital so that gains in the productivity of labor at least offset declines in the average and marginal productivity of land. Mark Elvin notes that the falling land to labor ratio in the medieval period led to the use of multiple cropping to increase per-hectare yields: quick ripening rice was imported from Vietnam allowing two crops of rice in the South and a dual crops of wheat and rice in the North.[7] A practice of staggering crops throughout the year was employed to reduce risks from natural disaster and to smooth

---

[6] Huang, P. (1985). The Peasant Economy and Social Change in North China. Stanford University Press, Stanford CA.

[7] Reference is to Champa rice which originated in India and found its way to China via Vietnam during the reign of emperor Zhenzong (992–1022). See Barker, R. (2011). "The Origin and Spread of Early-Ripening Champa Rice: It's Impact on Song Dynasty China" *Rice* 4:184–186.

out the use of labor[8]; and *"...it seems that a number of fine discoveries are due to bizarre experiments and simple caprice, or even to negligence and mistakes...The little extra efforts and knacks, inventions and discoveries, resources and combinations, which have caused people to exclaim at miracles in gardens, have been transported on a large scale out into the fields and have done marvels"*.[9]

DuHalde observes in 1741 that *"there is no part of China that can properly be said to be barren; and some parts are naturally so fruitful, that they yield a crop twice in a year; and others again owe their fruitfulness to the indefatigable toil of the husbandmen. But as the quantity of land proper to be cultivated is not very great in mountainous provinces, it is no wonder that hose which are more fruitful, should scarcely be sufficient for the maintenance of such a multitude of inhabitants"*.[10] DuHalde observes further along the lands of the great river *Kiang fi* (modern day Jiangxi) the marvels of canals, and the diligence with which fields are *"cultivated with care and labor of which none but the Chinese are capable"*. He observes the growth of multiple fruit cultivars and figs which were 'grafted' to trees. He noted the varnish tree that produced a sap used by artisans, the tong-chu tree which provided a varnish used in preserving wood, a tallow-tree whose pulp is used to make candles, and a white-wax tree onto which worms affix themselves to produce a wax more durable and valuable than bee's wax.

In his general description of Chinese agriculture, DuHalde's 1772 report describes the land pressures then already existing on the plains that *"neither hedge nor ditch is to be seen, and but few trees, so much are they afraid of losing an inch of ground"*.[11] He records the terracing of mountainsides already underway, and the methods of loosening stones on rocky mountains and using them to make little walls within which they level with good soil. He notes the laboring of constructing reservoirs to feed rice fields below and the invention of a 'hydraulic engine' to move water up

---

[8] Elvin, M. (1982). *"The Technology of Farming in Late-Traditional China"*, Chapter 2 in "The Chinese Agricultural Economy", Edited by R. Barker, R. Sinha and B. Rose, Westview Press, Boulder Colorado.

[9] Elvin M. (1982). *Op Cit*, page 13, cited from unnamed missionary in *"Mémoires Concernant les Chinois* (Paris, Nyon, 1776–1814). (Sic).

[10] DuHalde, P. (1742). The General History of China; Containing a Geographical, Historical, Chronological, Political and Physical Description of the Empire of China, Chinese Tartary and Tibet., Volume 1, 3rd edition. J. Watts, London, page 8.

[11] DuHalde, P. (1772). "The Chinese Traveler Containing a Geographical, Commercial, and Political History of China" Printed for E. and C. Dilly, London, page 211.

from canals into the fields or terraces. He observes the use of salt, lime, ashes, and natural animal and human dung and urine, and the practice of burying balls of hogs' hair and indeed human hair to invigorate the land, although they had yet to discover mineral fertilizers such as marl.

But it was DuHalde's description of population and land that Malthus latched on to in his (1798–1816) *Principle of Population*. The patriocracy that gave rise to the singular focus on the propagation of male heirs, the veneration of long-dead ancestors and the social demand that all children be married off, and the pragmatism of marrying early at times when subsistence is least likely with the knowledge that children are bound to maintain parents are all grounds for rapid population growth unique to China. But with a largely agrarian economy the land is continually sub-divided and distributed to successive heirs so that even the wealthiest of landowners would see their heirs reduced to poverty within three generations.[12]

Not surprisingly, the conditions of poverty in China in the late eighteenth century differed little from conditions in the early twentieth century. Malthus' reporting of conditions then would not materially be different from newspaper accounts in 1921: "*It is well known that extreme misery impels people to the most dreadful excesses…that mothers destroy or expose many of their children; that parents sell their daughters for a trifle; that there should be such a number of robbers…and that in times of famine which are here but too frequent, millions of people should perish with hunger, without having recourse to those dreadful extremities…*".[13]

But Malthus also took care not to equate China's woes with those of Europe: "*It cannot be said in China, as in Europe, that the poor are idle, and might gain a subsistence if they could work. The labours and efforts of these poor people are beyond conception. A Chinese will pass whole days digging the earth, sometimes up to his knees in water, and in the evening is happy to eat a little spoonful of rice, and to drink the insipid water in which it was boiled*".[14]

It is unsurprising that with DuHalde's and Malthus' observations China's agricultural economy would find itself entrapped in a cycle of poverty. The Malthusian poverty trap derives from the mathematical reality that little wealth can be accumulated when the rate at which the popu-

---

[12] Malthus, T. R. (1888). An essay on the principle of population: or, A view of its past and present effects on human happiness. Reeves & Turner, page 104.

[13] Malthus, T.R. (1888). *Op Cit*, page 105.

[14] Malthus, T.R. (1888). *Op Cit*, page 105.

lation increases is greater than the rate at which new lands can be cultivated. By the late 1700s, and hundreds of years before that, the terracing of even the rockiest of mountains suggest that land-population pressures persisted across China. If one accepts the proposition that an industrial economy flows from the wealth derived from a flourishing agricultural economy, it is not surprising that the Needham Puzzle is rooted in China's agricultural development. Persistent poverty in agriculture ultimately deprives the general economy from much needed savings and capital, while an abundance of labor suppresses the need to innovate. The notion of innovation suppression should be considered as a relative consideration since DuHalde's observations clearly show some degree of evolution in scientific and engineered agriculture through the 1700s, but at a pace then surpassed by Europe. Needham's claim on the other hand was that by the year 1400, China's agricultural and industrial might far exceeded that of Europe.

3.3 Low-Level Equilibrium Traps

Several demand-failure models have been developed to explain the lapse in agricultural innovation in China. Prominent among these is the model put forth by Elvin, but before this were Nurkse and Nelson. Nurkse (1952) makes the argument that balanced growth rests ultimately on the need for a balanced diet.[15] The imbalance results, at least in part, to the inelasticity of demand for consumables at low, real income levels, so that almost all goods are seen as necessities. Thus begins the circular relationship in low-income economies that the inelasticity of demand leaves little capacity to save, and thus the capital to invest, and thus the tendency to low productivity. The lack of buying power impedes any incentives to invest in a diversified industrial base that would ordinarily provide complementary goods and services so that the new entrepreneurs become each other's customers and slowly extract themselves from the deadlock of a low-level equilibrium trap.

Drawing on this, Nelson (1956) defined what he refers to as a low-level equilibrium trap.[16] A low-level equilibrium trap arises when the population growth rate equals the rate at which capital stock is accumulating. Under such an economy the amount of capital per worker is not increasing

---

[15] Nurkse, R. (1952). Some international aspects of the problem of economic development. *The American Economic Review*, 42(2), 571–583.

[16] Nelson, R. R. (1956). A theory of the low-level equilibrium trap in underdeveloped economies. *The American Economic Review*, 46(5), 894–908.

and the economy cannot grow. Capital in Nelson's model includes inputs to the production process plus the land available for cultivation. Even if capital inputs stagnate, capital can still be increased by bringing more land into cultivation, but as more land is brought into production there is an increasing difficulty that new lands would be of equal productivity to previous lands. Capital formation, changes in population, changes in output, and the social, political, and economic organization of the economy ultimately determine various equilibria where changes in population equal changes in output. Changes in population are bounded by the maximum biological rate and it is assumed that this arises only after a period of time at which per capital output was substantially higher than a subsistence rate. The boundary to the low-level equilibrium poverty trap is distinguished by the boundary of subsistence; that is (typically underdeveloped) economies in which output per capita is at or below subsistence, versus those (typically developing or developed) in which output per capita is above subsistence. The low-level equilibrium trap relates to low income-low technology states and is a stable equilibrium—an equilibrium that persists—when the population growth rate intersects the output growth curve from above.

Once a low-level equilibrium is established, escaping the trap is not immediate. If the trap begins with the change in population intersecting the change in output from below then the trap will remain until the change in output again exceeds the change in population. This can come about by an injection of capital into research and development, infrastructure, or the development of new markets to spur on demand. But until that happens, the output per capita is declining and in the Malthusian sense this can also come about by declines in population due to emigration and famine.

The crucial insight from Nelson's Malthusian Trap model is representation of the existence of persistent poverty traps that arise from the relationship between changes in population and changes in output or income. Hagen (1959) throws a bit of cold water on the underlying thesis by noting that only in the United States and Canada in the nineteenth and twentieth centuries when vast lands were available for cultivation did a rise in income actually stimulate population growth.[17] In no country did the population growth rate ever exceed the rate of growth in aggregate out-

---

[17] Hagen, E.E. (1959). Population and economic growth. *The American Economic Review*, 49(3):310–327.

put, although he does note that in the case of China population growth resulted from the introduction from abroad of sweet potatoes, peanuts, and early ripening rice that would allow the cultivation of lands that could not previously support population.

Nonetheless, China seems to stand out as being a country that over time expanded lands, while not pushing the technological frontier to keep pace. As mentioned, it is unlikely that that there were no technological advances in China during this agricultural phase, but not at the pace observed in Europe or North America for example. John Lossing Buck provides such a comparison from farm surveys conducted across China in the 1920s.[18] In China, he notes, aside from land, the chief factor in agricultural production is labor, whereas in the United States the capital investment in improved tools and farm machinery plays an important part. On labor versus technology, one hour of labor produced 1.1 kg of corn in China and 45.5 kg in the United States , and for wheat it was 1.6 kg/man-hour in China, and 39.4 kg/man-hour in the United States, and for rice was 2.2 kg/man-hour and 18.7 kg/man hour in China and the United States respectively. The multiples of labor required in China per man-equivalent in the United States to produce 1 hectare of crop was 5.61 for cotton, 5.83 for potatoes, 14.11 for corn, 23.1 for winter wheat, and 7.09 for soybeans.[19] Because of the land/capita problem the technologies adopted in the United States would be impracticable in China. The fixed costs of a tractor and gang plough to cover 60 hectares of land, cost about $4.75/ha with operating costs of $10.43/acre in the United States. In China the costs of ploughing a field with water oxen was about $4.00/ha.[20] This, of course, is the central element to the Needham Puzzle. For his part, Buck notes that: *"But because of the dense population, the Chinese farmer is doomed and all that can be done is to make the most out of an unfortunate situation"*,[21] and later *"The remedies for this too small size of farm business are difficult to find...As China becomes modernized, it is inevitable that industries will develop and a certain number of the country people be absorbed into them. Yet it can scarcely be hoped that sufficient numbers of them be absorbed as to relive the present agricultural situation very much. The*

---

[18] Buck, J.L. (1930). Chinese Farm Economy: A Study of 2866 Farms in Seventeen Localities and Seven Provinces in China. University of Chicago Press, Chicago Illinois, pages 147–148,
[19] Buck (1930). *Op Cit*, pages 230–233.
[20] Buck (1930). *Op Cit*, page 315.
[21] Buck (1930). *Op Cit*, page 314.

best future solution of the problem seems to be in some method of population control, and the best immediate solution, more intensive methods of raising crops and the growing of crops that produce more food per unit of land. Such productivity, however, will also be useless if population continues to grow".[22]

3.4 High-Level Equilibrium Traps

Nelson's model is essentially a static short-run model. As the technological, economic, and political environment changes so too would conditions leading into new equilibrium traps, or exiting existing equilibrium traps. An alternative model is Elvin's proposition of a high-level equilibrium trap. We should start off discussing Elvin's (1973; with Sinha (1973)) theory of 'high-level' equilibrium traps since this pertains most closely to the China problem of interest.[23] In Elvin's model he uses the term 'high-level', rather than 'low-level' to describe an equilibrium in which all innovations towards a maximal level of agricultural productivity have been exhausted at both the intensive an extensive margin. A low-level equilibrium assumes primitive technology so that output can be increased by simply introducing more labor into the market. Elvin notes that productivity per mou in 1368 was about 140 catties of grain (1 catty is about 500 grams), rising to 224 by the 1770s. It then fell to a little above 200 catties and rose to 240 catties by the mid-1800s. Connecting a line between the 1368 and 1850s highs approximates the potential output available given the levels of technology available. That for almost 500 years actual production did not (with records available) breach this potential, led Elvin to reconsider the underlying dynamics and diffusion of output per capita, while recognizing still that China had agricultural

---

[22] Buck (1930). *Op Cit*, page 424.
[23] Elvin (1973). *Op Cit*.
Sinha, R.P. (1973). Competing ideology and agricultural strategy: current agricultural development in India and China compared with Meiji strategy. *World Development*, 1(6), 11–30.
See also Elvin, M. (1984). Why China failed to create an endogenous industrial capitalism. Theory and Society, 13(3), 379–391.
Elvin, M. (1972). '*The high-level equilibrium trap: the causes of the decline of inventions in the traditional Chinese textile industries*', in W. E. Willmott (ed.), Economic Organization in Chinese Society. Stanford University Press, Stanford CA.
Elvin M. (1996). "Another History: Essays on China from a European Perspective" The University of Sydney East Asian Series #10. Wild Peony, Broadway, NSW, Australia.

practices that were more advanced in terms of pre-modern technology than other countries.[24]

In the China context, Elvin notes that the late traditional economy, starting perhaps in the fourteenth or fifteenth century (dates that correspond with the Needham Puzzle), was incapable of changes through internally generated forces, which focused on China's obsession with male heirs and family lineage. This led to outcomes of population increase regardless of whether or not aggregate output could sustain it. As population rose so too did the pressures on arable land which was in fixed supply. In early phases of population growth the population could be supported by expanding agricultural production, but the land expanded into likely had increasingly lower productivity. Eventually, the combination of decreasing labor productivity (involution) on a diminishing land base resulted in a population that could exist only at the margin. As populations increased the cost of labor fell relative to investments in capital, removing any economic incentives to develop labor-saving technology. In addition, as poorer quality land came to be cultivated the rental value of that land— its marginal value—also fell so that the demand for technology also fell. As lower productivity land was being brought into production for an increasing rural population, the retention held back for household consumption as a proportion of total output would also increase. Thus, the proportion of output that made its way into urban and industrial centers was decreasing relative to population increases there. Prices at the market centers would then have risen, causing a decrease in real wages which would in turn reduce demand for other non-food items. And so events went in a spiral that removed economic incentives to expanding entrepreneurship and technological, scientific, and economic innovation. With a stagnation in innovation an equilibrium trap was inevitable as the rate of increase in potential output fell below the rate of increase in population and labor. Instead, farmers adopted one scale of technology, the efficacy of which diminished as population increased. Then a higher level of technology was adopted and used until it could no longer support the population. Even good public works would have diminished as taxing lower output per capita became increasingly more regressive. In this model the increasing labor to land ratio coupled with a lack of demand for new technology led to a high-level equilibrium trap.

---

[24] See Sinha, (1973). *Op Cit*, fn 62, page 19.

Elvin's model is speculative and not all scholars are in general agreement. Tang[25] is skeptical of this citing Buck's (1937)[26] survey to suggest that output was below maximum potential so at least as late as the mid-Republican period China might have escaped the trap. Huang agrees somewhat with Elvin's notion that a failure to continually adapt new practices or develop new technologies can lead to periodic traps in which a failure to innovate combined with population pressure can lead to a high-level equilibrium trap, but he dismisses the idea that population alone is the driver, and that agricultural conditions cannot be understood in the absence of interdependent relationships between the natural environment and the sociopolitical order.[27] The point of departure may lie in the concept of involution. To Huang (it appears that) involution is a consequence of exogenous forces, including population growth and land quality that drives diminishing returns to labor, whereas to Elvin (it appears that) involution is a consequence of endogenous forces that lead to a choice not to innovate, until it is necessary to do so when population growth absorbs any surplus.

Lin is not in agreement with Elvin's case for a high-level equilibrium trap. Lin's argument is that regardless of location there will be distributions of innovation recognized by chance and experience, or developed by enlightenment and experimentation, suggesting along the way that technological innovation requires a diffusion process across time. This would be true in China as well as Europe. Alternatively, Lin argues that the Needham Puzzle arose from institutions in China that created bureaucracy and customs that no longer rewarded innovation. This was particularly acute in the post-Confucian era following the Sui (589–617) and Song dynasties (960–1275) when the enlightenments of science were replaced by rote memorization of Confusian scripts to pass the civil service examinations. To achieve high order in Chinese society it was the knowledge of the scripts, and not the perpetuation of what underlay the scripts, that was most important. The best and brightest were forced to forgo investigations into science, technology, and engineering.

---

[25] Tang, A.M. (1979). China's agricultural legacy. *Economic Development and Cultural Change*, 28(1), 1–22.

[26] Buck, J.L. (1937). Land Utilization in China: A Study of 16,786 Farms in 168 Localities, and 38, 256 Farm Families in Twenty-two Provinces in China, 1929–1933. Commercial Press, Limited, Agents in the United States, The University of Chicago Press.

[27] Huang (1985). *Op Cit*, pages 182–184.

In many respects, Justin Y. Lin's argument supports earlier views by A.M. Tang that feudalism in Europe likely led to a dampening of agricultural innovation, while at the same time in China, feudalism had long disappeared in favor of private ownership. As feudalism disappeared in the seventeenth and eighteenth centuries, just at the time the industrial revolution took off, there was every incentive to accumulate and apply scientific agriculture to the cultivation of food for an ever-increasing European population. Meanwhile in China, post-Confusion conservatism and the laser focus on civil service examinations stymied scientific innovation so that the maximum potential product diminished in proportion to the population.

3.5 The Anthropological View

Elvin's pathway to a (high-level) equilibrium trap is very consistent with the anthropologic approach of Boserup (1975; see also Darity 1980).[28] Boserup assumes that farmers are intentional in their adoption of technologies and innovations; as population pressure on land increased then new practices that may have arisen by serendipity or experimentation may be put on hold until necessary so that the farmer could maximize cultivation as a best management practice until there are population-induced diminishing returns. At that point, a newer technique can be put into action. After some time the farmers will become adept at the new technology and retain that until once again diminishing returns to population (and perhaps the land itself), forces adoption of a new technology or management practice. Clawing back to the Needham Puzzle, both Elvin's and Boserup's conclusions (and Perkins' to some extent) imply that the demand for new technology becomes more inelastic as population increases approach the carrying capacity of the previous innovation. At this point, innovation must come at any cost, to avoid falling into a below-sustenance poverty trap. Once achieved, and the new technology is adopted and food pressure is relieved, the demand for innovation becomes more elastic—at least with respect to population—so that grand innovations diminish for lack of demand.

---

[28] Boserup, E. (1975). The impact of population growth on agricultural output. *The Quarterly Journal of Economics*, 257–270.
Darity, W. A. (1980). The Boserup theory of agricultural growth: a model for anthropological economics. *Journal of Development Economics*, 7(2), 137–157.

Elvin is not specific about how technology evolves, but as Darity points out Boserup's view was counter-Malthusian in the sense that causality moves from population to agricultural intensification, for example (Darity citing Simon 1977) *"in India and China over a period of years before this century.... When population grew, the output of the society grew too.... Eventually reaching the same per-capita level as before the spurt of population. But during long periods when the population did not grow, the level of living also did not grow, but rather stayed the same."*[29]

Elvin's path to an equilibrium trap was similar. Elvin for example, provides an outer convex curve that is diminishing, but represents the potential at each population tick. The potential is never exploited as invented but made available as needed. Eventually the methods of practice available diminish as population increases until potential output intersects population growth giving rise to the equilibrium trap. In other words, when population is rising, increased agricultural intensification, including the expansion of new lands, can only go so far. In terms of Darity's critique of Boserup's conjecture, had Boserup made allowances for the diminishing quality of land—a Malthusian-Ricardian concern—the failure to innovate, coupled with exogenous risks of any sort, would have led to at least some outcomes that would have paralleled Malthus.

Consequently, where Elvin and Boserup depart is that Boserup's intensification path always stays ahead of population pressure and thus avoids the equilibrium trap. In fact, Darity's dynamic interpretation of Boserup's anthropology reveals an unstable equilibrium that is sensitive to initial conditions. In one world, Boserup's evolution guarantees perpetual poverty, while in another world wages rise sufficiently high to absorb excess output.

There is also the possibility that in China frequent catastrophes that led to population declines could halt innovation in agricultural development. As a process of recovery farmers would stick with what they knew on a de-population induced reduction in land use but at the intensive margin of the best management practices most familiar to them. Thus, even though new approaches to intensification might have been available to the surviving population there was no need to adopt them. Because innovation is a staged affair it may well be the case that the Needham Puzzle as it relates to agricultural practices did not evolve because uncertainty about

---

[29] Simon, J. (1977). The economics of population growth. Princeton University Press, Princeton, NJ, page 137.

the natural and geopolitical world would make farmers averse to adopting new but unfamiliar practices.

Boserup argues that as the rural population increases one approach to achieving balance is to migrate. This can be facilitated by infrastructure and public investment that would make trade more accessible and discourage the pattern of growing for subsistence. (China had the market system for hundreds of years via Skinner.) If the per capita share of agricultural output declines, there is likely to be—at least from time to time—instances when non-farm wages exceed the returns to agriculture forcing a migration. This will continue until per-capita returns to labor in the subsistence sector rise via a de-population effect equaling the competing wage rate.

Hagen on population resurrects the Malthusian point of view and reminds us that in the modern era the expansion of health facilities and medicine has lowered death rates significantly. Maximum birth rates are probably at 45 per 1000 and in many peasant economies the rate is above 40 per 1000 or 4%.[30] But the death rate can be just as high. When populations in peasant economies rise it is probably because death rates fall. Also there might be a population increase when incomes rise. In earlier economies, the abundance of land would allow populations to increase without a decline in per capita income. This might occur so long as land is available but if Elvin's neo-Malthusian model is correct, as land increases bring in more unsuitable land, per capita output would decrease. By the time the population recognizes that no more cultivation is possible, savings are so depleted that there is little left to invest in alternative technologies. Hagen's observations of industrial economies in that the *"Malthusian result did not occur generally, but it did not occur anywhere"*[31] fail to consider the conditions and time period under which Malthus considered populations.

3.6 Equilibrium and Poverty Traps

A resurgent view of the Malthusian Trap in more recent years has opted for the more broadly defined 'poverty trap'. In fact, to our sensibilities the use of the term poverty trap is preferable to the Malthusian Trap or its neo-Malthusian counterparts because it does not exclude output to population dynamics at the macro level, while allowing simultaneously for a

---

[30] Hagen (1959). *Op Cit.*
[31] Hagen (1959). *Op Cit*, page 315.

micro, short-run focus. Perhaps more important is that it opens the economics to random influences in the small and in the large and thus widens the range of policy options to include credit, insurance, and other forms of agricultural stabilization and social welfare.

In the poverty trap literature a dynamic equilibrium exists when a unit of well-being (income, assets) neither increases nor decreases in real terms between one period and the next. If there exist multiple equilibria, i.e. at high levels of well-being and low-levels of well-being, then at least one equilibrium must be an unstable equilibrium. An equilibrium exists as an attractor of sorts in which economic forces, good or bad, will move a household away from that initial equilibrium into an alternative state. How long the household remains in that state depends on degrees of resilience and asset dynamics. If conditions require the sale of productive assets, likewise, a better-off household might face an adverse shock, but local economic and growth forces will ultimately drive things back to the initial steady state.

The particular problem addressed in Carter and Barret was the differentiating control of income/expenditure measures which by pure randomness can rise and fall as markets and ecology dictate.[32] Categorizing poverty (or other measures for that matter) can be useful for de-marking various conditions of poverty. Static assessment, that is examining a population in a moment in time, is a first-generation process that can distinguish various classes of the population, i.e. the percentage of poor or the percentage of non-poor.[33] Exogenous factors such as drought or floods are difficult to weed out if the same conditions hold for all. Second generation measures of poverty might include detailed information on the same population over a period of time, and can thus measure how members of a population switch from one level of poverty or well-being, to another, for example from one asset quintile to another, over time.[34] The information this might provide depends upon the nature of shocks over

---

[32] Carter, M.R., and C.B. Barrett, (2006). The economics of poverty traps and persistent poverty: An asset-based approach. *The Journal of Development Studies*, 42(2), 178–199.

[33] For origination of first, second, third, and fourth generation poverty measures see Carter and Barrett (2006), *Op Cit.* Figure 1, page 180. Carter and Barret were actually seeking to classify econometric approaches to measuring poverty traps. We are taking a few liberties in our discussion.

[34] This is the approach used in Zhou, L., and C.G. Turvey, (2015). Testing Asset Dynamics for Poverty Traps in Rural China. *Canadian Journal of Agricultural Economics*, 63(1), 129–162.

the period of measurement, but an eventful period will have quite different results than an uneventful period if the objective is, for example, to capture resilience to economic shocks.

Third and fourth generation measures explicitly include exogenous shocks, presumably randomly distributed across populations with weak correlation, and/or independent across time and highly correlated (strongly covariate) across populations.[35] Third and fourth generation measures target asset dynamics—particularly production assets—and the conditions of risk that bring about the loss of productive assets (e.g. by death if livestock, or pawn sales for others) as well as the duration and conditions in time before the affected population re-accumulates assets and resumes production to the level of initial conditions. Understanding asset dynamics under conditions of risk allows for more granular approaches to policy prescriptions such as insurance, or expanding access to credit.[36] These are fundamentally structural changes to the agricultural economy. In contrast, shifts in income or expenditure cannot so easily be determined to be structural or just bad luck. The distinction is that first generation measures may simply result from random or stochastic factors (stochastically poor), and it is only after income, and then savings, are eroded that food, health, education, and other necessities must be met by the sale of consumable and then productive assets (structurally poor).[37] Recovery of the sale of productive assets is not instantaneous, at least not for the poor, who typically have less access to credit to either prevent the sale of productive assets or to re-accumulate once the causal stochastic event has passed. It takes time, and this is why asset dynamics are so important in the poverty trap framework, and particularly with respect to the existence of multiple equilibria that correspond or parallel the macro models.

---

[35] Systemic or covariate risks may affect large populations at a moment in time, e.g. floods or drought. These are also referred to as systemic risks.

[36] Examples of how understanding risk, and measuring asset loss or famine for purpose of insurance see Chantarat, S., Barrett, C. B., Mude, A. G., & Turvey, C. G. (2007). Using weather index insurance to improve drought response for famine prevention. *American Journal of Agricultural Economics*, 89(5), 1262–1268 and for an example of a fourth generation approach that measures resilience and asset dynamics with insurance in place, see Chantarat, S., Mude, A. G., Barrett, C. B., & Turvey, C. G. (2017). Welfare impacts of index insurance in the presence of a poverty trap. *World Development*, 94, 119–138.

[37] This claim appears to be validated by Kumar, C. S., Turvey, C. G., & Kropp, J. D. (2013). The impact of credit constraints on farm households: Survey results from India and China. *Applied Economic Perspectives and Policy*, 35(3), 508–527.

3.7 Multiple Equilibria and Fractal Poverty Traps

If there are multiple equilibria in a low-level equilibrium, or poverty traps which explain poverty dynamics, then there must also exist an inflexion point above which the poor can escape from poverty and below which a wealthier house can be driven to persistent poverty. In the fractal sense of Barrett and Swallow, a poverty trap is one in which multiple simultaneous equilibria exist in much the same way as the equilibrium trap literature suggests.[38] In the Barrett and Swallow context, fractal poverty traps can exist simultaneously at multiple scales (micro, meso and/or macro) and are self-reinforcing through feedback effects. The essential element of a fractal poverty trap is that the pattern repeats at all scales of aggregation; that is the forces which drive farm households into poverty by a particular dynamic are the same forces that drive a country into poverty. The forces are endogenous to each other and are self-reinforcing.

Depending upon scale the policy implications are quite different. At one level, capital investment linked to investment at the intensive or extensive margin can lead farmers in poverty to at least a steady state in which savings above consumption are non-negative. Investment can be through extension services, promoting use of different seed varieties, and/or developing implements to improve labor efficiency on a higher scale. Progressively, these elements of capital investment will ultimately be rewarded with reduced poverty rates, intensity, and duration. These may be sufficient for the higher-income farms, because for these farms, the policy regime would include contingent markets and credit that can be used to offset shocks or to provide liquidity through credit when it is needed most. These are probably more highly developed for the higher-income farms, so (as discussed in Chap. 1) progressive policies in the modern era based on financial inclusion hope to keep impoverished households from sinking deeper into poverty. The interlinkages described in Barrett and Swallow to describe a fractal poverty trap are more metaphoric in nature than mathematically precise. But this does not mean that their informal approach does not have a broader meaning.

Barrett and Swallow's notion of fractal is due to endogenous scaling and interlinkages, and in this is very similar to Nelson (1954) in the sense that assets are short-run static. If farm sizes are equal then the asset dif-

---

[38] Barrett, C. B., and B.M. Swallow, (2006). Fractal poverty traps. *World development*, 34(1), 1–15.

ferential must be in the technologies employed given the levels of technology available. Huang and Willis view the low- and high-level traps in terms of productivity at the intensive margin.[39] A high-level equilibrium exists for those who have utilized, to the economic maximum, output and income. Low-level may not have the savings or resources to invest in existing technology and practices. While economically speaking we would anticipate that the same shocks affect high- and low-equilibrium farmers in a similar way, with differences in intensity the higher group might end up in a lower economic state by selling consumable and then production assets. The less-resilient lower group could find itself stuck in an even lower poverty trap.

3.8 A Stochastic-Dynamic Model for Low-Level/High-Level Equilibrium and Poverty Traps

We discussed several models related to low-level equilibrium traps that could explain the sustained level of low-technology agriculture. This originated with Malthus and moved towards Boulding, Elvin, and other economic models. Conceptually, Elvin's model made sense at the level of principle but it was driven largely by anecdote rather than a foundational theory. Nelson, on the other hand, provided a theory with certain desirable properties, including a capacity constraint which we can assign to the limitations on land, but it lacked key measures of uncertainty that we think are far more critical to the understanding of agricultural and population growth.

The current models of low-level equilibrium and poverty traps are essentially short-run models. Elvin's high-level equilibrium model does account for the longer term, as does the Malthusian Trap model discussed in the previous chapter. Collectively, these models provide valuable insights into the linkages between population, land, and productivity but how do these aspects of poverty evolve over time and can they answer the basic question of how China got to be in its dismal condition in the early Republican era? To answer this question we move to a more technical discussion of stochastics and dynamics that brings most of these ideas together and develop, and then simulate, a stochastic dynamic model starting around the year 1400 for a period of 500 years bringing us approximately to the turn of the twentieth century, which is the starting point for the end of the Qing dynasty and the start of the Republican era.

[39] Huang, P. (1985). *Op Cit.*

We are inclined at this point to use the term 'poverty trap' in a generic way that avoids the necessity of defining a steady-state equilibrium. A poverty trap exists when an individual is either in, or falls into, a state of poverty which persists over time and from which it is difficult to escape. A poverty trap deals not only with the magnitude of poverty (income below a threshold), or the frequency of poverty (measured by the percentage incidence in a population) but the nature and duration of poverty. The nature refers to the conditions that give rise to poverty, while the duration refers to length of time that one remains in poverty.

As hinted above, the concept of equilibrium in a stochastic world is difficult to rationalize since nothing is ever stable. Instead, from any particular set of initial conditions the stochastic path sets a trajectory towards some distant locus to which it oscillates in some random fashion. This point in the future becomes more elusive as future time is extended, largely due to certain variance rules associated with non-stationary time paths. As this random path progresses towards a defined moment in time the variance is reduced in a linear or fractional way, until some point in time is observed and described by real data points. In the interim there are a multitude of paths, in fact an infinite number of paths upon which random and seemingly independent shocks can change economic trajectories in a permanent way. As we suggest in Chap. 2, where China ended up in 1921 is not due to any single factor but the accumulation of seemingly random effects which accumulate in China's history. Each event has the effect of shifting the population-land-economic dynamic in setting a new trajectory which may be exacerbated or reversed by subsequent random events. We are not alone in this view. For example, Perkins notes that if it were not for the Taiping rebellion in the middle of the nineteenth century that reduced the population by as many as 20 million, the rising population might have otherwise outstripped the ability of Chinese agriculture to produce adequate food supplies.[40] While cause and effect might well explain the Taiping rebellion with some determinism at the local time scale, when looked upon over the course of hundreds or thousands of years of economic development it is but one of many random events or shocks that was unforeseen in the future, but consequential to that which followed.

As the agricultural economy evolves there are times in which a number of things happen to define the state of farmers. At the macro or meso level there are states of nature which cause whole populations to bifurcate from

---

[40] Perkins, D.H. (1969). *Op Cit*, pages 28–29.

relative prosperity to relative poverty in ways that except for natural resilience and grit are beyond the control of any single farmer or population of farmers. Agriculture is unique in this way. Only rarely are agricultural risks independent across farmers. In the natural and political world, the reality is that risks are correlated across many farmers at one time.

In the equilibrium trap literature, the boundary between economic surplus (gains in income, savings, and consumption) and poverty states (low income, depleted savings, low consumption) is determined by the boundary of the output to population ratio that describes bare subsistence. Below this line affected households fall into a state of below-subsistence poverty which has numerous impacts on population and productivity. Malthus, as described previously, was very much concerned with these states since it took time for wages and prices to adjust. Meanwhile, the lack of food beyond that which might have been stored can lead to drastic reductions in population through migration and mortality.

These states of nature can be viewed in a random world as excursions, and how long they persist depends upon the nature of the shocks that occurred, the intensity of the shocks, and the duration. In some years, a drought may cause distress but abundance in the following year can reverse conditions. The number of people who die in the interim depends upon resilience. Consequently, the dynamic evolution of agriculture forms a stochastic differential equation of the Ito type, which appears to be fractional in typology. By fractional we mean that certain measures such as output or population or ratios of the two do not follow a random walk in the classical Brownian sense of, say, a stock market. Instead, the nature of things as described by Malthus interacts in ways that are self-reinforcing. Thus events of politics and nature are not simply independent random draws but are characteristically correlated across time in a systematic manner. For example, if population growth is dependent on the capacity of the land to feed its population and the resilience of the population to calamities and conflicts, then in the absence of social safety nets and access to medical services, populations will rise and fall as nature dictates in a mean reverting way. Even when faced with calamities, resilience can see populations grow in time, especially when necessities are abundant. But then comes a second interfering dynamic and that has to do with the land base. It is evident by all we know that as China's population grew in time, more land needed to be cultivated. For some period of time land was not binding in mass, but as more land was tilled, the quality of that land diminished. Ultimately, by 1900 virtually all land was in some form of cultivation, and had been for centuries before then, although some authorities suggest that the land capacity peaked in the middle of the nineteenth century. Yet the contouring of mountains in Shandong, Jiangsu, or Gansu suggests that the capacity to cultivate anything close to new fertile lands disappeared centuries earlier. Nonetheless, the conditions of increasing cultivation of ever-decreasing land quality while land was abundant would at some point in time exhaust the agricultural land base bringing about different shades of dynamics that once started could not so easily be reversed, at least with the levels of technology available.

3.8.1 Population Dynamics

Under the Malthusian argument, population growth is based on the natural growth rate comprised of birth, death, and migration rates, $g = (\mu_P - d - m)$. We assume that population growth is based on this natural growth rate, but also mitigated by the capacity of agricultural output to feed the population, P^*, and random effects arising from natural and man-made calamities and conflicts. Here, $P_t^* = \frac{Y_t}{c}$ is the ratio of aggregate output divided by per capita output requirements. We state this as a geometric Brownian motion in continuous time with ϕ being a measure of resilience that can exacerbate or moderate the population to capacity ratio[41]

$$\frac{dP}{P} = g\left(1 - (1-\phi)\frac{P}{P^*}\right)dt + \sigma_P dZ_P \qquad (1)$$

The ratio $(1-\phi)\frac{P_t}{P^*}$ captures the adjustment due to food supply with $0 \leq \phi < \approx 1$ as a resilience adjustment. As P^* increases relative to population $\frac{P_t}{P^*}$ declines, which increases the population growth rate. This moderates population growth as Malthus describes, in the sense that as food becomes abundant population increases, while constraints of food supply,

---

[41] The dynamic is close to Boulding's and other specifications. He measures the population above subsistence but also includes what he refers to as an improvement coefficient to capture technological change, and a scarcity coefficient to capture resilience. Boulding (1955). *Op Cit*, pages 199–201.

including frequent famine, reduce population growth rates. Whether this is due to decreasing birth rates versus increasing death rates is difficult to discern.

3.9 Agricultural Output

We assume that agricultural output per unit of land (mou, acre, hectare) is determined by labor and capital employed. We start off with the standard output model of labor and capital, $Y = AP^\alpha L^\beta$. We assume that population is proportional to labor supply and land is proportional to capital. However, as discussed this conventional function is unsustainable in the long run because of the diminishing capacity of land productivity as the amount of land increases, and the necessity of human capital to adapt to these conditions. We thus depreciate the elasticity of land by defining

$$\hat{\beta} = \beta - \lambda_L L \qquad (2)$$

and

$$\hat{\alpha} = \alpha + \lambda_P L \qquad (3)$$

Where λ_L and λ_P are the rates of productivity depletion and human capital appreciation respectively. When $\lambda_P \geq \lambda_L$ the model avoids the problem of involution as described by Huang

$$Y = AP^{(\alpha+\lambda_P L)} L^{(\beta-\lambda_L L)} = AP^{\hat{\alpha}} L^{\hat{\beta}} \qquad (4)$$

or

$$\mathrm{Log}(Y) = \mathrm{Log}(A) + (\alpha + \lambda_P L)\mathrm{Log}(P) + (\beta - \lambda_L L)\mathrm{Log}(L) \qquad (5)$$

Note also that the production elasticities do not adjust linearly in time but with respect to land. Land evolves randomly in time but ultimately has a geographical maximum that places a real boundary on the upper limits of land. An obvious drawback to this construction is that this assumes that growth in human capital diminishes as land approaches its natural boundary. Thus, this model will likely underestimate growth in human capital beyond the years at which land is bounded from above.

3.10 Technological Innovation and Output Uncertainty

To get around this problem we address technological innovations and output risk through the adjustment (intercept) value of A. Perkins too makes allowance for the intercept to grow with innovation in time, but in a deterministic way.[42] We assume that output grows at the rate μ_A, but is subject to random events σ_A. This we describe by the following Brownian motion

$$\frac{dA}{A} = \mu_A dt + \sigma_A dZ_A \qquad (6)$$

Where dZ_A is a Wiener process. Ultimately, we follow Justin Y. Lin's lead in correlating the output growth with population so regardless of the land boundary there remains a mechanism for output to adjust in real time to population changes beyond the land constraint.

3.11 Output Dynamics

There are three principal drivers of aggregate output in the above discussion. These are population dynamics and technological innovation. Both of these are described by stochastic differential equations. The third principal driver is the output function itself which feeds off land dynamics and population growth, as well as technological innovation. To extract a dynamic model for output we apply Ito's Lemma and the stochastic calculus

$$dY = \frac{\partial Y}{\partial A}dA + \frac{\partial Y}{\partial P}dP + \frac{\partial Y}{\partial L}dL \\ + \frac{1}{2}\left(\begin{array}{c}\frac{\partial^2 Y}{\partial A^2}dA^2 + \frac{\partial^2 Y}{\partial P^2}dP^2 + \frac{\partial^2 Y}{\partial L^2}dL^2 \\ +2\left(\frac{\partial^2 Y}{\partial A \partial L}dAdL + \frac{\partial^2 Y}{\partial A \partial P}dAdP + \frac{\partial^2 Y}{\partial L \partial P}dLdP\right)\end{array}\right) \qquad (7)$$

---

[42] Perkins (1969). *Op Cit*, Mathematical Supplement, pages 79–84.

Using $\dfrac{dY}{Y} = \dfrac{dA}{A} + (\lambda_P \text{Log}(P) - \lambda_L \text{Log}(L))dL + \hat{\alpha}\dfrac{dP}{P} + \hat{\beta}\dfrac{dL}{L}$ we obtain the following first and second order conditions

$$\dfrac{\partial Y}{\partial A} = \dfrac{Y}{A}$$

$$\dfrac{\partial Y}{\partial P} = \hat{\alpha}\dfrac{Y}{P}$$

$$\dfrac{\partial Y}{\partial L} = Y\left(\lambda_P \text{Log}(P) - \lambda_L \text{Log}(L) + \dfrac{\hat{\beta}}{L}\right)$$

$$\dfrac{\partial^2 Y}{\partial A^2} = 0$$

$$\dfrac{\partial^2 Y}{\partial P^2} = \dfrac{Y}{P^2}\hat{\alpha}(\hat{\alpha}-1) \qquad (8)$$

$$\dfrac{\partial^2 Y}{\partial L^2} = Y\left(\left(\lambda_P \text{Log}(P) - \lambda_L \text{Log}(L) + \dfrac{\hat{\beta}}{L}\right)^2 - \dfrac{(2\lambda_L L - \beta)}{L^2}\right)$$

$$\dfrac{\partial^2 Y}{\partial A \partial P} = \hat{\alpha}\dfrac{Y}{AP}$$

$$\dfrac{\partial^2 Y}{\partial A \partial L} = \dfrac{Y}{A}\left(\lambda_P \text{Log}(P) - \lambda_L \text{Log}(L) + \dfrac{\hat{\beta}}{L}\right)$$

$$\dfrac{\partial^2 Y}{\partial L \partial P} = \dfrac{Y}{P}\left(\lambda_P + \hat{\alpha}\left(\lambda_P \text{Log}(P) - \lambda_L \text{Log}(L) + \dfrac{\hat{\beta}}{L}\right)\right)$$

Also, by Ito's Lemma we have $\left(g\left(1-(1-\phi)\dfrac{P}{P^*}\right)dt + \sigma_P dZ_P\right)^2 = \sigma_P^2 dt$, and

$$(\mu_A dt + \sigma_A dZ_A)\left(g\left(1-(1-\phi)\dfrac{P}{P^*}\right)dt + \sigma_P dZ_P\right) = \rho_{A,P}\sigma_A \sigma_P dt \qquad (9)$$

With dA and dP defined by their respective stochastic differential equations we need a term for changes in land. We assume that land is driven by

$L = \dfrac{cP}{P^*}$ where c is the per capita consumption of agricultural goods. This we assume constant so that the change in land is

$$dL = \frac{c}{P^*} dP \tag{10}$$

Substituting for dL, dA, dP and for convenience $L = \dfrac{c}{P^*} P \rightarrow \dfrac{L}{P} = \dfrac{c}{P^*}$, further rearranging yields

$$\frac{dY}{Y} = \left(\begin{array}{l} \left(\mu_A + \left(\hat{\alpha} + L \left(\lambda_P \text{Log}(P) - \lambda_L \text{Log}(L) + \dfrac{\hat{\beta}}{L} \right) \right) \mu_P \right) \\ + \dfrac{1}{2} \left(\begin{array}{l} \left(\hat{\alpha}(\hat{\alpha}-1) + L^2 \left(\left(\lambda_P \text{Log}(P) - \lambda_L \text{Log}(L) + \dfrac{\hat{\beta}}{L} \right)^2 - \dfrac{(2\lambda_L L - \beta)}{L^2} \right) \right) \sigma_P^2 \\ + 2L \left(\lambda_P + \hat{\alpha} \left(\lambda_P \text{Log}(P) - \lambda_L \text{Log}(L) + \dfrac{\hat{\beta}}{L} \right) \right) \\ + 2 \left(L \left(\lambda_P \text{Log}(P) - \lambda_L \text{Log}(L) + \dfrac{\hat{\beta}}{L} \right) + \hat{\alpha} \right) \rho_{AP} \sigma_A \sigma_P \end{array} \right) \end{array} \right) dt + (\sigma_A dZ_A + \sigma_P dZ_P) \tag{11}$$

There are two components to this Ito process. The first bracketed term is the expected rate of growth in output which is determined by the contemporaneous amounts of land and population, the variance in population, and the correlation between population and technological growth. We can see that the variance of this process is given by the joint relationship between output and population, including the covariance between the two. This correlation is driven by Justin Y. Lin's argument that as the population increases there will likely be more geniuses born and thus more innovation.[43] Also included are the rates of appreciation and depreciation in human capital and land quality, and importantly the initial elasticities.

The second component of the equation is the variance term which captures the variation in output, via the intercept A and population P, and the covariance between the two. This Wiener process implies that the variance of the change in output per unit of time (in this case yearly) is determined by

---

[43] Lin, J.Y. (1995). *Op Cit*, page 271.

$$\sigma_A^2 + \sigma_P^2 + 2\rho_{AP}\sigma_A\sigma_P \tag{12}$$

More specifically, the dynamics are driven by the drift term which has several components:

(a) $\mu_A + \left(\hat{\alpha} + L\left(\lambda_P \text{Log}(P) - \lambda_L \text{Log}(L) + \frac{\hat{\beta}}{L}\right)\right) g\left(1 - (1-\phi)\frac{P}{P^*}\right)$ is the natural drift rate where $\mu_P = g\left(1 - (1-\phi)\frac{P}{P^*}\right)$ is the mean reverting rate for population

(b) $\hat{\alpha} + L\left(\lambda_P \text{Log}(P) - \lambda_L \text{Log}(L) + \frac{\hat{\beta}}{L}\right)$ scales the population growth rate to changes in land and capital. If $\lambda_P = \lambda_L = 0$ then the term boils down to $\alpha + \beta$ which equals 1 as constant returns to scale so that the natural drift would collapse simply to $\left(\mu_A + g\left(1 - (1-\phi)\frac{P}{P^*}\right)\right)t$

(c) We need to keep in mind precisely the role that λ_P, λ_L plays in our model. The first appreciates human capital and learning whereas the second captures the Malthusian Trap by reducing the output elasticity from land as new and poorer quality land is brought into production. If we assume these to be static, then growth in output is dependent only on the natural rates of innovation and population and the production elasticities. For example, if $\lambda_P = \lambda_L = 0$ then the equation collapses to the native form

$$E\left[\frac{dY}{Y}\right] = \mu_A + (\alpha + \beta)\mu_P + \frac{1}{2}\left(\left(\beta - \alpha + (\alpha + \beta)^2\right)\sigma_P^2 + 2(\alpha + \beta)\rho_{AP}\sigma_A\sigma_P\right). \tag{13}$$

If it is further assumed that the initial condition shows constant returns to scale then this reduces even further to

$$E\left[\frac{dY}{Y}\right] = \left(\mu_A + \mu_P + \beta\sigma_P^2 + \rho_{AP}\sigma_A\sigma_P\right). \tag{14}$$

Note that this includes the covariance effects presumed by Justin Lin so that as population grows so does innovation because a higher population will provide a larger pool of innovators and entrepreneurs.

As for the relationships themselves, if the economy is to maintain scale neutrality in terms of the production elasticities then $\lambda_P = \dfrac{k - \alpha - \beta + \lambda_L L}{L}$ which suggests that at any scale $\lambda_P \geq \lambda_L$. In other words if the production coefficient for the initial agriculture economy was $k = 1$ then $\lambda_P = \lambda_L$. If the economic goal was to achieve better than constant returns to scale then for $\dfrac{\Delta k}{\Delta L} > 0 \rightarrow \lambda_P > \lambda_L$.

If we assume that $\dfrac{\hat{\beta}}{L}$ is arithmetically negligible then the crucial term in the drift of the stochastic differential equation for growth is $\lambda_P \text{Log}(P) - \lambda_L \text{Log}(L)$. This should always be positive so long as $\lambda_P = \lambda_L$ and per capita land is greater than 1. Conflicts, calamities, and catastrophes can from time to time violate this presumption, but rearranging terms $\dfrac{\lambda_P}{\lambda_L} \geq \dfrac{\text{Log}(L)}{\text{Log}(P)}$ or $\lambda_P \geq \lambda_L \dfrac{\text{Log}(L)}{\text{Log}(P)}$. Thus as λ_P rises above λ_L, not only does the rate at which human capital rise relative to the depletion of land quality, but perhaps more importantly the slack between the two, i.e. $\lambda_P - \lambda_L > 0$, lowers the chance that the growth condition $\dfrac{\lambda_P}{\lambda_L} \geq \dfrac{\text{Log}(L)}{\text{Log}(P)}$ will be violated even when the population growth rate exceeds the rate at which new lands are brought into production.

3.12 Fractional Poverty Traps

dY/Y describes the stochastic differential equation for output. It follows a random walk. In fact, with certain boundary conditions and population reversion it is characteristically a fractional Brownian motion. This is important. Because the system is driven by stochastic processes, low-level equilibrium or poverty traps do not exist as fixed-point equilibrium in such a system but rather a barrier below which output cannot sustain the population at even the most rudimentary rates. We would not say this is an equilibrium in the ordinary sense of the term equilibrium, which implies some form of steady state. Under stochastic conditions the Nelson-type equilibrium is a pass through point. Instead a poverty trap might better be defined by the length of time that a population remains below the sustenance barrier.

3.13 Operationalizing the Simulation Model

The model presented above results in an intertemporal stochastic differential equation of an Ito form. The drift term, which defines the trajectory of agricultural output growth, is highly endogenous in the sense that population adjusts to land and capacity, which then feeds back into the land equation to determine how much land is actually necessary. As presented it assumes certain contemporaneous adjustments which are impracticable and unrealistic from a modeling point of view. We start with the following initial conditions which are drawn largely from Huang's reporting on Hebei and Shandong. There he reports combined population of 7.183 million persons in 1393 and 68 million in 1913. Over 520 years the exponential growth rate was 0.4323%/year. Citing Perkin's estimates of land in 1502, Huang argues that about 88.721 million mou would be appropriate for 1400 and this is capped to 238 million mou at the turn of the twentieth century.[44]

Models based on certain forms of Brownian motion (random walks) are notoriously difficult to converge to real-world observations because by design there is an infinite number of possible pathways emanating from the initial conditions. To at least get convergence at the mean we can algorithmically search for original parameters that would at least converge on average to the observed outcome. Thus, we calibrate the natural population growth rate to be .71%/year over 500 years from 1400 to 1900 so that given an initial population of 7.183 million the mean simulated population in 1900 is 68 million. This also yields a net population growth rate of 0.4037% over 500 simulated years which compares favorably to the actual 0.4323% actual growth rate between 1393 and 1913.

We model population in year 1 of the Monte Carlo simulation using the mean reverting Brownian motion

$$P_t = P_{t-1} e^{\left(g\left(1-(1-\phi)\frac{P_{t-1}}{P^*_{t-1}}\right) - \frac{1}{2}\sigma_P^2 + N(0,1)\sigma_P \right)} \quad (15)$$

Where g = 0.0071 is the natural growth rate, ϕ = 0.25 is a measure of resilience (with 1.0 showing no resilience and 0.0 being fully resilient), $P^*_{t-1} = \frac{Y_{t-1}}{c}$, the capacity of aggregate output divided by per capita con-

---

[44] Huang (1985). *Op Cit*, Appendices B and C.
Perkins, D. (1969). *Op Cit*.

sumption (c = 1,037.53 $kg/year$), is the capacity of the land to support the population at subsistence, σ_P = 0.05 is assumed to be the annual volatility in population meaning that the population might increase or decrease by 5% in approximately 68% of sampled years. This may appear large but with the frequency of floods, droughts, famine, plague, and war as well as random movements of populations immigrating or emigrating, it may not be as unreasonable as one might think. Finally, since we are assuming log-normality in population $N(0,1)$ is a randomly drawn standard normal deviate.

The output function is modeled in the following way. We assume as in our model a Cobb-Douglas form

$$Y_t = A_t P_{t-1}^{(\alpha + \lambda_P (L_{t-1} - L_0))} L_{t-1}^{(\beta - \lambda_L (L_{t-1} - L_0))} \tag{16}$$

The intercept term is not a constant as is usually the case in this kind of equation, but as discussed above it allows for technical innovation to increase aggregate output at the rate of μ_A = 0.002 per year. This number is loosely based on reported numbers for growth in wheat yield by Elvin. The volatility in aggregate output of 5% is assumed. It may be significant at the very local level but across two provinces there would likely have been spatial correlation and covariance between good and bad years that would moderate risk. The intercept is modeled as a Brownian motion. The volatility component of this random walk is used as the source of exogenous variation on output. However we add an additional component to this by correlating the randomness in this part with the randomness in the population equation to capture Lin's conjecture

$$A_t = A_{t-1} e^{\left(\left(\mu_A - \frac{1}{2}\sigma_A^2\right) + N(0,1)\sigma_A\right)} \tag{17}$$

We set the parameters as follows; α = 0.1668, β = 0.8332, λ_P = 0.00000186, λ_L = 0.00000186. These assume constant returns to scale. The parameters for human capital growth and land depreciation were calibrated to initial conditions. This ensures that over time the elasticity for labor increases at the same rate that the elasticity for land declines to ensure constant returns to scale at each time step. Finally, we use $(L_{t-1} - L_0)$ to scale the human capital and land depreciation properties. We do this because the initial values were calibrated to initial conditions which presumed the initial land base of 88.721 mou.

With output determined, the population capacity is computed using $P_t^* = \dfrac{Y_t}{c}$. Land dynamics evolve as follows

$$L_t = L_{t-1} + \frac{c}{\hat{Y}_{t-1}}(P_{t-1} - P_{t-2}) - \frac{cP_{t-1}}{\hat{Y}_{t-1}^2}(\hat{Y}_{t-1} - \hat{Y}_{t-2}), \tag{18}$$

where

$$\hat{Y}_t = 0.5\frac{Y_{t-1}}{L_{t-1}} + 0.5\frac{Y_{t-2}}{L_{t-2}} \tag{19}$$

is output per mou. This we smooth over two previous years on the assumption that farmers have some sense of rational expectations. Smoothing land in the same way makes the land dynamic less choppy while allowing for some lag between the time of an event or shock and a decision to increase or decrease the land base.

3.14 Some Results from Monte Carlo Simulation

We operationalize the above model using Monte Carlo methods for 5000 iterations over a time span of 500 years initialized to 1400 and concluding in 1900. Under the stochastic model presented above it is assumed that the actual history and evolution of population-land-output dynamics is driven largely by chance. The reality is that the historical path could have been altered at any point by a random shock to output, or population that was good, bad, or neutral. The driving force is the stochastic differential equations which follow Brownian motion with time-independent shocks. Essentially this means that in the course of China's agricultural history, anything can happen at any time; history is a random walk.

Casting the problem as a random walk also alters our view of equilibrium. In the sense of Nelson and others, an equilibrium is a steady state—a point of attraction of largely deterministic economic forces that once reached, remains in place. In a stochastic world the point of equilibrium, measured in various ways by land to population, or output per capita, is fleeting. It is a point of breakeven that is breached from above or below, but is transitory.

In Figs. 3.2, 3.3, and 3.4 we present three simulations. The upper-left quadrant plots the stochastic and dynamic paths of population and land. The output to land ratio is provided in the upper-right quadrant. Land per capita is provided in the lower-left quadrant and the capacity to population ratio in the lower-right. Capacity is measure by the population that can be sustained by agricultural output and is a traditional measure of the equilibrium trap. When this ratio is greater than 1 the economy will generally thrive. However when this value falls below 1 outcomes are dire: there is not enough food to support the population. This is the entry point of a poverty trap. How long a poverty trap persists is determined not only by population and land adjustments but also random events. A poverty trap is thus defined as an excursion below the equilibrium capacity line.

Figures 3.2 and 3.3 are interesting because the final population after 500 simulated years approximates the observed population in the 1900, and as well the land assumed to be under cultivation at that time. While both start and end up at the same place, the pathways are remarkably different. Figure 3.4 is provided to illustrate an outcome that was possible, but comes nowhere close to the observed conditions in 1900.

The output to land ratio is the aggregated output per mou. In our model we made some allowance for innovation, but depreciated the elasticity of land while increasing human capital, i.e. the elasticity of labor, to compensate. But in a random growth model from time to time disaster strikes, whether from a natural calamity or war the model does not differentiate, but it does capture the periodic booms and busts in China's agricultural history. Land per capita adjusts. This can be through a population increase relative to land, or the abandonment of land. In Fig. 3.2, for example land hits the natural limit after 300 years, or about the year 1700 as simulated. But once this maximum is reached there are periods of abandonment which could result from transitory increases in output relative to population, or declines in population. The capacity per capita in Fig. 3.2 shows a period of relative prosperity up until year 200. There is then a 50-year excursion into a poverty trap, a slight recovery, and then an extended poverty trap as the capacity to population ratio falls. In essence the population is growing at a rate in excess of the cultivation of new land and aggregate output. This extended poverty trap never recovers.

The simulation in Fig. 3.3 is similar, except that in this model land does not reach its maximum boundary until year 450, or the middle of the

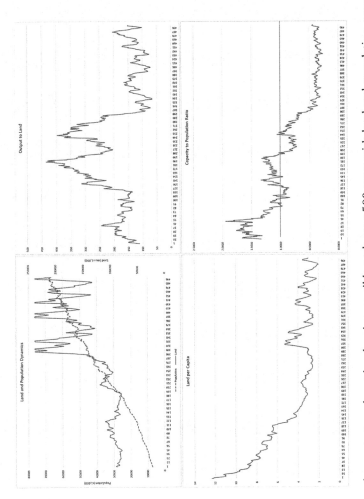

Fig. 3.2 Fractional poverty trap dynamics showing possible path over 500 years with land and population, upper left; output to land on upper right; land per capita, lower left; and capacity to population ratio, lower right. Start and endpoints approximate China's observed growth. Poverty trap dynamics illustrated in lower right, where excursions below values of 1 indicate below subsistence living standards. In this scenario land reaches its maximum about 300 years in, or around the year 1700. Beyond that the combination of low innovation and high output risk causes periodic rises and falls in land cultivated. Output uncertainty, the continual rise in population, and the land constraint results in a poverty trap that extends for nearly 300 years with this simulation

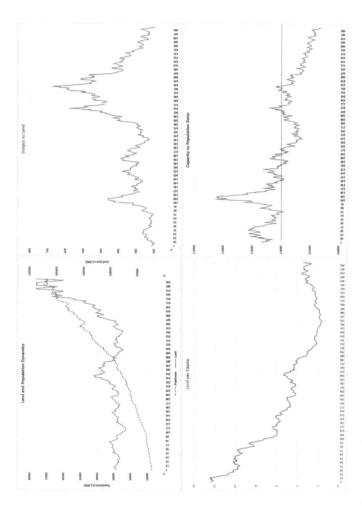

Fig. 3.3 Fractional poverty trap dynamics showing possible path over 500 years with land and population, upper left; output to land on upper right; land per capita, lower left; and capacity to population ratio, lower right. Start and endpoints approximate China's observed growth. Poverty trap dynamics illustrated in lower right, where excursions below values of 1 indicate below subsistence living standards. Note that in this example land reaches its maximum in the mid-1800s which is when some experts conclude the maximum was reached. The combined rise and fall in output, together with the rise in population, ensures in this particular path that by the 1900s farmers were locked into a poverty trap

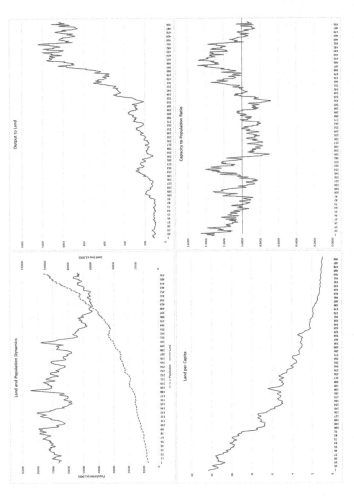

Fig. 3.4 Fractional poverty trap dynamics showing possible path over 500 years with land and population, upper left; output to land on upper right; land per capita, lower left; and capacity to population ratio, lower right. Start and endpoints differ from observed population and land use in China in 1900. In this scenario large gains in output due to technological innovation reduce the need to cultivate lower-quality land, while providing sufficient capacity for population growth. Poverty trap dynamics illustrated in lower right, where excursions below values of 1 indicate below subsistence living standards. Here we observe an excursion pattern that oscillates about the subsistence line

nineteenth century. Again with this particular iteration randomness in output reveals a chaotic path in output per capita. Again, under this set of circumstances the capacity to population ratio falls into the poverty trap at around year 365 (1765) and remains there until year 500 (1900).

Figures 3.2 and 3.3 are dire, but in terms of the question posed in Chap. 2—how did China's agricultural economy get to its condition in 1921?—illustrates how randomness in populations, productivity, and innovation can explain the conditions. But if chance is the driving force then under this model alternative pathways were feasible. Figure 3.4 ends with a population of about 77 million supported by only 67 million mou. In fact the land base in 1900 is less than it was in 1400. Why is this? The output per capita in Fig. 3.4 had a good run, and increased almost exponentially throughout this period. This could be a combination of strong innovation, good luck, or both but as output increased faster than the population, the amount of land required decreased. There was still variance, but the capacity to population ratio shows more positive excursions. Poverty traps still existed now and again, but not to the same extent as the other simulations in Figs. 3.2 and 3.3.

Again these are only simulations. Actual records on land cultivated, population, and output are scarce and dubious, so we can only presume what actually happened in China. By observation and anecdote we know that lands in Shandong and elsewhere were contoured many hundreds of years ago so it is unlikely that hitting the land capacity was a recent phenomenon in the mid-1800s as some have suggested. If the maximum was reached in 1600–1700 then it is not unreasonable to conjecture that any drought, plague, or war would lead to abandonment of mountain plots that were labor intensive. The continual parceling of land across generations as the population grew has repeatedly been asserted to explain the poverty conditions at the turn of the Republican era.

3.15 Fractional Poverty Traps

A fractional process is a stochastic process which has some form of entrenched memory. A Brownian motion is a stochastic process without memory in the Markovian sense that random shocks from one period to the next are independent of each other. A fractional Brownian motion will exhibit varying degrees of positive or negative correlation across these shocks. If correlation is positive the process is said to be persistent; if it is negative it is said to be mean reverting or ergodic.

A convenient means of estimating system memory is the Hurst coefficient, H. For $H = \frac{1}{2}$ the system is Brownian motion, for $0 < H < \frac{1}{2}$ the system is mean-reverting, and for $\frac{1}{2} < H \leq 1$ it is persistent, with long-run memory. The boundaries at 0 and 1 are rarely met in nature with 0 being pure white noise and 1 being almost perpetually reinforcing.

A straightforward way to understand the meaning of H is through the scaled variance ratio. In essence if we take the logarithm of an outcome variable (e.g. population, land, capacity/population ratio) by conversion, and then take the differences across all years of measurement, after conversion to logarithm $\{x_2 - x_1, x_3 - x_2 \ldots x_t - x_{t-1} \ldots x_{500} - x_{499}\}$, then the average percentage change across years is given by

$$E[x_t - x_{t-1}] = \frac{1}{T} \sum_{t=1}^{T} (x_t - x_{t-1}) \tag{20}$$

and its variance by

$$\sigma^2 = Var[x_t - x_{t-1}] = \frac{1}{T} \sum_{t=1}^{T} ((x_t - x_{t-1}) - E[x_t - x_{t-1}])^2 \tag{21}$$

The scale of measurement is 1 (because of a one-year difference) and it is assumed in a Brownian motion that the variance holds across all years and that shocks between years are uncorrelated. There is no memory in the system and in this sense a Brownian motion is also a Markov process. But if we examine outcomes on a different scale, will the Markov property hold? In other words, at different timescales will evidence of intertemporal correlation show up in a systemic way. Consider in our modeling case the timescale of 500 years. Then the difference in the outcome variable between year 500 and year 1 is $x_{500} - x_1$. We can rewrite this by adding zero's along the way, i.e.

$$x_{500} - x_1 = (x_{500} - x_{499}) + (x_{499} - x_{498}) + \ldots + (x_2 - x_1)$$

or

$$E[x_{500} - x_1] = E[x_{500} - x_{499}] + E[x_{499} - x_{498}] + \ldots + E[x_2 - x_1] = TE[x_t - x_{t-1}] \tag{22}$$

The variance term is more complex because there may be some correlation between changes across time. If this is the case then the system is no longer Markovian, but has some systemic memory in the system. It is still a random walk process but instead of being a geometric Brownian motion it is a fractional Brownian motion. The variance term is given in long form by

$$Var[x_{500} - x_1] = \sum_{t=1}^{T}((x_t - x_{t-1}) - E[x_t - x_{t-1}])^2$$
$$+ 2\sum_{i=1}^{T}\sum_{j=1}^{T}((x_i - x_{i-1}) - E[x_i - x_{i-1}])((x_j - x_{j-1}) - E[x_j - x_{j-1}]), i \neq j$$
(23)

Where the term $2\sum_{i=1}^{T}\sum_{j=1}^{T}((x_i - x_{i-1}) - E[x_i - x_{i-1}])((x_j - x_{j-1}) - E[x_j - x_{j-1}])$ is the covariance across all time steps. This covariance should be zero if all shocks are identically and independently distributed (i.e. a geometric Brownian motion) but will be negative if correlations are negative (thus decreasing overall variance) and positive if correlations are positive (thus increasing overall variance).

The relationship across the two timescales is given by

$$Var[x_{500} - x_1] = Var[x_t - x_{t-1}]T^{2H}$$
(24)

Where H is the Hurst coefficient of interest. If the system is memoryless then $H = \frac{1}{2}$ and the variance of the 500-year timescale will be 500 times the one-year time scale. Rearranging to solve for H, we use

$$H = \frac{1}{2} \frac{\text{Log}\left(\frac{Var[x_{500} - x_1]}{Var[x_t - x_{t-1}]}\right)}{\text{Log}(T)}$$
(25)

in our simulations. The variance ratio in the numerator will collapse to T if there is no correlation or covariance. In this case the numerator and denominator cancel out, $Var[x_{500} - x_1] = 500 \times Var[x_t - x_{t-1}]$ and $H = \frac{1}{2}$: a geometric Brownian motion. But if $Var[x_{500} - x_1] > 500 \times Var[x_t - x_{t-1}]$ then the numerator will have some value T+n so that the variance ratio

Table 3.1 Simulated Hurst exponents for population-land-output dynamics

Population	0.701	Persistent
Capacity/population	0.368	Mean reverting
Output	0.512	Slight persistence
Innovation	0.50	No correlation
Land	0.603	Persistent
Output to land	0.535	Slight persistence
Output/population	0.368	Mean reverting
Land/population	0.654	Persistent

will be greater than 1 and $H > \frac{1}{2}$. Likewise if $Var[x_{500} - x_1] < 500 \times Var[x_t - x_{t-1}]$, then the variance ratio in the numerator will have some value $T - n$, and $H < \frac{1}{2}$. From the simulations that generated Figs. 3.2, 3.3, and 3.4 we computed the Hurst coefficients as follows (Table 3.1).

What we find is that the macro forces are, as modeled, fractional. Population, land, and land per capita have elements of long memory. This suggests that to some degree events in the present will have some statistical relationship to events in the future, perhaps in an unseen or indescribable way. In general, higher Hurst coefficients will tend to have much longer excursion paths, perhaps indefinite one way or another. In other words, if we witness a rise in population this is more likely to persist longer into the future before reversing itself: likewise with land. But with land we have to take note of the geographic limitations that act as an upper boundary. It is not surprising for those simulated paths such as in Fig. 3.2 that reach capacity sooner rather than later that this capacity will reverberate in future years, declining and then reversing itself. The interaction between land and population is therefore an interesting one. Our initial specification of the population dynamic as a mean reverting process is indirectly driven by land, and this appears to dominate as population on its own or without the land capacity constraint would naturally rise and fall in response to shocks and the intensity of resilience that the population has available to it.

The land to population ratio is also a common measure in the equilibrium trap literature. We find this to be persistent at 0.654. As a general measure it is not purely random but characterized by longer-than-random excursions. If the ratio is on the rise then it will tend to continue rising for a longer period of time than one would expect with a purely random model; likewise when it is falling it will likely persist and fall for a longer period of time than a purely random model.

The capacity to population ratio (and the output to population ratio) is our key measure for fractional poverty traps, oscillating around a ratio of 1 which is the subsistence line. We find this to be highly mean reverting with $H = 0.368$. This is a classic Malthusian result. What it suggests is that the ratio reverses itself much quicker than would be expected under a purely random measure. That is, if the capacity to population ratio is rising, this induces population growth, which puts pressure on land, so the ratio soon enough reverses itself. Likewise if the ratio is falling as a result of some catastrophe then the population adjusts by reducing the growth rate or increasing mortality until subsistence is once again reached.

In our interpretation of a fractional poverty trap, we thus consider the number of times that the capacity/population ratio falls below 1 in a fixed period of time and once below the line, how long before it reverses itself. This again will naturally be tied to the land, the time required before all arable land is cultivated, and the innovations and random shocks applies to the output of this land. In Figs. 3.2 and 3.3 we can see that as the population rises relative to land ($H = 0.654$) this has the effect of pushing the capacity ratio below 1, and for a much longer period of time. Figure 3.4 on the other hand does not hit the land capacity and in this scenario we can observe a different pattern of reversals in the capacity ratio.

3.16 Summary

In this chapter we have strayed somewhat from the topic of agricultural credit by expanding on some ideas related to equilibrium traps. In 1930 Buck wrote: "*A small business, the result of over-population, especially in those regions periodically subject to famine from drought, flood insect pest, or like causes means little reserve for the years of crop failure. Farm population in such localities fare well if crops return even average yield, but crop failures, especially in successive years, spell ruin for all but the most prosperous. This situation is aggravated by the absence of the same credit, marketing and transportation facilities which would also make possible the enlargement of the farm business*".[45] Our point was to describe in an historical way how conditions so dire were observed in 1921 when the topic of agricultural credit was popularized as a means to solving some of agriculture's

---

[45] Buck, J.L. (1930). *Op Cit*, page 425.

problems. What Buck describes suggests that if equilibrium traps exist, many Chinese farmers were caught in them. But whatever situation these farmers found themselves in, exogenous risk factors were not a trivial part. Our attempt in this chapter was to merge the economic drivers of the various theories of equilibrium and poverty traps with dynamics and stochastics to provide a broader understanding of how China ended up the way it did in the Republican era. The literature provided some good guidance, from the earlier work of Malthus and Ricardo to modernist views of Nurkse, Nelson, and Elvin. While insightful, the prevailing models of low- (or high-)level equilibrium traps were all short-run models. Our history, on the other hand, was a long one, and as described in the previous chapter subject to so many random events from drought and flood to war and dynasties that the equilibrium trap models were seemingly incomplete.

It is impossible to replicate China's agricultural history, but enough hints were in these papers to offer guidance to developing a more structured dynamic model that took into account some of the risks and uncertainties that arose, and through this process perhaps gain a better understanding of the forces of poverty traps rather than the absolute causes.

We started by defining stochastic differential equations for population and innovation, accounting for the Malthusian observation that as populations grow poorer land is brought under cultivation. But from Elvin comes the notion that progress must be made in cultivation practices and the acquisition of human capital to sustain the population as more land is brought under cultivation. So, as the marginal quality of land declines, we make allowances for marginal gains in human capital so on average as land and populations increase at least constant returns to scale are maintained. We defined capacity/capita and built into our model dynamic adjustments in population that responded to rises and declines in the capacity of land to feed the population. This was all modeled as a stochastic process which takes a fairly complex form and which we describe as being fractional.

The idea of a fractional poverty trap in our context is that dynamics and structural constraints interact over time in a persistent manner. Once land hits its maximum capacity and population adjusts accordingly this constraint adds a form of memory to the system. We see that by our measure of the Hurst coefficient that measures tied to land and population have random shocks that are correlated over time—there is memory in the system and this memory drives excursion patterns. Typically the higher the

Hurst coefficient the more likely that current observed conditions would persist longer into the future than for lower Hurst coefficients.

Our main measure of poverty trap is the capacity to population ratio, which is closely tied to the land to population ratio used in the literature. We find this to be a mean-reverting fractional process and thus abscond with the terminology introduced by Swallow and Barret of the fractional poverty trap (they used fractal, but with the same meaning). A fractional poverty trap in our context is the consequence of a random process falling below the level of subsistence (capacity ratio = 1) and remaining there for some period of time. Our simulated measure of $H = 0.368$ indicates that it is a mean reverting process so that mathematically a poverty trap will ultimately be reversed. The lower the Hurst coefficient the more likely it will be reversed sooner than later, at least in a probabilistic sense. Nonetheless, the model suggests that poverty traps are not necessarily a permanent state, even though a poverty trap might appear as such over decades or even centuries. Eventually the forces of economies and population will cause a reversal path to escape the poverty trap.

A final note to the reader. We find Figs. 3.2 and 3.3 equally plausible. But in a model of this type there are millions of possible paths that could have provided similar initial and final conditions. Should a series be drawn with reliable population, land, and output measures for China (or elsewhere) it would be possible to measure the actual Hurst coefficients. Perhaps of more immediate interest is the modeling and measurement of poverty traps to determine if indeed they are 'fractional poverty traps' as proposed in this chapter.

CHAPTER 4

Traditional Forms of Credit in Rural China

4.1 Introduction

The rural financial problems of Republican China are bound up to a considerable extent with the 4000 years or more of history of the Chinese people. To understand and appreciate the evolution of modern rural financial institutions, it is both necessary and interesting to consider historical developments in rural credit or forms of credit that peppered China during the decades and centuries prior to the Republican era. A historical retrospective not only provides some colorful and innovative approaches to providing credit access to farmers but also provides context as to why the innovations in cooperative credit that started to emerge in 1921 China are historically significant.

"*Institutions*" as we use the term "*are regularities in repetitive interactions among individuals. They provide a framework within which people have some confidence as to how outcomes will be determined…Institutions are not persons, they are customs and rules that provide a set of incentives and disincentives for individuals. They entail enforcement either of the self-enforcing variety, though codes of behavior, or by third party policing and monitoring… Institutions arise and evolve because of the interaction of individuals. The growing specialization and division of labor in a society is the basic source of institutional evolution…a basic source of institutional change is fundamental and persistent changes in relative prices, which lead one or both parties to contracts to perceive they could be better off by alterations in the contract…*

© The Author(s) 2018
H. Fu, C. G. Turvey, *The Evolution of Agricultural Credit during China's Republican Era, 1912–1949*,
https://doi.org/10.1007/978-3-319-76801-4_4

individuals form organizations in order to capture gains arising from specialization and division of labor. Individuals may form contracts with each other, either voluntarily or through coercion, which specify terms of exchange. When a number of contracts fall under an overall, umbrella contract, they compose an organization".[1]

Traditional China had been an agrarian nation for centuries, dating as far back as 2737 B.C., sharing a recognition of the supreme importance of agriculture as the basis of the people's subsistence and the source of the government's revenue. In this chapter we want to step back and explore the institutions and methods by which farmers and emperors established the means to address the liquidity and credit needs of farmers in good times and bad. The 'institutions' that evolved include granaries, the *Qian Hui* (money-loan society, known in modern times as ROSCA, rotating savings and credit association), pawn shops, the *Qian Zhuang* (money shop) and *Piao Hao* (old-style native private banks), and private money lenders. These were rarely subjected to legislative requirements, and most of their credit activities were not regulated by governments.

4.2 Granaries and Traditional Rural Credit

In 1939 Nicholas Kaldor developed a theory of speculation in which he argued that speculators were people with better than average foresight who step in as buyers whenever there is an excess in supply, store commodity, and then release the commodity whenever there is a rise in price resulting from a shortfall in yield. Speculation in this form served as a mechanism to smooth intertemporal supply and reduce price variability. Ten years later in 1949, the Stanford agricultural economist Holbrook Working put forth a theory on the price of storage for grain. The argument made by Working was that storage involved stocks of grain that must be carried from one date to another in such volume that direct economic reward must be offered. Working argued that storage itself had value, a return that which, in the extremes of abundance or deficit, provided a return that moved inversely to market prices and market conditions. As supplies increased, reducing market prices, farmers would seek storage in the hopes that prices would rise in future. But the greater the demand for storage, the greater the cost of storage, removing on margin incentives to

---

[1] North, Douglass C. (1986). The New Institutional Economics. *Journal of Institutional and Theoretical Economics*, 142(1).

postpone sales to the future. On the other hand, in times of drought or reduced supply farmers would have every incentive to sell into the spot market, and as storage capacity increased, the cost of storage declined accordingly, providing an incentive to remove stock from current supply to be marketed at a future date. Both Kaldor and Working brought forth the argument that storage not only provided smoothing benefits across time, but also smoothing across space. A central storage facility could remove excess supply from areas of abundance to increase supply in regions of deficit so storage not only provided a stabilizing force across time but space as well. A final aspect of this modern theory of storage is something called convenience. Convenience refers to stocks of grain that are held in storage, even when all market signals suggest that a sale would be profitable, to ensure that the owner of the grain has immediate access to the grain at the moment it is needed.[2]

Although we view Kaldor and Working as capturing the essentials of a modern theory of storage, the theory appears to have been put into practice in literal form in China nearly 2000 years ago. While the formal markets with forward economic signals (e.g. forward contracts of futures markets) were not, so far as we know, part of China's early market model, we are not making too much of a stretch by equating the modern practice of speculation with the ancient practice of hoarding—the economic outcome was the same. Landowners with private storage could buy grain when supply was abundant at harvest and store the grain until household stores were depleted and prices rose. These merchants became the usurers of the day. As the final household stores were used to sow the fields, farmers would have to wait until harvest, starving in the meanwhile. The only recourse was to borrow from the private granaries at high prices on loan at usurious rates. If the farmer had no cash or barter he would have to repay the value of the loan plus interest in grain equivalents that at harvest was priced far below the price at planting. This is an ancient equivalent to the modern-day practice of toxic finance which leads, then and now, to an economic death spiral.[3] Entrapped by the immutable laws of economics

---

[2] Kaldor, N. (1939). Speculation and economic stability. *The Review of Economic Studies,* 7(1), 1–27.

Working, H. (1949). The theory of price of storage. *The American Economic Review,* 1254–1262.

[3] Red Herring (2001). Death by Finance, April 11, 2001 …Toxic finance involves what is referred to as a "toxic convert," which is a financing measure of last resort commonly used in the wake of the Nasdaq crash in 2000. In one example an entrepreneur, desperate for cash,

that persisted in the day, the greater the harvest, the lower the price, the more grain to be paid, so that no matter what the condition the farmer was left with a meagre result. If the harvests failed, which was China's frequent tragedy, the farmer would have to double down on more debt, accelerating the spiral, or give up the land entirely.

As a result, China developed a granary or warehousing businesses both in principle and practice long before the Europeans. Among its ancient warehousing facilities there were three important types of granaries known as *ever-normal granary (Chang Ping Cang)*, *charity granary (Yi Cang)* and *community/local granary (She Cang)*.[4] These granaries were organized with two main objectives, namely, the preservation of grain during years of plenty and the distribution of grain during years of scarcity and were maintained and operated as a relief measure against emergencies, rather than commercial organizations for mercantile purposes. To the best of our knowledge from the first of these came the term 'ever-normal granary' in the Western Han dynasty between 202 B.C. and 8 A.D. Then, a government system of storage was developed with the express purpose of 'normalizing grain-sale' and 'normalizing grain-purchase' during the reign of Han Wu Di (156–87 B.C.) to make "*the myriad things be unable to fluctuate in price*".[5] Around 604 A.D. at the beginning of the Sui dynasty, when emperor *Wen Di* ordered public granaries to be built in all towns and ordered all families, in proportion to their subsistence, to provide each year a quantity of rice and grain which was to be distributed in times of scarcity.[6] The value of convenience—the immediate access to

---

agreed to an exchange of $17 million in cash for $19 million's in common stock. The catch to a toxic convert is that the investors were entitled to the $19 million in stock, regardless of the price per share. It was not uncommon that the investors would then short sell the stock driving its price down, diluting the position of the original owners. The private investors running the scheme were in the industry as the 'grimmest of reapers', as were perhaps the usurers in ancient China. Accessed 8/23/2016 at share. http://www.placementtracker.com/News/PR%2004.11.01%20-%20Death%20By%20Finance2.html

[4] Zhongqi Wu (1992). A short history of Chinese Grainaries, Chinese Storage & Transport, V.2.

[5] Zhou, Shuangxi (1996). History of Grain in Ancient Times, Chinese Commerce Publishing House.

Fu, Hong (2009). "Development of Modern Rural Financial Institutions in Republican China". Chinese Material Publishing House, Beijing. Even before this there are records showing some basic elements of 'normalizing grain-sale' were practiced as early as the Spring and Autumn periods of China's development.

[6] DuHalde, (1741), page 387.

stores of corn and rice which limited famine and mitigated social unrest—was well understood. The role of storage with mercantile value was not developed for a few hundred years after.

4.3 Ever-normal Granary (*Chang Ping Cang*) and Formal Credit

The ever-normal granary was one of the earliest types of granaries constructed and maintained with government funds. The demand for credit fluctuated from year to year because of harvest variations, and even during the farming year fluctuated on a cyclical basis. Before the spring sowing, farmers borrowed small sums on a short-term basis and repaid these loans after the fall harvest. Towards the end of the winter when last year's grain was exhausted, farmers were often on the verge of starvation. Poor farmers who suffered from agricultural shortages and seasonal imbalances in grain supply and demand during planting season suffered near famine conditions through much of Chinese history. A reliable source of credit was required to finance the interval between sowing and harvest and crowd out speculators. These speculators would lend to farmers at usurious rates and, upon default, would seize farmers' land which farmers had been forced to use as collateral.

To deal with the instability brought by shortages and famines, the early Chinese rulers relied on government-owned ever-normal granaries which stored grain at a constant supply to reduce price manipulation. These granaries also provided the needed liquidity to farm households through credit access and borrowing during sowing to stabilize and smooth consumption through harvest. At harvest the farmer could sell or trade grain, store grain at the farm for household consumption, or store grain as a future reserve. As the ever-normal granaries took shape farmers could start to arbitrage seasonal price fluctuations. At harvest when prices were low, they would sell what was necessary for a basic standard of living or to pay off debts, and place the rest in storage. Since under normal expectations the price would rise as household stores were consumed, farmers could deposit grain, borrow against the grain stored, and then at the next planting (or before or later) remove the grain, sell it at higher-than-harvest prices, and repay the loan plus interest. If for some reason the price did not rise or the farmer could not repay the debt, the stored grain was forfeited. It is not clear if forfeiture erased the debt entirely, but it is more than likely that the farmer would not have been allowed to borrow in principal an amount that exceeded his amount stored. Instead, the farmer would deposit grain equivalent to the total loan plus interest, receiving only the principal in cash. It is also unclear if at that time farmers could voluntarily default if grain prices fell below the total liability value. If so, the early granaries of China will have provided some of the first examples of an imbedded put option, or contingent claim, in a credit contract.[7] It is fair to assume that the cost of storage was fixed within the interest rate so, unlike the modern-day theories, the cost of storage did not transmit a market signal. If the returns to storage were determined freely and competitively then so too would the cost of storage reflect periods of abundance and scarcity. With costs of storage linked to interest rates, and interest rates fixed by fiat, it is evident that the ever-normal granaries were not designed to send and receive market signals. Rather, the fixing of storage costs can be seen as an intertemporal swap of storage risks in the sense that the inevitable rise and fall of storage costs that come with harvests of abundance and scarcity are averaged across the possibility of outcomes into a single fixed rate. This in turn added further stability to the use of credit.

4.4 Charity Granaries (*Yi Cang*), Community Granaries, and Farmers' Mutual Aid System

The second popular granary in ancient China was known as the charity granary (*Yi Cang*). The charity granaries coincided with an enlightened sense of giving and welfare at the time.[8] These were publicly funded gra-

---

[7] Which is how one of the world's largest granaries in the present era, the Commodity Credit Corporation (CCC) in the United States operates. With the CCC a target price is set below which farmers can voluntarily default on the 'target loan' which is equivalent to selling the stored grain to the CCC at the higher-than-market target price. See Gardner, B. L. (1977). Commodity options for agriculture. *American Journal of Agricultural Economics*, 59(5), 986–992 or Turvey, C. G., Brorsen, B. W., & Baker, T. G. (1988, December). A Contingent Claim Pricing Model for Valuing Nonrecourse Loan Programs and Target Prices. In *American Journal of Agricultural Economics* (abstract Vol. 70, No. 5, pages 1197–1197).

[8] Benevolent societies, commonly named *t'ung-shan hui* or 'societies for sharing goodness', developed around the Late Ming and early Qing dynasties and expanded beyond the charity granaries to assist impoverished widows, bury the unclaimed dead, set up soup kitchens, and provide capital to merchants and doctors. See Smith (1987). Page 309.

Smith, J. F. H. (1987). Benevolent societies: the reshaping of charity during the late Ming and early Ch'ing. *The Journal of Asian Studies*, 46(02), 309–337.

naries by local people who donated part of their wealth to the public welfare. The oldest evidence for the charity granary is the system adopted by the Emperor Wen Di (581–604) of the Sui dynasty in 585. He retained part of the taxes to stock the commonly founded local granary at the suggestion of Zhangsun Ping, the minister of revenue (度支尚书). The charity granary was first operated in districts by private initiative, but were also founded in prefectures where the local government took over the organization. It was regulated that rich households would donate one dan of grain, middle-income ones 7 dou (0.7 dan), and households with lower incomes 0.4 dan.[9]

Charity granaries became widespread during the Tang dynasty (618–907). Emperor Tai Zong commanded in 628 that each member of the nobility, i.e. bearers of the titles of King or Duke, was to donate 2 sheng per mou, to serve as grain for the charity granaries. In 651 the rule was expanded to each household and the amount of grain to be donated depended on the income with a ceiling rate of 5 dan of grain. Special regulations fixed the reduction of this quota in years of bad harvest. The smaller charity granaries supplemented the larger system of ever-normal granaries that was founded in the early period. In combination the system was called the ever-normal charity granary, at least in the early decades of the ninth century. Not all dynasties followed the same organizational methods.[10]

The Southern Song (1127–1279) dynasty increased these fees by a donation of various types of silk fabric. In 1186 the great Neo-Confucian philosopher Xi Zhu, in whose home district Chong'an a great famine had occurred, donated the huge amount of 600 dan to the local granary as a loan to farmers who borrowed in summer and repaid at 2% interest (half during a small famine, no interest during a big famine) usually in winter. He submitted to the emperor proposals for the organization of this system and suggested expanding the system of community granaries in 1181. As he proposed, the system would be organized by local gentry who relied on the support of the district magistrate; local granaries and the ever-normal granaries would mutually lend grain in case of need; and granaries would also be allowed to give credit, at an interest rate of 2 dou per dan of rice (20%). Emperor *Xiaozong* (1162–1189) accepted the proposal and ordered this kind of mutual assistance to be realized. After 14 years in

---

[9] Zhou (1996). *Op Cit.* One dan is a measure of weight ranging from 180 to 360 kilos depending on local measures. One dou is 1/10 of a dan.

[10] Xu Liu (1975). Old book of the Tang, Beijing: ZhongHua publishing house.

operation, principal and interest of 3100 dan of grain was gathered which was then stored at a granary owned by local farmers according to Zhu Xi's suggestion.[11]

The Yuan dynasty required a payment of 5 dou of grain for free persons and 2 dou per serf. During the Ming period (1368–1644), the charity granaries were privately organized. Twenty or 30 households formed one 'community', with a community head, a community leader, and a vice leader, who organized the collection of grain for the community granary, according to three different ranks of income. Apart from the quota, each household paid a loss surcharge of 5 he (a unit of currency, 合).

The Qing dynasty (1644–1911) subjected the system to public supervision, while the organization was left to the local communities. In 1729 an imperial decree even forbade official interference in the system. The term 'charity granary' was only fixed in 1679 when the Emperor Kangxi (1661–1722) defined that charity granaries were granaries in cities, while those in smaller, more rural communities were called 'community granaries' the purpose of which was quite similar to that of the charity granary. Yet in the organization of these two types, there was no great difference. In the second half of the nineteenth century the system of charity granaries disintegrated more and more, heavily affected by the destruction during the Taiping Rebellion.[12]

In the late Qing period the village council selected several peasants to manage the village granary. They were responsible for collecting and preserving grain in the granary. One sheng of millet per mou of land for every household every year was required. The scheme was that in poor harvest years peasants could borrow grain by merely signing a statement of the amount they wished to borrow and when they would return the grain. In 1917 the county government ordered all villages to organize granaries. Many villages refused to do so and evaded carrying out the order by bribing officials or deceiving them. In 1936 the granary system was discontinued and its disappearance may be attributed to the fact that collecting grain contributions was more difficult because fewer peasants owned their land; and peasants renting land were unable or unwilling to contribute.

---

[11] Zhiping Chen. (2016). The design and change of Zhu Xi's Community Granary. *Researches in Chinese Economic History*, 6.

[12] Liping Bai. (2013). Emperor Kangxi and the construction of Community Granary, *Beijing Social Science*, 5.

Furthermore, increased taxes may have made it difficult for peasants to continue to support this organization.[13]

4.5 MONEY-LOAN SOCIETY (*QIAN HUI*) AND INFORMAL TRADITIONAL RURAL CREDIT

Since at least 1977 there has been much study of rotating savings and credit associations. The term ROSCA was coined by Fritz Bouman who had observed numerous reports starting around 1962 that revealed rotating savings and loans associations as a worldwide phenomenon.[14] With his interest piqued, Bouman began to search the literature and found that these ROSCAs were found in almost every society under some form of economic development and developed under a number of names including the financial aid society (FAS),[15] cooperative loan society,[16] money loan association,[17] and mutual savings society.[18]

The Chinese equivalent of the money-loan society known as Qian Hui, or He Hui, was (and in some places still is) a popular institution for informal rural credit with a long history in China. It was observed prior to 1899 by Arthur Henderson Smith (1845–1932), a missionary of the American Board of Commissioners for Foreign Missions who spent 54 years in China and who wrote in his book *Chinese Characteristics*: "*Among the most characteristic examples of Chinese capacity for combination are Loan Societies, which seem everywhere to be found*".[19] One of the first Chinese nationals to study rural credit in China wrote in 1928 that: "*These (money loan associations) are friendly clubs found in every county making loan transactions*".[20]

---

[13] Ramon H. Myers (1970). The Chinese Peasant Economy: Agricultural Development in Hebei and Shandong 1890–1949, Harvard University Press, Cambridge MA.

[14] Bouman, F. J. (1977). Indigenous Savings and Credit Societies in The Third World. A Message. *Savings and Development*, 1(4), 181–219.

[15] Fei, Hsiao-Tung, Peasant life in China: A Field Study of Country Life in the Yangtze Valley, London: Routledge & Kegan Paul Ltd.

[16] Arthur H. Smith (1899). Village Life in China: A Study in Sociology, Einburgh and London.

[17] Hsu, Chi-lien (1928). Rural Credit in China. 12 *Chinese Soc. & Pol. Sci. Rev.* 1.

[18] Gamble, Sidney D. (1954). Ting Hsien: A North China Rural Community, California: Stanford University Press.

[19] Arthur H. Smith. (1899). *Op Cit*.

[20] Chi-lien Hsu. (1928).

4.5.1 Green Sprouts Policy

As for the origin of the money-loan society, it might have evolved from the Green Sprouts Policy which was used to expand credit access to the rural poor with members mutually guaranteeing each other's loans during the Northern Song dynasty (906–1279).[21] The Green Sprouts Policy was a rural financial practice conceived by a Chinese reformer, Wang Anshi, an influential politician as well as a scholar. Wang emerged from a rising new group of Southern bureaucrats with a strong utilitarian bent, who challenged their more conservative, large-landholding colleagues from the North. At age 21 Wang earned his *jinshi* ('advanced scholar') degree in the civil service examinations. After working as a local government official for nearly 20 years, Wang concluded that the unlimited annexation of land weakened the economy. In 1058 Wang submitted to Emperor Renzong his "Ten Thousand Word Memorial", which contained rudiments of his later policies and political theories; no action was taken on his proposals, which were aimed at the bureaucracy. Wang asserted that more capable officials with skills suited for their duties should be trained and recruited. Wang entered central government in 1060, but not until the succession of Emperor, Shenzong did he achieve a powerful rank close to the throne and gain the trust of the imperial ear.

When Wang was appointed as Magistrate of Yin County that faced rural economic problems, he witnessed that farmers had no alternatives to usury. Wang attempted to initiate an interest-bearing loan model instead of the interest-free poverty alleviation loan that was commonly used to address economic distress and to preserve the limited resources of the county.[22] The model was first applied in Hebei, Henan, and Anhui provinces. According to the Green Sprouts Policy, farmers were loaned money by the government according to their needs in wheat and millet during the planting and growing season when farmers needed help most. The loan was known as 'Green Sprout Money' because it was issued when seeds put forth green sprouts, and was repaid after harvest in grain or cash with a fixed interest of 20–30% per loan. Money and grains from government-run ever-normal granaries and great charity granaries were

---

[21] Zongpei Wang. (1935). ROSCAs in China, Nanjing: Chinese Institute of Cooperatives.
[22] We are unclear as to the reference to the 'interest free' loans referred to in this statement. This may be referring to the private granaries that we discussed above or simply interest-free loans by the benevolence societies that were springing up here and there throughout that period.

used to establish the system. Farmers were classified into five grades based on their property and creditworthiness. This may also be among (if not) the first examples of self-help groups with mutual liability to obtain microcredit, superseding Muhamad Yunus's Grameen Bank by about 900 years. Similar to Grameen-style lending to the poor in the present day, borrowers were organized into five- or 10-person groups with all members mutually guaranteeing each other's loans. Wang's approach had two breakthrough conceptual insights into agricultural finance. First, as a government official he looked at the farm problem not through the lens of charity, which is a short-run solution, but through the longer-term implementation of farm policy by providing government sponsored loans. Second, he conceived a group-based loan model with members mutually guaranteeing each other which provided some insight and inspiration for financial aid societies/ rotating savings and credit associations and ultimately credit cooperatives. Anshi Wang's unconventional idealism through the Green Sprouts Policy and other 'New Policies' of 1069–76 sparked an academic controversy that continued for centuries.[23]

4.5.2 Money-loan Society (Qian Hui)

The money-loan society, *Qian Hui* in Chinese, was a financial aid society that came into being as a supplementary mechanism when the system of mutual allowance was inadequate. The system of mutual allowance was

---

[23] This debate was actually a continuation of a centuries-old debate. In 597 B.C. during the Tcheou dynasty there were two philosophers *Yang* and *Me*. Yang believed that all men should be loved alike, with strangers treated and loved as much as the nearest kin. Me, on the other hand, would have no man care about anyone except himself, nor be concerned about the welfare of the rest of mankind, including the emperor (DuHalde 1742, Page 329). Me's approach is reminiscent of Adam Smith's invisible hand in The Wealth of Nations: "*By pursuing his own interest he frequently promotes that of the society more effectually than when he really intends to promote it*". Me's self-interest seems to refer to absolute self-interest even in non-economic terms. Adam Smith's self-interest was in economic terms. At any rate the wedge between benevolence and self-interested behavior persisted through Wang's time, and as between Yang and Me, conflicts arose between Wang and the proponents of the charity granaries. Like Smith and the economic part of Me, Wang believed that free charity distorted market signals and encouraged borrowing for fancy rather than necessity. By charging interest rates, farmers incentives to borrow changed, and it was no longer in their self-interest to borrow unnecessarily, nor was it in their self-interest to become imprudent and complacent in reliance on free loans from the charity granaries.

Smith, A. (1776). An inquiry into the wealth of nations. Strahan and Cadell, London.

found chiefly in cases of temporary deficiency and among relatives or friends when the creditor was confident in the ability of the debtor to repay within a short time. Small sums of money could be borrowed from relatives or friends for a short term without interest since most borrowers had kinship relations who were bound by social ties to look after each other's welfare in traditional China. But when a large sum was needed, it was difficult to borrow from one individual and to repay in a short time. Hence the financial aid society came into being. Such a society was organized on the initiative of the person who needed financial help, and members who joined the society were considered as having rendered help to the organizer. Being a voluntary association, a *Qian Hui* was organized and dissolved easily without any government sanction or concern.

The money-loan society (*Qian Hui*) was a mechanism for collective saving and lending. It was not entirely satisfactory as a means of credit, but did illustrate a widespread faculty for cooperation in rural areas.[24] In simple terms, the money-loan society was an informal pre-cooperative microfinance group of individuals who agreed to meet for a defined period in order to save and borrow together. The one who called the first meeting was designated the Head of the Society, while other members were called Foots of Society. The members of the society depended on both the sum of money needed by the organizer and his social network. All details of the money-loan society, including amounts of capital, subscription of each member, number of members, dates of payment, duration, drawings, rate of interests, etc. were contained in a passbook which was presented to each member by the organizer and was the only kind of legal instrument used. Everyone subscribed his portion except the one whose turn it was to draw. The organizer who was in immediate need drew the sum of money collected at the first meeting. The sums collected at subsequent meeting were to go to the other members of the society in turn. Basically, each member by turns was able to access a larger sum of money during the whole term of the money-loan society *and* could use it for whatever purpose he wished. Those who took the sum earlier were more akin to borrowers, while those who took it later, were akin to lenders. There were three methods to fix the order for the use of the common fund and thus drawing rights could be arranged. Accordingly, the money-loan society was basically classified into three types: *Yao Hui* (dice-throwing society), *Lun*

---

[24] J. B. Tayler, Potentialities of cooperative movement in China, 21 Chinese Soc. &Pol. Sci. Rev. 1, 1937–1938.

Table 4.1 Types of *Qian Hui*

Province	Type of *Qian Hui* (%)						
	Yao Hui	Lun Hui	Biao Hui	Seven stars Hui[a]	Eight worthiness Hui[b]	Five wise men Hui[c]	Others
Jiangsu	45.8	16.1	10.4	11.6	3.4	2.7	10.0
Zhejiang	45.6	30.7	7.7	5.1	3.2	3.2	4.5

Source: Central Institute of Agricultural Experiment, Ministry of Industry (1934), Report on Rural Area, Vol. 2, No. 11

Note: [a]Seven-Member Hui, [b]Eight-Member Hui, [c]Five-Member Hui. All these were blends of *Yao Hui*, *Lun Hui*, and *Biao Hui*

Hui (rotating society), and *Biao Hui* (bidding society). Some societies were a blend of these three types.

4.5.3 Dice-throwing Society *(Yao Hui)*

In the dice-throwing society, the order for the use of the common fund was fixed by lot or by throwing dice. It was the most popular one in the Anhui, Zhejiang, and Jiangsu provinces according to a survey conducted in 1934 (see Table 4.1). The dice-throwing society (*Yao Hui*) can be divided into two groups: an amounts-increasing society and a subscription-decreasing society. In an amounts-increasing society, as it progressed, amounts of money collected were increased with interest from the Foots, though subscription of each member was fixed.

4.5.4 Amounts-increasing Society *(Duiji Hui)*

There were two kinds of amounts-increasing societies: single-stacked and double-stacked. In the 1934 survey single-stacked amounts was the only society adopted in rural areas because the double-stacked approach was too complicated to be popular. For example, in an 11-member amounts-increasing society (10 members plus the organizer of the society), the interest was collected in advance and took the form of a 'bank discount'. For each term the interest was assumed to be one-fifth of the subscription.[25] The flow of funds is more easily seen in tabulated form, as in Table 4.2.

[25] Arthur H. Smith. (1899). Village Life in China: A Study in Sociology, Edinburgh and London, Oliphant, Anderson & Ferrier.

Table 4.2 Subscription of members in a single-stacked amounts-increasing society

Meeting	Organizer	No. 1	No. 2	No. 3	No. 4	No.5	No. 6	No. 7	No. 8	No. 9	No. 10
1st	(100)	10	10	10	10	10	10	10	10	10	10
2nd	10	(82)	8	8	8	8	8	8	8	8	8
3rd	10	10	(84)	8	8	8	8	8	8	8	8
4th	10	10	10	(86)	8	8	8	8	8	8	8
5th	10	10	10	10	(88)	8	8	8	8	8	8
6th	10	10	10	10	10	(90)	8	8	8	8	8
7th	10	10	10	10	10	10	(92)	8	8	8	8
8th	10	10	10	10	10	10	10	(94)	8	8	8
9th	10	10	10	10	10	10	10	10	(96)	8	8
10th	10	10	10	10	10	10	10	10	10	(98)	8
11th	10	10	10	10	10	10	10	10	10	10	(100)
Total subs per person	100	100	98	96	94	92	90	88	86	84	82
Balance	0	−16	−14	−10	−6	−2	+2	+6	−10	+14	+18
IRR[a]	0.00%	4.86%	5.02%	5.44%	7.69%	3.00%	2.19%	3.05%	3.32%	3.45%	3.51%

[a]The internal rate of return, IRR, gives the discount rate that sets the net present value of the sequence of cash flows equal to zero. But IRR is a wobbly measure when the sequence of cash flow changes signs (+ to − or − to +) more than once. The IRR shown satisfy the definition locally for all members except member 5. Member 5 had an indeterminate and unstable IRR. We have imputed 3% which gives an NPV of −1.56 for this member

At the first meeting, each member pays 10 the sum of 100, accepted by the organizer. In the second period the members 2–10 each pay a reduced amount of 8 while the organizer pays 10, the total summing to 82. This 82 is received by the 1st member. In the 3rd meeting the organizer and 1st member each pay 10, while members 3–10 each pay 8. The sum of 84 is then handed to member 3. And so it continues with members who had received funds paying 10 thereafter and the remaining each paying 8 until they in turn receive payments. The organizer repays exactly 100 over time (plus feasts at each meeting). The 1st member is worst off having paid in 100 over the 11 periods, but received only 84 in return for a deficit of 16 (−16). In fact it is not until the 7th meeting that member 6 profits from the scheme. The last member pays in 82 over the time period, but receives 100 in period 11, so a gain of 18 (+18).

This may seem a puzzling result. Why would a member be willing to contribute for a sure loss in some instances? It appears that Chinese farmers had a good sense of the time value of money well before it became a commonplace concept. In the last row of Table 4.2 we compute the internal rate of return (IRR) for the cash flow sequence. The IRR is the discount rate that when applied to the sequence of cash flow provides a breakeven to all contributions and remittances. So long as the opportunity cost of money in its next best alternative is less than the IRR the investment benefits the members. Remarkably, the organizer has an IRR of 0% which is myopic in the sense that it ignores the time value of money, but clever in the sense that the organizer gets his loan at zero interest. But for members 1–5 who contribute more than they receive, nominally, it can be seen that this is not entirely irrational. Member 1 loses 16 but has an IRR of 4.86% per period. So long as the 82 received at the 2nd meeting can be invested with a net return of greater than 4.86% the member will benefit. Of course, there were not many investments but if the money-loan society avoided having to borrow from a usurer who might charge 18% to 20% or higher per period, it makes economic sense. Member 10 on the other hand receives payment in the last period for an IRR of 3.51%. Thus, even though the last member receives more cash-in-hand than predecessors, if the opportunity cost is greater than this, for example having to borrow at usury rates because of the subscriptions, it is actually a losing proposition from an economic point of view. Clearly, from an economic point of view the organizer is a pure borrower, while the last member (whether desired or not) is a pure creditor. In between, from left to right each members take on a diminishing debtor to increasing creditor position. While establishing the order by random means might be socially fair if all farmers were in the same economic condition, it would appear to be more socially optimal if farmers could self-identify and be ranked according to debtor needs and creditor desire.

There is risk however: one rule of economics appears to have been broken. As observed, the earlier a member collected on the loan, the less was the cash return on investment, but the IRR peaked at 7.69% for member 4, a mixed borrower-lender. On the other hand, the final recipient received all money in a lump sum with interest upon it. It was to a member's cash advantage to seek repayment as late in the drawing as possible. But it was far from being the case that interest was the primary motivator for being last or later in the draw. Like any ROSCA, the society tied up savings that could not otherwise be used, and the later the draw the greater the likelihood that the Hui would fail or be disbanded because of death, war, drought, flood, reneging, and any other manner of calamity that might befall farmers. These matters were not really taken into account for the last member, who was in the most perilous position, seemingly received no additional compensation for the risk he bore. But the investor who needed money and might never be sure of getting as much as he needed upon any better terms and risk than this, might gladly take it as soon as he could get it.[26]

4.5.5 Subscription-Decreasing Society (Suojin Hui)

In a subscription-decreasing society, each member's subscription decreased according to the order of collection at each particular meeting as determined by the following formula:[27]

Member's sum − [Organizer's subscription + (Number of debtors × debtor's subscription)]/Number of depositors

Member's sum − [Organizer's subscription + (Number of debtors × debtor's subscription)] / Number of depositors

Since the amount collected was constant, the difference between the amount of subscription and the amount of collection was the interest either paid on the loan or received from the deposit. Suppose the organizer gathered 14 members, each of whom subscribed 10, thus he got 140 in all at the

---

[26] Shan, Qiang. (2002). A study on Hehui in regions south of the Yangtze River in mordern era, Research in Chinese economic history, Vol. 2.

[27] Fei, Hsiao-Tung. (1939). Peasant Life in China:A field Study of Country Life in the Yangtze Valley, London: Routledge & Kegan Paul Ltd.

Table 4.3 Subscription-decreasing society

Order of collection	Amount of subscription	Amount of collection	Average rate of interest per half year (%) for loan	for deposit
Organizer	182.00	140.00	2.2	–
1st	88.47	70.47	2.1	–
2nd	86.85	70.47	2.3	–
3rd	85.10	70.47	2.6	–
4th	78.96	70.47	2.0	–
5th	74.71	70.47	1.5	–
6th	71.99	70.47	1.0	–
7th	69.06	70.47	–	2.0
8th	65.62	70.47	–	3.4
9th	62.70	70.47	–	2.8
10th	57.08	70.47	–	3.1
11th	51.41	70.47	–	3.4
12th	44.91	70.47	–	3.6
13th	38.43	70.47	–	3.8
14th	31.06	70.47	–	4.0

Note: At the 11th meeting, the sum of subscription of the organizer and the debtors had already exceeded member's sum of collection. The depositors need not pay anything but share the new surplus. The principal of distributing the surplus is that, excluding the organizer and the collectors of the first four meetings, all the members will have a share in proportion to the order of their collection. For instance, in the 11th meeting the collector of the 5th meeting will get a share of 0.11 or 5/110 of the total surplus (2.432). But the three depositors in that meeting, whose order of collection is still not certain, will have an equal amount of 13/110 of the surplus

first meeting. The society would meet twice a year. At each successive meeting, one of the members would collect a sum of 70 as a debtor and would repay at each succeeding meeting 5 of capital and 1.5 of interest (6.5 in total). The calculation was complicated by the fact that the member's sum was reduced to half of the organizer's own. Thus the organizer's subscription would be equally divided among the members (6.5 ÷ 14 = 0.464). The collector's sum was 70 + 0.464 and the other member's subscription was 6.036 (6.5 – 0.464). The organizer's and the debtor's subscriptions and the member's sum of collection are constant (Table 4.3).

4.5.6 Rotating Society (Lun Hui)

The rotating society (*Lun Hui*) was a different type of ROSCA in the sense that the order for the use of the common fund was discussed and determined in advance, usually by seniority. Usually the number of mem-

Table 4.4 Subscription of each member at every meeting in seven-member rotating society

Meeting	Member						
	Head	Foot 2	Foot 3	Foot 4	Foot 5	Foot 6	Foot 7
1st	(30)	7.5	6.5	5.5	4.5	3.5	2.5
2nd	7.5	(30)	6.5	5.5	4.5	3.5	2.5
3rd	7.5	6.5	(30)	5.5	4.5	3.5	2.5
4th	7.5	6.5	5.5	(30)	4.5	3.5	2.5
5th	7.5	6.5	5.5	4.5	(30)	3.5	2.5
6th	7.5	6.5	5.5	4.5	3.5	(30)	2.5
7th	7.5	6.5	5.5	4.5	3.5	2.5	(30)
Total sus per person	45	40	35	30	25	20	15
Balance	−15	−10	−5	0	+5	+10	+15
IRR[a]	12.98%	15.96%	12.00%	0.00%	11.99%	15.90%	20.21%

[a]The internal rate of return, IRR, gives the discount rate that sets the net present value of the sequence of cash flows equal to zero. But IRR is a wobbly measure when the sequence of cash flow changes sign (+ to − or − to +) more than once. The IRR shown satisfy the definition locally for Foot 2 through Foot 6, except for Foot 3. Foot 3 had an indeterminate and unstable IRR. We have imputed 12% which gives an NPV of −1.71 for this member

bers of a rotating society was fewer than other societies, ranging from 6 to 11. The most common was the seven-member plan, which was called in some places the 'Club of the Seven Worthies' (*Qi Xian Hui*).[28] The subscription of each Foot was decreased in descending order, the earlier subscribing more, and repaid with interest. The head of an old rotating society might not pay any interest but would provide a feast at each meeting, once a year usually, while the head of a new rotating society would have to pay interest as would other members.

Take a new rotating society of seven persons as an example, with a sum of 30. The subscription and balance of each member is illustrated in Table 4.4. The organizer receives the full sum at the first meeting. But the amount contributed by each member is determined by their foot position. Foot 2, labeled such because the member will receive payment at the 2nd meeting, will pay 7.5 while Foot 7 pays only 2.5. Note that there are two schedules in Table 4.4. The first schedule (to the right of the diagonal) shows fixed subscriptions for those yet to receive a payment. The subscriptions to the left of

[28] Qiang Shan. (2002). *Op Cit.*

the diagonal show the subscriptions to be paid after receiving the payment and this is seen to be $1 less than the pre-payment subscription.

In the last two rows we compute the gross contribution by each member. As with other societies, the earlier one is paid the lower the return. For example, Foot 2 and Foot 3 actually lose in nominal cash, the 1st paying 40 but receiving only 30, and the 2nd paying 35 but receiving only 30. Foot 7, who must wait seven years and absorb any risks of disbandment or collapse, pays only 15 but receives 30 for a nominal gain of 15.

In the last row we compute the internal rate of return for the cash flow sequence. In this set up (compared to Table 4.2) the organizer, while losing 15 nominally, has a beneficial IRR of 12.98% on the society. This can be viewed as the pure compounded interest (actually a synthetic opportunity cost) paid on the loan, and so long as this rate was lower than the next best source of credit, the organizer was better off under this society. Also, in this society, the last member, who is a pure investor, has an internal rate of return of 20.21%. So long as the opportunity cost of money was less than 20.21% the member was receiving a positive return to capital, and a risk premium of 7.91% above the organizer's effective borrowing rate.

4.5.7 Bidding Society (Biao Hui)

In a bidding society (*Biao Hui*), the members who had not received money from the society might bid for the privilege of receiving the amount to be collected at the current or next meeting. Each member was assigned a number written on one side of a piece of paper; on the other side the member wrote an amount he would be willing to receive from the other bidding members. The lowest bidder was given the fund at each meeting.[29] In some instances, the interest was open to competition by auction. Each one announced orally or deposited a slip in a box noting what he was willing to pay for the use of the fund for one term, with the highest bidder winning. It was often the case that the bid amounts changed through the years the society functioned.[30] The changes, together with the changes in the amount each member received from the society and the amount he contributed to it, are illustrated with the following example.

---

[29] Gamble, Sidney D. (1954). Ting Hsien: A North China Rural Community, Stanford University Press, Stanford.
[30] Gamble. (1954). *Op Cit.*

A man who needed 120,000 cash to meet some special business expenses invited 30 of his friends and relatives to join a mutual saving society. At the first meeting, the members discussed the organization, the rules, and the regulations of the society. It was decided that the society would meet every four months and it would continue for 10 years. The interest was open to competition by auction at each meeting and the highest bidder could get the fund. Each member should contribute 4000 cash when the society first met. The organizer was to receive the amount collected at the first meeting. The sums collected at subsequent meetings were to go to another member of the society according to bid. Figure 4.1 shows how the amounts received by the successful bidders at different meetings generally increased because nominal prices increased as the years went by and showed a wide variation. Thus it would seem that the members were figuring on a fairly set rate of discount.

As with other societies with longer-term loans there was a high probability that before the whole term of years elapsed there would be some occurrence to disturb the very unstable financial equilibrium of the members. This could be any number of calamities, but Gamble tells a story of how fluctuations in silver and copper prices affected the society.[31] For example, prior to 1917, the silver-copper exchange rate was relatively stable, but after that copper coinage depreciated so rapidly that the average exchange rate went from 1207.4 cash per dollar in 1917 to 3750.7 in 1927. All the saving society payments were made in terms of copper cash, but the change in exchange rate could not influence the purchasing power of the sums the members paid to and received from the society. The rapid depreciation of copper currency caused a big drop in the value of the society's fund even though the amount of cash increased at almost every meeting (Figs. 4.1 and 4.2). Combined with continual wars, famines, and floods the money-loan society (*Qian Hui*) fell out of favor. As long as there was a matching between real contributions and real withdrawals the schemes could operate with some stability; but with increasing instability, many members would be obliged to make contributions as negotiated at the first meeting but were unable to recover money with equivalent consumption value. In the late 1930s, for example, the money-loan society in Sichuan facing sharply increasing interest rates (e.g. from 2% to 4% or even 6%) was hard to organize as members preferred shorter time horizons of

---

[31] Gamble. (1954). *Op Cit.*

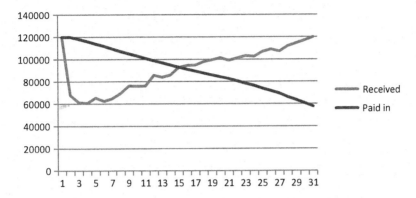

Fig. 4.1 Bidding society, copper value of amounts of received and paid in

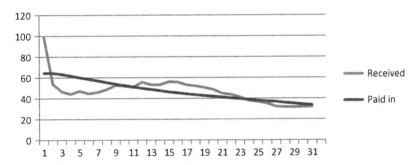

Fig. 4.2 Bidding society, silver value of amounts received and paid in

eight or six months, but not 12 months as before.[32] To ensure the repayment of funds given to the members, the rules of the saving societies required that each member furnished two guarantors before he received money from the society. Some societies also required that the members pledge land as security for the amounts they received.[33]

---

[32] Xiao, Zheng. (1977). Materials on Chinese Lands in 1931, Chengwen Press, Vol. 42.
[33] Gamble. (1954). *Op Cit.*

4.5.8 Pawn Shops (Dian Dang)

The pawn shop was a typical financial institution which extended small loans against movable personal property deposited with it as security for a stipulated period of time. The origin of pawn shops dates far back in the history of China. There are numerous stories grouped into four categories regarding their origin.[34] There are claims that the pawn shop originated as far back as 770 B.C. to 476 B.C. At this time there were only small pawn shops. From the Song dynasty it is written in '*Shuo Wen*', a classic on Chinese etymology, that the pawn shops of today originated from the monasteries of the Song period. Larger pawn shops as they are now known began to appear in the period between the Ming and Qing dynasties. From the Qing dynasty comes the story that pawn shops originated in jails where a number of criminals who had been sentenced to long terms of imprisonment attempted to make a living within the jail by lending money to new criminals at the rate of interest of 20% or 30%. As a result, old-fashioned Chinese pawn shops usually had a wooden railing and a tall counter without a single opening, with two sentries stationed at the front gate, appearing much like a jail. Also, since many pawn brokers were also Anhui merchants, many were inclined to think that pawn shops originated in Anhui Province. This is supported in part by the history of Chinese business, which had the merchants of Anhui along with Shanxi, Zhejiang, and Guangdong provinces enjoying great prosperity throughout several ancient dynasties.

Ultimately, pawn shops were usually owned by rich families and wealthy merchants. Pawn shops dealt in movables and did not keep a large amount of capital on hand as a bank does. Poor people who had little or no credit standing could hardly secure any loans from banks when money was needed badly, and the way in which they could solve the problem of financial difficulty was to approach a pawn shop with their belongings, because it was always ready to lend money on security. So an old Chinese proverb stated: "*The pawn shop is a poor man's back-door*".[35]

In the Republican era, pawn shops were popularly called *Dian Dang*. Generally speaking, pawn shops were classified into four categories based on the amount of capitalization and on the rate of interest to be charged

---

[34] Mi, Gonggan. (1936). A Study on Pawn Shop, Shanghai:the Commercial Press.
[35] Liu, Qiugen. (1995). History of Pawn Shops in China, Shanghai Classics Publishing House, Shanghai.

Table 4.5 A comparison of different types of pawn shops in the Republican era[a]

	Dian and Dang	Zhi	Ya
Amount of capital	10,000–80,000 dollars	Around 10,000 dollars	500–1000 dollars
Rate of interest	1.6–3% per month	1.8–6% per month	1.8–6% per month
Period of expiration	18 months	6–12 months	4–8 months
Amount of loan	50% of the value	60% of the value	60% of the value
Brokerage	1 or 1.5 cents on every dollar	1.3–1.5 cents on every dollar	Not specified
'Square parcel' charge	1 cent for every dollar	1 cent for every dollar	1.3 cents for every dollar
Kinds of securities accepted	All accepted except checks, watches, shoes, stockings, and jewelry	All accepted except valuables	All accepted except valuables

[a]Chow, C. P. (1938). Pawn shops in Shanghai, The Central Bank of China Bulletin, Vol. 4, No. 3

on loans: *Dian*, *Dang*, *Zhi*, and *Ya*.[36] Basically speaking, *Dian* had the largest amount of capital, offered the longest period of redemption, charged the lowest rate of interest and gave the highest estimate on the value of goods. And then came *Dang*, *Zhi* and *Ya* in order. Yet, as time went on, no sharp line of demarcation could be drawn. In Jiangsu Province, *Dang* had to pay 500 dollars for its license fee, *Zhi* 300 dollars and *Ya* 100 dollars. *Dian* and *Dang*, larger in scope than *Zhi* and *Ya*, were distinguished from each other in three aspects (Table 4.5):

1. *Dian* could not refuse any large loan on valuables when presented for a sum far below their actual worth, but *Dang* could freely decline such an offer on the ground that the sum required was in excess of its capitalization.
2. *Dian* was only equipped with one straight counter; *Dang* had two counters joined together at one end in the shape of an L.
3. In the case of *Dian*, the rate of interest was 20% and the time limit for the expiration of the right of redemption was 20 months, but those charging a higher rate of interest and granting a shorter period of redemption were named *Dang*. *Zhi* and *Ya* were distinguishable

[36]We use the word *dian* in its present-day usage. In the Republican era this is known as *tien*, Likewise we use *zhi* in the present day but in the Republican era this was known as *chih*.

by the amount of tax (actually a license fee) they paid. *Ya* was smaller in size than *Zhi*, the time limit for redemption being as short as a few months and the rate of interest as high as 39%.[37] Originally, *Ya* was not run by proper merchants, but by a gang of military criminals to exact unreasonably high interest charges.

Being a special type of business, the equipment of the pawn shops was also special. Even in the Republican era the imagery of a jail remained. Usually in front of an old-fashioned pawn shop was erected a red wood railing without any opening. Customers had to enter the shop by a small side-entrance. Inside the premises there was an exceptionally high counter so that outsiders could not command a clear view of what was on the opposite side, while the staff working inside the counter could only see the heads of the customers. Both the railing and the counter were said to have been purposely erected in order to prevent robbers. Inside the counter-hall was placed a wooden tablet representing the God who brought prosperity to the pawn shop. There were four counters or desks from which the daily business was operated. In the rear part of the counter-hall the manager was situated on the right and the cashier, accountant, and pawn-ticket recorder on the left. In the middle was a spacious platform where the value of securities was estimated. Behind the counter-hall there was a courtyard for sorting the securities and further back was a warehouse where clothing was stored. In addition, there was a reception room, a telephone room, a jewelry room, and a warehouse for sundry goods.

Most farmers resided in villages some distance from a market town, so access to pawn shops was difficult. In most cases pawn shops were found only in the towns.[38] Consequently for small loans, peasant farmers relied heavily on and borrowed mainly from friends and relatives. For larger loans the farmers would travel to the market towns where larger loans could be more easily obtained, and at better terms, than wealthy villagers could provide. Market town merchants/pawn shops charged slightly lower interest rates than private moneylenders.[39]

According to the regulations governing the business of pawn shops, no indemnity was paid by a pawn shop for any loss due to war, robbery, flood, or fire which were regarded as *force majeure*. And in spite of its long his-

---

[37] Chow C. P. (1938). Pawn shops in Shanghai, The Central Bank of China Bulletin, Vol. 4, No. 3.
[38] Gamble (1954). *Op Cit.*
[39] Ramon H. Myers. (1970), page 243.

tory and the popularity of pawn shops among the common people, the numbers of pawn shops, total value of pawned goods, and amount of pawn shop taxes collected decreased rapidly in the Republican era when rebellions, revolutions, and wars broke out here and there in China. Of about 7000[40] pawn shops in China in 1812, only around 4500[41] remained in 1930s, and about 270[42] in 1947. The amounts of pawn shop taxes collected declined sharply. Taking a typical pawn shop in Hunan Province as an example, 20,589 silver dollars were collected in 1915, 1651 silver dollars in 1919, and only 200 silver dollars in 1930s.[43] Pawn shops or native banks could turn unredeemed collateral or security, such as jewelry, furniture, clothes, land and so on into cash easily in good years but in the 1930s they could not dispose of the pawned goods so easily because of a rapid deterioration in economic conditions, and many had to close down owing to a serious shortage of circulating funds.

4.5.9 Traditional Native Banks and Chinese Currencies: Piao Hao *and* Qian Zhuang

Native banks, located principally in Tianjin, Jinan, Beijing, Xiamen, and Qingdao, had branch banks in the county seats of districts specializing in wheat, cotton, and peanuts. Their loans to merchants played an important role in financing the growth of these staple trades. With native banks, credit merchants were able to send their brokers to various market towns to purchase industrial crops and grain. This bank credit made up a large share of their working capital to make purchases, hold stocks, and then sell to factories, exporters, and other merchants. In terms of agricultural finance, it should be noted that merchants did not extend loans to peasant farmers while native banks were restricted to financing trade rather than production.[44] Nonetheless, native banks were critical to the funding of raw supplies used by farmers, and the marketing channels, wholesale markets, and processors required on the other side.

[40] Liu, Qiugen. (1955). History of Pawnshops in China, Shanghai Classics Publishing House, page 257.

[41] Lu, Guoxiang. (1936). Estimation of Amounts of Capitals of Pawnshops in China, Monthly of Farmers Bank of China, Vol. 3, No. 4.

[42] Yearbook of China. (1948). China Yearbook Press, page 1235.

[43] Gonggan Mi. (1936). Pawn shops, The Commercial Press (CP), pages 196, 242.

[44] Myers, Ramon H. (1970). The Chinese Peasant Economy: Agricultural Development in Hebei and Shandong 1890–1949, Harvard University Press, Cambridge, MA.

Traditional native banks in China can be divided into two groups: the Southern group, namely *Shaoxing Qian Zhuang*, and the Northern group, namely *Shanxi Piao Hao*. The Shanxi native banks were of the orthodox Southern group. Their activities and influence had developed to such an extent that they were considered as the leaders of all the native banks in China. The origin of Shanxi native banks dated back to the Qing dynasty when merchants from Shanxi Province were travelling all over the country. The merchants may be roughly classified into two groups; one called the shipping group which conveyed different kinds of commodities from one place to another by water; the other was the camel group which used camels to carry goods to inner and outer Mongolia and Moscow, Russia (along the silk road). Between the Emperor *Qianlong* (1736–1795) and Emperor *Jiaqing* (1796–1820) regimes, there was a dye-stuff store *Ri Sheng Chang* in Tianjin, operated under the proprietorship of Luetai Lei, a Shanxi merchant. As Lei had to make frequent business trips to Sichuan, Shandong, Hunan, and Shanxi provinces, he began to feel the inconvenience of carrying along with him cash money, usually silver or gold, for the settlement of business transactions. Being a talented businessman, he organized a *Hui-hua-zhuang* –a sort of clearing house—in Sichuan to perform the function of a domestic exchange. From then on, the difficulty of shipping large sums of money from one place to another had been eliminated. The charge for remittances was fixed by the bank according to the prevailing market condition, and through this process native banks made huge profits. And to facilitate the domestic exchange business, more than 30 branches of these banks were organized in important commercial cities. At their peak there were no less than 26 Shanxi native banks, each with established branches in nearly all principal cities and ports. Among these were well-known names such as Ri Sheng Chang bank, Yu Tai Hou bank, Yu Feng Hou bank, Yu Sheng Chang bank, and Bai Chuan Tong bank.

All the Shanxi banks were financial institutions with unlimited liability whether organized on a proprietorship or partnership basis. The manager was given full power to handle the business of the bank and stockholders could not interfere with the management and personnel problems. Basically a statement of accounts was presented to the proprietor or proprietors for approval once a year.[45]

---

[45] Fu, Hong. (2009). *Op Cit.*

Domestic remittances were always the main focus of their business. Besides handling domestic exchanges, native banks also sought to obtain the privilege of acting as the depository of public funds of provincial governments. At that time, Shanxi bankers were at the peak of popularity and many notables of the imperial family and government entrusted the banks with a large amount of money on deposit. The steady increase of deposits made it possible for the Shanxi bankers to extend loans and widen their sphere of activities. Loans were largely made in important cities and sea ports and confined to the money shops and big merchants. The relation between Shanxi banks and the officials of the Qing dynasty were stressed in Beijing and other important cities. The Shanxi bankers were quite capable and social, maintaining cordial friendships with imperial families, for example Yu Sheng Chang and Prince Qing, and Bai Chuan Tong and Viceroy Zhidong Zhang, and the managers of Shanxi banks often associated with local officials to promote their business. However as the Qing dynasty came to its end in 1911, the Shanxi native banks, *Piao Hao*, with close ties to the Qing regime, experienced great losses as loans and advances made directly to the Manchu government, as well as to important officials, went unpaid. Furthermore, as more modern means of transport and communications were adopted in China, demands for credit expanded considerably and with the *Piao Hao* unable to meet the demand, other types of financial institutions, including joint-stock banks, emerged. With increased competition, the native banks were unable to adjust to the banking activities and demands of a domestic exchange and their role in China's evolving financial development throughout the Republican era was largely diminished.[46]

The Southern native bank, known as *Qian Zhuang* meaning literally 'cash shop', also had a long and creditable record in the history of Chinese banking. It first appeared in some cities in Zhejiang Province, particularly in Ningbo, Shaoxing, and Shanghai. As to its origin, some historians regarded it as originating from exchange stores in the 1850s, while others suggest it originated from the extension of loans by Ningbo merchants in Shanghai before 1843.[47]

---

[46] Jianhui Huang. (2002). History of Shanxi Piaohao, Taiyuan: Shanxi Economy Press.
[47] George H Chang. (1938). A Brief Survey of Chinese Native Banks, The Central Bank of China Bulliten, Vol. 4, No. 1.

The chief function of *Qian Zhuang* was buying and selling currencies since there were various chaotic currencies since the Ming dynasty (about 1430), including copper token coins, taels based on silver bullion, dollars, 'small-coin' silver, 'big-money' small coin, and various forms of paper currencies in circulation. The tael as a Chinese currency unit varied in weight and quality from place to place. There were no less than 67 recognized standards of tael in use. In an article on currency, exchange, and banking in Julean Arnold's 'Commercial Handbook of China', Mr. Passeri stated in 1918: "*The currency in China is chaotic; it forms the most complicated mixture of heterogeneous mediums of exchange, from a weight to a coin, which has ever existed in any one country*".[48] This was true, as up to 1933 China was seriously handicapped by its unwieldy, chaotic, and unregulated monetary system, or rather lack of system in the Western sense. The lack of standardization was remedied by the establishment and operation of *Qian Zhuang*. *Qian Zhuang* met the needs of exchanging money so well that "*under these grave disabilities the wonder is that the Chinese are so accustomed to these annoyances that their burden appears scarcely felt, and the only serious complaint on this score comes from foreigners*"[49]

Qian Zhuang had undergone several major changes throughout the Qing dynasty and became an important institution across the interior regions of China. The native bank was organized on either a single proprietorship or partnership basis with unlimited liability. Partners of native banks varied from 2 to 10 in number with 4, 5 or 6 being most common. Since partners of a native bank assumed full responsibility for the bank's debts, the guarantee and protection offered by native banks were not limited to the full amount of their paid-up capital. A native bank absorbed capital investments and money deposits, focused on monetary transactions of all descriptions, dealt with extension of loans and adjustment of the pecuniary supply and demand in the money market. In a word, a native bank possessed the essential features of a modern bank, except it was organized and managed on a simpler basis.[50] Furthermore, while native banks assisted one another when depositors requesting withdrawals exceeded cash-on-hand, the lack of a central bank provided no protection when panic hit the business community. With insufficient capital and

---

[48] Cited from L. Y. Shen. (1938). Chinese currencies: old and new. The Central Bank of China Bulletin, Vol. 4, No.1, page 10.

[49] L. Y. Shen. (1938). *Op Cit.*

[50] Chang, George H. (1938). A Brief Survey of Chinses Native Banks, The Central Bank of China Bulletin, Vol. 4, No. 1.

inflexible, traditional management, most native banks could not withstand the onslaught of foreign banks in China. A few money shops survived by converting to modern banks but this came with diminished lending to agriculture. Loans to agriculture by *Qian Zhuang* were not unusual. For example a Shandong farmer when asked where he got credit stated that it came from money shops in Jinan. But after 1928, this source of credit evaporated when the money shops were converted into banks under the Nationalists. These banks made only large loans of over 1000 yuan, which automatically excluded the farmers.[51]

4.6 Mortgaging Land, Usufruct Rights and Merchant Credit

Though farmers borrowed small sums of money from close friends or relatives and repaid quickly without interest, large sums of 100 yuan or more were borrowed from merchants or wealthy families in different ways. One method was called *Chih-ti chieh-chien* which worked in the following way. The borrower looked for a go-between and financial guarantor who was a reputable, honest man and knew who had money and who was willing to lend. When the go-between located a lender, he brought both parties together to discuss the terms of the loan. Once the amount of the loan was agreed, the borrower offered a piece of land, usually valued at half the loan, as security in case he was unable to repay. The interest rate was 2–3% per month, and loan and interest charges had to be paid within a year, usually right after the harvest. The borrower continued to use his land as before, but if he failed to repay on time, the land had to be sold or offered as a mortgage to repay the lender.

Another way, called *tien*, involved mortgaging land.[52] Mortgaged land is the equivalent to renting land. It is obtained by lending the owner of the land an amount probably no greater than 50% of the land's value. The

[51] Duara, Prasenjit, Culture Power and The state Rural North China, 1900–1942, Stanford University Press 1988, page 271.
[52] The term *tien* as used by Myers (1970) and refers to a mortgage but not of the usual sort. In actuality the term mortgage in his context can be interpreted in the modern sense as a usufruct loan. If interest is charged and the loan not repaid then the holder of the mortgage receives a usufruct right to use the land for his own purpose until the loan is repaid. If interest is not charged then the usufruct right is assigned at the time the loan is made and the holder of the mortgage has immediate use of the land until the loan is repaid. Buck (1930, page 67) notes that the number of usufruct mortgages was quite low, accounting for only 1.2% of total capital recorded in his surveys.

'lender' or mortgagee then has use of the land until the loan is repaid.[53] Again the go-between brings borrower and lender together to discuss the amount of land to be mortgaged, the land's present worth, and the size of the land. The land was valued according to prevailing prices and the expected harvest, and some fraction of that value, usually around two-thirds, was then agreed upon the loan. The farmer mortgaging the land did not pay interest because the lender receiving the mortgaged land had the right to use it until the loan was repaid. The period of mortgage was usually three to five years, but there were cases when the period was longer. If the loan was not repaid, the farmer could not redeem the land. The practice of *tien* had been extremely common during the late Qing dynasty when farmers had more land and the mortgage period was only one to three years. In the early 1930s there were fewer cases of mortgaging land and the mortgage period was longer, because the farmers had less land to mortgage and redeeming land had become more difficult. Finally if mortgaging land proved insufficient to obtain the desired amount of money the land was sold to obtain cash. The farmer only did this if he had exhausted the above methods and still needed cash. The household head sold the land after the harvest and, again, he found a go-between to find a buyer to arrange the terms of sale. Once a buyer was found, a deed was drawn up and signed by the seller, the go-between, and the buyer. The buyer paid all taxes or levies on the land. This credit system was complex and the role played by the middleman was crucial. In a society where individuals were without the protection of property, using a third party to introduce, arrange, mediate, and guarantee was instrumental in minimizing risk and ensuring that transactions would be conducted honestly and agreements obeyed.

A holder of mortgaged land could transfer it to another person. Just as one's land was regarded as near-money, so too was mortgaged land. The mortgage period was usually 3–4 years, but sometimes as long as 6 or even 10 years. If after a long period in which it was obvious that the borrower would not repay his loan, the holder of mortgaged land could dispose of the land and realize a capital gain on the original loan transaction. Land that could not be redeemed was sold. Such cases were rare, and usually occurred if a farmer holding mortgaged land suddenly found himself in

---

[53] Buck, J.L. (1930). Chinese Farm Economy: A Study of 2866 Farms in Seventeen Localities and Seven Provinces in China. University of Chicago Press, Chicago Illinois, pages 67–68.

need of cash. The method of transferring land had not changed during the Qing period. A farmer wanting to sell land sought out a middleman who knew how to handle these transactions. The farmer told him of the reason for wanting to sell, and a document was drawn up indicating the amount of land and its present value. The middleman with this document now looked for an interested buyer. Once a buyer was found, negotiations commenced on the selling price. When this was agreed upon, someone was called in to survey the amount of the land to be sold. After that, a second document, indicating the amount of land, size, and location was signed by seller, surveyor, and middleman. This document became the basis for drawing up a final land deed which indicated the amount of land and its value and signed by buyer, seller, and middleman. An enclosure was added to this document stating the fee the buyer paid to the seller when the transfer was concluded. The buyer took the document to the local tax office and paid the land deed tax. The transaction was recorded and a red stamp was affixed to the deed indicating the legality of transfer and payment of deed tax. Henceforth the new owner paid all taxes on the land.[54]

Land carried two meanings depending on how the household used it. First, land represented a form of savings or near-money for the household because of the type of informal credit system previously discussed. Second, land which had been reclaimed, irrigated, and tilled represented capital for the household.[55] When cash was scarce and land was regarded as near-money, claims to land were used to acquire cash. Land was the key asset used to obtain credit. Myers stressed the importance of peasants using land to acquire credit. When peasants had extra cash they immediately purchased land. For the farmer, purchasing land meant security for his family, ensured continuation of the family line as land was transferred to sons, and brought social status. Buying land meant exchanging money for an asset easily converted into money if the need for cash arose later. Land represented a safe store of value and commanded purchasing power in terms of the credit or cash it could obtain. According to the National Land Survey Commission Report of 1937, land was the principal form of security used by peasants in Hebei and Shandong in 1936 to obtain credit. It was rare that land reverted to the moneylender if these small loans were not paid. The peasant mortgaged additional land to pay his debt.[56] Peasants

---

[54] Myers (1970). *Op Cit*, page 95.
[55] Myers (1970). *Op Cit*, page 167.
[56] Myers (1970).

might hoard copper, cash or silver for short periods, but as the rate of exchange between these two currencies always fluctuated, peasants could not predict with certainty which currency they should hold. There was no such problem where land was concerned.

4.7 Lease Contracts

The land holding philosophy in China at the turn of the twentieth century was that land was to be held for the benefit of the community, and that no one person should control more land than can be cultivated. In keeping with this, the Qing demanded, under penalty of forfeiture, that excess lands be rented out.[57]

Land tenancy in China is an important factor in economic development. There were three types of rental system: the share system, cash-crop system, and cropper system.[58] The most common system was the cash-crop system where a definite amount of grain, by measure, was given as rent each year either in grain delivered to the landlord or in cash equivalent.

The share system varies across China, but a typical approach would be a 'half and half' system. The landlord provides seed as well as land and buildings. About a third of landlords will also provide fertilizer. A few landlords might also provide work animals, but most resisted because human labor was abundant and cheap. The cost may accrue to the farmer, but the payment is delayed until the crop is harvested. Upon harvest, the landlord (or agent) would meet with the farmer (perhaps also with a feast provided) on the threshing floor and divide the harvest. Some landlords may also have required an additional amount for seed provided.

Under the cropper system the landlord typically provides everything except labor and hand tools. The farmer was recognized as the manager, but the landlord might also have provided input. Across all systems, the percentage of total receipts received by the landlord was about 40.5%, ranging from a low of 24.6% in one Jiangsu county to as high as 66.6% in *Wutai* County in Shanxi.[59]

---

[57] Hsu, Chi-lien (1928). "Rural Credit in China" *Chinese Social and Political Science Review*, Vol. 1 :1–15.
[58] Buck, J.L. (1930). *Op Cit*, pages 147–148.
[59] Buck (1930). *Op Cit*, Table 2, page 148.

In Buck's (1937) survey of farm households he finds that about 17% of Chinese farmers are pure tenants, 54% pure owners, and the remainder, about 29% both owned and rented land.[60] Tenancy was lowest in the wheat-growing areas, including the North China plains with only 6% of farmers being pure tenants, 76% being owners, and 18% mixed owner/tenants. In the Southern rice areas tenancy was higher with 25% renters, 38% owners, and 37% both owning and renting. The rental arrangements followed a share cropping pattern, but the nature and details of the lease contracts are not well known, although the nature of tenancy was such that in the South landlords resided in cities distant to the fields they owned, while in the North, landlords were more than likely to reside with the villagers who were also their tenants. Absenteeism did affect contract enforcement, especially during bad times when, in the South, it would not be unusual for the landlord's agent to face abuse.

Most rental arrangements were short run and under standard contracts. Rent could be paid in money and/or produce with the price fixed if in cash or stipulated as a proportion of the principal crop if in shares. Although the farm may also produce subsidiary crops, the rent is levied only on the principal crops. On the best lands the share would be 50% but the negotiated share would then diminish in proportion to land quality thereafter. At harvest the landlord is usually represented by an agent who would receive their share. Paying at harvest eliminated the liability to the landlord, but unless rent was specified by a specific weight of the principal crop, the landlord and tenant shared crop yield and market price risks proportionately. In addition, the expectation was that the landlord would pay the taxes

These were traditional rental arrangements. However, we came across a couple of lease arrangements that were very sophisticated and detailed which provides some additional scope to the lease as a financial arrangement with features which were to the farmer's benefit.

4.7.1 The Manchurian Lease

The first lease was used in Manchuria and reported by the Chinese Eastern Railway and South Manchurian Railway and translated from Russian and

---

[60] Buck, J.L. (1937). *Land Utilization in China: A Study of 16,786 Farms in 168 Localities, and 38,256 Farm Families in Twenty-Two Provinces in Chia, 1929–1933.* University of Nanjing, Nanjing China, University of Chicago Press, Chicago, Illinois, Table 6.2, pages 33, 34.

Japanese.[61] Most of the land reported was privately owned and rented out to peasants to farm. Ownership was historic, from the days of the Manchus who allocated land to the elites and which had since been transferred across generations by inheritance. In practice the holdings were so small that the peasant farmer needed to rent land from larger landholders (mixed-type farmers).[62] Other farmers simply rented all their land and were technically landless. The rents on land high and contractual. A land lease of 10 years was not uncommon. During the first five years the farmer paid nothing or very little but in years 6–10 it was expected that the farmer shares the produce with the landlord. The units of measure are vague. One dan is a measure of weight ranging from 180 to 360 kilos depending on local measures. One dou is 1/10 of a dan. In year 6 the peasant contributes 8 dou (8/10th of a Dan) per shang or approximately 1 dou per mou which is approximately 27 kg/mou (more or less) usually split equally between soybean, millet, and kaoliang. In the seventh year the peasant would contribute 1 dan or 20% more than the previous year (approximately 32.4 kg/mou). In year 8 this increased by 2 dou, year 9 by another 2 dou and in the 10th year it was 1 dan and 6 dou (1.6 dan) per shang or 51.8 kg/mou more or less. In many cases the owner provided the peasant with an unfurnished hut while the peasant provided furnishing, livestock, and implements. The 10-year lease was a contract but if the owner wanted to sell the land the farmer had the right of first refusal. If the farmer had no tillage implements then the owner would have furnished these tools, but would have required a rent of 25% after two or three years. In other instances, the peasant simply received a salary of $250–300 per year (Harbin dollars).

A second type of leasing was at a fixed rate where the peasant provided 2.2 dan (also referred to as tan) per *shang* (1 *dan* = average of 270kg, 1 *shang* = 10 *mou*) or about 27kg of soybean, millet, and kaoliang per *mou*. This farmstead might come with a hut, a well, and a mill. In more remote areas the rent might be decreased to 1.2–1.5 *dan* per *shang*.

Under the contract the tenant was required to hire coolies to work the farm depending on its size. The coolies were mostly transients from Shandong, Hubei, and other areas to the South. Coolies were to be fed and housed and received $1–1.50 (harbin) per day or up to $200 (harbin) for the season. The farmer would also be required to save seed for future

[61] China Weekly Review, June 6 1931, pages 16–18 "The Plight of the Manchurian Peasant" by A.A.R. (anonymous). The information reported here is translated from uncited documents prepared by the Chinese Eastern Railway and South Manchurian Railway and translated from Russian and Japanese.
[62] The unit of land here is a shang which equals 15 mou. Land ownership ranges from 1 mou to several hundred shang.

plantings and this was gathered at the rate of 2–2.5 dou/shang for soybean with an opportunity cost of about $2 (harbin)/shang. The cost of livestock might be as much as $6/shang. Taxes amounted to an additional $1.20/shang but this varied widely.

There were no credit associations (at the time of the report in 1931), or if there were they were rare under Japanese occupation. If a peasant borrows from a landowner he might have paid 25–30% per annum but if he used the village usurer it might have been as high as 50–60% per annum. The typical usurer would collect the interest up front. For example, with a $100 loan the farmer would receive only $40 or $50 but would be required to repay the $100 in full. Alternatively, the tenant-farmer could purchase inputs on credit with terms ranging from 2% to 5% per month for up to 6 months.[63]

---

[63] The reality was that earning a profit for the tenant was still very difficult and with many hurdles and too many intermediary agents: the farmer will carry his stock in native, horse driven, double-wheeled carts to the nearest populated center; the inn owner then acts as middleman and negotiates a price on behalf of the seller; or the grain dealers send out agents to the inns to negotiate directly. The peasant delivers the goods on payment of cash or simply leaves it in the hands of the innkeeper.

But another problem arises in that payment is made in strange Kirin provincial dollar notes, Heilongjiang provincial dollar notes, Mukden provincial dollar notes and the Harbin dollar notes. These almost operate as different currencies in and with different exchange rates. The peasant borrows money when it is at its lowest level in the summer and pays it back when it is at its highest level, losing purchasing power along the way. There are also reports of forward sales. The marketer will negotiate for soybean seed in July when the price is lowest for delivery in November when the price is highest. Because there is no forward pricing the farmer cannot hedge the price and is locked in to the lower price. Future deals were officially banned but still widely practiced.

For farmers that live some distance from the central market the additional cost of cartage must be borne by the farmer (who also usually pays a lower rent but must also pay taxes when passing from one district to another). Other taxes can be steep ranging from 2.3% to 3.4% depending on region and on top of this a tax of perhaps $6 per carload. The taxes can amount to as much as 10% of the value of the grain paid by the merchants but no doubt passed on to farmers.

Because of taxes and fees the farmer even in the best years might receive only 40% of the Free on Rail price of the commodities sold with the remainder being absorbed by taxes, fees, cartage, commissions, bribes, and so on.

Banditry is a widespread problem. It is infrequent but when it occurs it is damaging. But because conditions are so bad for so many peasants they actually become part-time bandits themselves. There is also widespread corruption when farmers add dirt to bulk-weight grain; marketers fudging the scales and adding further weight to exporters, and so on, and these activities lead to price discounting.

4.7.2 Changchun Lease Arrangements

This sub-section describes two lease arrangements as contracted by the Changchun Land Cultivation Company.[64] The first is between the landowner and the Changchun Land Cultivation Company and then between the Changchun Land Cultivation Company (CLCC) and the Korean farmers.[65]

4.7.3 Between Landowners and CLCC

1. Lease was on 500 hsiang with one hsiang = 1.66 acres for a period of 10 years.
2. Annual rent was 1.2 Chinese piculs of rice per hsiang of uncultivated land and 2 piculs for cultivated land, fixed for 5 years.
3. In times of drought the rent can be deferred, accrued, and paid in the following year.
4. Government taxes and various official fees on the land shall be paid by both parties.

---

[64] Yang, Solon S.C "Eye Witness Account and Analysis of Wanpaoshan Incident". *China Weekly Review*, August 1 1931, pages 339–342. This section is based on a description of a lease agreement that was central to the July 2, 1931, Wanpaoshan incident. The incident arose from the leasing of lands to Koreans under Japanese protection for growing rice. Our interest in this particular article is the detailed lease arrangement which can be used as an example of lease arrangements from a landlord in Manchuria.

[65] Under item 6 in the following list it should be noted that the irrigation ditch described cut across the lands of some 41 farmers who had no interest in the lease arrangement at all. Apparently CLCC/Koreans simply started digging ditches across these private lands without consent and under Japanese direction. This canal stretched for 7 miles by 15 feet wide by 8 feet deep destroying 2000 mou of land (333 acres) and putting an additional 40,000 mou at risk of flood. The Wanpaoshan incident resulted from the landowner protests. Changchun was the transfer point between the Japanese controlled South Manchuria Railway and the Soviet controlled China Eastern Railway and also home to a significant Japanese garrison. Under the orders of the Japanese, the Korean farmers, growing rice, were digging an irrigation canal drawing water from the Yitung River under Chinese protest. Failing to halt construction, 500 farmers armed with hoes, rakes, and scythes stormed the Korean settlement and destroyed the ditches. Japan responded by sending the military, evicting the farmers and maintaining control over the area. Ten Chinese farmers and two mounted policemen were killed. Meanwhile, as the news of the attack hit Soule, Koreans and Chinese clashed resulting in 44 Chinese deaths and one Korean dead.

Editorial, "Japan Uses Koreans in New Plan to 'Conquer' Manchuria" *China Weekly Review*, July 11 1931, pages 208–209.

5. While a landowner could transfer the deed to the land, the integrity of the lease on that land could not be transferred.
6. The rice farms under contract were to be irrigated by means of drawing water from the Itung River. The construction of a dam and ditches was to be measured in hsiang and landowners were to receive a payment of 3 piculs of rice per year for each hsiang for 10 years.
7. Water would be drawn only in the autumn with any controversies or incidents being the responsibility of CLCC (an interesting clause removing liability from Japanese or Koreans).
8. CLCC would be responsible for the building of bridges across dams and ditches.

4.7.4 Between Koreans and CLCC

9. The unit of land was to be assessed as 24 kung = 1 hsiang, a kung being a Korean area measure
10. Rent was to be 2.3 piculs of rice for cultivated land and 2 piculs of rice for other land (CLCC would net 0.8 piculs for cultivated land and 0.7 piculs for uncultivated land).[66]
11. The destruction for crops from any catastrophe will be considered a matter of fate by both parties (liability falls on CLCC; essentially an imbedded catastrophic put option to the Koreans).
12. Both parties were to be make special arrangements for payment of rent with minor calamities resulting in only partial destruction.
13. Plants for houses, etc. and areas of public use were exempt from rent.
14. Annual rent for space occupied by ditches and dams was to be 3 piculs/year (no net gain to CLCC).
15. After 10 years all buildings, dams, and ditches were to be returned to landowners to dispose of or keep at their discretion.
16. Guarantors shall control the land in case the rent is not paid on time or in case of embezzlement (liability falls on CLCC as presumed guarantor).
17. In addition to the rice land an additional 500 hsiangs of uncultivated land will be made available to tenants at a rate of 2 piculs/ hsiang (no net gain to CLCC).

[66] 1 picul = 1 dan = 50 kg.

18. Other fields would be made available to 'present' tenants at 2 piculs/hsiang.

4.8 Summary

At the end of the Qing dynasty and the turn of the Republican era the absence of formal credit arrangements resulted in a multitude of semi-formal and informal credit relationships. The earliest channels of credit were provided by the construction of networks of granaries across China, which provided not only a mechanism to smooth consumption and stabilize markets, but also enabled farmers to borrow against stored grain with the grain held as collateral. China also saw some of the first structures of Rotating Savings and Credit Associations (ROSCAs) with numerous forms of money-loan societies (*Qian Hui*). These might have evolved from the Green Sprouts Policy as early as the Northern Song dynasty (906–1279).

Progress towards more formal approaches saw the emergence of pawn shops and native banks; the latter did not directly make loans to farmers, but eased trade along East-West routes such as the Silk Road. Other financial arrangements such as land leasing ranged from very simple cash and share contracts to some very sophisticated long-term arrangements.

In order to appreciate the challenges faced in developing formal credit institutions for farmers in the Republican era, it is important to have some sense of this history. ROSCAs and other forms of *Hui* did not entirely disappear but as credit societies and credit cooperatives developed alongside new government-sponsored banks and financial institutions their need was displaced, and credit would become more standardized. The nature, type, and scope of new types of financial institutions in the Republican era are discussed in the following chapters.

CHAPTER 5

Emergence of Modern Rural Financial Institutions in the Warlord Era: 1912–28

5.1 Introduction

In this chapter we explore the early institutions of the Republican era and the attempts by the Chinese government to obtain credit in support of China's agricultural economy. The most significant effort was the establishment of the Agricultural and Industrial Bank in 1915. This was unique at several levels in that the banks could issue bonds to finance agricultural development, and also raise capital in support of a variety of credit associations—the first we believe where cooperative credit was linked to a bank charter.

Other institutions developed, but it is also fair to say that at the onset of the Republican era in1912 China's financial system was in disarray—a mess by global standards at the time. This was not a consequence of the revolution that ousted the Manchurian Qing dynasty, but of events that preceded it by many decades. Within the Republican era there was the period of disorganization between 1912 and 1913, the period of reorganization from 1914 to 1915, and the period of adjustment that started in 1915 and, as illustrated throughout this book, continued through 1949.[1]

To understand the state of China's financial system some background is required into the politics before and after the end of the Qing dynasty in

---

[1] Ts'ai, K'O-Hsuan. (1928a). Financial reform in China. *Chinese Social and Political Science Review*, 12, 259–271.

1911 and the start of the Republic in 1912. Events include the loss of tariff autonomy to the 'powers' following the Opium Wars, the imposition of likin, and the tumult of the warlord era. Only when these major elements of political economy are considered can the challenges to developing a financial system in the early Republican era be understood.

5.2 Tariff Autonomy and the Likin Tax

The wobbly financial foundation on which the new republic was formed resulted to a large extent on the lack of tariff autonomy. This originated in 1842 with the Treaty of Nanjing following China's defeat by the British in the Opium Wars. By treaty it was agreed that a 5% duty and 2.5% transit dues would be placed on imports, with no further taxation on the transportation of goods to the interior provinces. The problem was that these duties were locked to commodity prices as they were in 1843, so in real terms as the price of silver fluctuated, and prices rose, the real value of the tariffs declined, to China's detriment. This was followed by the second of the unequal treaties in 1858 with the Treaty of Tianjin in which a consortium led by the British and joined by France, Russia, and the United States imposed reparations for a skirmish in Guangzhou. The treaty revised that of 1843 extending the number of commodities not subject to tariff, and that goods personally consumed by foreign nationals would also be duty free. Following the Boxer Rebellion in 1900,[2] China was forced to accept a large and crippling indemnity to be paid over 40 years. To raise funds for these indemnities the foreign powers forced China to raise imperial maritime customs to 5%, and assign native customs duty and the salt tax to be used to secure the indemnity. These remained in place until 1918, despite an attempt by the new government in 1912 to renegotiate the terms. Ostensibly, because tariff rates were locked to prices circa 1900, as prices rose the actual duty was 3.5% while the indemnity obligation remained fixed. To meet the indemnity demands, China requested a 12.5% tariff at the Washington Conference in 1922, but this was ultimately rejected.

Until the powers relinquished claims to the Boxer Rebellion and other indemnities in the mid- to late 1920s, the unequal treaties between 1842 and 1900 hampered financial development in China. The Qing dynasty, guilty of its own excesses, relied on provincial taxes, with little coming in from imports which would otherwise be a reliable source of revenue. The

---

[2] Tan, Charles C. (1967). "The Boxer Catastrophe" Octagon Books, NY.

Table 5.1 1882–1931 imports and exports in China, unit: thousand customs tael[a]

Year	Imports	Index	Exports	Index	Import and export	Index
1882	77715	100	67337	100	145052	100
1891	134004	172	100948	149	234952	162
1901	268303	345	169657	252	437960	302
1911	471504	607	377338	560	848842	585
1921	906122	1166	601256	893	1507738	1039
1931	1433489	1845	909476	1351	2342965	1615

Source: T. R. Banister, 1931, *Op Cit.*
[a]A unit of measure used in imports and exports. 1 customs tael = 37.91 g

powers—Great Britain, Russia, France, Japan, Germany, and the United States—were not moved by the turmoil and success of the revolution, removal of the Qing dynasty, and establishment of the Republic to alter their stance. By 1922 for every dollar of debt owed by China, 74.2% was secured by customs revenues or surplus.[3]

With the foreign powers gaining increased access to China's interior markets through treaty ports, China made the decision to introduce a likin tax against domestically transported goods. The likin tax was introduced during the Taiping Rebellion in 1853 as a small tax of one tenth of 1% on goods transiting between one province and another. It was soon expanded across China but at rapidly appreciated rates of 3% at the departure station and 2% at inspection stations. Likin was limited to 10% per province but this was rarely adhered to and collections of 15–20% were reported. By the Treaty of Tianjin, however, the foreign powers had free movements of goods to the interior after paying the import duty fixed at 2.5%. Thus every incentive to interprovincial trade and competition was eroded, while foreign goods were able to flow in unabated. Perhaps more critical was that goods and commodities from the interior could not profitably reach international markets, creating significant trade deficits and robbing China of much-needed foreign exchange. This too would reduce the amount of tax collected and further strain central government revenues from provincial remittances. To get a sense of the magnitude of the trade problem, Table 5.1 provides indexed trade data for a variety of years between 1882 through 1931.[4]

[3] Ts'ai. (1928a). *Op Cit.* calculated from Table 1, page 266.
[4] Banister, T. R. (1931).The history of Chinese international trade in the last century, General of Chinese Maritime Customs Service, pages 244–245.

Starting in 1882, about 30 years after the first likin taxes were imposed, China's imports significantly lagged imports. By 1901, the year after the Boxer Rebellion,[5] the index value of imports favored exports by 345–252%. By the end of the Qing dynasty and the start of the Republican era in 1911 both imports and exports had increased, but exports still favored imports by 607–560%.

The likin was established as a temporary measure, but with the demands of the powers and the extraction of tariffs and customs duties and so on, the likin tax remained in place. The Chinese tried to negotiate relief from its obligations to lessen or eliminate the likin in 1902, 1916, 1919, 1922, and 1925 but no agreement could be reached that would accommodate the lost revenue, regardless of the economic gains that would result. It was not until 1929 that the Chinese, having been released of the Boxer indemnities by most of the major powers was able to eliminate the likin and attempt to grow the economy through interprovincial and international trade.[6]

5.3 Currency Chaos

A final aspect was the bewildering use of multiple currencies in China. Currency issues were not a new problem. About 620 A.D. in the Tang Dynasty there was the first attempt to standardize coinage by creating a coin inscribed with Chinese characters '*Kai-yuan*' meaning 'usher in a new era'.[7] This set a standard for coinage, but ever since the days of the Mongols,

---

[5] The Boxer Rebellion of 1899–1900 brought together a number economic and social forces that led to a group called 'the Boxers' to rebel against foreign powers. Superstition and certain martial arts made many peasants feel invulnerable to foreign bullets. Frustrated by drought and pressures from increased taxation due to indemnities demanded by the powers hit a pinnacle when in June of 1900 a force of Boxers converged on Beijing and, with support from the Empress Dowager Cixi, laid siege to the foreign legation for 55 days before a coalition of foreign troops quelled the riots. Because of damage to property and persons during the Boxer Rebellion, the foreign powers made further financial demands of the Qing. See
Tan, Charles C. (1967). *Op Cit.*,
Perry, Elizabeth. (1980). "*Rebels and Revolutionaries in North China, 1845–1945*", Stanford University Press, Stanforf, CA.

[6] Ts'ai, K'O-Hsuan. (1928b). Financial reform in China: Part II. *Chinese Social and Political Science Review*, 12:567–581.

[7] Lee, Frederick E. (1926). "Currency, Banking and Finance in China" United States Department of Commerce, Trade Promotion Series #7, Government Printed Office, Washington DC. Reprinted in book form, 1982 Garland Publishing Inc, NY.

960–1125 A.D. paper currency came into vogue. By the Republican era the currency situation was chaotic. S.R. Wagel, writing in 1889 stated *"The subject of Chinese currency demands not a brief paragraph but a comprehensive essay, or rather a volume. These chaotic eccentricities would drive any occidental nation to madness in a single generation or more probably such gigantic evils would speedily work their own cure. In speaking of the disregard for accuracy...100 cash are not 100 and 1000 cash are not 1000 but some other and totally uncertain number, to be ascertained only by experience"*.[8]

It is bad enough that a coin count in one region may be totally different in another, but also complicating matters is that coins were minted in terms of copper, silver, and gold. Farmers were paid in copper but their purchasing power depended on the exchange rate with silver, which in turn had a value determined by its exchange rate with gold. Banks issuing notes might link the notes to silver or gold, so the exchange rate of copper—the unit of currency most often used for paying wages—could easily change from one day to another depending on the spot exchange of copper to silver or copper to gold. So long as copper, gold, and silver were highly correlated the exchange rate would be stable. But as the correlations weakened the exchange rates became more volatile. A wholesaler purchasing in silver would increase or decrease the copper price to the laborer or farmer depending on the copper to silver price ratio. Even if demand and supply remained reasonably constant retail prices could swing wildly depending on the copper to silver price ratio, and the silver to gold price ratio. Another example is with the tael, which is a unit of measurement (not a currency although at times currency might be described in tael units) based on a weight of silver of a given fineness representing the standard for all banking and commercial operations. But even the tael might differ by region. In 1923, for example, 1000 Shanghai tael was equivalent to 964.5 Wuhu taels, 965 Suzhou taels, 990 Hankou taels, 960 Nanging taels, and so on.[9]

There is some hint that Gresham's Law took hold in China, but not in the usual way. In 1914 Yuan Shikai introduced the dollar yuan. At that time the most prominent silver coin was the Mexican dollar, and soon after the United States issued a trade dollar that weighed more than the Mexican dollar, the idea being that it would replace the Mexican dollar because it contained more silver. However, Chinese characteristics being what they were, the Chinese paid little attention to the silver value and

---

[8] Cited in Lee, Frederick E. (1926). *Op Cit.*, page 10.
[9] Lee, Frederick E. (1926), page 17.

focused only on the weight. The lower-weighted yuan and Mexican dollars remained in circulation while the US trade dollars were melted down.[10]

Banks often obtained rights to print their own money but not only might the notes be based nominally on silver or gold, but they rarely had a mechanism of exchange. In other words, at the beginning of the Republican era, and through at least the 1930s, there was no monetary system in China that could be understood by mortal men. In this book we do discuss currency now and again, and more intensely in terms of communist controlled base-area currencies vs the Japanese puppet currency and the Kuomintang (KMT) national currency during the Sino-Japanese war (Chap. 11). By the end of the War of Liberation in 1948, China finally managed a stable single currency, the renminbi (RMB), after previously non-exchangeable base-area currencies were merged along with banks, and the Chinese national currency collapsed under the weight of hyperinflation.

5.4 The Beginnings of Financial Reform

The Manchu dynasty created a defective system of finance in which the central government generated none of its own revenue. Instead, it depended entirely on monetary transfers from the provinces to defray administrative and military expenditure. There was a loyalty oath, and if any province reneged on its payments they faced the threat of Manchu troops overthrowing the provincial government and enforcing payment. However, when Sun Yat-sen took interim power as the first president of the Republic under the banner of the KMT, otherwise known as the Chinese Nationalist Party, he was not in a position to enforce payments and so a process of decentralization opened up and the provinces withheld payments for their own use that would otherwise have gone to the central government. Although Sun Yat-sen is often regarded as Father of the Revolution or Father of the Republic, his provisional presidency was short lived, By early February 1912 Yuan Shikai (Shih-kai), a Qing militarist and loyalist had negotiated a deal in which he became provisional president if he could negotiate the abdication of the child-emperor Puyi. This he did by the signature of the Empress Dowager on February 12, 1912. Thereafter, the government resorted to foreign loans. With the loans in place, the government could move forward, with one of the first reforms targeting the task at financial reforms and financial sector development.

[10] Lee, Frederick E. (1926). *Op Cit.*

There was a short-lived second revolution in 1913 in which a faction of the KMT rose against the Republican party that supported Yuan Shikai.[11] Throughout 1912 Sun Yat-sen sought to establish a National Assembly comprised of provincial appointees and led by a prime minister with a public role separate to that of the president. Elections slated for 1913 were held with the KMT winning most of the seats in the house and senate. Yuan Shikai was largely dismissive of the parliament and without consulting them entered into a reorganization loan of £25 million from Great Britain, France, Russia, Germany, and Japan. But this money was not put to national use, instead supporting Yuan's Beiyang army.[12] Parliament, alarmed at the dictatorial powers being exercised by Yuan Shikai, sought his removal and in response provincial armies loyal to Sun and the KMT rose against Yuan who then mobilized his army against the KMT forces, ultimately defeating them. With this defeat, Sun and his acolytes fled to Japan, and with the parliament ostensibly leaderless and powerless, Yuan expanded his powers. Yuan's ambitions to return to a monarchy were realized when in December 1915 he declared himself emperor. Followed by derision and revolt and declarations for independence by several provinces this was short lived and by March 1916 he abdicated the emperorship, returning China to a republic. He died three months later, but not before his actions led to a 12-year period between 1916 and 1928 known as the warlord era.

Upon the defeat of the KMT in 1913, the Republicans found themselves in a much stronger position and moved towards restoring the system of contributions used by the Qing dynasty. The 1914 budget provided for strict supervision over the receipts and expenditures of the provinces, and any surplus was ordered to be returned to Peking (Beijing). By 1915 the provinces were ordered to pro rate remittances on a monthly basis and the Beijing government specified certain sources of revenue such as title deeds inspection fees, stamp tax, wine and tobacco tax, and broker's license fees as being exclusively for the central government.

[11] Zarrow, P. (2005). "China in War and Revolution: 1895–1949" Routledge, London, UK.
[12] Zarrow, P. (2005). *Op Cit.*
The term '*Beiyang*' refers to the Northern ocean and was used to refer to the armies of the Qing dynasty. After the fall of the Qing the Beiyang government referred to the government in Beijing before the Nationalist government of the KMT exacted power and moved to Nanjing. Even with the KMT in power, beyond 1928 the term *Beiyang* was used to refer to an opposition government made up of Northern warlords, who wanted to seat the government in Beijing. In the current context, in the regime of Yuan Shikai, the term *Beiyang* imputes a kind of loyalty to the Qing and ruling Manchus. This loyalty led Yuan Shikai to declare himself Emperor in late 1914.

The financial problems stabilized and the Republicans found themselves with a financial surplus. With this surplus the government began issuing loans through highly subscribed bonds, secured by the 'tax' remitted by the provinces. But this lasted only as long as Yuan remained President. Once he declared himself emperor the provinces refused to remit their taxes and some also seized revenue from the various taxes and levies dedicated to the central government. With this began the chaos of the warlord era, and a continued dysfunction and disorganization of much needed financial reforms.

For years to come the lack of tariff autonomy, the burden of foreign and domestic loans, the burden of likin taxation, the lack of proper division between central and local revenues, excessive military expenditures, and wastefulness in public expenditure weighed down the pace of financial reforms.[13] Between 1912 and 1915 borrowing was secured against custom duties and surplus. The custom agent would collect the customs, deduct the amount required to satisfy the indemnity sinking fund and other secured obligations, with the surplus being passed on to the government. But as the debt increased, these surpluses were used to secure new loans so that the amounts in surplus rapidly diminished. Consequently, defaults on loans increased and the accrued interest on non-performing loans only added to the burden.

5.5 The Warlord Era

The warlord era starting around 1916 led to almost 12 years of political and economic chaos.[14] Yuan, a militarist at heart, encouraged the provinces to develop their own armies. The rise of militarism gave rise to changes in provincial governance where generals rose to power and leadership. Indeed much of the debt between 1912 and 1916 was due to the excessive militarization of China. In 1912 the percentage of total expenditure on the military was 33.87%, by 1919 it was 41.68%, and by 1923 it was 64%.[15] Things became even worse in the provinces. In Jiangsu, 1923, military expenditure was 41%, in Shandong it was 59%, in Shanxi it was 80%, 84% in Henan, and 94% in Hubei).[16]

[13] Ts'ai. (1928a). *Op Cit.*
[14] Zarrow, P. (2005). *Op Cit.* Chap. 4.
[15] Ts'ai. (1928a). *Op Cit.*, Table 2, page 269.
[16] Ts'ai. (1928a). *Op Cit.* Table 3, page 269.

Ultimately this might have been managed had Yuan not declared himself emperor, losing support from the provinces along the way. Rather than forwarding remittances, taxes, and fees the provincial governments began holding that money back to support provincial armies fearing that the rising debt and expenditure would leave them unpaid. These sums, which were $11.180 million in 1915 dwindled to $969,000 by 1917 and nil thereafter. After Yuan abdicated and died, China was weakened considerably and with no central power governance disintegrated into warlordism.

With loss of central command in 1916 the warlord era was almost inevitable and a military structure was part of China's governance under the *Dujun* system.[17] Each province had a civil governor and a military governor, a *Dujun*, the former appointed by civil examination and the latter through the military ranks. With the provincial military under his control the *Dujun* could easily usurp control from the civil governor and in many instances they were one and the same. The *Dujun* were more often than not illiterate and uneducated but through force of spirit were able to rise through the ranks. With the forces at hand they would collect private taxes and retain the remittances that were supposed to go to the central government. If ever they were unseated by the national army or some other opposing force they would simply disband into a bandit force, creating havoc along the way.

5.6 Towards a Coherent System of Agricultural Credit

We provided, in Chap. 4, a brief overview of attempts at rural credit in China over the past 2000 years. The challenge that China faced at the dawn of the Republican era was the establishment of a coherent financial system out of a dysfunctional and incoherent one. At the time of the revolution there were only seven modern banks in China, with single or multiple branches, and all of these were in large urban and population centers. In 1912 there was no sense of urgency for agricultural credit but there was a sense of urgency to reform the system left by the Qing dysnasty. The tasks were to obtain tariff autonomy and eliminate the likin system, consolidate foreign and domestic debts, establish a proper division between central and local revenue, reduce wasteful expenditure, reform the tax system, and develop national industries.[18] At best, efforts were made but

---

[17] Ts'ai. (1928a). *Op Cit.*
[18] Ts'ai. (1928b). *Op Cit.*, page 567.

the best China could do, at least through to the end of the Northern Expedition in 1928 and the beginning of agricultural reconstruction, was to hobble together certain laws and regulations that would lay the foundation for a sound system.

The late Qing dynasty began to encourage industry and promote modern national credit institutions aimed at lending long-term loans to improve agriculture productivity. But it was not until 1911, the last year of the Qing dynasty, that China's first specialized bank lending to agricultural and industry sectors was formed. The Property Increment Bank of Jinpu was founded on March 1, 1911 in Tianjin as a private bank run by a well-known salt merchant Shiyu Li. The bank continued in operation through 1937, but was eventually shut down when the Japanese occupied Tianjin in 1937.[19]

The next attempt at agricultural credit occurred when the regulations governing the Industry Orientation Bank was promulgated by the Beiyang government in 1914. This bank was aimed at establishing a nationwide financial institution to promote and finance industrial sectors including agriculture, forestry, and agribusiness. The attempt however fizzled with the turmoil of 1914 and turned out nothing without enforcement, because the Beiyang regime proved unable to assert real control over the national economy and fiscal revenue.[20]

These efforts notwithstanding, the most interesting development as it pertains to agricultural credit was the establishment of the Agricultural and Industrial Banks in 1915.

5.7 The Agricultural and Industrial Banks

The first attempt towards a system of agricultural credit in the Republican era was regulations governing the establishment of Agricultural and Industrial Banks in October 1915.[21] In promulgating the law the Minister of Finance at the time stated:[22]

---

[19] Zhaofu Liu (1995). Tianjin Annels, Tianjin:Tianjin acodemy of social sciences publishing house.

[20] Jiannong Zhu (1945). The origin and development of rural financial system in China, Financial Knowledge, Vol. 4.

[21] Hsu, Chi-Lien. (1928b). The Rural Credit in China (continued). *Chinese Social and Political Science Review*, 12, 273–286.

[22] Hsu, Chi-Lien. (1928b). *Op Cit.*, citing The Banker's Weekly, 3(102–103): page 46, circa 1915.

Our country is unusually rich in natural resources. It is a great pity that they are hardly touched by men. In order to develop our natural resources, it is necessary to establish Agricultural and Industrial Banks all over the country so as to provide capital for the developing of our vast hidden wealth. The regulations for the Chinese Agricultural and Industrial Banks are hereby enacted. They consist of seven sections and forty-six articles...

What is included in the act turns out to be a recurring theme in China's attempts to provide rural credit. What appears is a combination, with Chinese characteristics, of the Raiffeisen system from 1800s Germany and the newly enacted Federal Farm Loan Act of 1916 in the United States which established land banks as a government sponsored enterprise.[23] While the government would establish certain committees to provide oversight of the banks, and the banks would have to make certain requests on capital management or setting interest rates, the government was under no obligation to provide capital, although it did purchase or subscribe to shares issued as part of the bank's capital. Unlike the US system in which large amounts of capital were provided by the treasury, the Agricultural and Industrial Banks in China had to raise $100,000 in capital with no less than 50% in cash.

In this way, the Agricultural and Industrial Banks were to mobilize capital and provide funds to be used primarily for agricultural and industrial purposes with a broad range of acceptable collateral including immoveable property, durable agricultural commodities including grains, hides, cocoons and silk, and with repayment terms of between one and five years. Commodities (including fishing) could receive loans of one year, while collateralized real estate could obtain a term of five years. Loan amounts were restricted to two-thirds of the appraised value of the security.

Loans were targeted to scale up agricultural drainage and irrigation, planting forests and protecting river banks, purchase of seed, fertilizers, and other raw materials for agricultural and industrial purposes, for transporting and holding exhibitions of agricultural produce, for acquiring and replacing agricultural land and industrial equipment, for repairing farm houses and industrial workshops, for buying cattle and building ranches, for buying seeds and equipment, and for raising fish and silkworms.[24]

---

[23] See United States Senate. (1914). Agricultural Credit. Report of the United States commission on Land Mortgage or Long-Term Credit and Personal of Short-Term Credit. Senate Document No. 380 Parts I, II, III, 63rd Congress., January 1914. Washington, DC.

[24] Hsu, Chi-Lien. (1928b). *Op Cit.*

A distinct feature of the Agricultural and Industrial Bank was its use as a policy bank. At the request of the government treasury it could act as fiscal agent to collect taxes needed for the treasury to redeem or repurchase bonds, notes, treasury certificates, and other obligations of the government. It could also purchase, hold, acquire, and dispose of the capital stock of any corporation concerned. It could partake in inter-bank transfers, by depositing funds in other banks to earn a higher rate of interest, and it could act as an agent for the Industrial Development Bank of China.[25]

Core to supplying capital was the right to issue bonds. The amount of bonds issued was to be no more than twice the paid-up capital with minimum issues of $5 and interest, determined by the bank, paid twice yearly. To maintain liquidity the amount of bonds redeemed could not exceed the amount of loans collected, or in other words any loans collected had to be applied to the redemption of loans. This also meant that the holder of the bond could not redeem the bond until it was called, but in the interim the holder could sell the bond to a third party through a registered broker in a secondary market.

The reality was that because any security had to be registered and insured, most of the security would be in the form of real estate of other fixed assets. The loans were made even more difficult by the underdevelopment of an insurance industry which would ration credit even further away from rural and agricultural settings. Once registered and insured, the bank could then issue debentures using the registered collateral as security, in the same way that bonds issued on behalf of the land banks in the United States were secured by the mortgages on farm real estate.

5.8 Agricultural Credit Associations

The Agricultural and Industrial Bank Act of 1915 also included a feature that permitted the bank to support credit societies such as the Agricultural and Industrial Workers' Credit Association and Agricultural and Cooperative Loan Association. This was quite different from the US system in which the land banks formed under the Federal Farm Loan Act of 1916 were to issue bonds for farm mortgages while the Intermediate Credit Bank enacted with the Agricultural Credit Act of 1923 was designed as a separate entity to provide capital for associations and cooperatives

---

[25] Hsu, Chi-Lien. (1928b). *Op Cit.*

(Production Credit Associations).[26] The first of these were established by the Tongxian Agricultural and Industrial Bank and Changpin Agricultural and Industrial Bank centered around Beijing in 1915. These are likely the first agricultural credit cooperatives in modern China.[27]

The Agricultural and Industrial Workers' Credit Association was a member association with all members being jointly liable for borrowed money. The association would be initiated by one or more borrowers, who would then recruit additional members to provide a guarantee. In this sense the arrangement was very much like traditional cooperative loan societies[28] (see Chap. 4) except for the first time the money was not to be advanced by members, but by the Agricultural and Industrial Bank. At the time the association was being organized, borrowers had to provide it with an itemized list of unencumbered property, including location, value, and any deeds. These were recorded by the association as a form of collective security. Association members were not all borrowers, but would participate in the event in case they might need to borrow at some future date, with reciprocity amongst members being understood. Members would provide names, ages, and location of their land or real property with valuations and number of houses, etc. and provide the deeds as evidence. All members were required to sign an agreement on joint liability. This material would then be taken by the chairman of the association to the bank for approval, and once approved the allowed funds would be released immediately to the borrower.

Once a borrower received the money he was obligated to report to the association how the money was spent. Loan repayment was expected to be timely since delays in payment or arrearages would affect the credit worthiness of all members. In the event that the loan was in arrears or nonperforming the association had the right to levy a substantial fine on the delinquent borrower.

---

[26] Stokes, W. N. (1973). "Credit to Farmers: The Story of Federal Intermediate Credit Banks and Production Credit Associations". Federal Intermediate Credit Banks, Farm Credit Administration, Washington, DC.
Turvey, C. G. (2017). Historical developments in agricultural finance and the genesis of America's farm credit system. *Agricultural Finance Review*, 77(1), 4–21.

[27] Hsu, Chi-Lien. (1928b). *Op Cit.*, Chapter VII, page 279. The Tonghsien and Changpin Agricultural and Industrial Banks (in Hsu these are Tung Hsien and Chang Ping) were model banks used to pilot the concept. Hsu does not provide an exact date for the formation of the banks, but textually it appears that the two associations were created around the same time as the two banks. Those banks were registered in January 1915.

[28] Hsu, Chi-Lien. (1928a). The Rural Credit in China. *Chinese Social and Political Science Review*, 12, 1–15.

5.9 Agricultural and Industrial Cooperative Loan Associations

The Agricultural and Industrial Cooperative Loan Association differed from the Agricultural and Industrial Credit Associations in that the target group was poorer farmers and artisans. By doing so the Agricultural and Industrial Banks could extend their reach into rural areas and to potential borrowers who lack the collateral requirements imposed on loan association members. The purpose of the Cooperative Loan Association was to 'assist' its members in borrowing funds for agriculture and industry. The Agricultural and Industrial Bank envisioned a network of Cooperative Loan Associations with an expectation that they would coordinate and work together. As a member of a cooperative it was expected that the association would 'introduce' the member to a bank and vouch for the member as being creditworthy. The advantage of such a system was that by vouching for its members the cooperatives would reduce adverse selection, and by group enforcement, moral hazard.

The associations were still required to record all owned lands, houses, and deeds as with the loan associations, but for farmers without adequate collateral it made allowances for loans made if three or more members supported the borrower. In these instances the member could borrow from the Agricultural and Industrial Bank under the name of the association on a special note.

The Agricultural and Industrial Loan Associations and Cooperative Loan Associations showed some success to the extent that the Tongxian (*Tung Hsien*) and Changpin (*Chang Ping*) Agricultural and Industrial Banks reported no bad debts between 1915 and 1918, but on the other hand the loan amounts may not have been so great. In 1918 the Tongxian bank reported six-month profits of $3475, while the Changpin Agricultural and Industrial Bank reported profits of $2501.[29]

Table 5.2 lists the various branches of the Agricultural and Industrial Banks circa 1927.[30] The original model held for six years but in 1921 it was decided that instead of having separate banks, there would be a single 'central' bank with branches. The Dawan (*Dai Wen*) Agricultural and

---

[29] Hsu, Chi-Lien. (1928b). *Op Cit.*, page 282 citing *The Bankers' Weekly*, 3(22), June 24, 1919, page 37.

[30] Economic Research Office of Bank of China. (1937). BanksYearbook, 1937, pages 12, 15.

Table 5.2 Agricultural and Industrial Banks before 1927

Name	Year	Head office	Branches	Paid-up capital (Yuan)
Tonghsien Agricultural and Industrial Bank	1915	Tong hsien	–	–
Changpin Agricultural and Industrial Bank	1915	Changping	–	–
Dawan Agricultural and Industrial Bank	1918	Dawan	–	–
Chinese Industrial Bank	1919	Shanghai	Nanjing, Hankou, Qingdao, Tianjig, Zhenjiang, Suzhou, Wuxi, Hangzhou, Wuhu, Jinan, Beijing	4,000,000
Zhonghua Industrial Bank	1921	–	–	1,000,000
Shaoxing Agricultural and Industrial Bank	1921	–	–	–
Agricultural land Commercial Bank	1921	Shanghai	Shanghai, Hankou, Nanjing, Changsha, Xiamen, Hangzhou	3,000,000
Huifeng Agricultural and Industrial Bank	1922	Wujiang	–	200,000
Zhejiang Industrial Bank	1923	Shanghai	Shanghai, Hongkou, Hankou, Hangzhou	2,000,000
Ouhai Industrial Bank	1923	Yongjia	–	250,000
Fenyang Agricultural and Industrial Bank	1924	–	–	–
Shenghsien Agricultural and Industrial Bank	1924	Shenghsien	–	106,900

Source: Economic Research Office of Bank of China (1937), *Op Cit.*

Industrial Bank had performed quite well over the years and was selected to be the central bank with an increase in authorized capital raised to $1 million. This was $800,000 higher than its original $200,000 paid-in capital, and to make the reorganization work, the government would subscribe two-fifths or $400,000.

The newly organized bank was renamed the Chinese Agricultural and Industrial Bank.[31] However, it is not clear to what effect the Agricultural and Industrial Banks actually contributed economically to agriculture. There is some evidence of loan deterioration. Between 1921 and 1923 confiscated property under lien increased from nil to $204,166 or about 7.3% of assets.[32] But whether these were agricultural or industrial assets are unclear. Also interesting is that in 1921 loans secured by mortgages were $11,415 rising by six times to $68,890. Unsecured loans increased more than three times from $41,500 to $143,965, while loans secured by chattel mortgages declined by 20% from $677,807 to $539,000. We cannot attach too much meaning to the increases or decreases, but the numbers do suggest that the Agricultural and Industrial Banks did provide unsecured loans and use chattel as originally planned in 1915. The small amount of mortgage loans relative to chattel loans illustrates the difficulties in mortgage credit at the time, especially with ambiguous valuations and underdeveloped insurance markets.

5.10 The Chinese Postal Savings Bank

The Agricultural and Industrial Banks were primarily lending institutions, using capital and bonds to raise funds to make loans. It does not appear that providing savings/deposits was either part of their mandate or a priority in their business model, although it does appear that they held deposits from other banks. The lack of savings and deposits remained a void in the early Republican era until 1918 with the inauguration of the Chinese Post Office Savings Bank. The idea behind the Postal Savings Bank had been around for years but a problem that needed to be overcome was the fact that by treaty the post office was manned mostly by foreigners so that expanding the powers of the Post Office would be akin to expanding the powers of foreigners.[33] The objective in establishing the Postal Savings Bank was to encourage *"the thrift of the people, to facilitate the deposit of small amounts and thereby to foster the people's virtue of savings"*.[34] To this end the Postal Savings Bank automatically provided a network of saving

---

[31] Hsu, Chi-Lien. (1928b). *Op Cit.*
[32] Hsu, Chi-Lien. (1928b). *Op Cit.*, page 283.
[33] Editorial. (1919). The Inauguration of the Chinese Post Office Savings Bank. *Chinese Social and Political Science Review*, 4, 364–377.
[34] Editorial. (1919). *Op Cit.*, page 368.

facilities throughout China, even to Class III post offices in remote areas. It was non-discriminatory and would accept pass-book deposits from the poorest farmers to the wealthiest gentry, illiterate and literate. The only real restrictions were that no more than $100 could be deposited in any month; the balance could not exceed $2000 including accrued interest (fixed then at 4.5% per annum); and 1–3 days' notice days was required for withdrawing funds over $200; and no more than two withdrawals could be made in each month.

5.11 Summary

The purpose of this chapter was to provide a brief background to the conditions facing China's financial sector, and the need for financial development, in the early years of the Republican era. As the Qing dynasty came to an end there were only seven modern banks in China, none of which it appears dealt with agriculture. The new Republic had several problems to solve simultaneously and these included political unification (which did not happen), stability in state revenues (which did not happen), and the development of a modern financial system.

Following 70 years of turmoil, in which unfair treatise by the foreign powers extracted tariffs, custom, duties, and salt taxes as well as other sources of finance to pay indemnities, there was little revenue going to the new revolutionary government in 1912. To offset the payments to the powers, the Chinese imposed likin duties on a temporary basis after the Taiping Rebellion which inhibited economic growth within China and dampened exports. The archaic system of collecting remittances from the provinces provided some funds through 1915 but beyond that these dwindled as China entered the warlord era.

Within the Republican era there was the period of disorganization between 1912 and 1913, the period of reorganization from 1914 to 1915, and the period of adjustment that started in 1915. The years 1912 and 1913 were financed by borrowing on international markets, and some progress was made in 1914 and 1915. Over the 1912–13 period only seven new modern banks were formed, this dwindled to only three in 1914–15. Despite the chaos of the warlord era, 26 new modern banks were formed between 1916 and 1919, and 30 between 1920 and 1923.[35] Most of these were of the industrial/commercial type but agriculture was

[35] Lee, Frederick E. (1926). From Modern Chinese Banks, pages 72–73.

not entirely ignored. The first attempt to create a bank for agriculture was in 1914 with the Industry Orientation Bank supported by the Beiyang government. The Beiyang government under President Yuan Shikai in 1914, aimed to establish a nationwide financial institution to promote industry including agriculture, forestry, and agribusiness. It failed because its Northern-centric focus and distrust of the yuan made it unpalatable to Southern provinces.

The Ministry of Finance tried again in 1915 with the Agricultural and Industrial Banks. Here the Ministry provided for two model banks, the Tongxian and Changpin Agricultural and Industrial Banks. In terms of agricultural finance these provided a critical turning point in China. First was the recognition that agriculture needed to be developed, and to develop it needed credit. But perhaps more important was the sponsorship by the Agricultural and Industrial Banks of the Agricultural and Industrial Workers' Credit Association and the Agricultural and Industrial Cooperative Loan Associations. For the first time these associations had specific outreach to farmers, including those that lacked collateral. Furthermore, it was the first instance in China where a commercial bank made loans to members, rather than the age-old tradition of cooperative lending in which members provided loans to each other. These ideas would manifest themselves in years to come. The blueprint for agricultural credit prepared between 1929 and 1933 (see Chap. 9) relied on a dual system with one branch issuing bonds for agricultural loans and the other extending and supporting cooperative lending. It also introduced the idea of group guarantees, which was prominent throughout the cooperative movement in the Republican era, credit association financing in communist-based areas, and in the modern era the use of group guarantees for Rural Credit Cooperative loans.

CHAPTER 6

Estimating the Demand for Farm Credit in the Republican Era

6.1 Introduction

Little is actually known about the factors that affected the demand and supply of agricultural credit during the Republican era, largely because data collection was rare and modern econometric techniques and the computing power necessary were simply not available. The most complete assessment was reported in John Lossing Buck's *Land Utilization in China* (which we will replicate presently).[1] The important questions for economists and specialists in agricultural finance revolve around how much was borrowed, for what reasons, and at what interest rates. Answers to these are partially furnished by Buck, but not in a form that is economically meaningful.

However, in 2000 a stack of boxes were found in the archives on Nanjing Agricultural University which contained hand-written spreadsheets with the actual household records of 4403 surveyed households.[2] This represents only about 25% of the 17,000 households surveyed by Buck and his team between 1929 and 1933, but contained in these are

---

[1] Buck, J.L. (1937). *"Land Utilization in China: A Study of 16,786 Farms in 168 Localities, and 38,256 Farm Families in Twenty-Two Provinces in china, 1929-1933"* University of Nanjing, Nanjing China.

[2] Kuribayashi, S. Edt. (2007). *"Restoration of Farm Survey of Rural China in 1930s and Comparison with the Present Sampling Survey of Chinese Farms"*, Final Report, Tokyo International University.

© The Author(s) 2018
H. Fu, C. G. Turvey, *The Evolution of Agricultural Credit during China's Republican Era, 1912–1949*,
https://doi.org/10.1007/978-3-319-76801-4_6

actual records of amounts borrowed for consumption, amounts borrowed for production, interest rates charged, special expenditures, and measures of farm size and productivity. Unfortunately, not all records had matching variables so ultimately not all records could be used. Nonetheless, the data, when input to a modern econometric model, provide new insights into credit demand and supply during the Republican era that until now was unobtainable.[3]

In this chapter, we put Buck's recovered data to the econometric test. The objective is to recover as best as possible the economic relationship between credit demand and interest rates, by specifying two endogenous equations for credit supply and credit demand. The interest rates observed and the quantities of credit observed represent an agreement between the borrower and lender and as such are simultaneously determined. We investigate non-productive or consumption loans, and also production loans, while taking into consideration possible endogeneity between credit and productivity as well. We define a demand curve as quantity dependent with interest rates as independent variables, and the supply curve as interest-rate dependent with loan quantity as an independent variable. In our three-stage least squares (3SLS) structure, loan amounts and interest rates are treated as instrumental variables when used as explanatory variables. We consider interest rates, agricultural productivity, and special expenditure such as for weddings and funerals as drivers of demand, and loan amount, productivity, crop yield risk, and source of credit as drivers of supply. Productivity is linked to credit amount and interest rates as well as farm size, productive and market animals, hired labor, and so on as productivity factors.

Our findings are rather interesting. The first finding is we find no statistical difference between special expenditure on weddings, funerals, birthdays, birth of sons and dowry between farmers who borrow and those that did not. Thus, against the conventional wisdom of the day, we cannot attribute debt to special expenditure as a matter of course. For sure it happens in some cases, and also for sure many farmers with such expenditures

---

Hu, Hao, Weiwei Zheng, Minjie Yu, and Funing Zhong. (2016). "*Buck's Original Data Mining and Integrating*" Mimeo, College of Economics and Management, Nanjing Agricultural University, Nanjing, Jiangsu.

[3] The reliability of the data has been explored, with positive affirmation, by Zhong, Funing, Hao Hu and Qun Su. (2007). "*Reliability of John Lossing Buck's Survey Data-A Preliminary Test of Grain Yields*" in Kuribayashi, S. Edt. (2007). *Op Cit.* Chapter 3.

might have liked to obtain credit but could not, but a broad sweeping statement that special expenditure was a strong source of credit cannot so easily be generalized. However, we can generalize that for the subgroup of farmers that made 'consumption' loans, these loans were driven by special expenditures, particularly weddings and funerals.

A second interesting result was that farmers who did borrow had an almost perfectly inelastic demand for credit. The most reliable of our results suggest that this nearly perfectly inelastic demand revealed little or no sensitivity to the actual interest rate. Farmers were interest rate takers. The lender on the other hand acted as a local monopolist of sorts, willfully increasing the interest rate as the amount of credit demanded increased. But we also find across a number of different types of lenders, no significant difference in the interest rate charged. Interest rates were about 3% per month or 36% per year, and for sure there was heterogeneity in rates set by suppliers, but by and large no one group could be singled out to be overtly exploitive. Either all lenders were usurers—or none were usurers—depending on whether one considers 3% or higher per month usury. Importantly this finding applies to friends and relatives. In other words, there was no statistical difference in the rates on offer from a friend or relative, a business, landlord or other type of lender.

6.2 Rediscovering Buck's Data

The discovery of Buck's *Land Utilization in China* was incomplete in that many variables and observations were lost to time (Table 6.1). Variables that were recovered include precious data on savings, credit and indebtedness, and special expenditure. Much of these data have been cross-referenced with the more granulated data provided in Buck's statistical volumes so we are confident that the data we used do in fact represent the true data employed by Buck. Where we lose representation, from a statistical point of view, is that the granular detail of all variables are incomplete, not because the data are part of the lost set, but because for whatever reason these data were not collected for all farms. Thus as we add more detail to the regressions which follow, the addition of one or more variables reduces the effective sample size on which the regressions were run. Here begins the econometric challenge of balancing sample size with the explanatory power of what are deemed causal and important variables.

In addition, the data were fragmented, which means data with the same content were scattered over several spreadsheets and files with similar content for households from different counties or matching the content for households within the same county, but with different farm identifications.

Table 6.1 Description of data tables in Buck's rediscovered data

No.	Title	No.	Title
1.	Size of family	14.	Changes in the use of fertilizers
2.	Able bodied (over 15 and under 60 years of age)	15.	Changes in kinds of fertilizers used
3.	Proportion of all farm and subsidiary works performed by family and hired labor, by men, women, and children	16.	Yields per mou of all crop
4.	Amount of distribution of livestock	17.	Most frequent yield per mou of the byproduct of important crops
5.	Relation of size of farm to crop mou per labor animal unit	18.	Most frequent yield of important crops by the soil type of irrigation
6.	Farm area devoted to different uses grouped by size of farm	19.	Utilization of crops by amount for each use
7.	Number and area of graves in farms	20.	Utilization of crops by percentage for each use
8.	Number, distance, and size (crop area in local unites) of plots and fields	21.	Utilization of minor crops by amount for each use
9.	Proportion of farm area rented	22.	Savings
10.	Crop mou area per farm	23.	Credit and indebtedness
11.	Number of mou of crop area devoted to various crops	24.	Special expenditure
12.	Amount of fertilizer produced on the farm		
13.	Amount and kind of fertilizer applied per mou		

Each variable, or variable grouping, was presented on a specific spreadsheet. Each spreadsheet would identify the variable, the village, and the farm identifier, usually a number between 1 and 100 since Buck attempted to collect 100 households for each Hsien (county) surveyed. The household identification required a particular ordering that had to be matched across multiple spreadsheets containing multiple variables. Ultimately we must trust that farm household #10 for village A and variable x, is the same household #10 for village A and variable y. We have no reason to believe otherwise; in fact Buck's frequent use of cross-tabulations in the statistical summary by farm size and so on demands that the ordering and numbering of households had to be consistent across the original variable spreadsheets. When the original paper spreadsheet data was digitized and transferred onto electronic spreadsheets, our final variable database with variables by column and household observations by row were matched by a unique computer-generated identification number coded for province+county+farm household. Summary statistics from the electronic spreadsheets were then compared to statistics provided in Buck's statistical volume for consistency. Through this procedure we are quite satisfied that the transcription from the original paper spreadsheets to an amalgamated electronic spreadsheet for econometric analyses is consistent and accurate.

The third step was to identify and repair problematic data. To achieve this, the digitizing team had to deal with a multitude of value issues (indecipherable writing, being revised several times, calculation mistakes, and missing data), words spelling issues (illegible handwriting of English letters) and Chinese dialect issues (unclear meaning), and Chinese characters in place of a number. Deeper data checking covered checking the size and value among different tables and Excel sheets. A vivid example of discrepancies that originally emerged with the Nanjing team, was a mismatching of averages in the original data with the averages in Buck's statistical summary on area measures. It was soon discovered that different counties used a different measure of mou. Buck actually provided a table of mou conversions and once these conversions were used to adjust the raw data for each farm in each county to a common mou (one-sixth of an acre or one-fifteenth of a hectare) the electronic spreadsheet data could be compared to the original data. Thus, even though different measures were used locally in 1929–1933 China, our econometric analysis is based upon a common measure, eliminating an unforeseen source of bias. It also provides some measure of comfort that a tremendous amount of care was originally taken by Buck and his team to ensure data consistency and inter-regional comparison. Others units to be converted were that of yield, distance and currency.

6.3 Summary of Buck's Rediscovered Data Used in Demand Analysis

Table 6.2 summarizes the data available to the analysis, the number of observations recorded with valid data, and summary statistics across all observations. Every observation measures each single household and the number of observations for each variable category such as interest rate

Table 6.2 Descriptive statistics of Buck's data used in econometric credit demand analyses

Variable names	Observation numbers (N)	Mean	Std.dev.	Min	Max
Dummy loan (0/1) (Chinese Currency)	3044	0.30	0.46	0	1.00
Total loan (Chinese Currency)	3044	28.65	108.10	0	2000.00
Total interest rate (%)	3044	1.08	2.64	0	50.00
Production (average production/year x *Mou*)	2024	20.74	17.53	0	220.66
Weighted interest rate (%)	3044	1.05	2.53	0	50.00
Weighted interest rate for indebted farmers (%)	840	3.82	3.57	0.33	50.00
Average interest rate (%)	3044	0.54	1.32	0	25.00
Average interest rate for indebted farmers (%)	839	1.95	1.88	.25	25.00
Consumptive loan (Chinese currency)	3044	21.54	90.63	0	2000.00
Consumptive interest rate (%)	3044	0.88	2.47	0	50.00
Productive loan (Chinese currency)	3044	7.11	49.34	0	1710.00
Productive interest rate (%)	3044	0.19	0.85	0	8.00
Farm area square	2125	4121.59	13,130.38	0	256,036.00
Farm square	2125	39.25	50.82	0	506.00
Labor animal	2127	1.60	2.21	0	24.00
Productive animal	2127	0.46	1.25	0	21.08
Relatives (0/1)	3044	0.05	0.21	0	1.00
Friends (0/1)	3044	0.04	0.20	0	1.00

ESTIMATING THE DEMAND FOR FARM CREDIT IN THE REPUBLICAN ERA

Informal business (0/1)	3044	0.11		0.31	0	3.00
Formal/semi-formal Business (0/1)	3044	0.01		0.10	0	1.00
All other borrowing sources (0/1)	3044	0.07		0.25	0	1.00
Wedding	4317	69.45		166.81	0	3500.00
Dowry	4319	19.84		76.09	0	1500.00
Birthday	4319	2.13		31.30	0	1500.00
Birth of son	4319	2.83		20.56	0	500.00
Funerals	4319	52.91		203.23	0	7000.00
Other special expenditure	4318	5.53		155.65	0	9800.00
Income from other sources (%)	1824	1.48		6.06	0	50.00
Yield risk (average production/ highest production)	2020	0.68		0.18	0	3.88
If hired labor (0/1)	1824	0.57		0.50	0	1.00
If subsidiary labor (0/1)	1824	0.62		0.49	0	1.00
Year 1929 first half	4421	.2721104		.4450968	0	1.00
Year 1929 second half	4421	.317349		.4654972	0	1.00
Year 1930 first half	4421	.3168966		.4653194	0	1.00
Year 1930 second half	4421	.3155395		.4647829	0	1.00
Year 1931 first half	4421	.2972178		.4570849	0	1.00
Year 1931 second half	4421	.2065144		.4048497	0	1.00
Year 1932 first half	4421	.2741461		.4461334	0	1.00
Year 1932 second half	4421	.2741461		.4461334	0	1.00
Year 1933	4421	.0226193		.1487033	0	0.00
Hebei	4421	.1164895		.3208473	0	1.00
Shanxi	4421	.1590138		.3657303	0	1.00
Liaoning	4421	.0239765		.1529931	0	1.00

(*continued*)

Table 6.2 (continued)

Variable names	Observation numbers (N)	Mean	Std.dev.	Min	Max
Jiangsu	4421	.0622031	.2415514	0	1.00
Zhejiang	4421	.0454648	.2083449	0	1.00
Anhui	4421	.065596	.2476026	0	1.00
Fujian	4421	.0242027	.1536953	0	1.00
Shandong	4421	.1142276	.3181234	0	1.00
Henan	4421	.0228455	.1494277	0	1.00
Guangdong	4421	.0452386	.2078506	0	1.00
Guangxi	4421	.0461434	.2098193	0	1.00
Sichuan	4421	.0226193	.1487033	0	1.00
Guizhou	4421	.0689889	.253464	0	1.00
Yunnan	4421	.0454648	.2083449	0	1.00
Shannxi	4421	.0226193	.1487033	0	1.00
Gansu	4421	.0452386	.2078506	0	1.00
Qinghai	4421	.0244289	.1543939	0	1.00
Ningxia	4421	.0226193	.1487033	0	1.00
Suiyuan	4421	.0226193	.1487033	0	1.00

(N = 3044) and farm area (N = 2125) differs due to the actual constraints of missing data. Thus, although we had 3044 households with valid data (including zero) on how much was borrowed, we had only 2125 observations with valid measures of land area. Including area in a regression immediately reduced the available sample to no more than 2125. Complicating matters even further, the actual number of observations available to run regressions is no greater than the Venn intersection of the valid and available data of all variables employed. The available data includes observations on credit and indebtedness, proportion of all farm and subsidiary works performed by family and hired labor by men, women, and children, amount and distribution of livestock, farm area devoted to different uses grouped by size of farm, number of mou of crop area devoted to variables crops, amount of fertilizer produced on the farm, yields per mou of all crop, savings, special expenditure, able-bodies men (over 15 and under 60 years of age), most frequent yield per mou of the byproduct of important crops, and amount and kind of fertilizer applied per mou.

6.4 Amount and Character of Farm Credit

As mentioned, our sample base is drawn from Buck's original sampling using the rediscovered household data. As a point of comparison we restate Buck's original tables from *Land Utilization in China* showing the amount and character of farm credit. These are found in Tables 6.3 and 6.4. Whereas Buck categorized loans based on agricultural growing region, we decided to use provincial markers instead.

Our data include a total of 4421 individual household records. Of these we have valid data on 3044 households with valid entries (non-empty) for credit use. Of these 3044 households a total of 902 or 29.6% of farm households reported debt of one kind or another (Table 6.5). Of these, 732 households (81.2% of borrowers and 24% of all 3044 households queried) borrowed for consumption purposes which included special expenditure such as weddings and funerals, etc. Only 220 households, or 24.3% of all borrowers, and 7.2% of sampled households borrowed for production purposes. This suggests that only 50 households, or 5.54% of borrowers, actually borrowed for both production and consumption purposes. Buck reported that about 39% of households in China had some form of debt with about 12% borrowing for productive purposes and 33% for unproductive purposes. So our sample is slightly biased with a smaller percentage of households borrowing for any cause but the proportions of

Table 6.3 Amount and character of farm credit and interest rate

15,112 farms, 150 localities, 142 Hsien, 22 provinces, China, 1929–33

Regions, areas and localities	Number of localities	Percentage of farms having credit for Productive purposes	Percentage of farms having credit for Unproductive purposes	Percentage of farms having credit for All purposes	Amount of annual farm credit (in yuan) for farms having credit for Productive purposes	Amount of annual farm credit (in yuan) for farms having credit for Unproductive purposes	Amount of annual farm credit (in yuan) for farms having credit for All purposes	Interest rate percent per month for credit extended for Productive purposes	Interest rate percent per month for credit extended for Unproductive purposes	Interest rate percent per month for credit extended for All purposes
China	150	12.0	33.0	39.0	19.0	61.0	80.0	2.6	2.7	2.7
Wheat region	68	9.0	32.0	38.0	18.0	53.0	71.0	2.9	3.2	3.2
Rice region	82	15.0	34.0	40.0	21.0	68.0	89.0	2.3	2.3	2.3
Wheat region areas:										
Spring wheat	13	9.0	50.0	56.0	16.0	52.0	68.0	2.9	3.7	3.6
Winter wheat-millet	20	6.0	28.0	32.0	13.0	49.0	62.0	3.0	3.3	3.2
Winter wheat-kaoliang	35	11.0	27.0	35.0	21.0	55.0	76.0	3.0	3.0	3.0
Rice region areas:										
Yangtze rice-wheat	31	18.0	44.0	51.0	20.0	74.0	94.0	2.3	2.3	2.3
Rice-tea	21	14.0	33.0	41.0	17.0	51.0	68.0	2.0	2.1	2.0
Szechwan rice	7	12.0	30.0	34.0	19.0	45.0	64.0	2.6	2.5	2.4
Double cropping rice	11	20.0	38.0	45.0	20.0	70.0	90.0	2.1	1.9	2.0
Southwestern rice	12	3.0	9.0	11.0	29.0	96.0	125.0	2.9	2.8	2.7

Source: Land Utilization in China Table 18, page 462

Table 6.4 Percentage of farms obtaining credit and percentage of credit for productive and non-productive purposes

15,212 farms, 151 localities, 143 Hsien, 22 provinces, China, 1929–1933

Regions, areas and localities	Number of localities	Percentage of farmers obtaining credit	Percentage of total credit for Productive purposes	Non-productive purposes
China	151	39.0	24.0	76.0
Wheat region	68	38.0	25.0	75.0
Rice region	83	40.0	24.0	76.0
Wheat region areas:				
Spring wheat	13	56.0	24.0	76.0
Winter wheat–millet	20	32.0	21.0	79.0
Winter wheat–kaoliang	35	35.0	28.0	72.0
Rice region areas:				
Yangtze rice–wheat	31	51.0	21.0	79.0
Rice–tea	22	39.0	25.0	75.0
Szechwan rice	7	34.0	30.0	70.0
Double-cropping rice	11	45.0	22.0	78.0
Southwestern rice	12	11.0	23.0	77.0

Source: Land Utilization in China Table 19, page 462

Table 6.5 Loan amount summary

Variable	Obs	Mean	Std. dev.	Min	Max
Total loan	3044	28.64592	108.1006	0	2000
Dummy loan	3044	0.2963206	0.4567091	0	1
Total loan for indebted farmers	902	96.67205	181.3378	0.5	2000
Consumptive loan for indebted farmers	732	89.55321	167.5994	0.5	2000
Productive loan for indebted farmers	220	98.38745	157.4922	2	1710

our sample are reasonably consistent with Buck's assessment. We do not rule out differences in counting loans between our approach and Buck's approach as a source of discrepancy (percentage of loans versus percentage of households having loans).

On average, including zero amounts, the average farmer in our sample borrowed $28.65 with a maximum of $2000. For farms having credit the loan amounts average $96.67 with those having consumption loans averaging $89.55 and those with production loans $98.39 (Table 6.5). In comparison, Buck found that indebted farmers owed about $80 on average with about $19 borrowed for productive purposes and $61 for unproductive or consumption purposes (Table 6.4). Our average of $96.67 exceeds Buck's of $80 by $16.67 which is a substantial margin. Again, the difference is due to calculation. Buck included zero values for production or consumption loans so long as the other had a non-zero value. The numbers we report exclude zero values which would be blended into Buck's averages. For example only 24.3% of borrowers borrowed for production. Multiplying this by $98.39 results in a loan amount of $23.91 which is close to Buck's $19. Likewise, with 81.2% of borrowers having average non-productive borrowings of $89.55 the weighted equivalent is $72.71 which is higher than the $61 reported in Buck. The not-insignificant difference is likely due to our double counting of borrowers who had both production and consumption loans which accounts for about 50 farmers.

The data included interest rates for each loan made. In Table 6.6 (and all that follow) we report the Weighted Interest Rate for indebted farmers (%), excluding records if the Weighted Interest Rate equals zero. We find that a simple average of (non-zero) interest rates charged on loans is 1.95%/month ($N = 839$). This treats each loan individually and independent of all others. But when the interest rates are weighted across all loans reported by farmers the weighted average interest rate is 3.82% ($N = 840$). The discrepancy can only be explained if the larger loans made to farmers come with significantly higher interest rates, a conclu-

Table 6.6 Interest rate summary (%)

Variable	Obs	Mean	Std. dev.	Min	Max
Weighted interest rate	3044	1.05	2.53	0	50
Weighted interest rate for indebted farmers	902	3.55	3.58	0	50
Consumptive interest rate for indebted farmers	732	3.68	3.88	0	50
Productive interest rate for indebted farmers	220	2.66	1.83	0	8

sion that comes abundantly clear in our econometric analysis. The interest rates are quoted on a monthly basis so a 3.82% weighted rate implies a simple annual rate of 45.84%, which is in the range of interest rates reported elsewhere in the Chinese literature. Although there were some differences in interest rates charged the differences in Buck's data do not appear to be great. The average rate of interest on productive loans was about 2.6% and higher for unproductive purposes. In some areas such as the Spring-wheat area there was a significant difference between the two with production loans having a 2.9% rate (per month) and unproductive loans having a 3.7% rate. Again, differences in measurement explain why our rates, measured at the household level, differs from Buck's at the loan level. For example suppose a farmer has a $10 loan at 2% and $90 loan at 4%. Buck's average would record an interest rate of 3%. In comparison, our weighted approach would be 2%*0.10 + 4%*.90 or 3.8% as a weighted average for the farm.

However this comes with a wide range from 0.33%/month to 50%/month. The upper range is seemingly unreasonably high. On investigation we note that 50% interest rate was applied to a $5 loan in *Wuwei*, Gansu Province. In fact, in *Wuwei*, there were 18 loans above 10%/month (11–50%). While 10%/month is still substantially higher than average, there is enough documentary evidence elsewhere which suggests that 10%/month was not out of the ordinary at that time. However, this might be true of Gansu because it was very remote. Furthermore, *Wuwei* was surveyed from January to December 1932, which means that it is possible that interests on loans were referring to loans made in 1931 while Gansu was still recovering from the drought and famine. During this period, it is possible that some usurers took advantages of farmers' plight and charged extraordinary rates. After considering the nature of data, we decided to keep what might appear to be outlier rates of interest. The high usury rates accounted for 18/680 of consumptive/non-productive loans, or 2.6% of the total. We also do not believe those high values in the consumption side of Buck's data in 1937–1937 would not have been double –checked.

6.5 Sources of Farm Credit

In most cases, farmers obtained credit locally and personally. Buck queried farmers on where they sourced credit (Table 6.7) and found same village (10%), relatives and friends, (39%), wealthy persons (6%), merchants (3%), farmers (5%), mortgagors (1%), shops(3%), in and near cities (5%), landlords

Table 6.7 Percentage of farms obtaining credit from the specified sources

15,212 farms, 151 localities, 143 Hsien, 22 provinces, China, 1929–33

Regions, areas and localities	Number of localities	Same Village	Relatives and friends	Wealthy persons	Merchants	Farmers
China	151	10.00	39.0	6.00	3.00	5.00
Wheat region	68	14.00	29.0	6.00	1.00	3.00
Rice region	83	6.00	48.0	5.00	4.00	7.00
Wheat region areas:						
Spring wheat	13	11.00	40.0	16.00	2.00	0.00
Winter wheat-millet	20	18.00	36.0	5.00	[a]	3.00
Winter wheat-kaoliang	35	13.00	20.0	4.00	2.00	3.00
Rice region areas:						
Yangtze rice-wheat	31	2.00	37.0	10.00	6.00	10.00
Rice-tea	22	7.00	49.0	1.00	3.00	14.00
Szechwan rice	7	0.00	53.0	8.00	0.00	0.00
Double cropping rice	11	13.00	46.0	0.00	5.00	0.00
Southwestern rice	12	9.00	74.0	5.00	0.00	0.00

[a]The amount is under 0.5

Source: Land Utilization in China, Table 20, page 465

Mortgagors	Shops	In and near the city	Landlords	Neighbors	Adjacent village	Other	Unknown
1.00	3.00	5.00	2.00	8.00	4.00	7.00	7.00
a	4.00	9.00	2.00	12.00	6.00	6.00	8.00
1.00	3.00	1.00	3.00	5.00	3.00	8.00	6.00
1.00	4.00	7.00	8.00	a	3.00	a	8.00
1.00	3.00	5.00	0.00	10.00	4.00	10.00	5.00
0.00	5.00	13.00	a	16.00	8.00	6.00	10.00
1.00	1.00	3.00	3.00	3.00	6.00	11.00	7.00
a	4.00	0.00	a	5.00	1.00	9.00	7.00
0.00	0.00	0.00	8.00	7.00	1.00	9.00	14.00
2.00	9.00	0.00	2.00	9.00	6.00	6.00	2.00
0.00	1.00	0.00	6.00	1.00	0.00	4.00	0.00

(2%), neighbors (8%), adjacent village (4%), others (7%), and unknown (7%). Unfortunately, Buck is quite unclear as to the nature of these loans. For example, assuming that most people in a village know each other, how is the 10% of borrowing in the same village different from friends or relatives or farmers; or how do wealthy farmers differ from mortgagors. In this case we know that often the wealthy person would issue a mortgage in the form of a usufruct loan, but wealthy persons and landlords have also been identified as usurers. We also do not know the extent of *Hui* in these villages or whether lending amongst friends and relatives, neighbors, or others in the village are contributing to a ROSCA.[4] Since none are identified explicitly as credit cooperatives, bank, or native banks we do not know precisely what the

---

[4] See Chap. 4 for a discussion of these traditional approaches to borrowing amongst farmers. ROSCA = rotating savings and credits association.

Table 6.8 Rescaled borrowing sources of indebted farmers

Relatives	17.85%
Friends	14.29%
Informal business	39.29%
Formal/semi-formal business	3.6%
All other borrowing sources	25%

nature of these loans or lenders is. Buck does admit that certain groups can be amalgamated and that is what we do. We define relatives, friends, informal business, formal/semi-formal business, and all other borrowing sources as distinct categories with the relative percentages in Table 6.8. Ultimately we use these as 0–1 binary variables in the supply regressions we run. The supply equation has the weighted interest rates as dependent variables and including the credit-source variables as control variables will allow a determination of whether the supplier of credit differentially applies interest rates.

6.6 Uses of Credit and Special Expenditure

Our demand equation has as the dependent variable the amount of loan taken as a function of interest rates and the uses of the funds. As previously discussed, credit was used for productive and non-productive purposes. Of the non-productive purposes we do not know how much was borrowed for food and other necessities of life, but Buck did collect data on special expenditure which we replicate in Table 6.9. The averages available in our sample ($N = 4319$) are provided in Table 6.10.

In our numbers we include all households even if they have zero special expenditure. Clearly, from an econometric point of view where special expenditure is a (possible) driver of farm credit, even if a borrowing household had no special expenditure the debt must then be assigned to productive purposes, which we observe, or non-special expenditure on food, shelter, clothing, health, or education which we do not observe. This is important. Throughout the Republican era, nearly all of the literature discusses the sometimes ruinous impact of borrowing for special expenditure on farm indebtedness and persistent poverty. Most important are the social effects of 'saving face'. This was discussed by Smith in *Chinese Characteristics* and evidence exists that it persists to this day.

Buck also parses out special expenditure according to farm size and shows that there is an inverse relationship between some special expenditure, particularly weddings and funerals, and farm size. In other words, smaller and

Table 6.9 Special expenditure (in yuan) per farm family on all farms, by region

15,316 farms, 152 localities, 144 Hsien, 22 provinces, China, 1929–33

Regions, areas and localities	Number of localities	Weddings	Dowries	Birthdays	Birth of sons	Funerals	Others	Total
China	152	127.0	96.0	63.0	30.0	102.0	499.0	152.0
Wheat region	68	90.0	67.0	51.0	29.0	97.0	708.0	131.0
Rice region	84	157.0	118.0	66.0	30.0	106.0	321.0	169.0
Wheat region areas:								
Spring wheat	13	107.0	70.0	41.0	29.0	75.0	–	112.0
Winter wheat–millet	20	97.0	40.0	45.0	14.0	73.0	1134.0	111.0
Winter wheat–kaoliang	35	80.0	80.0	64.0	42.0	118.0	617.0	149.0
Rice region areas:								
Yangtze rice–wheat	31	123.0	108.0	62.0	22.0	101.0	226.0	162.0
Rice–tea	22	173.0	136.0	50.0	27.0	100.0	528.0	172.0
Szechwan rice	7	72.0	80.0	43.0	41.0	88.0	–	112.0
Double-cropping rice	12	305.0	169.0	114.0	53.0	130.0	100.0	247.0
Southwestern rice	12	115.0	85.0	86.0	26.0	115.0	145.0	137.0

Source: Land Utilization in China Table 22, page 468

Table 6.10 Special expenditure of household sample

	N	Average (including zero)	Std. dev.	Min	Max
Wedding	4317	69.45	166.81	0	3500.00
Dowry	4319	19.84	76.09	0	1500.00
Birthday	4319	2.13	31.30	0	1500.00
Birth of son	4319	2.83	20.56	0	500.00
Funerals	4319	52.91	203.23	0	7000.00
Other special expenditure	4318	5.53	155.65	0	9800.00

poorer farmers spend proportionately higher amounts on special expenditure, most likely to improve social status. Ultimately we will show that this holds true, but in a discriminating way. With special expenditure the social pressures are so critical and saving face so engrained in Chinese culture that, at least for weddings and funerals, the demand for cash is almost perfectly inelastic. This means that the lender can discriminate and charge higher interest rates for increasing borrowing amounts: the more that is borrowed, the higher the interest rate charged!

6.7 Livestock

We also include in our assessment a variable to capture whether or not the farm has livestock. Livestock can be classified as labor animals (e.g. donkeys) and productive animals. Labor animals (e.g. cattle, oxen) are raised for plowing, cultivation, and transportation, while productive animals are raised for household consumption (meat, eggs) or to be sold in the village market. Working livestock can also be an indicator of wealth, with larger farmers more likely to require animal power, while smaller farmers use family or, if affordable, hired labor.

Table 6.11 summarizes the livestock holdings of our farmers. Only 2127 of the households had valid records for livestock, with the remainder having no entry. We believe that the missing observations were not collected, rather than zero values, and were treated as such. However, we find on average that of these farmers the average number of labor animals was 1.60 per households, and only 0.46 productive animals per household. In most cases the productive animals were small-stock including poultry.

As a point of comparison we replicate Buck's tables in Tables 6.12 and 6.13. There appears to be a regional distribution of working animals

Table 6.11 Livestock holdings of sample farms ($N = 2{,}127$)

	N	Average (including zero)	Std. dev.	Min	Max
Labor animal	2127	1.60	2.21	0	24.00
Productive animal	2127	0.46	1.25	0	21.08

Table 6.12 Factors indicating the type of use of land—livestock and fertility maintenance

Data used for determining the two agricultural regions and the eight agricultural areas

Factors indicating the type use of land

Livestock and fertility maintenance

Regions, areas and localities	Percentage distribution of animal units for all animals having 10% or more of such units	Animal population (animal units per crop animal acre)	Percentage of all animal units which are productive animal units
China	Oxen, 34; water buffaloes, 22; hogs, 13.	0.34	25
Wheat region	Oxen, 37; donkeys, 20; mules, 14; sheep, 11.	0.28	22
Rice region	Water buffaloes, 38; oxen, 31; hogs, 17.	0.39	28
Wheat region areas:			
Spring wheat	Sheep 28; oxen, 21; donkeys, 15; horses, 11; mules, 11.	0.6	36
Winter wheat–millet	Oxen 37; donkeys, 21; sheep, 14; mules, 13.	0.22	25
Winter wheat–kaoliang	Oxen, 40; donkeys, 21; mules, 16.	0.19	15
Rice region areas:			
Yangtze rice–wheat	Water buffaloes, 42; oxen 24; hogs, 15.	0.19	30
Rice–tea	Water buffaloes, 32; oxen, 43; hogs, 20.	0.32	25
Szechwan rice	Water buffaloes, 12; oxen, 53; hogs, 31.	0.32	35
Double cropping rice	Water buffaloes, 44; oxen, 32; hogs, 15.	0.35	24
Southwestern rice	Water buffaloes, 49; oxen, 14; hogs, 14.	1.28	28

Source: Land Utilization in China, page 36

Table 6.13 Factors indicating the type of use of land—size of farm business

Data used for determining the two agricultural regions and the eight agricultural

Regions, areas, and localities	Factors indicating the type use of land		
	Size of farm business		
	Crop area per farm (acres)	Crop acres per man-equivalent	Animal units per farm
China	3.8	2.6	1.34
Wheat region	5.1	3.2	1.37
Rice region	2.8	2.1	1.32
Wheat region areas:			
Spring wheat	7.3	3.5	2.76
Winter wheat–millet	3.7	2.8	0.98
Winter wheat–kaoliang	5.1	3.3	1.11
Rice region areas:			
Yangtze rice–wheat	3.5	2.3	0.97
Rice–tea	2.2	2.4	0.97
Szechwan rice	3.1	1.9	1.35
Double-cropping rice	2.3	1.7	1.31
Southwestern rice	2	1.3	3.18

Source: Land Utilization in China, page 36

dominated by water buffalos, oxen, donkeys, mules, and horses for production, and hogs and sheep dominating for food. Farms also had chickens and other poultry, but in smaller numbers. Across China 25% of farm animals were productive animals (Table 6.12). Table 6.13 shows that Buck found about 1.34 animals per farm which is similar to our sample of 1.60 animals per farm.

6.8 Size of Farm Business

We find that on average farmers in our sample had 39.25 mou of land (about 6.5 acres) with the largest being 506 mou. Only 2125 of farm households in our sample had valid entries for land. As a point of comparison, Buck's data, replicated in Table 6.13, reports China-wide farm size of about 3.8 acres, which is lower than our sample. Land holdings vary across China with 5.1–7.3 acres in the wheat region areas and 2–3.5 acres in the rice-growing areas.

In our model we argue that credit demand, credit supply, and agricultural productivity are endogenous to each other. Households with greater productivity might have greater savings and less of a demand for non-productive loans, or a larger demand for production loans. Larger farms with more land would have more collateral and therefore might be able to access credit at lower rates from creditors. In terms of simultaneous ordering it may also be the case that farms are larger because they could, for one reason or another, access credit. We also include in our regressions an additional term that squares the number of mou. This addition is included to get some idea of the relationship between productivity and land holdings and economies of size. It is possible that given the limited resources available, farming larger tracts of land results in diminishing returns with labor or productive animal units constraining the amount of land that could be efficiently cultivated.

6.9 AGRICULTURAL PRODUCTIVITY

Our measure of agricultural productivity is based upon the total weight of crop harvested on the farm. This measure was also used by Buck and we were constrained by our yield data that was presented in units of a jin, which is approximately 500 grams or about 1 pound. The farms themselves were very diversified and many crops might have been grown by only one farmer in a county. The bulk of the weight harvested would come from the common crops grown by most farmers in a county.

Following Buck, we create a productivity measure that sums the total weight of crop harvested by each farm. This includes not only grains such as wheat, sorghum, and rice but also vegetables and fruit. This presents two problems. The first, as mentioned, is the commingling of crops into a single measure. The second is the heterogeneity in crop type, not only between villages, but also provinces and agricultural regions. On the first part, we recognize the intra-farm disparities that might result, but note also that in most cases the crops that dominated the county and region, also dominated the productivity measure. On the second, we do include additional 1–0 binary variables to account for regional differences in dominant cropping patterns. From our data there were 2024 households with production data. All data were converted from a local weight measure to the common jin measure and all land was converted from local mou to common mou. We find that on average farms produced 20.74 jin/mou

Table 6.14 Factors indicating the type of use of land—production

<table>
<tr><th colspan="2" rowspan="3">Regions, areas, and localities</th><th colspan="8">Data used for determining the two agricultural regions and the eight agricultural areas</th></tr>
<tr><th colspan="8">Factors indicating the type use of land</th></tr>
<tr><th colspan="8">Production</th></tr>
<tr><td></td><td></td><td>Crop yield index</td><td>Yield of wheat (bushels per acre)</td><td>Yield of rice (bushels per acre)</td><td>Production of grain-equivalent per man-equivalent (kilograms)</td><td>Production of grain-equivalent per capital of farm population (kilograms)</td><td>Wages of farm year labor, including value of food and other perquisites (in yuan)</td><td>Land value per acre, 1930 (in yuan)</td><td>All taxes per acre for medium-grade land (in yuan)</td></tr>
<tr><td colspan="2">China</td><td>100</td><td>16</td><td>66</td><td>1393</td><td>446</td><td>83</td><td>24</td><td>–</td></tr>
<tr><td colspan="2">Wheat region</td><td>95</td><td>15</td><td>53</td><td>1231</td><td>345</td><td>75</td><td>17</td><td>5.16</td></tr>
<tr><td colspan="2">Rice region</td><td>101</td><td>16</td><td>67</td><td>1556</td><td>406</td><td>87</td><td>31</td><td>–</td></tr>
<tr><td colspan="2">Wheat region areas:</td><td></td><td></td><td></td><td></td><td></td><td></td><td></td><td></td></tr>
<tr><td colspan="2">Spring wheat</td><td>84</td><td>12[a]</td><td>–</td><td>787</td><td>220</td><td>75</td><td>8</td><td>3.64</td></tr>
<tr><td colspan="2">Winter wheat–millet</td><td>86</td><td>14</td><td>55</td><td>1112</td><td>284</td><td>77</td><td>12</td><td>4.82</td></tr>
<tr><td colspan="2">Winter wheat–kaoliang</td><td>92</td><td>15</td><td>51</td><td>1444</td><td>426</td><td>74</td><td>28</td><td>5.79</td></tr>
</table>

Rice region areas:							
Yangtze rice–wheat	98	17	63	1357	483	89	24	—
Rice–tea	86	11	59	1665	489	100	28	—
Szechwan rice	1087	23	75	1662	712	62	31	—
Double-cropping rice	101	15	42	1281	497	101	53	—
Southwestern rice	139	22	97[b]	1830[b]	616[b]	68	43	6.24

[a]Spring wheat

[b]The yield of rice is exceptionally high in two localities where the soil is especially fertile. The local measure of land is also rather indefinite and the conversion to acres may not be quite correct. Therefore, the production of grain-equivalent may also be higher than actual.

Source: Land Utilization in China, page 37

with a standard deviation of 17.53 jin/mou and a maximum of 220.66 jin/mou. Keeping in mind that our productivity index is not precisely equivalent to that used by Buck, we provide as a point of reference Buck's Table 6.14 on productivity measures.

6.10 Yield Risk

We have written at length on the many calamities faced by Chinese farmers, but how these calamities translate into crop yield losses at the farm level is not easily calculable. Buck, however, made an attempt at capturing yield risk by asking farmers about their highest yield in memory, which could then be compared to current productivity. Using these measures we find that, on average, at the time the survey was undertaken, agricultural production was about 68% of best production, with a standard deviation of 0.18. As a risk measure, we would expect that households with low yields relative to historical highs would be in a precarious situation in regards to savings, which would be depleted, and access to food, which would be scarce and rising in price. This we surmise would increase the demand for credit. On the other, the higher the yield risks, the less likely that potential lenders would actually receive timely repayment. These two, not mutually exclusive, economic forces would likely result in more inelastic demand and supply relationships meaning, as a matter of practice, that farmers in distress would willingly pay a higher interest rate in order to obtain much-needed liquidity and that creditors would charge a higher interest rate than would ordinarily be charged under better conditions. These better conditions would be captured by a rising value of the yield risk ratio to 1.0 (and higher if current production exceeds previous historical highs).

6.11 Hired Labor and Subsidiary Labor

Also critical to agricultural productivity is the use of labor. Labor can include household or family labor, and hired labor in terms of contributing to increased or improved productivity. During idle periods, excess household labor might be employed in subsidiary work or wage labor. Labor use differed across regions. For example Buck notes that one-fifth of all labor is performed by women with the ratio being 31.6% in East Central China and 11.8% in North China, with the latter percentage most likely due to the prevalence of foot binding in North China, particularly in the Spring Wheat Area, where the binding was so tight as to compel women to do the field work on their knees.[5] Although we did have data on labor equivalents and hired labor, we took into consideration the possible multi-collinearity between hired labor in units and farm size and other wealth/size covariates. Thus we include only a 1–0 binary variable to capture hired labor and subsidiary labor. The first captures the excess demand for labor which would be positive so long as the value of labor to agricultural productivity exceeded the prevailing wage rate, while the

Table 6.15 Factors indicating the type of use of land—farm labor

Data used for determining the two agricultural regions and the eight agricultural areas

Regions, areas and localities	Factors indicating the type use of land		
	Farm labor		
	Man-equivalent per farm	Number of months of idleness per able-bodied man	Percent of total income from subsidiary work
China	2	1.7	14
Wheat region	1.9	1.8	16
Rice region	2	1.7	13
Wheat region areas:			
Spring wheat	2	1.7	19
Winter wheat-millet	1.6	1.7	15
Winter wheat-kaoliang	2	1.9	15
Rice region areas:			
Yangtze rice-wheat	2.2	1.9	13
Rice-tea	1.6	1.6	13
Szechwan rice	2.2	0.6	21
Double-cropping rice	2.3	1.7	12
Southwestern rice	2.1	1.9	9

Source: Land Utilization in China, page 36

[5] Buck (1937). Op Cit., page 292.
Buck, J.L. (1930). "Chinese Farm Economy: A Study of 2866 Farms in Seventeen Localities and Seven Provinces in China" University of Nanjing and University of Chicago Press, Chicago Illinois, page 235.

second captures an excess supply of labor with value in non-agricultural activities that provides greater value than using that labor on the farm would provide. Subsidiary work would most likely arise during periods of idleness, but could also be employed by less productive household members such as children, the elderly, or women with bound feet. We provide Table 6.15 from *Land Utilization in China* to provide a sense of the labor demand, idleness, and subsidiary work we capture with these variables.

6.12　Time and Regional Variables

Buck's study took place in one of the more tumultuous periods in China's history. The period between 1929 and 1933 saw an almost relentless sequence of natural and man-made calamities ranging from drought and famine, floods, insurgencies by communists, civil war and strife, Japanese annexation and military action. It thus matters when and where Buck collected data since these may have a bearing on the results. To be sure, Buck would not send his survey teams into war-torn areas, or areas held by communists, or even to drought or flood-stricken areas, so for the most part we would expect that our investigations into credit supply and demand would be under near, or perhaps more aptly, relatively normal conditions. Nonetheless, these artifacts of man and nature that might have affected the agricultural economies at the places and times of the events cannot be ignored. To give a sense of the events facing China's farmers over this period we provide a simplified summary in Table 6.16 which identifies the event (and in the case of drought and flood, the year following an event) and provinces affected.[6]

We know from Buck's statistical summary when and where surveys were taken and to capture the effects we developed two sets of binary variables. We define nine time zones, identifying whenever the specific household data were recorded. They are: first half year in 1929, second half year in 1929, first half year in 1930, second half year in 1930, first half year in 1931, second half year in 1931, first half year in 1932, second half

---

[6] The data provided in Table 6.16 are our own compilation from multiple sources, but largely from the reporting in *China Weekly Review*, a weekly English language news magazine. All news items between mid-1928 and late 1933 were scanned for event information, including drought, famine, floods, bandits, communist activities, anti-bandit/anti-communist activities, warlord actions, anti-Japanese activities, and so on. Locations and dates were collated as best as possible to the provinces and time schedule of the survey periods as reported by Buck.

Table 6.16 Summary of calamities facing Chinese farmers

Province	Major drought	Major drought (t+1)	Major flood	Major flood (t+1)	Communism	Communist suppression	Civil war	Northern war	Japanese/Manchurian
Shandong	0	0	1	0	1	0	0	0	0
Shansi	0	1	0	0	1	0	0	0	0
Hebei	0	0	0	0	0	0	0	0	0
Guangdong	0	0	0	0	1	1	0	0	0
Shandong	0	1	0	0	1	0	0	1	0
Hebei	0	0	0	0	0	0	0	0	0
Guangxi	0	0	0	0	1	0	0	0	1
Hebei	0	0	0	0	0	0	0	0	0
Suiyuan	1	0	0	0	0	0	0	0	0
Liaoning	0	0	1	0	0	0	0	0	0
Shansi	0	0	0	0	0	0	0	0	0
Yunnan	0	0	0	0	0	0	0	0	1
Ningsia	0	0	0	0	0	0	0	0	1
Shansi	0	0	0	0	0	0	0	0	1
Guizhou	0	0	0	0	0	0	0	0	0
Shansi	0	0	0	0	0	0	0	1	0
Shandong	0	0	0	0	0	0	0	0	0
Shansi	0	0	0	0	0	0	0	0	0
Qinghai	0	0	0	0	0	0	0	0	0
Shansi	1	0	0	0	0	0	0	0	0
Sichuang	0	0	0	0	0	0	0	0	0
Shandong	0	1	0	0	0	0	0	1	1
Hebei	0	0	0	1	0	1	0	0	0
Guizhou	0	0	0	0	0	0	0	0	1
Hebei	0	0	0	0	0	0	0	0	0

(continued)

Table 6.16 (continued)

Province	Major drought	Major drought (t+1)	Major flood	Major flood (t+1)	Communism	Communist suppression	Civil war	Northern war	Japanese/Manchurian
Shansi	1	0	0	0	0	0	0	0	0
Gansu	0	0	0	0	0	0	0	0	1
Shandong	1	0	1	0	1	0	0	0	0
Yunnan	0	0	0	0	0	0	0	0	1
Guangsi	0	0	0	0	1	0	0	0	1
Qinghai	0	0	0	0	0	0	0	0	1
Zhejiang	0	1	0	0	1	0	0	0	0
Zhejiang	0	0	0	0	0	0	0	0	1

year in 1932 and year 1933. We also know the village/county, province, and agricultural region and create corresponding binary variables for them as well. All told our sample includes observations from 17 provinces including Hebei, Shanxi, Liaoning, Jiangsu, Zhejiang, Anhui, Fujian, Shandong, Henan, Guangdong, Guangxi, Sichuan, Guizhou, Yunnan, Shaanxi, Gansu, Qinghai, Ningxia, and Suiyuan.

The specific events will not be captured by the regional identifiers alone, for these will also capture the provincial politics and agricultural conditions generally present. However, the combination of the provinces and times not only makes an allowance to control for fixed provincial effects but also the random effects of the calamities that occurred across time.

Buck said very little about these calamities. In both *Chinese Farm Economy* and *Land Utilization in China* the narrative is passive and neutral and never discussed in the context of what impacts these might or might not have had on agricultural productivity and credit. To be fair, the survey part of *Land Utilization in China* as well as the randomization of localities to be surveyed was developed in 1928, just as the drought in the North was beginning and before any of the events occurred. Again, Buck avoided sending surveyors into distressed areas and even suspended the survey, setting his enumerators to work on flood relief in 1931. Nonetheless, these events should not be treated as production or credit neutral and our econometric approach sheds some light on the effects. A related problem is that we do not know within the six-month time spans we define whether a particular village was surveyed before, during, or after an event. A farm surveyed in the spring of one year would most likely refer to management practices and harvests for the previous year, while households surveyed at the end of a calendar year would likely respond in terms of the current year's harvest. To capture some of these effects we also include a variable to capture households surveyed the year after a drought or flood event. This would be meaningful for the 1928–30 Northern drought and the 1931 Yellow and Yangtze River floods which were so severe that full recovery in the next crop year would have been unlikely for many farmers.

Although Buck did not correlate data with the events, he did query farmers on the extent of catastrophes. These are provided in Table 6.17. The first line in Table 6.17 summarizes across China, reporting that on average a Chinese farm household survived three famines in its occupants lives, each lasting on average about 11 months, resulting in 5% of the population facing starvation and forcing 13% emigrate. On top of this

Table 6.17 Factors indicating the type of use of land—crop production and crop risk

Regions, areas, and localities		Data used for determining the two agricultural regions and the eight agricultural areas									
		Factors indicating the type use of land									
		Crops			Frequency of crop failures						
	Types of farming	Percent of crop area in winter crops	Percent of crop area cropped	Frequency and extent of famine within memory of informants					Calamities (floods, droughts, insects, war, wind and frost) occurring between 1904 and 1929, causing a loss of 20% or more of the crop, but not causing a famine		
	Percent of crop area in each crop appearing in the type for the region or the area as a whole			Number of famines per household	Duration of famines (months)	Percentage of population		Number of families	Percentage of Hsien crop	Number of calamities per locality	Percentage of all crops destroyed
						Emigrating	Staying				
China	Rice, 33; wheat, 29; and cotton, 7.	41	49	3	11	13	Chapter 10.5	a	67	16	43-54
Wheat region	Wheat, 40; millets, 27; cotton, 8; and kaoliang, 15.	35	27	3.6	13	14	8	1	77	21	40-57
Rice region	Rice, 68.	46	66	2.5	9	11	1	a	57	13	40-55

Wheat region areas:								
Spring wheat	Millet, 34; Irish potatoes, 10; spring wheat, 18.	a	7	2.6	22	19	14	1	86	20	25–53
Winter wheat–millet	Wheat, 40; millet, 31; cotton, 9.	40	18	4.3	14	14	12	1	81	15	35–61
Winter wheat–kaoliang	Wheat, 46; cotton, 9; millet, 23; corn, 16; kaoliang, 19.	43	39	3.4	11	13	4	a	72	24	37–51
Rice region areas:								
Yangtze rice–wheat	Rice, 58; cotton, 13; wheat, 31; barley, 19.	62	65	3	9	20	1	a	68	11	34–60
Rice–tea	Rice, 73; rapeseed, 13.	42	69	2.6	7	9	1	0	53	22	48–60
Szechwan rice	Rice, 41; opium, 11; rapeseed, 13; corn, 14; wheat, 19.	52	67	4.6	7	5	1	a	52	9	20–80
Double-cropping rice	Rice, 90; sweet potatoes, 12; sugar cane, 6.	8	76	0.4	12	a	a	0	22	9	50–60
Southwestern rice	Rice, 60; opium, 19; broad beans, 17; corn, 14.	43	52	2.2	11	8	4	0	71	10	39–70

[a] The amount is under 0.05

Source: Crops, Land Utilization in China, pages 34, 35

each region on average faced 16 calamities with the percentage of crop yield destroyed ranging between 43% and 54%.

6.13 Estimation Method

We have previously mentioned that the relationships between credit demand, credit supply, and agricultural productivity are endogenous. By endogenous, we really mean that they feed off each other. Our demand equation has amount borrowed as a function of the interest rate on the loans and under normal conditions we would expect that the higher the interest rate the lower will be the demand for credit. But the interest rate has to be agreed upon between the borrower and the lender and the lender might well set the rate depending, among other things, on the amount borrowed. A higher loan amount might come with a higher interest rate, but with this higher interest rate the borrower may reassess and reduce demand, which in turn will cause a revision in the interest rate offered and this will continue until a deal is struck. Likewise a farmer may have some savings with which to purchase seed or hire labor, but to obtain higher levels of economic efficiency it may be economically advantageous to borrow. Again, a dynamic arises between the borrower and lender in which a loan amount is requested and an interest rate offered, and if the interest rate extracts too much from the marginal value of production resulting from the loan then the borrower will revise accordingly and reduce the request, and this will continue until a bargain is reached that returns a profit to both borrower and lender. In this way the demand for inputs drives a demand for credit. But if the bargain between borrower and lender succeeds in increasing output and profits then as credit demand feeds production, production in turn feeds credit demand.

Our modeling approach is a three-equation simultaneously determined system of equations with credit demand, credit supply, and agricultural productivity being treated as endogenous. To accommodate endogeneity we employ 3SLS, which is an appropriate instrumental variable technique when the error term is correlated with one or more explanatory variables. This is a reasonable assumption since we are assuming that the many extraordinary events between 1929 and 1933 are common sources of exogenous force that impact all three elements one way or another. From a statistical point of view the 3SLS estimator is biased in small samples but is consistent and asymptotically more efficient than single-equation estimators. Thus, it has desirable large sample properties.

The three equations to be estimated for credit demand, credit supply, and productivity respectively are:

$$\text{Loan Amount}_i = \beta_0^1 + \beta_2^1 \text{ Interest Rate}_i + \beta_2^1 \text{ Productivity}_i$$
$$+ \beta_3^1 \text{ Wedding}_i + \beta_4^1 \text{ Dowry}_i + \beta_5^1 \text{ Birthday}_i + \beta_6^1 \text{ Birth of Son}_i + \beta_7^1 \text{ Funerals}_i$$
$$+ \beta_8^1 \text{ OtherSpecial Expenditures}_i + \beta_9^1 \text{ Time}_i + \beta_{10}^1 \text{ Region}_i + \varepsilon_1$$

$$\text{Interest Rate}_i = \beta_0^2 + \beta_1^2 \text{ Loan Amount}_i + \beta_2^2 \text{ Productivity}_i + \beta_3^2 \text{ Yield Risk}_i + \beta_4^2 \text{ Relatives}_i$$
$$+ \beta_5^2 \text{ Friends}_i + \beta_6^2 \text{ Informal business}_i + \beta_7^2 \text{ Semi Formal Business}_i$$
$$+ \beta_8^2 \text{ All other borrowing sources}_i + \beta_9^2 \text{ Time}_i + \beta_{10}^2 \text{ Region}_i + \varepsilon_2$$

$$\text{Productivity}_i = \beta_0^3 + \beta_1^3 \text{ Loan Amount}_i + \beta_2^3 \text{ Interest Rate}_i + \beta_3^3 \text{ Farm Area}_i + \beta_4^3 \text{ (Farm Area)}^2_i$$
$$+ \beta_5^3 \text{ Labor Animals}_i + \beta_6^3 \text{ Productive Animals}_i + \beta_7^3 \text{ Income from other source}_i$$
$$+ \beta_8^3 \text{ Hired Labor}_i + \beta_9^3 \text{ Subsidiary Labor}_i + \beta_{10}^3 \text{ Time}_i + \beta_{11}^3 \text{ Region}_i + \varepsilon_3$$

The credit demand equation has (with the exception of one model variant) the actual loan amount as the dependent variable and interest rate as the key endogenous independent variable. We include productivity to capture agricultural productivity and also include special expenditure. Much of the literature on credit in this era, anecdotal as it is, points to special expenditure as a major driver of farm debt, particularly for weddings and funerals. Wedding expenditure arises if a daughter is being married. The expenditure will typically be paid by the girl's parents. But when a girl leaves a household, the family also loses a source of household labor and thus a dowry was often paid to the girl's household as a form of compensation. The time and region variables are random-effect binary variables for each of nine (six month) periods between 1929 and 1933. The region variables are fixed-effect binary variables representing the provinces.

The second equation is the credit supply equation. This equation is interest rate dependent, with the interest rate determined by the lender depending on a number of factors including the (endogenous) loan amount, the (endogenous) productivity of the borrower, and to capture uncertainty the yield risk variable. We also include the source of the loan. Here we want to examine whether the source of the loan matters. Typically we would expect that borrowing from friends and relatives would come at lower interest rates than formal and semi-formal businesses which could include usury rates. The random and fixed-time and region effects are also included to account for exogenous factors that could affect credit supply.

If a loan was made in a region facing drought or military incursion, it is possible that this would affect loan supply.

The third equation captures farm productivity effects and includes the (endogenous) credit effects of loan amount (a source of liquidity with which to purchase inputs or labor), and interest rate which is a cost of doing business. We also include factors of production such as farm area (and its square to capture economies of size and scale), labor animals and hired labor. Productive animals, subsidiary labor, and other income are also included to capture product substitution effects. The region and time effects again capture the location (approximate) in agricultural regions and again the time effects to capture shorter-term random effects.

We examine several variants of this model. The first model includes all respondents regardless of whether they were indebted or not. The dependent variable is equal to 1 if a loan was in place and zero otherwise. The interest rate in the supply equation is the weighted interest rate assigned to borrowers and zero otherwise. This is equivalent to a linear probability model. Normally, problems of this type would use a Logit, Probit, or Tobit function at least for the demand equation, but in a systems approach blending a non-linear regression in a 3SLS with linear regressions can result in unstable standard errors. The LPM will generally provide the same story as the marginal effects of the Logit/Probit/Tobit models but suffers from a predicted value that can (and most likely will) fall outside the {0,1} bounds of a probability distribution. Since we are interested in the explanatory power of the regression rather than a prediction, we can live with this sin. More problematic is the inclusion of interest rates and loan amounts in the first place. As will be seen the coefficients of interest rate in the demand equations are positive and the coefficients of loan size in the supply equations are positive because, as a tautology, a zero loan is assigned a zero interest rate for non-borrowers while a positive rate is assigned a positive loan amount for borrowers. The coefficients in this first equation have no economic meaning and are included simply as control variables. Rather, what we are interested in with this binary demand structure is to get some idea of other factors that might affect whether a farmer borrows or does not borrow.

This is not the case for the remaining three models we present. The second model includes all loans, the third model considers only consumption loans and the fourth model considers only production loans. These models include only borrowers and in these we seek to understand not only the economic relationships between loan amounts and interest rate to see whether demand is downward sloping and supply upward sloping, as theory suggests, but also the household and economic drivers of agricultural credit demand and supply in China's Republican era.

6.14 ECONOMETRIC RESULTS: WHO IS BORROWING?

The results in Table 6.18 relate to a simple question: who are the borrowers and are there differences between the characteristics of borrowers or non-borrowers? The interpretation of the coefficients should be interpreted in the context of an increasing or decreasing likelihood of borrowing. Both ordinary least squares (OLS) ($N = 1718$) and 3SLS ($N = 1314$) regressions are provided. The greater reliance is on the 3SLS model. The more detailed results follow, but the overall finding is that, generally speaking, there is little difference between the borrower and non-borrower sub-groups. From the demand equation it does not appear that we can justify sweeping statements that special expenditure on wedding, funeral, birthdays, dowry's etc. leads to credit use. We find that whether a farmer faces a special expenditure cannot be used as a matter of course to explain why a farm household borrows. Sometimes they do, sometimes they do not—with no statistical leaning one way or the other. We do find that, at a reasonable level of statistical reliability, higher productivity farmers are more likely to borrow. This paints a somewhat different story than the conventional wisdom might suggest. We cannot conclude that special expenditure is a driver of credit use, but can conclude that productivity is. When we consider the production equation in Table 6.18 we can observe the endogenous relationship between credit demand and productivity. Farms that borrow tend to be more productive, and more productive farms tend to borrow. We also find a size effect. Larger farms tend to be more productive and thus borrow more, and other factors that contribute to productivity such as hired labor and labor animals also then contribute to credit use.[7]

---

[7] In the 3SLS credit demand function, if there is more loan supply in the agricultural credit market, there will be more farmers conducting borrowing behavior (coefficient of 3SLS interest rate = 0.2058877, P-value = 0). However, from the nearly perfect inelastic relationship between productivity and loan demand in the second graph, productivity does not have much of a role in impacting farmers' decision to borrow (P-value of 3SLS production = 0.103).

Important time variables are year1930h2 (Coefficient = 0.1273513, P-value = 0). Important region variables are Shanxi (Coefficient = 0.2838039, P-value = 0.049), Guangxi (Coefficient = 0.4342342, P-value = 0.055), Yunnan (Coefficient = 0.324354, P-value = 0.098),

Table 6.18 Binary model of agricultural credit

Dependent variable (Bold)	OLS		3SLS	
	Coefficient	P-value	Coefficient	P-value
Dummy loan				
Independent variable				
Weighted interest rate	0.0708975	0	0.2058877	0
Productivity	−0.0010522	0.317	0.0071722	0.103
Wedding	2.66E–07	0.993	−0.0000167	0.74
Dowry	−0.0000916	0.016	−0.0000516	0.645
Birthday	−0.0001437	0.003	−7.42E–05	0.737
Birth of son	−0.0004156	0.002	−0.0001806	0.618
Funerals	−4.00E–06	0.854	5.94E–07	0.987
Others	−0.0012864	0	−0.0005987	0.885
Year 1929 h1	0.1995966	0		
Year 1930 h1	0.1350179	0.259	−0.2972795	0.164
Year 1930 h2	0.1280955	0.007	0.1273513	0.059
Year 1931 h1	0.2065745	0.058	−0.3391054	0.172
Year 1932 h1	0.1927577	0.041	−0.3282276	0.141
Hebei	−0.1256535	0.168	0.1853788	0.228
Shanxi	0.032017	0.69	0.2838039	0.049
Guangxi	0.0326866	0.718	0.4342342	0.055
Guizhou	−0.0912546	0.194		
Yunnan	−0.0521477	0.513	0.324354	0.098
Gansu			−0.772441	0
Qinghai	0.1402073	0.143	0.4191007	0.044
Ningxia	0.1552007	0.051	0.3736906	0.013
Suiyuan				
Number of obs = 1718			Number of obs = 1314	
F(19, 1698) =			Parms = 19	
Prob > F =			RMSE = 0.5620071	
R-squared = 0.4672			"R-sq" = −0.1529	
Root MSE = 0.37116			chi^2 = 812.45	
			P = 0.0000	
Dependent variable				
Weighted interest rate				
Independent variable				
Dummy loan	0.6902606	0	0.9349819	0.763
Productivity	0.0162211	0.331	−0.0043298	0.87
Yield risk	−0.2709193	0.349	−0.071816	0.848
Relatives	1.510982	0	1.776068	0.352
Friends	3.442942	0	3.473832	0.195

(*continued*)

Table 6.18 (continued)

Dependent variable (Bold)	OLS		3SLS	
	Coefficient	P-value	Coefficient	P-value
Informal business	2.942236	0	2.53253	0.166
Formal/Semiformal business	1.775289	0	2.76759	0.355
All others	2.507147	0	2.698801	0.258
Year 1929 h1	−0.0217677	0.958		
Year 1930 h1	4.29044	0	0.2017773	0.869
Year 1930 h2	−0.1524913	0.252	−0.4218242	0.199
Year 1931 h1	3.695907	0.001	−0.2648421	0.874
Year 1932 h1	4.258063	0	0.2931026	0.813
Hebei	−4.042747	0	0.3350961	0.764
Shanxi	−4.141461	0	0.1036986	0.929
Guangxi	−4.11885	0	−0.3016163	0.839
Guizhou	−4.560338	0		
Yunnan	−4.461356	0	−0.2643724	0.809
Gansu			4.430215	0
Qinghai	−3.861846	0	0.1658326	0.925
Ningxia	−4.931953	0	−0.7634071	0.424

Number of obs = 1717

F(20, 1697) = 87.75
Prob > F = 0.0000
R-squared = 0.5625
Root MSE = 2.0831

Number of obs = 1314
Parms = 19
RMSE = 2.371333
"R-sq" = 0.5374
chi^2 = 1350.74
P = 0.0000

Dependent variable
Productivity
Independent variable

Dummy loan	−1.795239	0.253	9.688896	0.007
Weighted interest rate	0.5608175	0.339	−2.313831	0.003
Farm area square	−0.0002232	0	−0.0002252	0
Farm area local mow	0.0881802	0	0.0922535	0
Labor animal	0.3980929	0.096	0.4016467	0.119
Productive animal	0.0820473	0.638	−0.0145744	0.955
Other income percent	403,455	0.129	0.0406555	0.498
Dummy hired labor	4.309383	0	3.3936	0
Dummy subsidiary	0.3550058	0.694	0.3100553	0.724
Year 1930 h1	−27.42663	0		
Year 1930 h2	−2.855484	0.037	−3.956419	0.018
Year 1931 h1	−6.763873	0.001	18.98447	0

(*continued*)

Table 6.18 (continued)

Dependent variable (Bold)	OLS		3SLS	
	Coefficient	P-value	Coefficient	P-value
Year 1932 h1	−11.66465	0	14.28114	0
Hebei	29.0319	0	2.976021	0.236
Shanxi	27.16659	0	0.729946	0.827
Guangxi			−26.44501	0
Guizhou	54.68648	0	30.75549	0
Yunnan	13.18848	0	−12.32866	0.002
Gansu	39.49775	0	27.37746	0
Qinghai	13.83657	0	−12.76711	0
Ningxia	26.86419	0	−0.5235277	0.888
Number of obs = 1321			Number of obs = 1314	
F(20, 1301) = 325.85			Parms = 20	
Prob > F = 0.0000			RMSE = 14.56467	
R-squared = 0.7755			"R-sq" = 0.7086	
Root MSE = 12.869			chi^2 = 4390.91	
			P = 0.0000	

Gansu (Coefficient = −0.772441, P-value = 0), Qinghai (Coefficient = 0.4191007, P-value = 0.044) and Ningxia (Coefficient = 0.3736906, P-value = 0.013). Gansu Province does not appear in a OLS credit demand function. In the 3SLS credit supply function, loan supply is very inelastic to loan demand (Coefficient of 3SLS loan amount = 0.9349819, P-value = 0.763), which implies Chinese farmers are price takers in the agricultural credit market. And productivity also does not impact loan supply demand (Coefficient of 3SLS loan amount = −0.0043298, P-value = 0.87). Gansu (Coefficient = 4.430215, P-value = 0) is the only valid independent variable while it does not appear in the OLS credit supply function. In the 3SLS productivity function, whether the farmer borrow money has a greatly positive impact on productivity because the coefficient of Dummy Loan is 9.688896, P-value = 0.007, which means when farmers take on more loans, the higher the productivity will be. It also might imply the loan amount was mainly used for productive purposes. The coefficient of loan supply (coefficient of interest rate = −2.31383, P-value = 0.003): the more loan supply, the less productivity will be. It implies informal borrowing sources (friends, relative, etc.) takes an important role in the loan supply side, otherwise if formal credit dominates the agricultural credit market, the increase in credit supply will not decrease productivity; for the money lender, those who spared some of their income or savings to lend to other farmers, the money they lent might have been planned for productive purposes previously. Among the other basic independent variables, the statistically significant ones are Farm Area Square (Coefficient = −0.0002252, P-value = 0), Farm Area (Coefficient = 0.0922535, P-value = 0), If has hired labor (Coefficient = 3.3936,

6.15 Econometric Results: The Demand and Supply of Agricultural Credit

The next sets of econometric results explain what are best considered the conditional demand for credit. In the previous section the assessment was based on all farmers for which data were available including farmers that were not indebted. Here we now reduce the focus only to the farms who reported agricultural credit. First we examine any type of debt, and then look more closely at whether the debt was for productive or non-productive purposes. Consequently the sample size reduces accordingly and the reader may want to keep this under consideration.

Table 6.19 shows the OLS and 3SLS results for total credit demand (productive and/or non-productive credit). The first regression is the demand equation, the second the supply equation, and the third the productivity equation. We focus again on the 3SLS results because they account for the endogeneity of demand, supply, and productivity. We find that more productive farms borrow more and that households with special expenditure for weddings and funerals also borrow more. We do not find that households with special expenditure on birthdays, birth of boy, or dowry lead to increased borrowing. The result is an interesting one because in the contemporaneous writings of the day there are many claims of farm households borrowing specifically for weddings and funerals. Our results support these claims.

Another point of note is that there is a positive relationship between the amount borrowed and the interest rates charged on loans. The interest rate charged on loans is determined by a number of factors including loan amount ($p = 0.166$) and yield risk ($p = 0.11$). On this latter point a higher number means that current productivity is getting closer to historical best yields so it does appear that the lender takes risk into consideration, charging a higher interest rate for higher-risk farms. However, with the 3SLS results we find no evidence that one source of credit charges an interest rate higher than any other when other things, such as time and province, are

P-value = 0). Important time variables are year1930h2 (Coefficient = −3.956419, P-value = 0.018), year1931h1 (Coefficient = 18.98447, P-value = 0), year1932h1 (Coefficient = 14.28114, P-value = 0). Important region variables are Guangxi (Coefficient = −26.44501, P-value = 0), Guizhou (Coefficient = 30.75549, P-value = 0), Yunnan (Coefficient = −12.32866, P-value = 0.002), Gansu (Coefficient = 27.37746, P-value = 0), and Qinghai (Coefficient = −12.76711, P-value = 0). Guangxi appears in 3SLS while not in the OLS production equation. On the other hand, Year1930h1 (OLS: Coefficient = −27.42663, P-value = 0) appears in the OLS not 3SLS productivity equation.

Table 6.19 Total loan for indebted farmers with time and region variables

Dependent variable (**Bold**)	OLS Coefficient	P-value	3SLS Coefficient	P-value
Total loan				
Independent variable				
Weighted interest rate	−0.5106107	0.338	14.53257	0.038
Productivity	0.1628833	0.611	2.888649	0.068
Wedding	6.68E−01	0	0.5694614	0
Dowry	0.0920703	0.597	0.0263822	0.861
Birthday	0.6717979	0.644	1.15E + 00	0.847
Birth of son	0.4722442	0.448	0.7112581	0.263
Funerals	3.08E−01	0	2.01E−01	0
Year 1929 h1	2.913435	0.433		
Year 1930 h1	−38.25168	0.488		
Year 1930 h2	−6.153648	0.834	20.75009	0.373
Year 1931 h1	40.72046	0.296	37.78344	0.573
Year 1932 h1	5.642136	0.859	−6.392555	0.936
Hebei	24.04278	0.552	−75.53818	0.095
Shanxi	−37.04501	0.339	−124.3306	0.06
Guangxi	4.373326	0.921	−13.17376	0.872
Guizhou	14.31937	0.649	−104.297	0.179
Yunnan			212.2831	0.019
Gansu	0.6157157	0.984	−249.4231	0.02
Qinghai	−30.49923	0.478	−99.0438	0.133
Ningxia	−20.7167	0.552	−92.71529	0.194
Number of obs = 439			Number of obs = 361	
F(18, 420) =			Parms = 18	
Prob > F =			RMSE = 119.8012	
R-squared = 0.6904			"R-sq" = 0.5757	
Root MSE = 95.9			chi^2 = 870.83 P = 0.0000	
Dependent variable				
Weighted interest rate				
Independent variable				
Total loan	0.0004069	0.539	0.0033668	0.166
Productivity	0.0754979	0.244	−0.078592	0.225
Yield risk	−2.674854	0.198	−2.533015	0.119
Relatives	0.155313	0.492	−0.2215084	0.687
Friends	−0.5745886	0.427	−0.2355776	0.702

(*continued*)

Table 6.19 (continued)

Dependent variable (Bold)	OLS Coefficient	OLS P-value	3SLS Coefficient	3SLS P-value
Informal business	0.7314436	0.038	0.5368589	0.307
Formal/Semi-formal business	0.4816642	0.191	0.2633986	0.731
All others	0.3265979	0.491	0.1510708	0.818
Year 1929 h1	3.906955	0.026		
Year 1930 h2	−0.7830909	0.112	−1.047519	0.294
Year 1931 h1	−3.856079	0.006	−0.3783078	0.891
Year 1932 h1	−3.822216	0.019	0.4274127	0.897
Hebei	4.534557	0.016	5.482501	0.004
Shanxi	6.080447	0.002	5.841284	0.042
Guangxi	8.406599	0	3.964342	0.312
Guizhou	6.686425	0.001	6.89809	0.028
Yunnan	6.038755	0	2.130672	0.611
Gansu	14.06407	0	15.11412	0
Qinghai	7.139634	0	5.524437	0.051
Ningxia	6.922309	0.003	5.337925	0.103

Number of obs = 440

F(20, 420) = 221.08
Prob > F = 0.0000

R-squared = 0.6750

Root MSE = 3.6091

Number of obs = 361
Parms = 19
RMSE = 4.342678
"R-sq" = 0.5738
chi² = 632.47
P = 0.0000

Dependent variable
Productivity
Independent variable

	Coefficient	P-value	Coefficient	P-value
Total loan	0.0018664	0.463	0.0109645	0.388
Weighted interest rate	0.7389451	0.324	−3.872628	0.025
Farm area square	−0.000107	0.133	−0.0000661	0.501
Farm area local mow	0.0482158	0.217	0.0417356	0.36
Labor animal	0.423825	0.466	0.5651593	0.488
Productive animal	0.4415527	0.549	−0.5611113	0.531
Other income percent	0.040442	0.66	0.0011485	0.995
Dummy hired labor	4.055596	0.001	2.872348	0.147
Dummy subsidiary	−1.763553	0.23	−1.189474	0.521
Year 1930 h2	−2.51142	0.286	−3.981249	0.376
Year 1931 h1	22.82909	0	16.08599	0.157

(*continued*)

Table 6.19 (continued)

Dependent variable (Bold)	OLS Coefficient	P-value	3SLS Coefficient	P-value
Year 1932 h1	25.29787	0	22.24962	0.094
Hebei	1.634978	0.663	17.02094	0.076
Shanxi	−4.073426	0.476	12.2727	0.364
Guangxi	−34.94398	0	−18.15344	0.211
Guizhou	0.5189212	0.947	22.11491	0.176
Yunnan	−24.52106	0	−15.76009	0.377
Gansu	1.184048	0.896	54.7489	0.022
Qinghai	−15.82887	0.002	5.272599	0.691
Ningxia Suiyuan	−10.32131	0.087	4.472979	0.759

Number of obs = 364

F(20, 344) = 86.68
Prob > F = 0.0000

R-squared = 0.8013

Root MSE = 12.016

Number of obs = 361
Parms = 20
RMSE = 21.8244
"R-sq" = 0.3049
chi^2 = 531.43
P = 0.0000

considered. However, the OLS results do suggest that informal businesses ($p = 0.038$) do charge a higher rate, although we place less weight on this result.

The loan-interest rate results are interesting. Taking the positive loan amount to interest rate from Eq. 1 and the positive interest rate to loan amount in Eq. 2 suggests that farmers are interest rate takers. In other words, this result can only be consistent if the actual demand facing the farmer is highly inelastic so that a higher interest rate does not affect the borrowing decision. This is especially true for weddings and funerals where failure to provide an appropriate feast would be culturally unacceptable and cause 'loss of face'. On the lender's side the decision on what interest rate to charge is quantity dependent; the higher the loan, the higher the interest rate charged with some adjustment for risk and some differentiation by use.[8]

---

[8] The observations of total loan for indebted farmers are targeted to those farmers who were indebted. The sample size is small (observations = 361) compared with the original dataset.

6.16 Econometric Results: The Demand and Supply of Non-productive or Consumption Credit

Results for consumption loans are reported in Table 6.20. Again we find with strong significance that weddings and funerals are key drivers of non-productive loans. But we also find that larger consumption loans are positively related to productivity. This holds when productivity and credit are treated endogenously but does not hold with the OLS regression. We also find, again, that the demand curve is upward sloping and significant in the 3SLS model, but not significant in OLS. These we see as the same thing and conclude as before that the demand is almost perfectly, if not highly, inelastic so that farmers willingly accept a higher rate on larger loans. To the extent that there is negotiation between borrower and lender the story weakens. We find in the supply equation no statistical relationship between the

In the 3SLS credit demand function, interest rate (Coefficient = 14.53257, P-value = 0.038) and production (Coefficient = 2.888649, P-value = 0.068both positively related with loan demand. The increase in money supply will also increase money amount demanded, which implies generally speaking farmers are willing to borrow and borrow behavior is a common to be seen for Chinese farmers at that time; increase in production also increase loan demand. In my opinion, the higher production, the larger farm size will be, which will stimulate farmers' need for money used for productive purpose. We also can see among the indebted farmers, special events like weddings (Coefficient = 0.5694614, P-value = 0) and funerals (Coefficient = 0.2014051, P-value = 0) will increase their credit demand while birth of sons reversely decreases the credit demand. All time variables are statistically insignificant. All region variables are Hebei (Coefficient = −75.53818, P-value = 0.095), Liaoning (Coefficient = −124.3306, P-value = 0.06), Yunnan (Coefficient = 212.2831, P-value = 0.019) and Gansu (Coefficient = −249.4231, P-value = 0.02). However, Yunnan does not appear in the OLS credit demand function. Secondly, all basic independent variables and time variables are statistically insignificant in 3SLS credit supply function. Loan demand does not impact loan supply, which verifies the inference the farmers are price takers and the higher production, the lower loan supply will be. Important region variables are Hebei (Coefficient = 5.482501, P-value = 0.004), Shanxi (Coefficient = 5.841284, P-value = 0.042), Guizhou (Coefficient = 6.89809, P-value = 0.028), Gansu (Coefficient = 15.11412, P-value = 0) and Qinghai (Coefficient = 5.524437, P-value = 0.051). However, year1939h1 (OLS: coefficient = 3.906955, P-value = 0.026) appears in OLS credit demand function instead of 3SLS function. In 3SLS productivity function, Loan demand does not have relationship with production. However, the more loan supply, the lower production will be. The other basic independent variables are all statistically insignificant. The only valid time period is year1932h1 (coefficient = 22.24962, P-value = 0.094). Important region variables are Hebei (Coefficient = 17.02094, P-value = 0.076) and Gansu (Coefficient = 54.7489, P-value 0.022).

Table 6.20 Consumption credit

Dependent variable (Bold)	OLS Coefficient	P-value	3SLS Coefficient	P-value
Consumptive loan				
Independent variable				
Consumptive interest rate	−0.2344526	0.63	19.12231	0.002
Productivity	0.1657111	0.56	3.771076	0.026
Wedding	5.79E−01	0	0.4581681	0
Dowry	0.0889123	0.635	0.0130958	0.93
Birthday	0.9983116	0.394	1.20E + 00	0.822
Birth of son	−1.24867	0.326	−0.5505292	0.64
Funerals	3.04E−01	0	1.94E−01	0
Others				
Year 1929 h1	2.425001	0.455		
Year 1930 h1	17.487	0.712	−258.2811	0.018
Year 1930 h2	15.25516	0.62	40.89557	0.117
Year 1931 h1	65.32261	0.001	−276.7796	0.005
Year 1932 h1	21.34468	0.055	−336.8034	0.001
Hebei	−28.27701	0.295	179.4723	0.031
Shanxi	−57.98391	0.001	170.5514	0.007
Guangxi	−6.34989	0.743	331.1812	0.001
Guizhou			207.7009	0.001
Yunnan	1.482697	0.969	551.327	0
Gansu	−16.77768	0.118		
Qinghai	−52.23498	0.028	195.6869	0.006
Ningxia	−30.3705	0.043	211.5881	0.002
Suiyuan				
Number of obs = 381			Number of obs = 315	
$F(18, 362)$ =			Parms = 18	
Prob > F =			RMSE = 133.5065	
R-squared = 0.7089			"R-sq" = 0.3950	
Root MSE = 87.491			chi^2 = 711.89	
			P = 0.0000	
Dependent variable				
Consumptive interest rate				
Independent variable				
Consumptive loan	0.0005842	0.485	0.004384	0.196
Productivity	0.0878831	0.21	−0.109683	0.147
Yield risk	−3.185998	0.169	−2.171547	0.234

(*continued*)

Table 6.20 (continued)

Dependent variable (Bold)	OLS Coefficient	P-value	3SLS Coefficient	P-value
Relatives	0.2931582	0.277	−0.2079623	0.711
Friends	−0.5190018	0.496	−0.1950251	0.753
Informal business	0.9270542	0.031	0.4542665	0.42
Formal/semi-formal business	0.7886978	0.142	0.252894	0.771
All others	0.6294758	0.161	0.2862689	0.678
Year 1929 h1	3.295705	0.082		
Year 1930 h2	−0.8595934	0.133	−0.9440116	0.447
Year 1931 h1	−4.119966	0.013	0.9192048	0.81
Year 1932 h1	−3.885705	0.031	2.025213	0.64
Hebei	5.074939	0.013	5.177187	0.035
Shanxi	6.200795	0.005	4.799157	0.217
Guangxi	7.666323	0.004	1.045889	0.835
Guizhou	6.399851	0.003	5.096017	0.218
Yunnan	6.113548	0.001	−0.042744	0.994
Gansu	13.93146	0	14.3845	0
Qinghai	7.331143	0	4.313716	0.264
Ningxia	7.367471	0.003	4.346178	0.312

Number of obs = 382

F(20, 362) = 126.00
Prob > F = 0.0000
R-squared = 0.6691
Root MSE = 3.827

Number of obs = 315
Parms = 19
RMSE = 4.812568
"R-sq" = 0.5255
chi^2 = 518.41
P = 0.0000

Dependent variable
Productivity
Independent variable

Consumptive loan	0.0037018	0.243	0.0178198	0.301
Consumptive interest rate	0.7777542	0.302	−4.059061	0.018
Farm area square	−0.0000867	0.272	−0.0000506	0.635
Farm area local mow	0.0383796	0.376	0.028991	0.57
Labor animal	0.3087556	0.613	0.4524751	0.585
Productive animal	0.6321546	0.42	−0.400096	0.674
Other income percent	0.1076263	0.396	−0.0030882	0.99
Dummy hired labor	3.801197	0.005	2.061805	0.316
Dummy subsidiary	−1.978248	0.212	−0.8249456	0.679
Year 1930 h1	−29.38809	0	52.89896	0.04
Year 1930 h2	−0.8802852	0.743	−2.895373	0.604

(*continued*)

Table 6.20 (continued)

Dependent variable (Bold)	OLS Coefficient	P-value	3SLS Coefficient	P-value
Year 1931 h1	−3.543324	0.422	72.17854	0
Year 1932 h1	−0.3640374	0.917	79.37668	0
Hebei	27.61863	0	−37.5833	0.053
Shanxi	21.78675	0	−44.35667	0.004
Guangxi	−7.475689	0.071	−77.4175	0
Guizhou	23.08524	0	−40.05429	0.004
Yunnan			−76.22105	0
Gansu	26.99077	0		
Qinghai	10.74549	0.011	−49.96959	0.001
Ningxia	14.93683	0	−50.81258	0
Number of obs = 318			Number of obs = 315	
F(20, 298) = 80.64			Parms = 20	
Prob > F = 0.0000			RMSE = 23.74518	
R-squared = 0.7971			"R-sq" = 0.1751	
Root MSE = 12.181			chi^2 = 413.88	
			P = 0.0000	

weighted average rate of interest charged and the loan amount ($p = 0.19$), and no significance in the OLS regression either. Nor do we find price discrimination amongst the various suppliers with none of them in 3SLS or OLS charging interest rates that statistically differ from the average.

When isolating consumption loans in this way it comes to mind that when a loan request for a wedding or a funeral is made, there is an inherent rate charged by all suppliers that is simply accepted by the borrowers. Unfortunately this explanation is inadequate since it does a poor job of explaining the demand-supply paradox for consumption loans. Recall that the same evaluation for total indebtedness supports the view of demand inelasticity without paradox. Another explanation, which we can only conjecture for as we have not seen this discussed in the contemporaneous literature of the time, is that there was in fact an excess supply of credit and farmers actually had bargaining power. The bargaining power could arise from social pressure and peer effects as well as reciprocity in the sense of today's lender is tomorrow's borrower. Social pressure would frown upon usury and this might place a cap on the interest rates charged. If a farmer could approach multiple lenders with excess credit they may have to compete at rates below the social maximum. Meanwhile, a farmer would not necessarily balk at the idea of paying a higher interest rate for a higher loan, for when the day comes that they become a lender (or had been in the past) they too would likely require the same.

Also interesting is the finding that neither productivity nor yield risk has a statistical impact (although both come with the expected negative sign) which suggests that at least from the supply side lenders do not put as much weight on these factors, likely because the special expenditure is unrelated to production and is deemed as a social requirement of village life. In the productivity equation we find that there is no relationship between special expenditure and productivity, which gives credence to the argument that special expenditure and production expenditure are not substitutes. This interesting results bolsters that argument that when regional differences and time frames are accounted for there is separability between consumption and production, at least when it comes to agricultural credit. It may be true that farmers have to give up other consumption items such as health or education, or even food, to repay the loans but do not sacrifice production along the way.

This does not hold true for the interest rates charged however. There is a negative relationship between interest rates and productivity and this is significant in the 3SLS equation ($p = 0.018$) but not the OLS ($p = 0.302$). From an economic point of view farmers may consider the loan principal, a source of liquidity, as being fungible. The rate of interest charged however is a necessary expense of celebrating the wedding or funeral, and the higher this rate the more the farmer has to give up in terms of inputs to the production process.[9]

---

[9] The sample size is still 315. Targeted survey takers are farmers who borrowed for consumption purposes. The results of the 3SLS credit demand function are similar to Table 6.20. Total Loan for indebted farmers with Time and Region Variables, interest rate (Coefficient = 19.12231, P-value = 0.002) and productivity (Coefficient = 3.771076, P-value = 0.026) both positively related to loan demand. That is to say, similar to Total Loan Version, loan demand increases with loan supply; loan demand also increases with productivity. We can also see among the indebted farmers, special events like weddings (Coefficient = 0.4581681, P-value = 0) and funerals (Coefficient = 0.1939465, P-value = 0) will increase their credit demand while the birth of a son reversely decreases the credit demand. Important time periods are year1930h1 (Coefficient = −258.2811, P-value = 0.018), year1931h1 (Coefficient = −276.7796, P-value = 0.005) and year1932h1 (Coefficient = −336.8034, P-value = 0.001). Important region variables are Hebei (Coefficient = 179.4723, P-value = 0.031), Shanxi (Coefficient = 170.5514, P-value = 0,007), Guangxi (Coefficient = 331.1812, P-value 0.001), Guizhou (Coefficient = 207.7009,

6.17 Results Analysis: Production Loan for Indebted Farmers with Time and Region Variables

The final investigation is on production loans, of which there are only 58 observations for the unrestricted model, hardly enough to be conclusive. Results are shown in Table 6.21. Here we find a negative relationship between interest rates and loan amounts, as would be expected in conventional credit theory. This holds in both the 3SLS ($p = 0.053$) and OLS ($p = 0.099$) models. We also find a positive relationship between productivity and loan amount ($p = 0.003$) suggesting that, as previously found, more productive farms tend to borrow more for production purposes. This is not symmetric though, since we do not find in the productivity equation that, unlike consumption loans, higher interest rates mean lower productivity. This suggest that as far as production is concerned the value of the input investment at least equals, if not exceeds, the cost of borrowing. (We also find, but with no specific interpretation, that there is a positive relationship between wedding ($p = 0.011$) and birth-of-son ($p = 0.057$) and production loans. This may be evidence of fungibility between production loans and special expenditure, but the granularity of the data does not support such a conclusion with any degree of comfort. It is safer to consider these as statistical artifacts.)

P-value = 0.001), Yunnan (Coefficient = 551.327, P-value = 0), Qinghai (Coefficient = 195.6869, P-value 0.006), and Ningxia (Coefficient = 211.5881, P-value 0.002). Guizhou province appears in the 3SLS credit demand function not in the OLS function while time variable year1929h1 appears in the OLS not the 3SLS. Similarly, in the credit supply function, loan demand and production cannot affect loan supply. All basic independent variables and time variables are statistically insignificant. The only two ones are region variables Hebei (Coefficient = 5.177187, P-value) and Gansu (Coefficient = −4.059061, P-value = 0.018). In the 3SLS productivity function, productivity has no relationship with loan demand while it has a negative relationship with loan supply, which verifies that Chinese farmers are price takers.

The other basic independent variables are all statistically insignificant. Important time variables are year1930h1 (Coefficient = 52.89896, P-value = 0.04), year1931h1 (Coefficient = 72.37668, P-value = 0), and year1932h1 (Coefficient = 79.37669, P-value = 0). Important region variables are Hebei (Coefficient = −37.5833, P-value = 0.053), Shanxi (Coefficient = −44.35667, P-value = 0.004), Guangxi (Coefficient = −77.4175, P-value = 0), Guizhou (Coefficient = −40.05429, P-value = 0.004), Yunnan (Coefficient = −76.22105, P-value = 0), Qinghai (Coefficient = −49.96959, P-value = 0.001), and Ningxia (Coefficient = −50.81258, P-value = 0). Among these Yunnan only appears in the 3SLS productivity function not the OLS equation.

Table 6.21 Productive loan for indebted farmers with time and region variables

Dependent variable (Bold)	OLS		3SLS	
	Coefficient	P-value	Coefficient	P-value
Productive loan				
Independent variable				
Productive interest rate	−13.81784	0.099	−55.33578	0.053
Productivity	0.4301687	0.694	5.440612	0.003
Wedding	2.23E−01	0	0.130652	0.011
Dowry	0.0906299	0.639	−0.0036724	0.988
Birthday	0		0.00E+00	
Birth of son	1.175789	0	1.049963	0.057
Funerals	2.90E−01	0.002	1.59E−01	0.224
Others				
Year 1929 h1	30.2709	0.218		
Year 1930 h1	−55.07195	0.668		
Year 1930 h2	0.7134642	0.985	46.6263	0.338
Year 1931 h1	11.21739	0.916	−79.99474	0.371
Year 1931 h2				
Year 1932 h1	35.43054	0.525	−47.79411	0.68
Hebei	75.14033	0.423	81.36491	0.446
Shanxi	58.75692	0.456	106.869	0.48
Guangxi	46.10739	0.54	246.2551	0.116
Guizhou	−7.706453	0.88	−132.4513	0.339
Yunnan	−9.285127	0.785	239.4167	0.105
Gansu			103.3964	0.651
Qinghai	38.42489	0.673	244.8395	0.159
Ningxia	−20.70702	0.548	32.9698	0.807
Number of obs = 73			Number of obs = 58	
$F(17, 55)$ =			Parms = 17	
Prob > F =			RMSE = 85.8562	
R-squared = 0.7475			"R-sq" = 0.5811	
Root MSE = 69.325			chi^2 = 163.24	
			P = 0.0000	
Dependent variable				
Productive interest rate				
Independent variable				
Productive loan	−0.0017912	0.086	−0.0034321	0.053
Productivity	0.0108236	0.332	0.0387461	0.064
Yield risk	−0.5487945	0.576	0.4501207	0.644
Relatives	−0.1924474	0.595	−0.3930662	0.512

(*continued*)

Table 6.21 (continued)

Dependent variable (Bold)	OLS Coefficient	P-value	3SLS Coefficient	P-value
Friends	0.5742167	0.168	0.6975957	0.129
Informal business	0.1524437	0.51	0.0507588	0.868
Formal/semi-formal business	0.1702209	0.532	−0.0465682	0.923
All others	0.1543696	0.595	−0.0490804	0.929
Year 1929 h1	2.50171	0.004		
Year 1930 h2	−1.062789	0.001	−0.3346021	0.505
Year 1931 h1	−2.497807	0	−2.336454	0.003
Year 1932 h1	−2.872495	0.003	−2.511676	0.05
Hebei	4.081876	0	2.623176	0.007
Shanxi	5.671531	0	3.984983	0.002
Guangxi	5.433001	0	4.598918	0.003
Guizhou	3.29561	0.014	1.30846	0.432
Yunnan	5.607441	0	4.121536	0.009
Gansu	7.268536	0	5.078707	0.001
Qinghai	6.216929	0	5.285053	0
Ningxia	4.133177	0.002	2.494583	0.078

Number of obs = 73
$F(19, 53)$ =
Prob > F =

R-squared = 0.9146
Root MSE = 0.83746

Number of obs = 58
Parms = 19
RMSE = 0.7673681

"R-sq" = 0.8891
chi^2 = 605.81
P = 0.0000

Dependent variable
Productivity
Independent variable

Productivity loan	−0.0285909	0.236	0.0057884	0.859
Productive interest rate	0.3019306	0.841	3.575461	0.409
Farm area squared	−0.0002404	0.052	−0.0001679	0.204
Farm area local mou	0.1741037	0.042	0.1299531	0.169
Labor animal	1.332393	0.572	0.70695	0.733
Productive animal	−1.57288	0.337	−0.6992099	0.67
Other income percentage	−0.1469099	0.352	−0.1079454	0.568
Dummy hired labor	5.324517	0.057	4.310013	0.096
Dummy subsidiary	−4.55999	0.273	−4.224089	0.315
Year 1930 h1	32.72912	0.124		
Year 1930 h2	−10.97899	0.153	−9.972679	0.059
Year 1931 h1	40.85605	0.003	13.48962	0.221
Year 1932 h1	34.21577	0.003	7.076156	0.638

(*continued*)

Table 6.21 (continued)

Dependent variable (Bold)	OLS		3SLS	
	Coefficient	P-value	Coefficient	P-value
Hebei	−16.65698	0.181	4.754758	0.788
Shanxi	−13.20614	0.024	5.403447	0.824
Guangxi	−63.21222	0	−39.36868	0.079
Guizhou	17.44856	0.018	41.34098	0.041
Yunnan	−24.23681	0.026	−10.37198	0.669
Gansu			12.36935	0.708
Qinghai	−39.7622	0	−23.05063	0.341
Ningxia	−21.55644	0.003	2.239625	0.907
Suiyuan				
Number of obs = 58			Number of obs = 58	
F(19, 38) =			Parms = 20	
Prob > F =			RMSE = 8.616028	
R-squared = 0.8987			"R-sq" = 0.8829	
Root MSE = 9.8973			chi^2 = 515.13	
			P = 0.0000	

On the supply side we find the relationship between loan amount and interest rates to be negative (p = 0.053). This contrasts with previous results that show a positive relationship between the loan amount and interest rates. The economic explanation for this result is that when it comes to production loans farmers have considerable market power in negotiating favorable terms for higher loan amounts. It is possible that lenders with excess cash would prefer to make a smaller number of higher-valued loans to reduce transactions, regularizing, and collection costs. But with only 58 observations we shouldn't over interpret. Indeed, this argument is weakened by the finding that higher productivity farms pay a higher interest rate (p = 0.064), even though there is no statistical support in the productivity regression for any relationship between interest rates and productivity (p = 0.409), let alone the loan amount and productivity (p = 0.0859).[10]

---

[10] The sample size is only 58. Targeted survey takers are farmers who borrowed for productive purposes. In this case, the higher the supply of money (Coefficient of interest rate = −55.33578, P-value = 0.053), the less demand for productive purposes. On the other hand, the higher productivity is (Coefficient = 5.440612, P-value = 0.003), the greater the demand for productive loan. Farm size and efficiency might play a role in this part. Wedding (Coefficient = 0.130652, P-value = 0.011) and Birth of Son (Coefficient = 1.049963, P-value = 0.057) are significant special expenditures. There is no valid time and region vari-

6.18 Discussion on Credit Demand and Supply

There is much anecdotal evidence about credit demand and supply in the lead up to the formalization of credit cooperatives and formal agricultural banking during the Republican era, but what is missing is a thorough examinations of the economic characteristics of credit supply and demand. The conventional wisdom was that farmers *en masse* had an excess demand for credit and were forced in desperation to borrow from usurers of one sort or another at exorbitant rates. Our findings dispel some of these notions.

The discovery of John Lossing Buck's credit data in 2000 provides the first opportunity to assess credit demand and supply. Over 4000 records were recovered and of these over 3000 had actual (useable) data on agricultural credit including production and non-production loan amount interest rates, productivity, risk, and special expenditure. From these we constructed four models, the first to investigate the characteristics of those that borrowed versus those that did not, and then from the sub-sample of those that borrowed the demand and supply relationships between total borrowing, borrowing for consumption (special expenditure), and borrowing for production. Although we present OLS results, we focus primarily on 3SLS results on the premise that supply, demand, and productivity are endogenously related.

able in the credit demand function. In the credit supply function, loan demand (coefficient = −0.0034321, P-value = 0.053) has a slightly negative impact on loan supply and the higher productivity (coefficient = 0.0387461, P-value = 0.064), the more loan supply will be. It makes sense because productivity means higher income and higher ability to provide loans. Important time variables are year1931h1 (Coefficient = −2.336454, P-value = 0.003) and year1932h1 (Coefficient = −2.511676, P-value = 0.05). Important region variables are Hebei (Coefficient = 2.623176, P-value = 0.007), Shanxi (Coefficient = 3.984983, P-value = 0.002), Guangxi (Coefficient = 4.598918, P-value = 0.003), Yunnan (Coefficient = 4.121536, P-value = 0.009), Gansu (Coefficient = 5.078707, P-value = 0.001), Qinghai (Coefficient = 5.285053, P-value = 0), and Ningxia (Coefficient = 2.494584, P-value = 0.078). In the 3SLS production function, productivity does not have a relationship with loan demand as well as supply which implies income and savings may first be used for productive purposes which ensures productivity. The sample size is too small to make the results convincing.

Among basic independent variables, the only valid one is If has hired labor (Coefficient = 4.310013, P-value = 0.096). The only important time period is year1930h2 (Coefficient = −9.972679, P-value = 0.059). Important region variables are Guangxi (Coefficient = −39.36868, P-value = 0.079) and Guizhou (Coefficient = 41.34098, P-value = 0.041).

Unfortunately, not all data from Buck were retrieved and for some variables we thought important there was no consistency in collection. Data such as farm size, for example, were not necessarily collected for all farms that had credit, and credit was not collected for all farms for which farm size was collected. This involved some sacrifices for statistical efficiency. When examining all loans we had only 361, 315, and 52 farms for all loans, consumption loans, and production loans respectively. This we understand is inadequate and we do our best not to oversell the results, and indeed provide the actual summary tables published by Buck in *Land Utilization in China* to provide requisite balance.

Nonetheless, there are some elements of credit demand and supply that we feel are robust and important. First, against the narrative that special expenditure leads to heightened credit use, we find no evidence that this is either necessary or sufficient. When using special expenditure in a regression equation with 1 for a borrower of any type of loan, and 0 for non-borrowers, none comes up significantly to explain which farmers borrow versus those that do not. Observing a farmer with a loan does not imply special expenditure, nor does an observation of a special expenditure imply that farmers are driven to debt. Of course we are being very general for we do not observe farms that wanted credit for a special expenditure but were not granted it. However, for the subsample that borrowed for consumption purposes, the evidence is strong that these loans were largely driven by special expenditures on weddings and funerals.

A second result that we believe to be important we draw from the more reliable second regression on total indebtedness. There we find a very interesting dynamic between supply and demand. We believe that the demand for credit is nearly, if not perfectly, inelastic, meaning that farmers are price takers at any loan amount. The lender exploits this inelasticity by increasing the interest rate as the loan demand increases, as a local monopolist might do. We find the same for consumption loans and offer some strong statistical evidence that the reasons that farmers borrow for non-productive use is in part to cover special expenditure on weddings and funerals. We have said before that this type of expenditure was very much a part of Chinese culture and status seeking as well for saving face. These results are very much in line with some of the discussions in the Chinese literature at the time.

Results for production loans are far less reliable, but interestingly show some degree of demand elasticity and negative slope. This is an appealing result, with the direction of causality going from higher interest rates to lower amounts borrowed. But on the supply side we also find a negative relationship in the causal direction of a large loan leads to a lower interest rate. If the observed interest rates were an autarky result we would expect that the supply result would be positive as found for consumption and total indebtedness. The results for production credit are unconvincing one way or another since by construction of the 3SLS structure, failure to explain one result means that all results are unreliable, even if at first glance they make economic sense.

CHAPTER 7

The China International Famine Relief Commission

7.1 Introduction

In Chap. 5 we discussed the promulgation of law in 1915 that brought about the Agricultural and Industrial Bank as a mechanism to direct credit to agriculture, and also lay the foundation for agricultural cooperation in credit. By all accounts, by 1921 or 1922 the Agricultural and Industrial Banks had faltered in their mission and there is little known record of material, large-scale, agricultural activity or successful and sustainable cooperatives. There were other attempts at cooperation throughout China during the early years of the Republican era which we discuss presently, but by all indications, at least around 1914–15, the Chinese government was considering the problem of how to direct credit to agriculture.

1921 saw the beginning of a different effort and one which has no connection to the Agricultural and Industrial Banks. The China International Famine Relief Commission was then dealing with famine across China, and as part of its reconstruction efforts started supporting the idea of cooperative credit. It was from these initiatives that much of the efforts towards cooperative credit in the Republican era can be credited. This chapter steps through the developments of cooperative credit in Germany and how these relate to cooperative credit in China, and the role that the China International Famine Relief Commission played in its development.

7.2 The Raiffeisen Model for Rural Credit

As mentioned, in the Republican era, and indeed even in the late Qing there was interest in the German Raiffeisen approach to agricultural credit. Conditions in China in the Qing dynasty and throughout the Republican era were in many dimensions worse than those that prevailed in Germany at the turn of the nineteenth century. German farmers had just come out of the era of serfdom and feudalism and were able to acquire farmland. However, emerging from an era in which credit was provided to landowners, there was no institutional structure for providing farm credit to smallholder farms.[1] With an expanding demand for credit in the early part of the nineteenth century, and no formal market to meet these needs, German farmers faced credit conditions that were exploitive and economically devastating. To remain operational farmers had little choice but to borrow from informal money sources or obtain store credit, failing at which little was left but to go out of business. Interest rates were usurious and ruinous, often exceeding 100% per year. Storekeepers, with localized monopoly power and a ready source of liquidity, would supply seed and fertilizer on credit and with no choice about quality or price. In bad years, when either the market or weather failed, the credit relationship became one of servitude as security became exhausted. If land was worth purchasing it would be assigned to the creditor by contract or public sale.

This was particularly acute in 1846–47 with famine widespread throughout Germany. Frederick William Raiffeisen, at age approximate 29, was sympathetic to farmers' plight and gathered sufficient funds for a cooperative bakery where peasants could purchase bread at about half the shopkeepers' prices. This was followed by a cattle-purchasing society and in 1849 the first cooperative loan bank, or local mutual credit bank, was formed. In the absence of personal security the cooperative offered a different structure of self-help and group guarantees with unlimited liability for indebtedness of all members of the society. No entrance fee or share obligation was required, unless it was legally obliged. The credit societies could be developed as a loan operation or as a supply cooperative which purchased inputs at lower cost and distributed them to members on credit. Loans could not be speculative and were not fungible, in the sense that they must be used for the intended purpose. Repayment was flexible to

---

[1] Turvey, Calum G. (2015). Historical Developments in Agricultural Finance. Mimeo, Dyson School of Applied Economics and Management, Cornell University.

meet the planting and harvest sequence of agriculture or the term of use if a productive asset.

The Raiffeisen rural banks could be of any size and made up of any mix of rich and poor farmers. The capital in the bank was obtained from deposits by members who would receive some interest in return. However, since credit demand was usually restricted to multiples of savings on deposit, alternative mechanisms of obtaining loan funds were required. To serve this purpose, Raiffeisen formed the Agricultural Central Loan Bank for Germany as a joint-stock company which spanned a network of 5000 local rural banks (in 1914).

In parallel, Chinese farmers faced an entirely new political and economic system following the revolution and fall of the Qing dynasty in 1911. While certain freedoms were promised farmers in the new Republic, farmers faced nothing but tumult for the next 37 years. Instead of unification, the demise of the Manchus resulted in the disbandment of provincial military forces. Governors under the Qing were also high-ranking military men with mixed loyalties to the New China. In many instances the provincial forces under their command were easily persuaded to switch loyalty away from the Peking government to the provincial governors who then governed as warlords. Elsewhere, tens of thousands of troops were demobilized and with no pension then formed bandit gangs who would prey upon farming communities. Indeed on banditry John Lossing Buck wrote to *China Weekly Review* in 1929 that upon meeting farmers in a tea house to discuss credit cooperatives a farmer said *"if any financial help is rendered to us now, it would only bring more harm than good, for our greatest distress and sorrow is no other than the bandits. We can neither work in the daytime or rest at night…well-to-do families have taken refuge in the city. Those who are poor…hurry away and hide with their children wet and cold, in the bushes and streams of the mountainside in spite of the mosquitos and snakes… many deaths have occurred. We do not grieve over the dead, for it is better to die of sickness than to be killed by bandits…we would rather die than suffer"*.[2]

The relation between farm life and policy throughout the Republican era was now coming to the fore in Nanjing. Harry Paxton Howard's oratory places the challenges in vivid context:[3]

---

[2] CWR v47 P73. John L. Buck.
[3] April 20 1929 P324–328 The Problem of China's Unification by Harry Paxton Howard.

> The peasantry are the backbone of the Chinese people. The cultivators of the soil are the greatest productive elements of the country. And it is they who are the worst sufferers from war when it invades their districts. The(y) have everything to gain from peace,-if it is a peace based upon enlightened policy and not merely on bayonets...A policy devoted to the interests of the peasantry is not mere altruism. Every thought of altruism may be cast to the winds (as it already appears to have been by many leaders unfortunately), and the stubborn and undeniable fact remains that a policy in the interest of the cultivators is the soundest and most intelligent policy that can be pursued...A class of cultivars feeling themselves the master of their own soil and free to enjoy the fruits of their labor is a sound basis for political and social stability. A class driven to desperation by rent, taxes and usury is a basis for an impoverished economy and perpetual discontent...A peasant policy is not a simple thing to be worked out particularly in the widely varying conditions throughout China. But if the essential aim is clarified the details become less complex. This aim must be devoted to the welfare of the actual cultivators of the soil. Whether owners, tenants or farm laborers, they must be dealt with as cultivators, – if they are. The cultivator feeds everyone else, whatever may be the form of land tenure...If the agrarian policy be taken as basic, a policy may be founded upon their fundamental necessities. The primary need is freedom from pillage – this making them a basic factor for peace. Beyond this there is required a policy which will free cultivation from taxation. Taxes should rest upon non-productive ownership rather than upon productive cultivation. The ratio should be according to the value of the land, not according to the value of its product...With the elimination of crushing rents and taxes on cultivators, comes the possibility of a positive program. Such a program has already been projected by the Kuomintang, but its realization still belongs for the most part to the future. The most essential features would appear to be (1) cheap credit, best of all in the form of co-operative credit unions; (a start on this has already been made.) (2) Cheaper goods, which necessitates the elimination of the various business and transit taxes which weigh so heavily upon commerce here, and could be furthermore assured by the formation of co-operative consumers' societies; (3) better prices for products, which could best be gained by cooperative marketing; (4) improved communications, which will make exchange easier and facilitate the production of surplus (but only if the cultivator can see himself receiving the benefit of this surplus); (5) better seeds, new crops, other technical improvements...

The reality, it appears, is that by the time of the Northern Expedition, Chiang Kai-shek realized the indisputable linkage between farming conditions and bandit, warlord, and communist insurgency. Farm policy, long ignored but for famine relief, was now viewed as a matter of national defense. It was in this era, and under these circumstances, that the push for agricultural cooperation took hold as a matter of policy.

7.3 Early Attempts at Cooperative Societies

Prior to the formation of the Nanjing government following the death of Sun Yat-sen in 1926 there were many attempts to form cooperatives.[4] The first push towards cooperation was penned by a journalist Xu Cang-shui in 1916 who wrote on consumers' cooperatives in department stores and a discourse on people's banks. The first consumer societies were formed in 1918 at Peking National University. By 1922 consumer societies such as the Shantou Rice Guild Consumers' Society, the Anyuan Miners Consumers' Society, and the Shanghai Employees' Cooperative Stores abounded. Other consumer cooperatives included the Shizhong Cooperative Book Store in Wuchang, and the First Cooperative Store in Ningbo in 1923, followed by the Shanghai Cooperative Consumer's Society in 1926.

Xue Xian-zhou was a German-trained economist at Futan University who was introduced to the Raiffeisen system during his studies, and consequently introduced the study of cooperatives into lectures. On October 22, 1919 Xue formed the Shanghai Peoples Cooperative Savings Bank at Futan University. This was the first cooperative savings bank in China. With its success Xue and his students promoted cooperation through the *People's Weekly*, a popular magazine that discussed the strengths and pitfalls of cooperatives. With this publication the cooperative movement began to expand throughout Shanghai, and expanded into Jiangsu, Zhejiang, and Hunan.

The first independent agricultural cooperative was the Chengdu Farmers' and Workers' Cooperative Savings Society formed in August 1921.[5] This cooperative was formed to further develop cooperative enterprises amongst farmers and workers, and was capitalized with a $5 per share, paid in three installments. Early attempts at building producer cooperatives were not so successful. The Datong Cooperative in Hunan,

---

[4] Yang, H.K. (1937). The Cooperative Movement in China. Central Bank of China Bulletin 3(2): 110–125.

[5] We have inserted the word 'independent' here since we know that various attempts at developing credit societies aligned with the Agricultural and Industrial Bank occurred around 1915.

the Peasants' Cooperative Society in *Shiosan*, and the Changsha Penmakers' Society were all ultimately closed down under laws that made it illegal or unlawful to organize workers' organizations.

The biggest push to cooperation before the efforts of the Kuomintang (KMT) in 1928 was through the China International Famine Relief Commission in 1921. The China International Famine Relief Commission was a philanthropic organization funded largely by overseas Chinese and Western philanthropists to provide famine relief as needed. In its relief efforts it began to investigate rural economic activities and discovered that the largest constraint to productivity and famine relief was a consequence of credit constraints. In 1922 the China International Famine Relief Commission called a commission to draft regulations for Rural Cooperative Credit Societies. The regulations, based on the principal of unlimited liability, were drafted by J.B. Taylor, a Briton, who was chairman of the China International Famine Relief Commission as well as Dean Reisner and John L. Buck from the University of Nanjing. Once approved, funds were released from the China International Famine Relief Commission for loans to societies formed by personnel of the committees as well as universities, including the University of Nanjing.[6]

7.4 THE CHINA INTERNATIONAL FAMINE RELIEF COMMISSION

The role that the China International Famine Relief Commission played in the development of agricultural credit cooperatives cannot be understated. In fact the China International Famine Relief Commission played a crucial role in the development and expansion of cooperatives throughout China, and was as influential as the KMT military's activities were following the Northern Expedition. Ultimately the activities of the China International Famine Relief Commission and the military's reclamation efforts were drawn into *Nong Ben Ju* (the Farm Credit Bureau) to form the cooperative arm of the Agricultural Credit Administration in 1936.

In 1921/22 drought and famine once again doomed the rural population of Henan, Shansi, Shandong, Shaanxi, and Chihli taking nearly

---

[6] Buck, J.L. (1973). Development of Agricultural Economics at the University of Nanjing, China 1926–1946. Cornell International Agricultural Development Bulletin 25, September 1973. Cornell University.

500,000 lives.[7] As horrendous as this sounds it was far less severe than the famine of 1876–79 which took an estimated 9.5 million lives and with 19.9 million of a total population of 49.9 million requiring some form of relief. This relief was taken up in large part by foreign missionaries and foreign donations in conjunction with whatever resources the cash-strapped Manchu government could muster. As famine relief took structure, subsequent famines in 1907, 1910–11, and 1911–12 saw the development and maturing of relief efforts. In addition, China's infrastructure took shape with the building of 6000 miles of railway (Mallory).[8] Earlier experiences with famine convinced relief agencies that simply providing money was not going to resolve the problem. First, injecting money into an income-depleted economy under famine conditions simply drove prices up as hoarders seeing desperation would release foodstuffs to the highest bidder. Second, in many famines the issue was not lack of abundance, but lack of access to food. While the economics behind famines have been explored in the modern era by notable economists, at the turn of the twentieth century the realization that famine was preventable was a revelation.[9] Sen (1981), for example, has made the case that food availability decline is not a satisfactory explanation for starvation and is not so much about there *not being* enough food to eat but a matter of *not having* enough food to eat.

Sen's modern notion of entitlement is very similar to Mallory's (1926) notion of 'margin of livelihood'.[10] In Mallory's study of famine in China he focused largely on the failure of economic systems that resulted in reduced supply and related price effects. Market failure of one sort or another could be attributed to overcrowding, surplus labor, lack of credit, usury, antiquated agricultural methods, depletion of soil fertility, intensive

---

[7] Peking United International Famine Relief Committee (1922) "The North China Famine of 1920–1921, with Special reference to the West Chihli Area" Commercial Press Works Ltd., Peking.

[8] Mallory, W. H. (1931). Rural Coöperative Credit in China. *The Quarterly Journal of Economics*, 484–498.

[9] Lin, J. Y., and D.T. Yang, (2000). Food availability, entitlements and the Chinese famine of 1959–61. *The Economic Journal*, 110(460), 136–158.

Ravallion, M. (1997). Famines and economics. *Journal of Economic Literature*, 35(3), 1205–1242.

Sen, A. (1981). Ingredients of famine analysis: availability and entitlements. The quarterly journal of economics, 96(3), 433–464.

[10] Mallory (1931) pages, 484–498.

cultivation, depletion of forests, poor communications, and inefficient transportation methods. But he also focused on social, political, and natural causes of famine, and argued that the solution to famine is also grounded in economic reforms to address specific market failures. In relation to the 1876–79 famine, the underlying source of the famine was failure of rains, but the cause of the famine was communication. As a result of this failure some 13 million perished from starvation, disease, and violence. With over 300,000 square miles affected, it took months for word to reach government authorities who were in a position to help. In addition, transport to afflicted regions was hampered by lack of transportation, despite the fact that massive amounts of relief were shipped to and stored at Tianjin. In November 1877, more than a year after the onset of the famine, Mallory cites the Chairman of the Foreign Relief Committee in Tianjin on the tragedy of having food available but not being able to deliver it: "*The Bund was piled mountain high with grain, the Government storehouses were full, all the boats were impressed for the conveyance of supplies towards Shansi and the Hochien districts in Chihli. Carts and wagons were all taken up and the cumbersome machinery of the Chinese government was strained to the utmost…the most frightful disorder reigned supreme along the route to Shansi (with) officials and traders all intent on getting their convoys over the pass…the track was completely worn out, and until a new one was made a dead block ensued. Camels, oxen, mules and donkeys were hurried along in wildest confusion, and so many perished or were killed by the desperate people in the hills, for the sake of their flesh…the way was marked by the carcasses or skeletons of men and beasts…No idea of employing the starving people in making a new or, improving the old road ever presented itself to the authorities…*".[11]

---

[11] Mallory (1926) *Op Cit.*, pages 229–30.

Mallory (citing J.E. Baker, Adviser to the Chinese Ministry of Communications) provides the food arithmetic of transporting grain on foot to a distant market. The assumption is that a typical man can carry 133 lbs (100 catties) on his back covering a distance of some 17 km/day (32.7 li). But for each day he requires minimally 2 catties of food, and assuming he brings along his family of four each requiring 1 catty/day for a total of 6 catties, or about 8 lbs of food per day, then several catties will have to be exchanged for other items (salt, food, clothes), amounting to 1.5 catties/day for a total of 7.5 catties or about 10 lbs/day total. Thus in about 13 days the entire stock being transported would be consumed with the maximum distance being covered in 6.5 days (in either direction), meaning that if the delivery market is greater than about 111 km distance the cost of transportation alone will consume the entirety of that which is being transported. Under famine conditions this would be even more precarious a trip since an addition to the drudgery of the hike would be roving bandits

In the swirl of these observations relief practices changed dramatically. Following the 1876–79 famine the American Red Cross utilized its famine relief funds in Shandong and Shanxi to pay able-bodied famine victims to construct roadways from railway lines to interior depots. The missionary organizations followed suit. The benefit was that by purchasing and transporting grain and foodstuffs from surplus granaries, the relief agencies could use that food to build the necessary infrastructure, resolving both of the problems discussed above.

In August of 1921, the Peking United International Relief Committee (PUIRC), which had administered and organized many of the famine relief efforts in China's North joined with the North China International Society of Famine Relief, the Chinese Foreign Famine Relief Committee, the Shandong International Relief Committee, the Shanxi International Famine Relief Committee, the Joint Council of the Hankou Famine Relief Committee, and the Hunan Chinese Foreign Famine Relief Committee to form a national trust fund for famine relief using excess donor funds.[12] The new organization was named the China International Famine Relief Commission. In part, the China International Famine Relief Commission saw its role as supplanting the government's efforts which in the post-revolutionary warlord era was in no position to deal with national emergencies. The China International Famine Relief Commission saw it role as not only being effectual in the direct delivery of famine relief but also in carrying out national programs on conservancy, including flood control, dyke construction, agricultural resource management, forestry management, and so on.

In 1922 the Commission commissioned a study by J.B. Tayler, a professor at Yanjing University (Qing Hua University) who prepared the final report with Carroll B. Malone at Qing Hua University.[13] The Commission's

and famine sufferers seeking out food, increasing the costs of transportation and reducing the likelihood that food would be delivered from remote surplus locations to famine stricken areas; the farmer would be as well off selling into the local surplus market at a fraction of the price offered in the famine area. The point being made is that even in the presence of abundance, the failure to develop infrastructure can exacerbate famine conditions. Even the presence of a formal graded pathway from remote regions that could support wheelbarrows or carts could reduce the opportunity costs, with greater volume being delivered over longer distances, in a shorter time period.

[12] Nathan, A.J. (1965) The History of the China International Famine Relief Commission: East Asian Research Center, Harvard University, Harvard University Press, Cambridge Mass.

[13] Malone, C. B. (1923). Study of Chinese Rural Economy, The. Chinese Soc. & Pol. Sci. Rev., 7, 88.

Committee on Credit and Economic Improvement sent requests to 22 educational institutions and ultimately compiled a team of 61 students from nine different universities to conduct field surveys in 1922. The objective of field surveys was to determine what the China International Famine Relief Commission should do to ameliorate the economic conditions under which "*so many of the people in the country live, and which are a very important contributing factor to the suffering due to famine, and to carry out ameliorative measures…(with the intent to)…improve their economic status and to broaden their basis of livelihood beyond entire dependence on agriculture, and to provide systems of credit for farmers which will enable them to secure loans at reasonable rates of interest*".[14] The investigation covered 240 different villages predominantly in Chihli with a number in Jiangsu, Shandong, Anhui, and Zhejiang.[15] The results reported by Malone and the *Ning Hua* University team in Chihli province were dire. Malone suspected that many farmers would underestimate income and assets for fear of provincial taxation, but so desperate were conditions that Malone remarked: "*Yet the sad part of it all is that while the individual figures are not reliable, the general impression is true. They are a people who live so near to the margin of existence that even in good years they are eating elm bark and gathering willow leaves for their winter rations. While this food may inure them to famine conditions and diet when the time comes and they have nothing else, their low standard of living and lack of any margin for saving and improvement precluded the possibility of progress. We cannot believe that they really do live on such low standard as the figures show, but neither can we understand how they could live on an income twice or even five times as large as they report, and I do not believe that the figures are that far from the truth*".[16]

Tayler, J. B. (1924). Study of Chinese Rural Economy, The. Chinese Soc. & Pol. Sci. Rev., 8, 230.

Malone, CB and JB Tayler, The Study of Chinese Rural Economy, CIFRC publication B-10, Peking, 1923

[14] Malone 1923 page 89.

[15] China International Famine Relief Commission. (1980). Herr Raiffeisen Among Chinese Farmers (Vol. 22). Dissertations-G.

Trescott, P. B. (1993). John Bernard Tayler and The Development Of Cooperatives In China, 1917–1945. *Annals of Public and Cooperative Economics,* 64(2), 209–226.

Tayler, J. B. (1937). Potentialities of the co-operative movement in China. Chinese Soc. & Pol. Sci. Rev., 21, 1.

[16] Malone 1923 Page 99.

7.5 Famine and the Household Economy

Tables 7.1 and 7.2 are drawn from Tayler's report.[17] Table 7.1 provides the population frequencies of net income for four locations, with the rightmost columns providing the cumulative frequencies. Tayler had estimated a poverty rate for a typical Chinese family at this time of $150/year, a number which excludes any expenditure that the household might on its own cover with its resources or labor. By this measure Tayler estimated that 64.3%, 62.4%, 62.1%, and 82.5% of Qinxian, Jiangsu, Suzhou, and Chihli households respectively were below the poverty line. Chihli, one of the hardest hit areas of households with net household income of $50 or less, one-third of the poverty line, had an astonishing 62.2% result.

Table 7.2 shows net income per mou of land holdings in various regions evaluated. The range of income varies greatly and an interesting observation is that the smallest land holdings appear to have the highest income per mou. This U-shaped relationship is a curiosity because conventional wisdom is that higher holdings will achieve some amount of economies of scale and/or size. But here, likely because of labor specialization and labor productivity, it has an alternative result. Unfortunately, the economic analysis that was to be completed by John L. Buck is lost to history and no available assessment has been found.

But this is not our point in providing these results. Keeping in mind that Tayler sets the poverty line at $150 for a minimum protein/calorie diet, he also shows that in Zhejiang (Qinxian), Jiangsu (three villages average), Anhui (Suzhou), and Chihli (four counties average) the numbers of mou required to exceed the poverty line from farming activity are (approximately) 8+, 11+, 35+, and 34+ respectively. Table 7.3 shows the distribution of farm household by land holdings for Jiangsu and Chihli. In Jiangsu about 67.8% of farm households have holdings below the Jiangsu threshold, while in Chihli somewhere between 77.6% and 89% of households had holdings below the poverty line.

7.6 Famine and Population

The consequences of these economic vulnerabilities had considerable impacts on population dynamics. Figures 7.1 shows the population density in Chihli (circa 1921) by age group. Tayler claims that this might pos-

[17] Tayler (1924b) ibid.

Table 7.1 Net income of famine-affected households

	Distribution of household income $/family/year (Tayler 1924b, page 251)							
	% of families				Cumulative %			
	Qinxian	Jiangsu	Suzhou	Chihli	Qinxian	Jiangsu	Suzhou	Chihli
<51	19.4	16.5	16.9	62.2	19.4	16.5	16.9	62.2
51	12.3	11.8	11.4	7.7	31.7	28.3	28.3	69.9
71	12	10.4	11.8	5.1	43.7	38.7	40.1	75
91	5.8	9.7	7.9	2.8	49.5	48.4	48	77.8
101	8.8	7.4	8.4	2.7	58.3	55.8	56.4	80.5
131	6	6.6	5.7	2	64.3	62.4	62.1	82.5
151	9.9	11.8	9.5	3.5	74.2	74.2	71.6	86
201	8.8	12	9	4.6	83	86.2	80.6	90.6
301	9.9	7.9	9.9	4.3	92.9	94.1	90.5	94.9
501	4.9	4.7	6.5	3	97.8	98.8	97	97.9
1001	1.9	0.8	1.1	1.3	99.7	99.6	98.1	99.2
2001	0.3	0.2	1.6	0.7	100	99.8	99.7	99.9
5000+	0	0.2	0.4	0.2	100	100	100.1	100.1

Table 7.2 Relationship between net income per local mou and land holdings

	$/mou	Size of holding (Tayler, Note 1 1 page 250)				
Size of holding	1–2	3–4	6–10	11–25	26–50	50+
Qinxian	35.6	18	14.6	9.8	7.7	5.1
Yizheng	27	19.1	13.2	9.8	7.4	
Jiangyin	19.5	18.9	19.1	18.9	18.4	
Wujiang	11.3	10.9	11.1	10.9	10.6	6.7
Suzhou	5.6	5	5.8	5.2	3.2	3.7
Zunhua	7	6.5	4.9	4	4	4.4
Tangxian	3.8	3.8	3.9	4.1	4.5	5.1
Handan	3.8	2.5	2.7	3	4.7	5.1

sibly be the first population survey of rural China and the discrepancies between males and females is quite startling as are the patterns among age groups as measured on the horizontal axis. The exact deaths from the famine are estimated to be 500,000 which is a fraction of deaths from previous famines, those in 1878–79 and 1907 being amongst the worst famines, globally, on record. Our analysis here is crude by any scholarly standard, but our interest here is to illustrate the challenges of famine itself

Table 7.3 Farm holdings in local mou

	Average size of farm holdings in local mou, Kiangsu and Chihli Villages			
	Jiangsu %	Chihli %	Jiangsu cumulative %	Chihli cumulative %
<3	10.5	12.6	10.5	12.6
3–5	25.4	20.3	35.9	32.9
6–10	31.9	22.3	67.8	55.2
11–25	23.2	22.4	91	77.6
26–50	6.1	11.4	97.1	89
51–100	1.5	6.9	98.6	95.9
>100	1.4	4.1	100	100

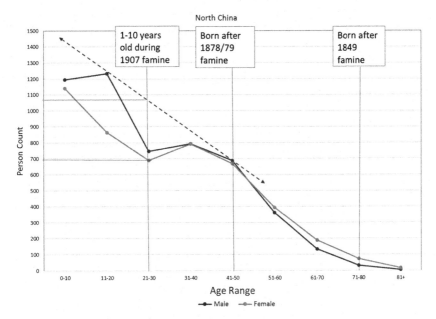

Fig. 7.1 Age distribution, 1921 male and female, North China

and the challenges faced by the various relief agencies operating in China. The dashed line joins the extremities of the male population from new birth to approximately 40–50 years of age. We assume a certain convexity in the population representation and naturally assume that under fairly normal conditions the male and female populations would be evenly split. We assume, perhaps falsely, from the data that the years following the 1907 and 1879 famines returned to normal birthrates so that any shortfall below the dashed line joining these points is abnormal, or what Tayler refers to as 'defect'. The defect is greater for females than males, but even so the population of young children in 1921/22 during and following the famine is about 18% below normal. The defect in population of those 21–30 years old were 0–10 years old during the 1907 famine, and this population shows a defect of over 30%. Some estimates of the 1907 famine put deaths at 24 million, nearly 5% of the crude estimates of China's population at that time; areas such as these reported would have been hit with devastating effect (Fig. 7.2).

Of course we should not presume that the supposed defect is any indicator of mortality. Tayler points out that the 11–20 year range is also the range of marriage and part of the female defection might be due to marriage and leaving the village, although presumably if this is true then there would also be an influx of new brides. Other sources of defection could be

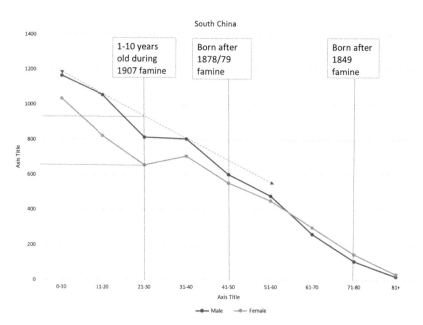

Fig. 7.2 Age distribution, 1921 male and female, South China

through childbirth, or a general exodus from the famine regions in search of food and relief. If this were the case for the 21–30 year-old bracket, this may also explain the simultaneity of the deficit in the 1–10 year-old bracket who would have been born to this group. Nonetheless, what the China International Famine Relief Commission found was troubling enough even in the absence of mortality.

The 1921 famine was a result of three factors. The source of the famine was drought conditions over the greater parts of Chihli, Shanxi, Shaanxi, and Henan and parts of Shandong. These were the same regions affected by the 1876–79 famine, but drought was not the cause of the famine. The first cause was the overcrowding of the land, with nearly 1200 people per square mile of land, with each piece of land being sub-divided and sub-divided, and each sub-division placing the farmer in greater peril with low income and limited accumulation of grain to smooth income. In the biblical sense the Joseph effect refers to seven years of plenty followed by seven years of want, but the equivalent Chinese adage was: "*There are no seven fat kine—rather only seven lean kine and then seven a little more lean*".[18]

The second cause was lack of alternative opportunities including wage labor. The vast number of people were smallholder farms dependent only on what could be raised from the land. With dwindling to non-existent food supplies and now diversified sources of liquidity the farmers could do little but sell what little they owned, including children, sisters, brothers, and wives. In the *Shuntefu* district of Henan of 1,395,000 mou of land, 187,000 mou were sold; of 42,663 animals owned before the famine, 30,034 were sold; with a population of 397,700, of which 160,119 were destitute even before the worst of the famine hit, 9252 children were sold. In the whole of the *Shuntefu* district it was estimated that 25,443 children were ultimately sold.[19] What land was sold provided very little. Land that sold for $100/mou before the famine sold for $3 or $4 per mou during the famine. The adobe huts in which farmers lived were destroyed so that the timber could be burned or sold. Even children fetched a meagre price. Of 112 cases reported sold in *Peng Cheng* in Chihli there were 41 girls, 40 boys, 21 wives, and 10 daughters-in-law: 25 sold for $3 and under, 38 for

---

[18] Peking United International Famine Relief Committee (Peking United International Famine Relief Committee) (1922) The North China Famine of 1920–1921 with Special Reference to the West Chihli Area. Commercial Press Works Ltd. Peking. Page 12. We are unsure of the etymology of the word '*kine*'. In old English it is the plural of cows, but as with the Joseph effect one can substitute the word 'year' to the same effect.

[19] PUIFR (1922) Page 15.

$7 and under, 36 for $12 and under, nine for $20 and under, and four for $20 dollars and under. In another region 188 sales recorded 110 girls, 34 boys, 35 wives, eight sisters and one daughter-in-law with 59 sold for $10 or under, 20 for $20 and under, 39 between $20 and $50, and five between $60 and $150.[20]

The third factor was the neglect of improvements in China which could have been made. In *Tingchow*, for example, farmers were starving because of drought, but ground water was available by well only 30 or 40 feet below the surface. The cost of digging the well was $90 but without the knowledge on the one hand and access to capital on the other, it was up to the relief agencies to sink over 1000 wells. Riverways too were neglected and allowed to silt. Indeed, W. Kirton, a reporter touring Jiangsu during the 1907 flood-induced famine, noted that not only were there dredgers moored on the river, but they had not moved in 10 years even though they were collecting dredging retainers. Here the failure at dredging the Yellow River and along the Grand Canal was corruption and administrative incompetence of the worst kind.[21] The accumulation of silt was largely due to deforestation of hillsides. Without dredging operations, flooding over wide regions of the Yellow River was frequent. Another cause was lack of communication. While communication had improved since the 1878–79 drought, areas with plenty of stockpiles of grain could not easily be identified and sent to famine regions. The organization of famine relief across the provinces with the Peking United International Famine Relief Committee alleviated this considerably in the 1920–21 famine and railroads facilitated shipments far greater than before.[22]

7.7 Conceptualizing Rural Credit Cooperatives

There is some dispute over exactly when the various relief agencies decided that agricultural cooperation would be beneficial as a measure of relief. The Peking United International Famine Relief Committee report in 1922 barely touches on agricultural credit except to say: "*Another contributing factor was the inability of the farmers to get credit at a reasonable interest rate. At such times in the country they have to give 3%, 4% and 5%*

---

[20] Peking United International Famine Relief Committee (1922) Page 89.
[21] Kirton, W. (1907). A silent war, or, The great famine in Kiangpeh. North China Daily News and Herald, Peking.
[22] Peking United International Famine Relief Committee (1922) Page 10.

interest per month, a very common occurrence. To have to borrow money under such condition (sic) is tantamount to economic crippling. Many families of average means will be crippled financially all their lives by the burden of debt incurred during famine, It is little wonder that there is a great rising tide of interest in measures which will alleviate these conditions".[23] And adding later, that loans were made at exorbitant interest rates, and when defaulted upon, the lender would take the child as payment.[24]

In the particular studies of Malone and Tayler cited above, both claim that the information collected on credit was inadequate to do any analysis. For example, Malone states explicitly that the Credit Committee aimed to find means to provide systems of credit for farmers,[25] but then reported that many families admitted that they owed money, with none confessing to be creditors who seemed always to live elsewhere. Tayler (1924b) noted that the Famine Relief Commission had already started organizing Rural Credit Societies in 1924, but this is probably referring to the initiatives at Nanjing University with Paul Hsu and John L. Buck. Nonetheless, in terms of the studies carried out, Tayler notes that the data on indebtedness was unsatisfactory and varied in reason and source across districts.

In famine regions, famine was a major cause of borrowing whereas in less-affected areas the cause was social expenditure such as for weddings and funerals.[26] Rates tended to be high averaging 2–3%/month in Qinxian, 1.6–1.7% in Wujiang, 3% in *Chanhua*, and 3% in *Tanghsien* Tangxian. The highest rates of 5 or 6% with as much as 10% at times was reported in *Chihsien* Qianxian, and 5% in *Chanhua*, and was sourced from local rich men, pawn shops, and grain dealers. The official rate was not to exceed 3%/month but at least one group of farmers in Chihli reported interest rates in excess of 100%/year.[27]

---

[23] Peking United International Famine Relief Committee (1922) page 10.
[24] Peking United International Famine Relief Committee (1922) page 87.
[25] Ibid page 89.
[26] Tayler (1924B) Page 256.
[27] Ibid.

7.8 JOHN B. TAYLER, JOHN LOSSING BUCK, AND RURAL COOPERATION

Although the first recorded credit cooperative in China was developed by Paul Hsu and John L. Buck at Nanjing University in 1923, it is more than likely that the idea of credit cooperatives as a solution to famine came from John B. Tayler, a Briton, who lived from 1878 to 1951.[28] Tayler was born in Liverpool and received bachelor and master degrees from the University of Liverpool in 1898 and 1901, and after a short stint in industry moved to China as a missionary in 1906. There he was administrator to a boys' school until 1917 when he accepted an appointment to head the economics department at Yanjing University in Peking. Having no formal training in economics, Tayler spent a year in preparation at the London School of Economics in 1919–20.

When the China International Famine Relief Commission was formed in November 1921, Tayler served as chair of the Committee on Credit and Economic Improvement. There he met fellow missionary Buck who was newly appointed to head the agricultural economics program at Nanjing College of Agriculture and Forestry. Both were enthusiastic supporters of cooperative credit.[29] Buck, raised on a New York farm, a student of agronomy, and one of a handful of agricultural missionaries between 1916 and 1921, was well entrenched in China's agricultural economy by 1921, whereas Tayler evolved into the role. In any case, neither Tayler nor

---

[28] Trescott, P. B. (1993). John Bernard Tayler and The Development Of Cooperatives In China, 1917–1945*. Annals of Public and Cooperative Economics, 64(2), 209–226.

Trescott, P. B. (1992). Institutional Economics in China: Yenching University, 1917–1941. Journal of Economic Issues, 26(4), 1221–1255.

There were many advisors to China over this period. The agricultural reformers are summarized in Stross, R.E. (1986) "The Stubborn earth: American Agriculturalists on Chinese Soil, 1898–1937" University of California Press, Berkeley CA.

See also Thomson, J.C. Jr. (1969) "While China Faced West: American reformers in Nationalist China, 1928–1937" Harvard University Press, Cambridge MA.

Spence, J. (1969). "To Change China: Western Advisors in China, 1620–1960" Penguin Books, NY NY.

[29] Trescott (1981), *Op Cit.* suggests that Buck became enthused about cooperatives from his meetings with Tayler, but Buck would also have been aware of the push for cooperative credit from his studies at Cornell where Liberty Hyde Bailey and George F. Warren were pushing cooperative credit as a matter of agricultural policy. Buck's Master thesis advisor in 1922/23 at Cornell University was W.I. Myers, another big promoter of cooperative credit, who would be appointed as the first governor of the Farm Credit Administration by President Roosevelt in 1933.

Buck were Western ideologues.[30] Tayler pushed the Yanjing economists to provide students with information regarding the Chinese economy and to demonstrate the relevance of Western economic analysis to China's problems. Similarly, Buck quickly realized that as an agricultural missionary that to teach or deliver agricultural extension on Western methods was useless. Ultimately, Tayler was an institutionalist in the traditional sense that economics was to have a public purpose. He wrote on a variety of topics including the economic circumstances and problems of the Chinese people and the relationship between the vastness of China's population, productivity, the lack of capital and enterprise, and the insecurity of property and life. He had no objections to being a social reformer and continually pursued projects, programs, and policies with a reformist and activist zeal. He was a proponent of scientific integration into China's agricultural and industrial sectors, including the use of experimentation at the village level to evaluate how production methods, infrastructure, and institutions improve livelihoods and general welfare.

When his realization that access to credit was constraining farm profits and contributing to poverty and susceptibility to famine occurred is not clear, but all evidence indicates that the problem of farm credit and the role that credit cooperatives might play in delivering credit to farmers was clearly a motivation behind the 1921/22 field studies described above. As mentioned, the field surveys cast little light on the traditional mechanisms of farm credit of the day, so it is unlikely that they, themselves, motivated the China International Famine Relief Commission's foray into credit cooperatives. Nevertheless, it would be with small error to suggest that once agricultural credit and credit cooperatives became an objective of the China International Famine Relief Commission that Tayler would reach out to Buck to provide the first grants to Nanjing College of Agriculture and Forestry to start the first rural credit cooperatives.

The push from the University of Nanjing came from one of Buck's students Paul Hsu. Leveraging the China International Famine Relief Commission funds Hsu began discussing rural credit with farmers and in 1923 organized the first China International Famine Relief Commission sponsored credit society called the Feng-Run-Men Rural Credit Society at Nanjing and another in *Keng* Village near *Hwaiyuen* in North Anhui in

---

[30] For more on American agriculturalists in China see Stross, R.E. (1986) *"The Stubborn Earth: American Agriculturalists on Chinese Soil 1898–1937"*. University of California Press, Berkely CA.

1924. The Nanjing cooperative was sponsored by a group of vegetable growers who used a $1000 capital grant to build a public privy from which the farmers could obtain fertilizer for their gardens. Funded by the China International Famine Relief Commission , Hsu also visited rural areas and conducted field surveys directed towards understanding credit and savings and organizations employed by farmers, resulting in two more cooperatives through the College of Agriculture and Forestry at the University of Nanjing. In addition, Buck, Dean Reisner, and Hsu guaranteed a commercial loan from the Shanghai Commercial and Savings Bank for 1925 and 1926 to start yet another cooperative. Following these successes, and despite reservations about the credit trustworthiness of farmers, the Shanghai Commercial and Savings Bank began to advance funds to new cooperative ventures well into the 1930s.[31]

The experiments in cooperation established by Hsu, Buck, and Reisner had a far-reaching impact in showing how cooperative credit societies could advance competition and level the playing field for poorer farmers. Ultimately, Hsu would be the first manager of the Farmers Bank of Jiangsu, which was capitalized by the provincial government with $1 million to finance cooperative enterprises. He was also to pen the first draft of rural cooperative legislation—the Provisional Cooperative Legislation for Rural Cooperatives—promulgated by the Jiangsu provincial government, and which established a blueprint for expanding cooperation well into the Republican era. Hsu eventually resigned to join the Bank of Communication and ultimately obtained a Master's degree in agricultural economics from Cornell University in 1932. The University of Nanjing continued its efforts in establishing cooperative societies through the 1930s, and even after the occupation of Nanjing by Japanese forces in December 1937. Then the university moved to Hankou and eventually to Chengdu in Sichuan.

7.9 Credit Relief and the Yangtze River Floods

Following the Yangtze River floods in 1931 the Flood Relief Committee of the National Christian Council provided a grant for Buck and others to take up relief work in *Moh Lin Kwang*, near Nanjing, and *Wujiang* in Anhui. This included establishing 11 simple credit cooperative societies with all monies paid back. During the flood, the Rural Church Committee of the National Christian Council had made emergency rehabilitation

---

[31] Buck, J.L. (1973) Op Cit.

loans to victims in flood regions. As this money was repaid, the council provided between $37,000 and $57,000 (depending on ultimate repayment of loans) to the University of Nanjing to continue its work on agricultural cooperation, and to provide the capital for new cooperatives.

A series of credit relief efforts were organized by the School of Agriculture at the University of Nanjing. Included in this relief was the establishment of agricultural banks and in fact a central agricultural bank was to be considered.[32] The Nanjing-managed relief had restored nearly 1 million mou of land using refugee labor (presumably with wheat payment) but in order to get farmers back on the fields an amortized loan system was established. Under this scheme farmers could borrow seed grain directly or money to purchase seed grain, fertilizer and/or implements for the planting of winter crops. These loans were to be administered by Ningshu Agricultural Relief Association *"to afford a permanent agency for promoting the agricultural and economic welfare of the rural population of this* (Ningshu) *region"*. One of the first projects was to colonize some uncultivated land in *Chuyung* Hsien (county) along the *Ching Hwei* River which was badly damaged during the 1931 floods. About 3500 mou was set aside to support about 150 farm families. Colonists would be provided a loan to cover the costs of seed and other inputs, food, and material for a shelter for the first year and this would then be repaid within a 3–5 year period.

In addition, short-term loans and mortgages were issued to rice farmers facing the low rice prices in spring of 1932. Farmers would have had to sell twice as much of their stores than normal, and this provided an opportunity to bridge the price gap with a loan. To guarantee the loan the farmers were required to deposit their cheap rice as a mortgage in one of 101 depots scattered across the area. It was reported that some farmers were walking as much as 30 miles with rice on their shoulders to get the loans. Most of the 3014 families assisted by the commodity loans held less than 30 mou of land. Larger farmers who had resources were not eligible. At most a farmer could deposit 1500 catties (1 cattie = 500 g or about one pound (lb)) and could receive up to $30 in credit of ($0.02/cattie or $2/dan with 1 dan equaling 100 cattie). Interest was set at 1% and loan terms were from 4 to 6 months. When the loan was paid the farmer would remove the rice from the depot. An average loan was about $15. Farmers would be issued a deposit receipt which itemized the transaction and its

---

[32] Editorial, "Some Practical Applications of Farm Relief" *China Weekly Review* February 4, 1933 pages 407–408.

terms and this was the only record of the transaction. The deposit receipt was transferable and could be sold to a third party and the rice released to the third party so long as the loan was repaid with interest. If the loan was not repaid then the rice would be auctioned.

In addition, Nanjing University reorganized cooperatives in the district to encourage wheat production using wheat cultivar #26 which was tested by Nanjing University to increase yields by 10–15%. In addition, #26 seed was loaned to farmers on the condition that they would follow certain cultivation practices in line with the cooperatives. Dean Lin stated: "*These cooperative societies are, in our opinion, most important, and we hope to make them a permanent feature of our work in the Ningshu district. Think of the hundreds of things that we could do for soil and crop improvement, animal breeding, forestry, and for general rural betterment through such societies. The solution of China's agricultural problem in my opinion lies in having such co-operative societies properly organized and properly directed*".[33]

At Chengdu the faculty helped in the establishment of 16 associations and then a federation of these associations with 5811 farmers involved. Cooperative credit federations would amalgamate the financial interests of various marketing cooperatives. Rather than each cooperative raising its own funds for credit, the cooperative credit federations would pool individual capital and resources, with unlimited liability for the protection of the whole. Thus if a single member of particular cooperative defaulted on a loan, that cooperatives members would be mutually liable; but if the entire cooperative collapsed then the remaining cooperatives would be mutually liable. Although we cannot state with certainty, it is highly likely that this approach to cooperative credit was modeled after the emerging push toward a jointly liable cooperative system in the United States that was being pushed by W.I Myers (Buck's MS thesis advisor at Cornell University, and the first Governor of the Farm Credit System in 1933).

During this period John B. Tayler continued to work on agricultural cooperation, but having handed credit cooperatives to Buck and Hsu, refocused his energy towards agricultural marketing cooperatives and industrial cooperatives. Trescott (1992) makes the case that Tayler, every bit the institutionalist and as head of the economics department at Yanjing University, sought to broaden the department's scope, although efforts at rural economy were by no means abandoned.

---

[33] Editorial, "Some Practical Applications of Farm Relief" *China Weekly Review* February 4, 1933 pages 407–408.

7.10 Summary

Although several efforts at cooperation were promulgated and developed between 1915 and 1922, much of the credit towards the development of cooperative credit societies goes to initiatives by the members of the International China Famine Relief Commission in 1921 and 1922. As said, there were several other efforts at cooperation, but the initiatives by the China International Famine Relief Commission and Nanjing University managed to establish protocols, rules, and regulations, and promoted cooperation in such a way that it stuck. With a handful of successes and experience, cooperatives loan societies soon became institutionally important in China, especially after 1928 when China moved towards rural reconstruction. The growth of cooperative credit societies and the development of other financial institutions dedicated to agriculture are discussed in the following chapters.

CHAPTER 8

Rural Reconstruction

8.1 Introduction

The term 'rural reconstruction' took its lead in the history books once the Kuomintang (KMT) and Chiang Kai-shek himself got involved in the cooperative movement, but prior to that date the work of the China International Famine Relief Commission followed by the initial efforts at Nanjing, Nankai, and Yenching universities was evident. The movement was originally described in old Chinese by *hsiang ts'un chien* which has the literal translation of construction, but despite the continued use of the term at the time, it was taken to mean reconstruction.[1] Thus there may be some confusion over a period of this history when 'rural construction' was in vogue, and another in which 'rural reconstruction' was used. What we have set forth in the previous chapters is more in line with the original usage of the term. Propelled by the China International Famine Relief Commission , cooperative credit societies were just a part of a package of initiatives designed to offer stability to farmers and to prevent, or at least minimize, the impact from the many and frequent calamities faced by Chinese farmers.[2] Preventive measures included road construction, and digging irrigation canals, ditches, wells, and dikes. Self-help and extension

[1] Hsu, Leanord. (1937). Rural Reconstruction in China. *Pacific Affairs,* 10(3), 249–265.
[2] Djang, Y. S. (1931). Credit Cooperatives in 1000 Villages. *Chinese Social and Political Science Review* 15, 161–170.

services expanded cultivation practices, introduced wheat hybrids, and promoted forestry and best management practices for soil.

The morphing towards the term reconstruction came about through a variety of calamities, catastrophes, and conflicts that China faced throughout the 1928–1932 period. The KMT recognized that China was facing diverse social forces that drove at least three political and economic objectives, or imperatives. The first was to increase production. The insularity of the Qing dynasty had left China with no industrial base and it lagged modern industrialization significantly. Despite the promise of Sun Yat Sen's three principles and the 1912 republic, China wasted an enormous amount of time and effort in transitioning to a democracy—including a brief attempt at returning China to a monarchy in 1914, followed by the warlord years, a common revolt against confucianism, followed by political compromises, the death of Sun Yat Sen, the Northern Expedition, famine in 1921, and 1928–1931, floods in 1931, further attempts at forming a new government in Peiping (Beijing) and Canton (Guangzhou), the rise of communism, and Japanese aggression. It was, by any measure, a mess and by the early 1930s China could not so easily rely on its primary and agricultural exports to balance trade exchange for goods such as kerosene, electrical appliances, wool, and food stuffs for which China was incapable of meeting domestic demand, despite its massive land resource.

The second objective was China's own salvation and this was none truer than after the annexation of Mongolia and the Northeastern Manchurian provinces in 1930/31 by the Japanese and further aggression in the South Shanghai conflict in 1932. Since the opium wars of 1840, the Sino-Japanese war of 1898, the Boxer Rebellion of 1900 and many incidents in between, the foreign powers set up a system of reparations that bled China's treasury at any opportunity. China's military was so inferior to the Western powers that no matter who caused an incident China would ultimately lose, and as was the principle at the time, the loser paid reparations to the winners. On many occasions a foreign power would do no more than float a gunboat up the Yangtze River to get China to submit. By 1931 the largest provincial and national expenditure was spent on military expenditure against bandits, communists, and warlords on the domestic front. On the international front, Chiang Kai-shek thought it better to keep the communists at bay in South China rather than to pit its limited and technically inferior arsenal against the Japanese. Increased productivity and reconstruction it was believed would ultimately protect China from outside influences.

The third objective was better local government and self-discipline. The rise of the communists and the establishment of soviets was recognized as a failure of the existing governance structure and inequalities between, and within, rural and urban communities. Cooperation and mutual aid societies were seen as a means to counter the more extreme reforms offered and imposed by the communists.

The reconstruction movement also dealt with institution building.[3] This was driven by private institutions emphasizing exploration and experimentation, and public (government) institutions emphasizing execution and standardization.[4] Private institutions included: (a) social or educational service agencies pushing rural centers to provide practical services to people; (b) universities, colleges and normal schools emphasizing the practice and dissemination of technical research and experimentation; (c) banks, including policy or quasi-governmental banks with interest in rural credit and some even having specialized departments for agricultural finance and cooperative lending; and (d) initiatives by individuals or groups to promote self-government and self-direction at the village level, including self-defense corps. In Henan the Federated Self-government Union of Zhenping, Xichuan, and Neixiang successfully suppressed a bandit-infested countryside using a village volunteer force of some 50,000 men.[5]

The government institutions at the time included the National Flood Relief Commission (NFRC) in 1931 to administer some $70 million in relief to the 25 million affected by the Yangtze River floods. This, in 1931, was the first time that the Chinese government provided a rural service on a national scale. Prior to this, as previously mentioned, the methods of famine relief and mitigation efforts came largely from private organizations such as the China International Famine Relief Commission. Even though the NFRC was short lived, it incentivized the national government to think more broadly about the institutional role that government could play in agricultural and rural development. Another government institution was the Rural Rehabilitation Commission which coordinated rural reconstruction work and brought about direct government involvement in agriculture by establishing the National Agricultural Research Bureau and the National Rice and Wheat Improvement Institute,

---

[3] Taylor, G. E. (1936). "The Reconstruction Movement in China" Royal Institute of International Affairs, London, UK.
[4] Leanord Hsu. (1937). ibid.
[5] Leanord Hsu. (1937). ibid Page 253.

launching agricultural relief efforts, promoting agricultural cooperation, and pushing taxation reform.[6]

A third governmental institution at the time was the *bao-jia* system of local self-government in areas under military control. Chiang Kai-shek recognized the link between rural economic and political reconstruction and military action. The *bao-jia* system was based on 10 (*bao*) and 100 (*jia*) households with collective responsibility for all for the wrongs of any one. From this, the *bao-jia* system was put to work in the building of infrastructure such as roads and irrigation, and improvements to agriculture, civic education, the organizations of cooperatives, and land registration. Other aspects of rural reconstruction included establishing local magistrates, building granaries, encouraging banks to participate in agricultural cooperation, establishing a postal savings and telegraphing system in rural areas where remittances could be sent and received, promoting and advancing health care, and modernizing and expanding railways and rail services including reduced freight for agricultural products,

The full extent of China's woes in the first years of the 1930s could fill volumes, and the full extent of reconstruction efforts and ultimately the emergence and evolution of rural credit cooperatives cannot be fully appreciated without at least some background as to the forces affecting China over this period.

8.2 Communist Expansion

What was once considered a bandit force of extremists was now a significant force moving in and out of territories, creating soviets along the way with purges of conventional leadership and the reallocation of land and wealth. As of mid-July 1931 the major battlefront between the republican forces and the communists was in the mountainous terrain of Jiangxi.[7] The government force alone included 30 divisions, a troop strength of some 300,000 soldiers against 42,000 Red Army troops with 18,000 rifles. The historical development of the communist activities included three phases. The first phase was doctrinaire and theoretical. This evolved into the Chinese Renaissance Movement during the 1920–23 period, although the ideas of communism were widely discussed before then. But

[6] Ibid.
[7] Yang Chien. (1931). Canton Rebellion Likely to Throw All china into Ranks of Communists. *China Weekly Review*, 57(July 25), 297–300.

the renaissance movement was academic and politically inactive and it was not until 1924–27 that communists actively sought political alliance with the KMT under Sun Yat-sen and were very active in Hubei, Hunan, and Jiangxi.

While alive, Sun Yat-sen was able to maintain a balance between the communists and the republicans but after his death in 1925, Chiang Kai-shek ordered a purge of communist party members. The Ironsides, who would later team up with Guangxi rebels, were joined by communist generals in 1927 and communist insurrections arose throughout Hubei, Hunan, and Jiangxi. By the end of 1930, 76 of 81 Hsiens (counties) in Jiangxi were either totally or partly controlled by the communists, with 33 fully Sovietized. Likewise in Hubei 50 out of 60 Hsiens and in Hunan 50 of 69 Hsiens were at some time or another under communist influence with 15 Hsiens being fully sovietized in Southern Hunan. Communist forces also had a presence in Anhui, Sichuan, Fujian, Zhejiang, Henan, and Shandong.

The rise of communism was actually a self-reinforcing mechanism in which the communists took advantage of political and military challenges facing the KMT when they struck. The Northern Expedition against the warlords Chen Fa-kui and Huang Qi-xiang in 1927, led to communist control of Canton (Guangzhou); the revolt of the Guangxi-Ironsides troops against the republicans provided an opening for the capture of Changsha, and the 1929–30 activities of the *Kuomenjun* led by Feng Yu-xiang and Yan Xi-shan created a void in Hunan and Jiangxi as government forces were diverted to Henan and elsewhere. This void provided freedom of movement that allowed the communists to develop skills in militarism while also developing the civilian rear-guard political machine required of propaganda and sovietization.

To a rural population, largely ignored, politically marginalized, and desperately poor the principles guiding the communists had a populist ring that to many peasants was attractive. These principles included the destruction of imperialism, confiscation of industries and banks of foreign capitalists; the unification of China and its indigenous nationalities; overthrowing the national government; establishing soviet rule involving a council of workers, peasants, and soldiers; enforcing an eight-hour work law, increasing wages, ending unemployment, enforcing social insurance, etc.; confiscation of all non-peasant land and redistributing farmlands amongst the peasants; improving the living conditions of soldiers and finding work and land for the people; abolishing all taxes levied by central and local governments and military authorities, and enforcing in their stead a graduated single tax on farm produce and other forms of income yielded by the land; and supporting the Union of Soviet Russia with the proletarians of the world.

In some instances what was promised was not precisely what occurred. For example, in eliminating taxes, the communists instead took a portion of physical grain harvested. But what was taxed was consumed and not necessarily sold. Consequently, to fund activities systems of fees and surcharges were put in place in addition to the forced surrender of grain when needed. On the other hand, improving the farm economy by farm reconstruction, improvement in irrigation, prevention of floods and droughts, supporting emigration to reduce farm population density, establishment of farmer's banks and cooperative societies to provide credit on easy terms, unifying currency and weights and measures, and maintaining efficient control of waterways were all designed to improve agricultural conditions and productivity. In Jiangxi much of these reforms were put in place including the removal and burning of all deeds and the removal of boundary markers to destroy all evidence of ownership boundaries. The land was redistributed to the able-bodied regardless of sex, and additional land was allocated to households for persons with disabilities and children under 16 by up to 25% of the normal allocation for the household. To aid in recruitment, land held by soldiers of the Red Army would be tilled by others. The labor class including poor and middle-poor peasants and workers were organized into unions. The middle- and upper-class gentry were excluded from all political activities for fear they would manipulate a class struggle in order to get land back. The bandit class, including the various societies (Hungman, Small Sword, Red Spears, etc.)[8] were absorbed into the soviet and the military so long as they renounced any authority other than the soviet.

After the 1928 Northern expedition, the KMT began the process of reconstruction, and saw the cooperative movement as a critical component in the overall strategy.[9] In February 1928 at the Fourth Plenary Session of the Central Executive Committee, Chiang Kai-shek and Chen Guo-fu proposed the organization of a special committee on cooperation.

---

[8] Perry, Elizabeth. (1980). "Rebels and Revolutionaries in North China, 1845–1945", Stanford University Press, Stanford, CA.
[9] This section relies heavily on H. K. Yang. (1937). The Cooperative Movement in China. *Central Bank of China, Bulletin*, 3(2), 111–125.

Later, in October 1928 the Central Executives of the KMT ordered all branches across China to include cooperative work as part of their political activities. By 1932 several other factors intervened including the Yangtze River floods in 1931 followed by the Japanese occupation of Manchuria in 1931, the Shanghai incident in 1932,[10] conflict between Nationalists and communists between 1930 and 1932, and on the financial front the hoarding and accumulation of silver by banks, at a time when credit was

---

[10] The so-called 'Shanghai Incident" of January 29, 1932 refers to the military clash between Japanese marines and China's 19th Route Army in Shanghai. The incident itself was the culmination of a great many stressors and a general distrust of Japan's intention to occupy Shanghai as it was presently doing in Manchuria. The Manchurian occupation and the massacre of Chinese civilians in Korea led to widespread boycotts of Japanese goods and services starting around July of 1931. The boycotts were enforced by organizations like the Anti-Chinese Boycott Association, which included harassing Chinese working for Japanese employers. On January 18, 1932 five Japanese including several monks were attacked by a Chinese mob in the Shanghai district of Chaphei. Two of the Japanese were wounded and one of them, a monk, died shortly thereafter. On January 20 a mob of 50 Japanese retaliated, burning down a towel factory and clashing with Chinese municipal police, wounding two and killing one. Three Japanese were shot by police, killing one. That same day Japanese residents sent a message to Tokyo requesting the Japanese government to send warships and troops to suppress the anti-Japanese movement. In the afternoon of the 20th the Japanese Consul-General presented an ultimatum to the Mayor of Shanghai who responded that two of the conditions, adequate control of anti-Japanese movements and the immediate dissolution of all anti-Japanese organizations, would prove difficult. Nonetheless, by January 24 Japanese reinforcements arrived off Shanghai while Chinese troop reinforcements moved into Chapei. Despite assurances by the mayor that indeed the final two conditions could be met, the settlement committee (Japanese) decided that the promise could not be enforced and imposed a State of Emergency. Around 11 pm on January 28 the admiral notified the defense council that it was going to move a detachment of marines into the Chapei region and that Chinese troops should remove themselves to the Western side of the Woosung railway station. Chinese troops refused to move as demanded and fighting broke out between Chinese regular troops and Japanese marines. The Chinese held their ground at the Woosung rail station until the Japanese bombed the rail station and surrounding buildings with incendiary bombs. By early March 1932 the Japanese had not only advanced through Shanghai but had extended their reach to about 45 km from Shanghai, deep into the farming countryside. By May 7, 1932, a Sino-Japanese truce was signed ending hostilities between Japanese and Chinese with Chinese troops remaining in the positions current at that time and Japanese troops returning to the international settlement in Shanghai.

Editorial, "League Committee's Report on Shanghai" China Weekly Review, February 13, 1932. Page 335–336.

Editorial, "The Ban on Japanese Goods in Honan" China Weekly Review, January 23, 1932. Page 258.

Editorial, "The Chinese-Japanese Battle-Front at Shanghai and Geneva", China Weekly Review, March 12, 1932. Page 41, 42–63.

crucial. From this started the reconstruction movement generally, and more to our point the realization by Chiang Kai-shek in the midst of the anti-communist campaign in Hubei in October 1932, of the importance of agricultural cooperation in rural reconstruction.[11]

8.3 Rural Reconstruction and the Chinese Communist Party

The General had little choice in the matter. The reality was that the KMT had to counteract the populist approach to rural development on offer by the communists.[12] The communists had two factions, the Stalinist faction which was militaristic and dominated by Zhu De and Mao Zhedong, and the more conciliatory Trotsky faction led by Chen Du-xiu. The Stalinist faction had dominated military activities in South China and it was through these areas that Chiang Kai-shek had to fight. Chiang had two challenges. The first was the rate at which the communists could mobilize military forces from the peasants and proletariat. In 1927 two communist commanders, Fang Zhi-min and Shao Shi-ping, left Nanchang for Southeast Jiangxi with seven rifles between them and in the three years that followed had amassed the 10th Red Army with 12,000 men and 3000 rifles. Likewise when Zhu De was driven from Jiangxi in 1927 to join up with Mao Zedong he escaped with just 200–300 rifles, but within three years he headed three communist forces with 30,000 men and 15,000 rifles. By 1931 what was considered a bandit force in 1927 had about 14 armies with 70,000 troops and 50,000 rifles, and using largely guerilla tactics occupied the movements of some 30 divisions of nationalist (KMT) forces throughout Jiangxi, Hubei, Hunan, Zhejiang, Guangdong, and Guangxi. Chiang Kai-shek needed a program of rural reconstruction in order to suppress the recruitment of disaffected peasants by the communists.[13]

The second motivator was that, by and large, the communists kept many of their promises in terms of land redistribution and the cancelling of debts to usurers and pawn shops. While the communists tolerated middle-peasants, they excluded and singled out the higher classes for attack. In so doing they maintained the class struggle required for

---

[11] Hsü, L. S. (1937). Rural Reconstruction in China. *Pacific Affairs*, 10(3), 249–265.
[12] Taylor, G. E. (1936). *Op Cit.*
[13] Yang Chien *Op Cit.*

revolution. To accomplish this, peasants were organized into various unions and mutual-aid societies.[14] These mutual aid societies were essentially cooperative ventures in the sharing of land, labor, and implements. At some times they operated as a collective, especially in areas where land titles and registrations were destroyed. Nonetheless, the formation of mutual aid societies brought together the labor supply of the lower peasants with the higher technology of the upper peasants. Rent and interest rates were negotiated to be reduced by 25%, with threats to lose access to the government granaries or bank loans for landlords or lenders who did not comply.[15] Within and across the soviets the communists had mobilized a formerly sanguine and largely neglected rural population, and Chiang Kai-shek recognized that by supporting cooperation the KMT could build upon a new rural order. The KMT also had to win over the peasants. When in retreat, for example, the communists would race to the mountains of Southern Jiangxi where they would be protected by the peasants.

Thus, in October 1932, Chiang Kai-shek took an interest in cooperation and issued regulations concerning the organization of rural cooperatives in recovered areas, as well as regulations concerning credit, utilities, consumers' and transportation cooperatives. To support this, Chiang Kai-shek established an institute to train people in the management of cooperatives throughout Henan, Hubei, Anhui, and Jiangxi. In November of 1932 the Military Headquarters Bureau dispatched representatives to help farmers organize rural cooperative preparatory societies along the lines of mutual aid societies. In April 1933 the Four-Provinces Farmers Bank was established in Hankou with a mandate to support agricultural cooperation and credit cooperatives. The Four-Provinces Farmers Bank ultimately became the Farmers Bank of China and moved to Shanghai.[16]

How successful the communists were in establishing cooperatives is not very clear. For example, H.K. Yang reports that a survey in 1932 indicated 22 societies in Anhui, 15 in Jiangxi, three in Hubei, and 17 in Hunan. He then attributes the propitious growth in societies to Chiang Kai-shek's declarations in October 1932. However, the timing of the reported survey and Chiang Kai-shek's declaration is not clear so this may be propaganda, since large swaths of Jiangxi, Hubei, and Hunan were occupied by

---

[14] Yang Chien *Op Cit.*
[15] Perry, E. J. (1980). Rebels and revolutionaries in North China, 1845–1945. Stanford University Press.
[16] H. K. Yang *Op Cit.* (see also Chap. 12 of this book).

communist forces throughout 1931 and 1932.[17] On the other hand, there is documentation in that establishing mutual aid societies the CPC would use pre-existing credit societies as a base and convert them to a new (mutual aid) purpose.[18] Whether or not these refined mutual aid societies also provided credit for undertaking cooperative activities is not clear.

8.4 Rural Reconstruction and Price Volatility in Copper, Silver, and Gold

Nonetheless, between the constructionists and the reconstructionists the focal point of rural credit became squarely focused on the cooperative movement. This was not done in isolation. As mentioned, China at that time was struggling with the development of the formal financial sector, which was particularly hard hit by the great depression in the United States, high volatility in the copper, silver and gold standards that defined China's multitude of local, provincial and national currencies, and also a weakening correlation amongst the three precious metals that caused wild swings in local, regional, and global prices for tradable goods. A local merchant trading in copper might go to a market center trading in silver, with the fair exchange determined by the ratio of the two; that is the exchange of silver for copper. Up to the beginning of the depression this worked well so long as the volatilities of, and correlation between, copper and silver remained reasonably constant. But markets changed. Locally the price of copper fell, while the price of silver rose, meaning high inflation as the local copper currency was exchanged for goods priced to silver (typically the Mexican silver dollar). Meanwhile, domestic agricultural commodities at the local level were priced to copper so that a merchant holding silver could scoop a larger quantity of commodities for the same expenditure.

8.5 Japanese Aggression, Bonds, and Credit

In times of peace, or at least in the case of China relative peace, Chinese government issued bonds were considered a safe investment, despite the fact that bond yields were more than 20%. But since the occupation by the Japanese of Manchuria on September 19, 1931 the bonds had been largely

---

[17] H. K. Yang *Op Cit.*
[18] Perry, E. J. (1980). Rebels and revolutionaries in North China, 1845–1945. Stanford University Press.

discounted at 30–40% of face value with yields ranging from 40% to 60%.[19] Prior to the Manchurian excursion the bonds held by Chinese were liquid with lenders offering loans at 9–10% using 60% of the bond value as collateral. But with the Japanese annexation of Manchuria, the bonds achieved junk status with virtually no remaining collateral value. Unable to use bonds as security, many bondholders were forced into bankruptcy because they could not obtain the required credit. At the national level, the Bank of China which normally held 40% of its reserve funds in bonds decided to replace government bonds with gold bonds and other securities backed by certain indemnity funds and deeds. The exact structure of the gold bonds is unclear, but presumably the bonds refer to bonds that are secured by gold deposits rather than bonds linked to the price of gold.[20]

Things worsened in 1932 during and after the Shanghai incident. The banking situation in Shanghai became perilous with freight destined for Shanghai being held at Japanese ports or in Hong Kong. Cargo, even when delivered, went unclaimed. Much of the problem was due to the fact that Chinese banks were unable to provide terms for short-run working capital to accept delivery. For example, the normal custom was for US cotton that was blended with inferior Indian and Chinese cotton to be delivered to factories with 10-day terms and then paid thereafter in cash drawn on a line of credit from a Chinese bank. Cotton imports in Shanghai amounted to $40 million monthly, with China being the United States's second largest customer. But with the Chinese banks unwilling, or unable, to lend against cotton purchases the cotton trade all but dried up as a result.[21] To alleviate the credit supply problem the United States government offered weavers and manufacturers of yarn and clothing three-year loans at 5% coupon payable in gold to purchase US cotton. In the midst of the depression surplus cotton in the United States was high, and prices were low, and below lower quality Chinese cotton. To avoid dumping, duties were imposed on imported American cotton.[22]

---

[19] CRW January 30, 1932, Pages 282–283 "Bondholders' Delirium" by B. Y. Lee. China weekly Review Volume 51 1931–1932.

[20] January 30, 1932 Page 286 "Bank of China to Convert Domestic Bonds into Gold Bonds" China weekly Review Volume 51 1931–1932.

[21] February 20 1932, Page 361 "American Cotton Imports Stopped by Trouble Here" China weekly Review Volume 51 1931–1932.

[22] June 17, 1933 Pages 112–113 "U.S. Cotton Loan as a Relief to Cotton Industry" by Y. Lee. CWR Volume 65, 1933.

(see also Page 134 Page 156)

Shanghai and the surrounding area was also home to about 106 silk filatures with 65 being in the devastated district of *Zhabei*. Several were totally destroyed, barraged by machine gun fire or looted by the Japanese. But a more important aspect of the problem was in access to credit. The filatures were turnkey operations relying on quick turnover of products for sale in order to survive and this also required working capital credit. However, with Shanghai banks no longer providing credit, silk production was severely hampered, especially in the purchasing of cocoons. In addition, with Japanese bombardment and occupation of major filature centers such as *Wusong*, *Jiangwan*, and *Zhabei* the indigenous populations had largely evacuated leaving no one to watch over cocooning, hatch silkworm eggs, or extract the silk. Estimates put the price of raw silk at $50/picul compared to between $80 and 95 in previous years. Further, for operators of the filatures any attempt to sell capital or cocoon-buying stations mostly failed due to lack of supply and processing facilities.[23]

8.6 Lack of Currency Control Within China

With these events the Chinese currencies and bond markets were in disarray. Most provincial governments issued bonds on silver, while the global standard was moving to gold. Chinese banks migrated towards the gold standard and as gold prices increased, provincial bonds decreased considerably in value as the price of gold rose. But many of the problems facing China between 1929 and 1934 were internal. What was happening in global metals and currency markets just exacerbated the problems.

One of the problems was simply the amount of silver currency available. For example, in 1930 with famine raging across North China, relief workers in Gansu were unable to use silver-based notes without a huge discount. The preferred cash was in physical silver. Physical silver had to be purchased in outlying areas and in some cases relief agencies actually mined the silver from the ground, and transported it directly to be minted into '3rd year *Yuan Shi-kai dollars*'.[24] Not only does this illustrate the complexities in the fluidity and liquidity of paper currency, but the notion that independent agents can simply mine and distribute currency of its

---

[23] Editorial, "Effects of War Upon China's Silk Industry", *China Weekly Review* April 9, 1932 Pages 181–182.

[24] Editorial, "Currency Confusion Affects Famine Relief Work" *China Weekly Review*, August 30 1930, Page 482.

own making, and independent of the central monetary authority would contribute not only to price volatility, but also— at least locally—to inflation. Elsewhere, farmers in Manchuria had to deal with payments made in strange dollars of Kirin provincial notes, Heilongjiang provincial notes, *Mukden* (now Shenyang) provincial notes, and Harbin notes. Farmers might forward contract in one currency, despite that fact that the currency was not recognized as, and must be exchanged for, local currency.[25]

8.7 THE YANGTZE RIVER FLOOD

The shortage of silver not only affected famine relief across Gansu, Shaanxi, and Shanxi in 1930 but in the summer of 1931 as rains elsewhere in China failed to cease, the Yellow and Yangtze rivers began to overflow. By August 26, 1931 the Yangtze River at Hankou was at 53.5 feet which was greater than the previous great flood of 1870/71 where the river rose to 50.5 feet. In fact it is reported that the last time water in the Yangtze was at 1931 levels was in the fifteenth century Ming dynasty. Much of central China was flooded with somewhere between 50 and 60 million people affected; 45 of 68 districts in Hubei were flooded with no crops left standing in 30 Northern districts, as were 24 districts in Shandong. The rice growing regions of Anhui province in the Huai (*Hwai*) Valley were devastated as the flooded area reached almost 100–150 miles from Chinkiang to the ocean.

In Hubei, 8000 were known to have been drowned and 10 million were rendered destitute. The destitute in Hunan, Jiangxi, and Anhui was estimated at more than 25 million. As at August 22, 1931 some 35,000 sq. miles of Hubei was under water with 5 million destitute. The number of refugees in Wuhan was 400,000, Hankou had 200,000, Wuchang 50,000, and Hanyang 30,000. Flood waters in Hunan covered 22,000 sq. miles with 2 million destitute and deaths from starvation and disease in Wuhan alone exceeded 1000 a day with corpses floating in the streets along with cats dogs and livestock, while the living were stranded in the second floors of houses that were still standing. Transportation in Wuhan was by sampan only. Chiang Kai-shek ordered all available military craft and commandeered private cargo boats to remove people from flooded areas.

---

[25] Editorial by A.A.R. (anonymous), "The Plight of the Manchurian Peasant". *China Weekly Review* June 6 1931 Pages 16–18.

Tragedy was rampant. On August 21, 1931, 1000 refugees housed in barracks were drowned when yet another dyke broke. In Sichuan, Chengdu and Chongqing were in as bad a shape as Wuhan and Hankou. About 10,000 of the river population, inhabitants along the Yangtze River, were believed to have been washed away. The Yangtze floods continued into 200 miles of dense farmland North of Nanjing and Zhenjiang (*Chinkiang*). This was due to the breaking of dykes along the Grand Canal. One section of the dyke in Northern Jiangsu gave way along an eight-mile stretch due to fierce winds pelting the water against the weakened dyke system. The number of dead by drowning was estimated at between 10,000 and 50,000. Cities were also affected particularly in Gaoyou(*Kaoyu*), *Shaobai*, Xinghua (*Hsinhua*) and Yangzhou (*Yangchow*). There was little warning when the dykes broke giving little or no time for inhabitants to seek safety. With most possessions lost by survivors they camped atop the remaining dykes with whatever could be salvaged. Elsewhere, thousands of refugees and animals found safety along elevated rail lines, and in refugee camps. Others remained in trees and rooftops while carcasses and corpses floated around them, raising fears of cholera. Even in areas that escaped the flood, nature's havoc continued with vast areas consumed by locusts leaving farmers destitute and in famine conditions.

The economic costs were tremendous. In the Wuhan district 160,000–163,000 houses had been submerged affecting 728,000–780,000 with 500,000 declared destitute and homeless requiring $30,000,000 (probably Mexican silver) for food and supplies in the following month. In September 1931, President Herbert Hoover announced 450,000 tons of wheat (or flour substitute) representing some 15,000,000 bushels of wheat would be provided by the United States for food relief at market prices and repaid over five years by 1936. It was reported to Hoover that the total food aid required through 1932 would be 100,000 tons to be distributed among 180,000,000 people affected by the floods. It was also reported that there simply was not enough food grain in China to meet the emergency, but as is so often the case in disaster relief this was not to say that grain and rice stock were not available. It was true that in the storage facilities of Manchuria all stores had already been sold (but still held in storage and available) while Japanese rice stocks were already lower than demand. Large quantities of soybeans were available from the Manchurian provinces but the soybeans had to be processed into food quality and soybeans were not normally part of the diet of Southern Chinese.[26] The national famine relief loan was estimated at $50 million.

8.8 Canton Rebellion

Chiang Kai-shek visited the flood area on August 28, 1931 and was sympathetic to the monetary demands for food, shelter, and medical assistance, and the costs of reconstruction and land reclamation. But still his focus was on communists and other rebel forces, claiming that communists had blown up a dyke to thwart advancing republican troops, drowning 20,000 communist villagers. In 1931 having both a horrendous flood and a civil war at the same time was in itself a tragedy of untold proportions. Despite the calamity of the Yangtze and Yellow River Valley floods, civil war expanded. The independent government in Beijing (Peiping) headed by Shaanxi Christian general Feng Yu-xiang and Shanxi general Yan Xi-shan in opposition to the KMT in Nanjing was, in June 1930, being mimicked in Canton (Guangzhou) in June 1931 where a Southern government independent of Nanjing was being considered. While Canton forces could do little against Nanjing, the Canton faction (rebellion) was joined or associated with the Guangdong and Guangxi military (rebel) groups who were already engaged against Chiang Kai-shek.[27] Chiang Kai-shek was mobilizing some 300,000 troops to oust communists from Jiangxi Province and with a possibility thereafter of moving on Canton. Communists forces across Jiangxi had already established 'soviets' in the standard way and farmer members of these soviets were urged not to protect the communist forces at all. Although in June 1931 no military action of significance was noted, the leaders of the Canton rebellion, fearing the worst from Nationalist forces, recalled all Cantonese troops loyal to the rebellion as well as allied Guangxi and Ironsides troops. Of immediate concern was the mounting of the Jiangxi offensive and the failure of the Canton rebels to win over the commanders of the 19th Route Army to their side. With a large force within hitting distance of Canton, thousands

---

[26] September 12 1931 Pages 45–46 "The American Wheat Loan and the China Food Crisis". CWR Volume 58, 1931.

[27] Editorial, "Canton Factions Resemble Peiping Rebellion" June 13 1931, Page 52 Volume 57, 1931.

of farmers and laborers were pressed into fortifying Canton with an encirclement of 300 miles of trenches, barbed wire and fortifications.[28]

However, with the Yangtze floods in July and August of 1931 the communists sought to take advantage of the logistical problems facing Chiang Kai-shek. A communique from Canton ordered all available soldiers to march into Hunan in the belief that Chiang Kai-shek could not mobilize enough troops from Hubei because of the floods. Nonetheless, reports indicated that Chiang Kai-shek was able to mobilize 150,000 troops to defend Hubei and Hunan against the Cantonese invasion. On September 16, 1931 it was reported that a force of some 50,000 Southern Rebel troops from Guangdong and Guangxi advancing in Hunan had been repulsed. Most of the fighting had been along the Hunan, Guangdong, and Guangxi borders where the rebel groups held several towns. It was anticipated that Cantonese forces would join with the Guangxi rebels to march on Republican forces. Some 40,000 Cantonese troops had already entered Hunan from the Guangdong North. It was further reported that the Cantonese troops were coordinating military activities with the communist forces. A battle between Zhu De and Mao Zedong's 8th Red Army and Republican forces claimed 7000 communists killed and captured. This was one of several battles in the region and was viewed by some commanders as the fiercest fighting yet between communist and republican forces.[29]

To fund its excursions the Cantonese government imposed a tax on all food shipments to Hong Kong, forcing rationing in Hong Kong and reducing demand for Cantonese produce (e.g. poultry). However, there was a significant impact on the Canton treasury with yields due to war risk so high that that the value of notes issued by the Canton Central Bank fell by 60% of their face denominations. To compensate, the Canton Finance Ministry increased taxes on tobacco, spirits, gambling houses, and firecrackers. These and other business taxes would soon be expanded to all of Guangdong.

---

[28] Editorial, "Chiang Kai-shek Heads 300,000 Troops in Anti-Communist Drive" June 27, 1931 Pages 132–136.
[29] Editorial, "Chinese at Home and Abroad Appeal for Peace as Canton Renews its Civil War" China Weekly Review September 19 1931, Pages 92–96.

8.9 Institutional Development and the Rise of Credit Cooperatives

We return to the push by Chiang Kai-shek to develop agricultural cooperatives in 1932 as part of rural reconstruction. As the constructionists had recognized 10 years earlier, Chiang Kai-shek saw the need for credit in rural China. With Chinese bond markets in disarray, a stifled and chaotic banking system, unsettled reforms in local currency standards, and no conformity in currency standards (copper, silver, gold) the move towards cooperative lending rather than bank lending appeared prudent. The credit cooperatives were locally run with amounts dispersed and amounts repaid always in local currency or acceptable tender. Cooperative guidelines could always ensure that transactions were entitled in the same currency so that neither lender nor borrower had to deal with exchange: a loan made in copper was repaid in copper, a loan made in silver was repaid in silver, and so on. Furthermore, since the cooperatives were, at least in 1932 through 1936, separable from the formal financial system and were largely dependent upon money circulation at the local (village) level, the credit cooperatives were largely immunized against the factors of influence against provincial and national banks. In times of turmoil, the protections inherent in local cooperation might have provided a degree of stability that might not otherwise be available from pure reliance on a formal banking system.

A second reason that cooperatives took hold lies in the nature of the Chinese character. Elsewhere we have discussed *hui*, currently known as a form of rotating savings and credit association (ROSCA) that had in one way or another existed in rural China since the Song dynasty a thousand years earlier (see Chap. 4). *Hui*, could not survive in rural China without an innate sense of trust amongst the various members. Almost always the *hui* were made up of local villagers, or at least individuals local or known to the organizer. In one of our examples in Chap. 4 the *hui* had 31 members, which required that the last member to receive the funds had to believe that the 30 previous members would pay their dues and ensure that he got his contribution. Adding to this is the tight network and market linkages between villages of kinship, clan, and common economic enterprise as outlined by Skinner.[30] In both Trayner and Skinner the strength of

---

[30] G.W. Skinner. (1977). *The City in Late Imperial China*, Stanford University Press Stanford, CA.

community was tied to the central market to which outlying villagers would trade. In Skinner's world the identification of a region was defined by the central market as an attractor and a point of common interest to outlying villages. Two villages a mile apart might have no communication because the one village might travel South to its central market, while the other traveled North. Trayner makes the case that the membership of the *hui*, while usually within a village, would otherwise draw from this central market. So not only was there trust in *hui* but also trust in trade.

Building on this trust, Trayner saw the central market also as a place of cooperation. This was especially true of market and supply cooperatives, since cooperation at the village level without a connection to a market was a fairly redundant and unsustainable exercise. This was not necessarily the case for credit cooperatives since the money lent and borrowed was fungible and could be used within the village or at the market. Nonetheless, the idea of a union of cooperatives defined by the market center would allow for the expansion of cooperatives. The cooperatives at the village level could then be unionized to what Trayner referred to as the rural municipality. The rural municipality is very much like the structures defined by Skinner. Trayner went further to suggest that the idea of cooperation, particularly in credit cooperatives, could then be expanded and linked like a spider's web to form a federation of cooperatives in which flows of funds could be moved amongst high demand and high supply unions or municipalities.

Federating the credit cooperative unions started around 1932 by the four provincial banks which were merged into the Farmers Bank of China, one of the four policy banks of the era. With this initiative the credit cooperatives could use their own capital to secure loans from the Farmers Bank, increasing credit available. This was similar to the evolving system of credit cooperation in the United States at that time in which a cooperative bank—a government sponsored enterprise—would match capital put up by farmer members to increase the supply of credit. A federated system of cooperation was formally developed with *Nong Ben Ju* (the Farm Credit Bureau, see Chap. 13) to formalize cooperation as the primary source of credit for Chinese farmers.

CHAPTER 9

A Blueprint for Credit Under Rural Reconstruction

9.1 Introduction

As early as 1915 with the foundation of the Agricultural and Industrial Bank (Chap. 5) there was tacit recognition of the need for agricultural credit. But these efforts waned, and it was not until the China International Famine Relief Commission in 1921 and 1922 examined the issue did agricultural credit take root as a viable economic initiative with strong political support. Political support came with the formal recognition of the importance of agricultural lending for rural rehabilitation and reconstruction as being consistent with the Three People's Principles or San-min Doctrine. The doctrine, often summarized as nationalism, democracy, and the livelihood of the people, was a political philosophy developed by Sun Yat-sen—the father of the revolution against the Qing dynasty in 1911 and the first president of the Republic in 1912—as part of a philosophy to make China a free, prosperous, and powerful nation. Sun Yat-sen delivered a famous speech in 1924 about Principles of People's Livelihood, stating that it was the requirement of Three People's Principles to build a Farmers Bank and expand credit cooperatives.

Eventually, agricultural credit and broader access to institutional credit for farmers became a guiding principle for the national government. China's banking system at that time was so underdeveloped that progress would be slow. As the failure of the Da Wan Agricultural and Industrial Bank to deliver any momentum in developing agricultural credit illustrated,

© The Author(s) 2018
H. Fu, C. G. Turvey, *The Evolution of Agricultural Credit during China's Republican Era, 1912–1949*,
https://doi.org/10.1007/978-3-319-76801-4_9

the change from an existing institutional arrangement to an alternative was a costly process especially if the economic incentives were not there. To deliver credit to agriculture in the early Republican period would have been costly and risky so it was unlikely that a market-based voluntary institutional change would occur. Sun Yat-sen's populist message under the Three People's Principles recognized the social benefits of pushing programs that might otherwise be unprofitable. Conventional wisdom would suggest that Sun Yat-sen was thinking about the greater good, but he might also have sensed pressure from the communists with whom he had aligned in the first effort to unify China, to promote agricultural reforms.

After Sun Yat-sen died on March 25, 1925 his militarist successor Chiang Kai-shek moved to purge the communists from the Kuomintang (KMT) and unify China's North and South by force. Social and economic change was not a priority. As a main threat and a very strong competitor to the KMT, the Communist Party of China (CPC), founded in 1921, spared no effort to obtain the support from farmers and workers and began to lead armed uprisings and build revolutionary base areas or soviets. By the summer of 1930, several large revolutionary bases had been built and developed. With the Jiangxi Central revolutionary bases and Hubei-Henan-Anhui revolutionary bases, there arose a sense of urgency for Chiang Kai-shek and the Nanjing nationalist government to pay more attention to the rural economy, especially rural finance.

Self-help was a mainstay of most forms of cooperation whether in technology transfer, manual assistance, or acquiring credit. From the foreign academic perspective John Lossing Buck believed that the missionaries, and presumably also academics and extension faculty at agricultural and forestry universities, would train the Chinese in such a way that they could continue their work and could train others themselves. Buck saw that the Chinese nation had to develop its own destiny without the humiliating encroachment of foreigners. Believing that *"some outside help would be useful"*, the Chinese had to be free to choose the ideas and the methods from the offerings of Western culture.[1]

---

[1] Pugh. (1973). page 40. Based on interview by James Pugh with Buck at Poughkeepsie NY, April 27 1973.

Pugh, J. (1973). J. Lossing Buck, American Missionary: The Application of Scientific Agriculture in China, 1915–1944, Honors Thesis, Swarthmore College, Swarthmore PA, May 1973.

Although Buck was sympathetic to some of the platforms of the Nationalist movement, the events of 1927 were discouraging and frustrating: "*The prevailing Chinese opinion is that the Nanjing Nationalist Government is skating on thin ice and may topple any time. All are agreed that the new Nationalist government (of Chiang Kai-shek) is no better than the old regime so far as corruption and personal ambition is concerned. Chinese returned students, our own students, and members of our faculty say that of the taxes that are collected only a small fraction ever as appropriated to the purpose for which they are raised. Military taxes go largely to commanders, not to pay the inadequately dressed and fed soldiers. The Chinese in charge of establishing the new Farm Loan Bank said that much of the new tax of $1.20 (mex) per acre is kept by the tax collector himself and that only as small amount will actually reach the bank*".[2]

By March 1929 Buck's opinion had changed: "*Since the coming of the Nationalist Government to Nanjing there has been an increased interest in the subjects of agricultural economics, farm management and rural sociology. This is evidenced by increased requests from government bureaus and other national organizations for information pertaining to agricultural economic conditions and for recommendations of graduates who have had training in the same subject. There is now a demand for a number of men who have specialized in these particular subjects*",[3] and by 1933 "*I found much more interest in what is now known termed in China "rural reconstruction work" than has existed during any previous time. I found everyone talking and writing about rural reconstruction, and the officials and government bureaus all attempting some type of rural improvement work, either on paper or in a more concrete way*".[4]

9.2 A Blueprint for Modern Rural Financial Institutions by the Nanjing Government (KMT)

So, by 1929 the KMT was facing pressure from multiple forces. On economic development there was the China International Famine Relief Commission and agriculturalists at Nanjing University pushing for a pro-

---

[2] "Lossing Buck Tells of Visit to Nanjing" Poughkeepsie Eagle News, Saturday, January 7, 1928. Page 3. Also Buck to friends, November 13, 1927, Presbyterian Archives, 82:33–7. Page 5. Cf Pugh page 42 in part.

[3] Buck, J.L. (1927). Personal report of April 1, 1928 to March 31, 1929. Presbyterian Archives. 82:32–18, P.3. cf. Pugh page 40–41.

[4] Buck, J.L. (1933). Personal report of April 1, 1932 to March 31, 1933. Presbyterian Archives. 82:46–11, P.1–2. cf. Pugh page 61.

gram of rural reconstruction led by an expansion of cooperative rural credit societies, there were Sun Yat-sen loyalists pushing the populist message of the Three Principles, and finally—and most important to Chiang Kai-shek—was the growing communist threat. Consequently, a meeting was called on December 5–11, 1929 by the Ministry of Agriculture and Mining, to develop a blueprint for an ideal rural financial institution system. The outline of the resolution was as follows:

 I. Main goals: To formulate the entire agricultural loan system, to set up central and local rural financial institutions, and to specialize in providing low-cost funds needed for agriculture so as to support the development of agriculture and the improvement of farmer life.
 II. Administration: The central government was to set up a Commission of Agricultural Finance, jointly organized by the Ministry of Agriculture and Mines and the Ministry of Finance, which was to be the supreme organ for the implementation of the system of agricultural loans. The duties of the commission were as follows:

 (a) To make regulations on the establishment of rural financial institutions in the country;
 (b) To assist in and supervise the progress of the rural financial institutions throughout the country;
 (c) To formulate various laws and regulations relating to rural finance;
 (d) To investigate the agricultural economic issues throughout the country;
 (e) To promote and reward various agricultural cooperative undertakings; and preparation of the Central Agricultural Bank.

 III. Organizations:

 (a) The central government was to set up an agricultural bank to subsidize the rural financial institutions in various provinces and to lend long- and medium-term agricultural loans;
 (b) Provinces were to set up provincial agricultural banks to subsidize the rural financial institutions in all counties;

(c) The county was to set up the County Agricultural Bank of China to make medium-and short-term agricultural loans;
(d) Farmers banks were to be organized by provinces and counties or farmer groups to provide short-term agricultural loans.

IV. Implementation:

(a) The nature of rural financial institutions at all levels was to be not-for-profit;
(b) The Central Bank of Agriculture was to be established using state-designated funds or grants;
(c) Local rural financial institutions were to be established with public funds;
(d) Credit lending by local rural financial institutions were to be limited to loans and credit cooperatives organized by farmers;
(e) The central and local rural financial institutions would have the right to issue agricultural bonds.

V. Laws and regulations: All kinds of regulations of the rural financial institutions, the regulations on the issuance of agricultural bonds, the regulations on agricultural cooperatives, and other laws and regulations relating to the system of agricultural loans were to be written and promulgated at an early date.

The blueprint outlined the principles to be employed in the formulation of various laws and regulations and detailed measures. There was a sense of urgency that experts be selected and a meeting of the Agricultural Finance Committee be established as soon as possible. This was the first time in modern China—and indeed in China's history—that a comprehensive plan concerning the entire rural financial system was prepared as a blueprint for long-term government policy. This latter point is important. The 1915 act that allowed for the Agricultural and Industrial Bank and related joint liability credit cooperatives was prepared as a means for private joint-stock enterprises to supply credit to agriculture and related businesses, with no mandated support from the government. However, it should be noted that in the law permitting the Agricultural and Industrial Banks, there were provisions for farmer credit cooperatives and the option for the banks to issue bonds secured by mortgages to raise capital.

9.3　The Rural Finance Discussing Committee

As one of resolutions above, the Rural Finance Discussing Committee was founded in April 1930, hired agricultural economic experts, appointed the relevant members, and held a meeting in which six resolutions were accepted including the Plan of the Agricultural Finance System and its implementation, a draft of the Central Agricultural and Financial Committee Organization, a draft of the Central Agricultural Bank, a draft of the Farmers Bank, a draft of Agricultural Insurance, and a plan to establish respectively the Agricultural Bank of China and the Farmers Bank.

The draft of the Central Agricultural Bank of China provided for its organization, scope of business, bonds, supervision, and other items. On organization, the Ministry of Industry and the Ministry of Finance were to work together to form a Central Agricultural and Financial Commission. The Central Agricultural and Financial Commission would have the responsibility for establishing the Central Agricultural Bank of China. The business objectives included support for the development of agriculture and lending to long- and medium-term credit undertakings such as agriculture and forestry, land reclamation, farmland irrigation and fishery.

The draft of the Farmers Bank stipulated the organization, business, supervision, subsidies, and withdrawal of provident funds from the bank. It was stipulated that the Farmers Bank was to be organized on cooperative principles and be organized from the bottom up to the county level, then the provincial and central levels. Its supervisors and the directors were to be elected by the competent agricultural finance committee, and its business objective was to provide credit to farmers and funds for the development of the rural economy.

Members of Rural Finance Discussing Committee called for a second meeting in March 1933, when they approved a plan to implement an Agricultural Finance System, drafted an Agricultural Granary Law, and revised other draft laws and regulations. The objective was to establish agricultural financial institutions that could provide credit for cultivation, fishery and animal husbandry, forestry, and other related loans. It urged establishing a Central Agricultural Bank Preparatory Office and agricultural granary. They recognized that rural deposits would likely be small and so to avoid credit constraints on agricultural loans they needed to increase the financing channels for financial institutions. To achieve this, it was recommended that the public donate grain funds[5] and that various financial institutions (banks, insurance companies, trust companies, savings associations) should be rewarded for making agricultural loans. It was also suggested that funds be made available from the Postal and Savings Bank and that a grain levy or import tax be applied to grain imports to provide funds for the proposed Agricultural Bank of China. Finally, they proposed the issuance of Agricultural Bank bonds.

Finally, recognizing that the loan types required short-term flexibility to match production cycles versus capital or land loans, the meeting classified loan types into long, medium and short terms. But this created an additional problem related to the liquidity matching of loan terms to loan sources (i.e. using short-term funds for making long-term loans, and vice versa). Due to the different loan terms, the meeting proposed to separate the proposed Agricultural Bank of China and the Farmers Bank into two agencies.

9.4 Characteristics of Modern Rural Financial System in Design

Figure 9.1 illustrates the system of rural finance conceived by the KMT government according to the above designs. Its structure was based on a binary rural financial system with central, provincial, and county level 'Agricultural' and 'Farmers' banks being complementary in terms of aggregate supply but differentiated by the nature of credit. The Agricultural Bank was to be responsible for medium- and long-term loans, while the Farmers Bank was to be responsible for short-term loans. Thus, the proposed Agricultural Bank of China, lending long-term and medium-term loans, was in some respects similar to the land bank system in various other

---

[5] During this period of the Republic, China faced economic decline, conventional sources of taxation were exhausted, and the fiscal order was chaotic. In addition to conventional taxes there were many random levies and excessive surtaxes imposed at local, provincial, and national levels. One of these was a temporary move forcing of 'donations' of grain referred to as the Grain Donation. This included merchant donations, shop donations, wine donations, opium donations, house donations, car donations, and more. The central decree stipulated that local governments at all levels, in promoting construction, should organize charitable and cultural undertakings. Donations would be collected in accordance with the uniform collection method, and the national and provincial governments also had provisions for the collection of donations. Youyi Zhang (1957), China modern agricultural and agricultural history data, Beijing: Sanlian Bookstore.

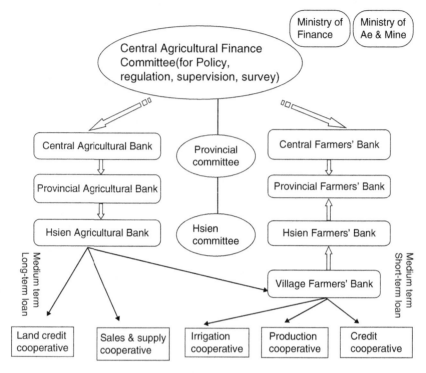

Fig. 9.1 Schematic of KMT blueprint for agricultural credit, circa 1933

countries, particularly the Farm Credit System in the United States. The American Farm Credit System operated as a Government Sponsored Enterprise (GSE), accepted government deposits and issued bonds secured by farm mortgages. Likewise the Chinese model, also designed to operate as a GSE, was overseen by the government and required capital from government funds or by issuing bonds that would have had some form of implicit or explicit guarantee. The Farmers Banks were more closely tied to America's Production Credit Associations in the sense that their funds would almost exclusively target the development and support of an underlying cooperative banking system, run by civilians. The Agricultural Bank was to provide capital for credit cooperatives as well as sales and supply cooperatives, but could also transfer funds to, and support the lending of, the village Farmers Bank. The Farmers Banks, operating at the village level, would provide credit at the farm level for active participation in irrigation, production, and credit cooperatives.

There were other differences as well. The Provincial Farmers Bank and Hsien Farmers Bank were envisioned as a unitary system since it had no branches. The Central Farmer's Bank and the Agricultural Bank of China were to establish headquarters and head offices in major cities and established branches and sub-branches in larger cities, counties, and larger towns across China, thereby forming a large network of banks. Because the Agricultural Bank was to be the main organ for agricultural credit policy its design was on a top-down basis, pushing credit to meet demand. The Farmers Bank was a bottom-up approach to credit demand, being driven by the establishment of cooperatives at the village level. The demand signals flowed from village to county to province. The central authority for the Farmers Banks was top-down only as it pertained to policies, laws, regulation, and oversight coming from the central government.

9.5 Summary

The initiatives taken by the KMT between 1930 and 1933 are illustrative of how policies towards agriculture were rapidly changing. These changes were seen not only as an economic imperative but a military one as well, as the communists were gaining traction in the rural South, and elsewhere in China. The blueprint also revealed a level of sophistication in understanding not only the role of credit in agricultural economies, but also the agricultural economy itself. It also opened the door for political action and the recognition that left to its own devices the emerging Chinese banking system was unlikely to have meaningful spillover effects for agriculture, at least in the immediate future. Agriculture was (and still is) highly risky and very expensive to originate and monitor loans. Consequently, there was wide-spread credit rationing of a prejudicial form that the private sector was not going to remedy.

The blueprint laid out a program of agricultural credit with direct government involvement and the development of new types of banks and cooperatives as a government sponsored enterprise. The government sponsorship of land banks and bond financing in the United States, as well as the expansion of capital for agricultural cooperatives followed, at least in principle, the cooperative model of the Raiffeisen model in Germany a century earlier.

Ultimately the blueprint was not acted upon to the extent laid out between 1930 and 1933. In 1935 the Farmers Bank of China was formed, but not along cooperative lines, although ultimately it did support cooperation in the 1940s. The Central Agricultural Bank—the first notion of the Agricultural Bank of China—did not take form, leading later in 1936 to the formation of *Nong Ben Ju* (the Farm Credit Bureau). The Farmers Bank of China and *Nong Ben Ju* are discussed in the following chapters.

CHAPTER 10

Evolution of the Cooperative Financial System: 1927–49

10.1 Introduction

Up until this point it is clear that the basic reason for changes in rural financial institutions during the Republican era was the shortage of financial supply or imbalance of rural financial institutions. In fact there was barely any supply and few economic incentives to create any balance between the rural and urban sectors. We have discussed in Chap. 5 the 1915 promulgation of the Agricultural and Industrial Bank, including a right to develop credit cooperatives, but by 1921 this had largely fizzled out. The push by the China International Famine Relief Commission and Nanjing University were the first true efforts to develop agricultural cooperation but there appears to be little initiative by the Kuomintang (KMT) at least through 1927 and after the Northern expedition (see Chap. 8). There is evidence from John Lossing Buck that the effort to mobilize resources towards agricultural credit were frustratingly slow in 1926, but by 1928 initiatives towards rural reconstruction were taking hold in Nanjing along the lines that Buck had proposed. However, it does not appear to be until 1932 that the KMT really pushed for agricultural cooperation and credit but this was not so much the Nanjing University initiative, but rather the realization that within communist-held soviets in South China, cooperative credit was rising in popularity. The nationalist government soon came to realize that what the communists had to offer was a sense of populism and agricultural reforms that had not previously been provided for farmers. The battle against the communists was not just about geography, but about economic reforms, and this included credit.

With this, the designation and execution process of financial sector development for rural areas during the period of the Nanjing national government was forced institutional change seen through the lens of military conflict, rather than other initiatives at modernizing the banking system based on macromonetary demands and ascendance to global trade. Consequently, the Farmers Bank of China gradually obtained a monopoly position in the development process of institutions serving farmers and agricultural development; meanwhile, to support credit cooperatives and credit unions the foundation of a Central Cooperative Treasury promoted the formation of a cooperative financial system. These treasuries, which emerged during the war years, were to ensure capital flows and liquidity for the cooperative system as a whole, becoming a crucial linkage between commercial lenders including the Farmers Banks of China which could then contribute capital to cooperatives, and the credit societies themselves, to provide a mechanism for funds to flow between surplus and deficit cooperatives across both county and provincial boundaries.

10.2 Administrative Structure of Cooperative Credit

"*In order to extend loans to farmers, banks usually had to organize cooperatives for the rural population in advance. Agricultural cooperatives with a healthy structure are of paramount importance, for without them, loans extended to the farmers might fall into the hands of selfish and undesirable members of the rural communities.*"[1] With this sentiment, the cooperative was introduced and considered as a great aid to improve Chinese economic organizations. Indeed, the Nanjing government regarded the cooperative movement as the very first step to carry on the Principle of People's Livelihood.[2] Both central and provincial governments advocated and encouraged all efforts engaging in the cooperative businesses. Jiangsu,

---

[1] Yijin Lin. (1941). Chinese Government Banks in War Time, The Central Bank of China Bulletin, V.7 No.1, p. 23.

[2] Principle of People's Livelihood was one of the Three Principles of the People, which also translates as Three People's Principles or San-min Doctrine established by Sun Yat-sen. The three principles relate to nationalism, democracy, and the livelihood of the people where livelihood sought sufficiency in clothing, food, housing, and healthcare.

Zhejiang, Shandong, and Hebei established special administrative structures responsible for the management of cooperative business affairs. This included registration of cooperative societies, making plans, investigation and statistics, personnel training, and assessment. Regional administrative sections were also established. The Rural Cooperative Committee in Henan-Hubei-Anhui-Jiangxi Field Headquarters for Suppressing Bandits (*Yu-E-Wan-Gan Sisheng Jiaofei Silingbu*) was established to promote cooperative business in these four provinces in 1934.[3] Finally a national administrative section referred to as the Division of Cooperation was established within the Ministry of Industry in June 1936.

10.3 Rules and Law

Before 1927 there were no special laws for cooperation other than what was ordinarily considered customary and a few clauses in Civil Law. The first governmental regulation, Provisional Regulations of Cooperatives, was enacted in Jiangsu in June 1928, followed by Provisional Regulations of Rural Credit Cooperatives in Zhejiang in July 1928. Between 1928 and 1934, 15 provincial regulations were enacted.[4] Henan-Hubei-Anhui-Jiangxi Field Headquarters for Suppressing Bandits enacted Rural Cooperative Regulations in the Bandit District and detailed rules for its implementation in October 1932.

The Nanjing central government enacted the Cooperatives Law in March, 1934 and its detailed rules for implementation were released in August 1935. The purpose of the Cooperatives Law was to regularize competent authority, determine various classifications for cooperatives, define the scope of business, and establish rules for associations of cooperatives. An Outline for County-level Cooperatives' Organization was promulgated in August 1940, which included an important clause stating that county-level cooperatives were to be the basic structure for developing the national economy. This broadened the mission of cooperatives from prior statements related to the improvement of members' livelihood and economic conditions as written in the Cooperatives Law six years earlier. In other words, starting in 1940 the role of cooperatives (and mutual

---

[3] The term 'bandits' in this context did not refer to roving warlords or robber forces, but specifically to communists operating in these areas.

[4] Jian-cheng Lai. (1990). Cooperative Movement in Modern China, Taiwan: Zhengzhong Press, p. 147.

aid) was elevated from a local purpose to a national purpose including promoting national economic policy.

The main provisions of the Detailed Rules of Cooperatives Law were as follows. First, the competent authority provided under Article 2 of the rules stated that: "*The competent authority referred to in this Law and these Detailed Rules and Regulations shall be the county government at the county-level, social bureau in municipal government, cooperative undertaking department, or the social department or the construction hall in provincial government, the Ministry of Civil Affairs in central government*". Second, the rules established three types of cooperatives including production, supply, and credit cooperatives. Third, the rules recognized the differences across businesses and business types. With specific reference to agricultural finance, they recognized that the business of credit cooperatives was directed to the circulation of finance and the purpose of making loans to their members for production and manufacturing. Fourth, for a cooperatives association, Article 42 stipulated that: "*The establishment of a cooperative association shall be based on the needs of the alliance in the business, but each and every one of the counties, every province and the whole country shall still have its own integrated association organization so as to meet the needs of the general public and the general public business needs*".

10.4 Funding Cooperatives

There were three main sources of funding for a cooperative organization. The first was the collection of funds of the cooperative, including the stock, deposits, and accumulation fund. The second was external capital, mainly from loan funds from administrative regulators and the banks providing rural credit, and the third was a cooperative financial system built specifically to finance its businesses.

In the earlier phases of the cooperative movement, external capital held an important position. However, the development of cooperatives mainly depended on the increase of self-collecting funds. Stock funds were the most basic source of funds for cooperatives and formed the basis for cooperative self-reliance. The share of cooperatives was paid by each member and required before they could use economic facilities. The average subscribed capital per member is shown in Table 10.1, and the shares of

Table 10.1 Average subscribed capital per member

Province	Capital up to June 1947	1940	1941	1942	1943	1944	1945	1946	June 1947
Total	20,644,291,355	3.5	5.2	9.2	23.7	44.7	84.8	306.1	1024.5
Jiangsu	1,795,289,670	–	–	–	–	–	–	3141.3	8268.2
Zhejiang	298,368,880	2.4	3.4	3.6	10.3	19.0	30.4	251.8	299.6
Anhui	266,465,583	4.2	4.7	8.3	15.1	28.7	51.7	260.9	289.0
Jiangxi	729,807,680	7.3	8.6	15.0	24.5	33.0	66.6	214.9	249.6
Hubei	591,039,606	2.0	2.7	10.1	10.9	41.2	94.6	188	398.5
Hunan	285,895,317	1.8	4.1	4.2	5.5	9.2	9.2	64.3	216.8
Sichuan	1,055,890,956	2.6	5.2	6.6	16.6	42.4	105.7	24.8	378.1
Xikang	6,235,953	5.3	6.8	6.8	11.2	21.7	29.4	44.7	49.4
Hebei	347,048,350	–	–	–	–	–	–	668.6	1501.7
Shandong	230,659,940	–	–	–	–	–	–	2727.2	4704.0
Shanxi	3,159,991,432	–	–	–	–	–	–	885.1	4292.8
Henan	1,025,237,963	3.4	6.9	14.8	28.7	41.8	45.6	55.0	443.6
Shaanxi	415,118,907	2.1	3.1	8.5	43.2	93.7	167.2	273.1	281.3
Gansu	66,911,121	3.8	5.2	7.0	33.0	60.0	116.0	116.0	116.0
Qinghai	23,346,311	–	–	–	–	–	294.2	295.4	330.1
Fujian	166,457,754	3.4	4.0	6.6	6.8	29.0	44.5	247.7	247.7
Taiwan	45,956,840	–	–	–	–	–	–	–	4452.3
Guangdong	1,619,686,981	2.3	7.8	9.3	35.5	47.4	61.0	180.9	1588.7
Guangxi	395,841,911	1.5	2.5	7.5	38.6	64.7	67.7	215.0	346.2
Yunnan	505,875,340	3.5	5.3	17.2	65.5	123.8	421.7	819.6	1405.2
Guizhou	291,959,495	2.6	3.4	8.1	16.8	33.7	57.4	169.2	294.5

(*continued*)

Table 10.1 (continued)

Province	Capital up to June 1947	1940	1941	1942	1943	1944	1945	1946	June 1947
Liaoning	831,547,750	–	–	–	–	–	–	–	7642.5
Jilin	111,788,050	–	–	–	–	–	–	–	15578.0
Rehe	10,212,840	–	–	–	–	–	–	–	598.5
Suiyuan	360,862,300	–	14.3	18.0	31.1	89.2	232.6	1490.5	5667.2
Ningxia	13,481,166	2.1	4.1	10.5	25.9	53.3	124.0	122.5	162.1
Nanjing	3,449,133,900	–	–	–	–	–	–	4080.4	36747.6
Shanghai	1,615,009,893	–	–	–	–	–	–	6608.4	10585.5
Peking	259,451,510	–	–	–	–	–	–	1092.4	1093.9
Tianjin	464,070,010	–	–	–	–	–	–	2208.5	2628.6
Qingdao	822,983,680	–	–	–	–	–	–	3410.3	10365.9
Chongqing	2,227,564,260	14.7	15.6	27.1	46.3	101.2	151.8	210.1	77241.4

Average subscribed capital per member ($)

Source: Institute of cooperatives of China (1947), Cooperative Movement in China, Liming Press, p. 13

national cooperatives over the years increased rapidly in nominal terms[5]—4120 times over the 10 years from 1937 to 1947—and the overall strength of the cooperative movement greatly increased. The amount of funds of a single cooperative also increased year by year. On average, the share of each cooperative was 113 yuan in 1937 and 127,470 yuan by 1947, an increase of 1128 times. In some years, like 1943 and 1947, there were extraordinary increases.

10.5 Cooperative Credit Associations (*Hezuoshe Lianshe*)

It was felt that if loans could be extended to a cooperative credit society, secured on the joint and several responsibility of all of its members who would supervise the extension and collection of loans to individual members, the cost of administration could be kept low, and the ultimate interest rate could be greatly reduced. Eventually these credit societies were to be coordinated through unions and the whole controlled by a central bank. The first credit union came into existence in 1925 with 10 member societies. These unions gave the members of the individual societies a feeling of solidarity which came from an association with large numbers of members and outreach and training courses for cooperators. It was thought that: "*It is quite possible that eventually, when the movement grows, the Central Bank will make loans only to the unions, and they in turn will reallocate the funds to their member societies*".[6]

A significant timestamp to the changes in policies of the national government towards cooperatives can be marked by the 1936 establishment of the first provincial cooperative bank. The development of the cooperative financial system of Modern China can thus be divided into two phases: before 1936, cooperative finance was dependent upon the banking system, including the newly formed Farmers Bank and other commercial banks. After 1936, capital and fund flows were obtained from the development of newly established associations of cooperatives, provincial level cooperative banks, and the Central Cooperative Bank.

---

[5] These included both real effects via expansion and efficiency, but the period following the Japanese invasion in 1937 and the civil war years had significant bouts of inflation. See Chaps. 8 and 14.

[6] Walter H. Mallory. (1931). Rural Cooperative Credit in China: a record of seven years of experimentation summary, *The quarterly Journal of Economics*, V.45 No.3.

10.6 Expansion of Cooperatives

After the outbreak of the war with Japan, the KMT vigorously promoted the establishment of a cooperative system. The establishment of associations of cooperatives and cooperative treasuries was an important part of the national government in building an independent cooperative financial system. Associations of cooperatives had mainly three levels, from the bottom up are: District Association, County Association, and Provincial Association.

Table 10.2 shows that the total number of associations at the provincial and county levels was increasing year by year. The district association was established earlier, developed rapidly between 1938 and 1943, and degenerated due to shrinking credit business after 1944. The county association was also established earlier, with numbers gradually increasing from 1938 to 1947. The number of provincial associations began to increase only after the provincial governments made great efforts from 1944 to promote the cooperatives.

By 1949 there were 170,181 cooperative credit associations throughout China. In addition to making loans, accepting deposits, and providing insurance for domestic animals, cooperatives had also established mechanisms for transmitting rural remittances in towns and villages. The cooperative society was not only an economic organization, but also a basic political and societal unit especially during the war years. Jiancheng Lai argued that the cooperative movement, "*Under different regimes, in different times and regions, has been used as an instrument of policy with different aims and means*".[7] As can be seen from Table 10.3, before the outbreak of the Anti-Japanese War, the areas where cooperative movements made much progress was North China (Hebei, Shandong, and Shanxi provinces), and the middle and lower reaches of the Yangtze River (Jiangsu, Zhejiang, Anhui, Jiangxi, Hunan, and Hubei). After the outbreak of the Anti-Japanese War, North China was occupied by Japan. Consequently, the regions and directions of the cooperative movements underwent significant changes (see Chap. 14). The Southwestern and Northwestern regions (Sichuan, Xikang, Shaanxi, Gansu, Guangxi, Yunnan, and Guizhou provinces) became major areas for cooperative development. The center

---

[7] Jian-cheng Lai (1990). Cooperative Movement in Modern China, Taiwan: Zhengzhong Press, p. 3.

Table 10.2 Associations of cooperatives 1938–46

Year	\multicolumn{3}{c}{Provincial-level associations of cooperatives}			\multicolumn{3}{c}{County-level associations of cooperatives}			\multicolumn{3}{c}{District-level associations of cooperatives}		
	No. of cooperatives	No. of members	Subscribed capital ($)	No. of cooperatives	No. of members	Subscribed capital ($)	No. of cooperatives	No. of members	Subscribed capital ($)
1938	–	–	–	45	–	–	694	–	–
1939	–	–	–	54	878	190,614	896	11,908	1,885,808
1940	–	–	–	104	2565	1,254,362	1099	15,028	1,297,259
1941	–	–	–	130	3367	1,675,038	1139	17,330	2,300,183
1942	–	–	–	164	3947	4,086,616	1093	14,601	1,299,130
1943	–	–	–	241	5563	25,027,459	1032	13,932	1,248,258
1944	5	107	4,223,950	369	7472	68,356,044	991	13,434	1,210,815
1945	9	354	64,300,173	459	11,049	204,522,692	965	13,763	1,163,924
1946	9	355	122,786,273	588	12,779	545,883,125	631	9123	2,168,630
June 1947	14	669	298,720,523	651	14,377	900,826,387	644	9135	2,248,630

Source: Institute of cooperatives of China (1947), Cooperative Movement in China, Liming Press, p. 5

Table 10.3 Geographical distribution of cooperatives

Year	1932	1933	1934	1936	1936	1937	1938	1939	1940	1941	1942	1943	1944	1945	1946	1947
Total	3978	5535	14,649	26,224	37,318	46,983	64,565	91,426	133,542	155,647	160,393	166,826	171,681	172,053	160,222	161,953
Credit cooperatives %	87.11%	78.49%	67.2%	58.8%	55.25%	73.6%	85.7%	88.2%	87%	84.9%	82.4%	48.1%	44.2%	38%	34.1%	30%
Jiangsu	1798	1911	2937	4077	3305	3305	2415	4024	–	–	–	–	–	–	333	805
Zhejiang	782	1139	1793	1972	1518	1195	1558	3299	4766	5709	5970	6468	7236	7641	5504	5537
Anhui	22	387	1463	2284	4125	4125	4098	4958	6742	7792	8900	9964	10,210	10,574	10,680	10,641
Jiangxi	15	489	1078	2038	3209	4614	7451	8390	10,387	10,853	11,033	11,361	11,382	11,041	7233	7221
Hubei	3	5	566	1228	1932	2717	5612	6607	11,062	11,926	13,440	14,340	16,071	16,522	16,682	16,858
Hunan	17	14	558	963	1985	3674	6111	7077	14,947	17,755	17,530	17,809	18,139	18,139	17,513	16,849
Sichuan	8	2	3	–	1322	2374	8236	166	24,146	23,599	23,586	24,349	22,663	23,400	24,981	25,473
Xikang	–	–	–	–	–	–	–	360	629	1162	1297	1291	1277	1231	1272	1337
Hebei	999	956	1935	6240	6663	6663	6045	16,693	–	–	–	–	–	–	520	699
Shandong	211	545	2472	3637	4985	4965	2597	360	–	–	–	–	–	–	103	304
Shanxi	19	7	190	453	69	69	44	6045	–	–	–	–	–	320	566	414
Henan	26	10	997	1761	3221	3484	4009	2597	7386	9747	9827	12,872	14,233	14,287	14,355	15,791
Shannxi	6	5	320	671	2066	4009	4659	44	9780	11,542	11,260	12,306	11,206	9345	8665	8529
Gansu	3	–	–	33	244	437	2562	4407	5561	6659	6752	6197	6105	5637	5637	5637
Qinghai	1	–	–	312	–	–	–	5378	–	–	–	–	–	218	281	288
Fujian	4	–	14	–	1946	2615	3353	4681	5171	5782	7730	–	9268	10,119	7522	7522
Taiwan	–	–	–	–	225	750	–	–	–	–	–	–	–	–	–	12
Guangdong	6	12	194	307	6	20	672	4025	1913	6639	8694	–	9994	10,722	11,291	12,427
Guangxi	2	8	8	14	3	129	507	–	16,334	19,066	15,601	–	13,625	13,692	10,565	10,215

Yunnan	27	–	–	–	35	1487	234	725	4806	6450	7266	–	7424	7162	6654	7063
Guizhou	4	–	–	–	–	–	4338	4532	9593	10,427	10,416	–	11,101	10,187	7174	5755
Liaoning	–	–	–	–	–	–	–	838	–	–	–	–	–	–	–	59
Jilin	–	–	–	–	–	290	–	6694	–	–	–	–	–	–	–	10
Rehe	–	–	–	–	290	60	5	–	–	–	–	–	–	–	–	30
Chahaer	3	–	–	–	60	–	59	–	–	–	–	–	–	–	–	–
Suiyuan	4	3	54	–	–	–	–	–	–	299	316	286	333	367	763	797
Ningxia	–	20	–	–	78	–	–	–	189	359	395	653	728	788	804	780
Nanjing	8	5	–	50	15	–	–	–	–	–	–	–	–	–	9	31
Shanghai	2	37	16	123	19	–	–	–	–	–	–	–	–	–	40	94
Peking	6	–	85	7	–	–	–	–	–	–	–	–	–	–	249	332
Tianjin	2	–	–	–	17	–	–	1	–	–	–	–	–	–	210	236
Qingdao	–	–	–	–	–	1	–	–	–	–	–	–	–	–	120	160
Chongqing	–	–	–	–	–	–	–	–	130	181	380	551	686	661	496	47

Source: Jian-cheng Lai (1990), Cooperative Movement in Modern China, Taiwan: Zhengzhong Press, pp. 98–99

Table 10.4 Summary of cooperative treasuries in various provinces over years

		Sichuan	Xikuang	Guizhou	Yunnan	Guangxi	Shaaxi	Gansu	Henan
Before 1937	Provincial-level CB	1							
	County-level CB								2
1937	Provincial-level CB	1							
	County-level CB	6							2
1938	Provincial-level CB	1							
	County-level CB	62		16			17		2
1939	Provincial-level CB	1							
	County-level CB	76	9	42		32	5		5
1940	Provincial-level CB	1				1			
	County-level CB	117	10	58	9	51	17	22	16

Hubei	Hunan	JIangxi	Zhejiang	Fujian	Chongqing	Total	Shutdown	Total	Loan balance (thousand ¥)
						1		1	250
						2		2	
		1				2		2	500
1	6	5				20	7	27	
		1	1			3		3	14,000
2	10	13	18		1	141	10	151	
		1	1			3		3	50,000
12	18	11	26		1	237	13	250	
		1	1	1		5		5	100,000
11	25	10	32	2	1	381	16	397	

of the cooperatives movement was Sichuan, which was the center of the war of resistance. The pace and development of cooperatives was also rapid in the middle and lower reaches of the Yangtze River even though these regions were also under the threat of war.

10.7 Cooperative Treasury (Hezuo Jinku) System

Although the number of cooperative societies grew rapidly their financial power did not grow that much due to a shortage of capital. Social elites appealed for a cooperative treasury[8] and an independent cooperative financial system. The main business of a cooperative treasury was to finance its members and offer a deposit service. The ultimate goal of cooperative treasuries was to establish a financial institute of the cooperative society, by the cooperative society and for the cooperative society. The first provincial-level cooperative treasury was founded in Sichuan Province in December 1936. On February 23, 1938, the Ministry of Economic Affairs amended the 'rules' announcing that subscribers to cooperative treasuries could be extend to Farmers Banks, local banks and other banks handling agricultural loans. The effect of this amendment was to increase cooperative treasury funds rapidly. In addition, the initiatives under *Nong Ben Ju* (Farm Credit Bureau) and the Farmers Bank of China, Bank of China, Bank of Communications, the Central Trust Agency, Association of Chinese Industrial Cooperation, and provincial and municipal governments also resulted in cooperative treasury activities. This was the golden age of the cooperative treasury. By the end of 1938, *Nong Ben Ju* led the establishment of 76 county-level cooperative treasuries. In January 1939, the Fifth Plenary of the KMT approved stepping up the "*promotion of the cause of cooperation*" and urged the establishment of a Central Cooperative Treasury and the readjustment of the businesses of the Farm Credit Bureau (see Chap. 13), the Farmers Bank of China, and the Agricultural Adjustment Branch accordingly. This was supported by the government that helped in its development. As a result, the numbers of cooperative treasuries, first established in 1939, grew rapidly, expanding to 175. By the end of 1940, 397 cooperative treasuries were established and 475 in 1941. By the end of 1941, provincial (municipal) cooperative treasuries were

---

[8] Basically the cooperative treasury was founded to finance cooperative societies, and was not for profit. It was some kind of cooperative bank, but was not named as a cooperative bank, because as Chiang kai-shek said, "*it's different from a bank in nature*".

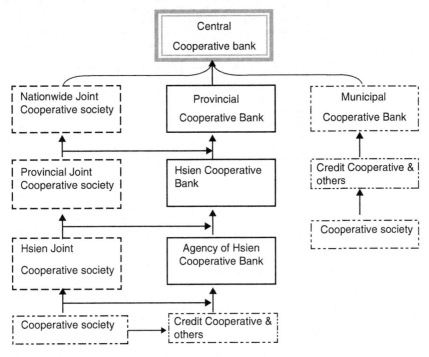

Fig. 10.1 Structure of the cooperative system

founded in Sichuan, Jiangxi, Zhejiang, Fujian, Guangxi, Yunnan, Gansu, and Chongqing. The Central Cooperative Treasury was founded in June 1946, and by 1947 it had about 49 branches across free China and was the fastest-growing segment of the rural financial system.

The cooperative financial system was originally a four-tier system as shown in Fig. 10.1, but after 1943 it switched to a three-tier system, in which the provincial cooperative treasuries, independent legal entities, were replaced by a branch of the Central Cooperative Treasury. A cooperative treasury was an ally of cooperative societies. The county-level cooperative treasury was subscribed to by all cooperative societies and its associations within the scope of a county; provincial-level treasuries were formed from aggregated county-level cooperative treasuries and provincial-level associations of cooperative societies within a province; a centralized cooperative treasury was formed by the aggregation of provincial-level cooperative treasuries and the national association of cooperative societies.

10.8 Differences Between the Credit Cooperative Association and Cooperative Treasury

The main differences between the system of cooperative treasuries and the system of credit cooperatives were as follows:

1. The credit cooperative associations were allies of credit cooperatives, and the cooperative treasury was the union of various kinds of cooperatives and cooperative associations.
2. Most credit cooperatives associations were organized with a bottom-up structure, while cooperative treasuries were structured as top-down organizations.
3. The credit cooperative associations were purely mutual financial institutions, while some cooperative treasuries were purely mutual-aid organizations, although there were still some cooperative treasuries run by official or public sectors.
4. In addition to a wider range of lenders, the size or amounts of loans issued by cooperative treasuries were larger than typically offered by credit cooperatives.
5. With the coexistence of credit cooperative associations and cooperative treasuries, the emphasis of the cooperative treasury's work was on the guidance of cooperative financial services, while the work of credit cooperative associations was on the guidance of community affairs.

10.9 Summary

By 1936 there were two initiatives of the KMT in operation: *Nong Ben Ju* and the Farmers Bank of China. Both initiatives had mandates to support agricultural development including infrastructure and storage facilities and the provision of credit to agriculture. Because of the war with Japan, and the civil war that followed, these initiatives did not have the intended effect nationwide, but as the war progressed there was increased reliance on agricultural credit and the formation of agricultural societies in unoccupied territories. 1936 saw the establishment of the first cooperative bank, which was a clear indication of how the KMT viewed agricultural cooperatives and cooperative credit societies in China's national development. The war years did not diminish the role of cooperative credit for agriculture and in fact providing farmers with access to credit became even more important in support of the war effort.

The constraint to the development of agricultural credit in this form was access to funds and a clearing mechanism. Laws, guidance, regulation, and oversight became critical. The legal framework was established formally in 1937, which set forth a rapid expansion of credit associations throughout China. By 1940 the role of cooperative credit societies was expanded from a microfocus on farm productivity and county development to become the basic structure for developing the national economy. To accomplish this and the funding shortage cooperative treasuries were formed. The cooperative treasuries superseded cooperative credit societies in terms of oversight and market development, but more crucially they became a financial linkage between commercial lenders including the Farmers Banks of China which could then contribute capital to cooperatives, and the credit societies, and provided a mechanism for funds to flow between surplus and deficit cooperatives not only across county boundaries, but across provincial boundaries as well.

A consequence of these initiatives between 1937 and 1949 was a rapid rise in the number of credit societies in free China, and the capital held by cooperative societies. To what effect the gains are real is difficult to discern because of periods of hyperinflation, but in Chap. 14 it appears that in real terms the farming sector held steady. Ultimately, the system collapsed under the weight of the war with Japan and the civil war as the national currency and monetary system collapsed. Nonetheless, the fabric of cooperative credit societies remained in principle and by 1950 new cooperative credit societies emerged that would eventually become the basis for the modern rural credit cooperatives.

CHAPTER 11

Chinese Communists, Border Currency, and Agricultural Credit during Wartime

11.1 Introduction

During the war of aggression with Japan, Japanese forces occupied large sections of land in both North and South China. As discussed in the previous chapter there was tremendous growth in the number of credit cooperatives in unoccupied territory. However, in occupied areas the numbers of credit cooperatives and societies dwindled to almost nothing having being shut down as Japanese commandeered positions in provincial banks, or outlawed the societies outright. What is not well understood is how farmers obtained credit in occupied territories.

This chapter explores a particularly interesting story of agricultural credit in China, which in several seemingly unrelated parts, occurred within the communist 'controlled' border regions that saw the Communist Party of China (CPC) issuing its own banknotes not only for its own transactions, but also for making loans.[1] The three component parts of

---

[1] There were a number of border regions established between 1937 and 1949. The most famous was the Shanxi-Hebei-Shandong-Henan (JinJiLuYu) border region. The Shaanxi-Gansu-Ningxia border region was centered around Yan'an. Others include the Shandong base area which covered most of the Shandong interior, beyond the border areas, Shanxi-Chahar-Hebei, Shanxi-Suiyan, Hubei-Anhwei-Henan, and Jiangsu. (Chahar and Suiyuan were absorbed into Inner Mongolia and modern Hebei.) See for example, Goodman, D.S.G (1994). "JinJiLuYu in the Sino-Japanese War: The Border Region and the Border Region Government". *China Quarterly* 140(December):1007–1024.

© The Author(s) 2018
H. Fu, C. G. Turvey, *The Evolution of Agricultural Credit during China's Republican Era, 1912–1949*,
https://doi.org/10.1007/978-3-319-76801-4_11

interest are the designation and administration of border regions, the issuance of currency within these regions, and the advent of agricultural taxation based upon units of grain. These will be expanded and linked together in this chapter to provide an overall sense of credit and credit systems in the base areas.

The issuance of currency in the border and base areas is interesting itself, but as the Sino-Japanese war progressed it is foolhardy to consider the monetary and credit institutions of the border regions, without considering the power structure and currency of the Nationalist government and the Japanese, particularly when as early as 1938 the three power centers each forbade people to use the others' currencies.[2] The role that agricultural credit played in the history of currency and banking in modern China is an innocuous one, but one that ultimately led to the formation of the People's Bank of China in 1948. We describe the conditions in the border regions, the rise of border currency and agricultural credit within the border regions, and the political posturing by the CPC and the Kuomintang (KMT) to jointly undermine each other's currency using direct and devious means in a way that can only be described as economic warfare.

11.2 Border Regions and Base Areas

The border regions were more of an administrative unit rather than a full-blown government. Nonetheless, they were a convenient political instrument of the wider CPC strategy during wartime (and beyond). These were designed to mobilize the war effort, provide support to the determination and collection of taxes, provide economic stabilization, direct economic warfare, and when necessary provide disaster relief against nature and war. The border regions were provisional in the sense that they were wartime institutions on the one hand, and undemocratic on the other.[3]

At the onset of the Sino-Japanese war in July of 1937 large parts of Eastern and Northern China were vacated by KMT troops. In Hebei, for example, both Beijing and Tianjin were taken over with barely a fight, the

---

[2] Campbell, C. and G.C. Tullock, (1954). "Hyperinflation in China, 1937–1949". *Journal of Political Economy.* 62(3):236–245.

[3] Goodman *Op Cit.* On the undemocratic aspect of provisional government, Goodman (page 1021) quotes Deng Xiaoping's appeal to democracy, his objection to totalitarian or one-party rule (as he saw the KMT), and that the leadership of the Party should ultimately be elected democratically.

nationalist forces retreating southward and virtually all forms of government disintegrating. The vacuum was filled by local armed groups including self-defense units, guerilllas, some remnants of the Chinese army, and on the other side, agents of the Japanese.[4] Within a year, Hebei and other provinces had been restored to some semblance of order by the communist Eighth Route Army. To the North formed the Shanxi-Chahar- Hebei Border Government. Central Hebei was under the control of the Eighth Route Army, while 54 Hsien (counties) in South Hebei were governed by the 115th Division of the Eighth Route Army. Only a handful of Hsien were actually under KMT control, and these did not recognize any authorities decreed by the communists. To the South in Shandong, Anhui, and Jiangsu there remained large numbers of KMT troops behind Japanese lines, but even so there were vast areas of land where local governments had failed, and the communists were able to organize guerrilla actions and gain a foothold in local governance.[5] Even so, it is important to keep in mind that it was under nationalist government orders that the Eighth Route Army halt Japanese advances South through Shanxi—which they did at the battle of Pingxingguan, to defend the Cheng-tai Railway, and to move the 115th Division into Western Shandong in late 1938.

Throughout this period there was political posturing by both the KMT and the CPC, and mischief on both sides. But in terms of hearts and minds, the communists were far more progressive, at least in the eyes of the peasantry. The Eighth Route Army had imposed a 'fair burden' taxation system whereas the KMT's approach to taxation was multifarious and regressive; the communists formed a 'Farmers' National Salvation Association' which opened up membership to the landless, while the KMT 'Mobilization Committee' had a property qualification which excluded all but the landlords and the rich; the communists employed guerrilla tactics while the KMT employed a gentrified police force called the Peace Preservation Corps. In so many ways the political, economic, and military rituals of the communists and KMT were so much at odds with each other that any form of unified governance behind Japanese lines was virtually impossible. In June of 1939, amidst a Japanese offensive in central Hebei, a KMT army under the control of General Zhang Yin-wu attacked 8th Route forces and guerrilla units, but were defeated. Later, through the

---

[4] Lindsay, M. (1945). "Conflict in North China: 1937–1943" *Far Eastern Survey*, 14(13):172–176, Goodman *Op Cit.*
[5] Lindsay (1945). *Op Cit.*

summer of 1939 and towards the end of the year, another KMT general, Shi You-san, who was in control of the 69th Army operating in Southern Hebei, collaborated with the Japanese and also attacked 8th Route Army forces. He was forced into retreat and later executed in December 1940 as a traitor. In September 1939, in the Hebei-Henan-Shandong border area the KMT authorized general Zhu Huai-bing's 97th Army to attack 8th Route Army forces in an attempt to split the army in Shanxi and Hubei.[6]

And so evolved three major power centers in China. The first was the nationalist government headed by the KMT, the second was the CCP, and the third was the Japanese puppet government. Operating mostly behind enemy lines and/or within Japanese controlled areas the communists sought a number of ways in which to find balance between political ideology, economic realities, and class structure. If the objectives of the communists were to establish a set of populist, mobilizational strategies for the remaking of Chinese society on democratic and egalitarian principles, these principles as applied were very much defined by conditions at the local level.[7] This was also hemmed in by some glaring contradictions, the most critical being between egalitarianism and unification. Egalitarianism was about the redistribution of resources (including land and wealth) to erode intellectual elitism and rural-urban inequalities.[8] Unification, on the other hand, was about community building, yet to accomplish this required interclass cooperation and consensus[9]; interclass cooperation required a more totalitarian effort while the consensus required greater democracy. Throughout the war years and beyond, balancing seemingly contradictory and mutually exclusive goals was a constant tension, and where along a spectrum between totalitarianism and democracy a policy, or program, was implemented depended very much on local forces and circumstances. Thus, throughout the border regions in wartime China similar approaches would arise with different results so that no single program was a panacea.[10]

We have seen previously that communist efforts at cooperation and agricultural credit predated the Sino-Japanese war and even the Long

---

[6] Lindsay (1945). *Op Cit.*
[7] Keating, P. (1994). "The Yan'an Way of Co-Operativization" *China Quarterly* v140(December):1025–1051.
[8] Selden, M. (1971). *The Yenan Way in Revolutionary China*. Cambridge, MA: Harvard University Press, 1971.
[9] Keating *Op Cit.*, page 1026.
[10] Keating *Op Cit.*

March.[11] In South China the communists undertook land reformation, redistribution, improved management practices, the formation of mutual self-help groups, and mechanisms to provide agricultural credit. The KMT, for its part, observed many of these initiatives and used these in the push for agricultural reconstruction, but as Japanese expansionism continued between 1937 and 1940 the breakdown in local governance virtually eliminated all forms of agricultural cooperation and credit. To achieve any semblance of self-reliance and self-sufficiency the communists in Japanese-controlled areas, and other border regions, had to quickly establish new institutions to fill the void. This involved a complex set of policies including issuing currency, establishing standard measures of grain yield for paying rents and repaying loans, and doing so with priorities on self-sufficiency and self-reliance. In this context, self-reliance meant virtually no trade with either the Japanese or Chinese nationalists beyond the border regions, and even within the border regions.

11.3 Agriculture, the 'Fair Burden' Tax, and the Grain Standard

Within the border regions the CPC found it necessary to rehabilitate the tax system which was generally corrupt and regressive, if taxes were being collected at all.[12] In many of the base areas owing to the military conflicts with the Japanese—and in some instances with the KMT—the administrative capacity to collect taxes was largely diminished. The CPC, however, knew that in order to mobilize the war effort taxes had to be collected. In the Shanxi-Chahar border region the CPC instituted the 'fair burden' (*he-li-fu-dan, ho-li-fu-tan*)[13] system of taxation which was based on ability to

---

[11] The Long March refers to the retreat from KMT nationalist forces by about 80,000 communist troops from their stronghold in Jiangxi Province along the Fujian border between 1934 and 1935. The march ended in Shaanxi Province where the communists established a stronghold at Yan'an. See Salisbury, H. E. (1985). *The Long March: The untold story*. HarperCollins Publishers, NY.
  The idea of 'The Yenan/Yan'an Way' as used in Selden (1971, *Op cit.*) and Keating (1994, *Op cit.*) suggest that the ideas of cooperation came about only after the Long March. This is not the case. The communists had attempted a variety of initiatives in their occupied areas well before consolidating power in Yan'an, Shaanxi.
[12] Much of the discussion in this section is drawn from Lindsay, M. (1970). "The Taxation System of the Shansi-Chahar-Hopei Border Region, 1938–1945" *China Quarterly* 42(April-June):1–15.
[13] This is sometimes also referred to as the 'equitable' burden system of taxation.

pay. There were two drivers to this policy. First, the local administrators set a tax quota at the level of Hsien, and this then trickled down to villages and then to villagers.[14]

The second driver was a shift from a currency base to a grain standard as the accounting unit. In the Shanxi-Chahar- Hebei border area the base grain was millet. In other areas it might have been a different crop or commodity based upon local advantage (e.g. wheat flour). Accounting records included two books, one with the records recorded in currency and the other with records based on millet equivalence. Even salaries were paid in millet with a small amount provided in cash for pocket money, but the cash allowance did not retain its values as well as millet (or other storable grain commodities) did.

This shift from paper to grain was not by happenstance, but was a deliberate move by the CPC in the early war years to preserve value and insulate the border regions from currency depreciation. As will be discussed later there is evidence that the natural hedge of grain as a store of value did insulate the border and base areas more than free China and Japanese controlled areas. Further, since each base area issued currency that was not exchangeable across base areas, using a grain standard as a unit of account was convenient in many ways. In one editorial, one of the complaints about the 8th Army/18th Division was that it just appeared to wander from here to there rather than engaging the Japanese. It is possible that troop movements were immobilized by the inability to exchange currency as troops moved from one border area to another: "*The existence of the various currencies with the fluctuation in exchange rate hindered economy and trade, and created great difficulties as well for the mobile warfare of troops*".[15] One of the solutions to this problem was the issuance of the CPC grain tickets or vouchers (*liang piao*) that soldiers would give to farmers or granaries in return for a given weight of grain. The farmer or granary would then deduct the sum of vouchers accumulated from soldiers from their fair burden tax liability.

---

[14] There would naturally have been some moral hazard in the final allocations. If the local power was in the hand of the gentry then they would likely shift more of a burden onto the peasantry, but if the local power was in the peasantry they would shift more of the burden to the gentry. Depending upon the situation, village leaders and county administrators might have to negotiate the quota allocation based on local conditions.

[15] People's Bank of China (1988). "Picture Album of the Renminbi" Compiled by Currency issuance department of the People's Bank of China. China Financial Publishing House. Beijing, page 8.

To operate on the grain standard the CPC had to define grain equivalents. In Shanxi-Chahar-Hebei, as mentioned, the unit of account was millet, and all other grains were measured in millet equivalents. These would vary across regions, but the basic idea remained. The tax system was then based on grain equivalents. The simplest approach was as discussed above based on the quota system, with each Hsien allocated a millet-equivalent quota which had to be met. A more sophisticated variant on this was formed in the Shanxi-Chahar- Hebei zone. There, the local administrators distinguished between cultivated (taxed) and uncultivated land (not taxed) and related assets such as stored grain (not taxed) or shares in cooperatives (not taxed). As a unit of area of cultivated land they defined a 'standard mou' as being the amount of cultivated land which on average produced 10 *shi dou*[16] or 750 kg of unhusked millet. Thus the tax was based on a local mou adjustment. For example, a farm on hilly land might produce only two-thirds the millet as a farm on a valley plain. The local mou on the hilly land would be 1.5 times the local mou on the valley land.[17] Thus, the tax burden on the lower productive hilly land would be spread over a larger physical land base than more productive valley land. This was viewed as being more equitable in the Shanxi-Chahar-Hebei area, than other areas in which a fixed quota might be assigned to a common measure of land regardless of whether it was cultivated or equally productive.

A measure of 'wealth power' (*fu-li*) was then defined by four standard mou. This measure of wealth was adjusted for a variety of things including costs of production and personal deductions for the number of people in a home and so on. A progressive taxation system was defined across 16 classes with the lowest class 1 being equivalent to half a wealth power and the highest class 16 having more than 81 wealth powers. Each class was assigned points with the first class being 0.8 points and the 16th class being 2.1 points. Each point was given a tax. In 1941 this tax was 1.2–1.3 shi dou of millet equivalent plus $1.50 in local currency plus some

---

[16] One shih tou is equivalent to 150 jin or 75 kg. So one standard mou would be the area required to grow on average 750 kg per year.

[17] Today, one mou is equal to one-sixth of an acre or one-fifteenth of a hectare. Perhaps one of the first mentions of local mou was by John Lossing Buck who faced the problem of converting local mou to hectare equivalents. Buck's statistical atlas lists the local mou conversion factor to achieve a one-fifteenth hectare equivalent for each village surveyed. A close inspection of these data would show an inverse relationship between productivity per hectare and local mou.

allotment of fodder for animals. These amounts would vary by year and circumstance with a lower tax employed after a calamity or catastrophe, and a higher tax following a good harvest. Other factors would include military conflict, troop deployments, and so on.

While being fair in terms of productivity and other adjustments, the CPC did not make allowances for landlords who had to pay tax not only on the cultivated lands but also on rental income. To avoid double taxation landlords would have had to cultivate the land themselves or sell land to tenants. Since tenants could hardly afford the land, many were forced off the land and pushed into the wage market or the army.

What is important here is the widespread application of the grain standard. The idea of collecting grain instead of money to pay taxes was not a new concept in wartime China. Indeed the KMT had been collecting grain in lieu of money for agricultural land taxes for years, while other industries and businesses had to remit taxes in cash. But the communists in the border and base areas went much further than this by extending the grain standard to all facets of the base-area economies including currency and agricultural credit.

11.4 Monetary Control in CPC Base Regions and Border Areas

By 1939 the provinces of Shandong, Hebei, and Henan were largely controlled by the Japanese. Within Japanese-held territory all credit societies were abolished and the legal tender, the Chinese National Currency (CNC) was banned. Farmers were forced to exchange CNC[18] and accept a new currency known as the puppet currency or Japanese Controlled Currency (JCC).[19] However, the Japanese had neither the troop strength

---

[18] CNC is China National Currency based on notes issued by the Central Bank of China, the Farmers Bank of China, Bank of Communications, and Bank of China.

[19] After the invasion of 1937 and into 1938 the Japanese issued currency for local tender tied to the Lian Yin Bank in Beiping, Hebei, Henan Shandong, and Shanxi, so notes of other banks had to be converted to Lian Yin bank notes. This required establishing a formal exchange program in occupied areas. For example a Huaxing yuan could be exchanged for one Lian Yin yuan at parity in 1939. In the beginning these bank notes were exchanged at par for legal Chinese currency. However the exchange value was not retained. The Huaxing yuan, for example, was tied to six English pence and then to the customs gold unit which was tied to the US dollar. The point being that not all Japanese-issued currencies held value because of different capital structures and also the failure of the Japanese yen in China to

nor administrative capacity to have full control of these provinces, particularly in the rural areas. Uncontested, communist forces were able to move South from their base in Yan'an, Shaanxi and establish base camps and soviets throughout the three provinces.

In April 1940 the Northern Bureau of the Central Committee of the CPC issued a document, *Instruction on the Financial and Economic Policies*, that identified various ways in which CPC-issued currency could be circulated. Although the CPC said that it had permission from the KMT Ministry of Finance to replace the JCC with a new currency in base areas, the KMT ultimately denied this. Nonetheless, the CPC on its own account decided upon a new currency that was exchangeable within the base area soviets but not with either the CNC or JCC. By doing so the CPC could essentially control all trade in and out of the base areas, discourage citizens in the base areas from emigrating, and perhaps more important discourage CPC soldiers from deserting.

Initially the CPC instituted currency policies to support military activities. They had likely learned a lesson from the Japanese in Manchuria. In Japanese-controlled areas the Japanese also established their own banks with their own currency. For example, in Manchuria on June 15, 1932 the Manchurian Central Bank issued Manchurian bank notes with registered capital amounting to 30,000,000 yuan and backed by paid-up capital of 7,500,000 yuan. The remaining capital base could be intangibles such as tax flows or fixed assets. Like the CPC, the Manchurian government had the problem of wanting to separate its currency from the Chinese yuan, and use a local currency tied to the Japanese yen. The purpose of issuing Japanese currency was to exchange it for KMT bank notes which were legal tender in international markets. The exchange was also a means of converting Chinese yuan to Japanese yen, allowing the Japanese to purchase military equipment from abroad so that the Manchurian forces were less reliant on Japan.[20] In other words, by issuing bank notes and establishing an exchange, the Manchurian government could then accumulate CNC (Chinese yuan) which could then be exchanged for English pounds

have the same value of the Japanese yen in Japan since the former was depreciated. In 1941, 39.5 Lian Yin yuan could be exchanged for 100 KMT yuan (legal Chinese tender).

[20] With the confiscated currency the respective governments did not destroy the money, but instead used it in markets for which it was still legal tender to purchase the other's goods. This had the effect of reducing supply, sometimes on a grand scale, but with all or most currencies in circulation, the increased money supply was also inflationary. See Campbell and Tullock *Op Cit*.

or American dollars in Shanghai and Hong Kong as legal tender. The new Manchurian currency could be exchanged for Japanese yen, but not Chinese yuan, yet Chinese yuan could be (and had to be) exchanged for Japanese notes. As an economic model this worked until the start of the Pacific war with the United States in December 1941, after which all foreign exchanges in China were shut down.

11.5 Currency Formulation in the Base Areas: The Formation of the *Luxi* Bank

The currency issued in base areas can generically be referred to as border currency. One of the first CPC banks in the base areas was established in May 1940 with the *Luxi* Bank in West Shandong which issued a form of currency called *luxi* currency. On April 15, 1940 an administrative office of the CPC was established in the Shandong base area in Northwest Shandong, West of Tai (sic). In January 1940 the 115th Division of the 8th Route Army established a supply center to bring food, clothes, and weapons to the base areas. They also brought in paper and ink. With the help of Weizhou Li, a local printer, the CPC began to print bank note in January 1940 and issue it in May of 1940.

In May 1940 the regional commander, Lv Lin of the administrative office near Tai, and head of the supply center, was nominated as the General Manager of the *Luxi* Bank and issued the *luxi* currency. In 1940 the *luxi* exchange rate with the silver dollar (official KMT Shanghai silver) was 5.3:1. If the exchange was in paper rather than coin then in 1940 the *luxi* exchange was 1:1 at par with the CNC, the fabi (fa means legal, bi means currency), which was issued in November 1935 secured by gold rather than silver). Thus, a farmer holding coin would exchange $1 silver and receive 5.3 *luxi* dollars, while a farmer holding paper CNC would receive only 1 *luxi* dollar.[21]

---

[21] These exchanges were not at all stable. By the time the war with Japan came to a close in August 1945, the exchange rate for silver was 112:1. By September 1947 it was 1200:1. Paper currency fared somewhat better, at least through 1948. By 1941 the exchange ranged from 1:0.9 to 1:0.65(or 1.11 *luxi* for 1 fabi and 1.538 *luxi* for 1 fabi), by 1942 1:0.74 to 1:1.77, 1943 ranged from 1:2.69 to 1:3.10, 1944/45 ranged from 1:3.67 to 1:3.5, 1946 1:5.05, 1947 1:26.94, 1949 1:20000. Cf. Picture Album of Bank Notes s issued by Beihai Bank and *Luxi* Bank. Compiled by Shandong Currency Association. 1998 (山东省货币协会编：北海银行暨鲁西银行货币图录, 齐鲁书社, 1998年版, page 259.

In August 1941 the management of the *Luxi* Bank was changed to civilian control. This broadened the emphasis of finance, enabling agricultural loans for seeds, fertilizer, and livestock and so alleviate poverty, and investment in irrigation and water conservancy projects. Loans had no interest rates when issued to poor farmers or water projects. Loans on agricultural production were 6% monthly. For a farmer to receive a loan there would have to be support from the village leader and a farmers union and be approved at district and then county level. By 1942 the interest rate increased to 8% per month. Between 1942 and 1945 there was a great famine so no interest payments were imposed. Many farmers fled because of famine and war so loans without interest were used to encourage farmers to stay.

Agricultural loans at the *Luxi* Bank were issued in currency with the expectation that the money would be spent almost instantaneously to avoid price rises through delay. High interest rates were no more than a stop-gap measure and were tied to ever-increasing deposit rates. But over many months this hardly kept up with inflation so in real terms farmers benefited from borrowing. To avoid adverse incentives to borrow and hoard, the accrued loan value was indexed to the commodity base (e.g. corn flour) so the final amount the farmer repaid was the principal, plus interest, multiplied by the change in the price of the reference commodity. This had the effect, approximately, of ensuring that what farmers borrowed and repaid was equivalent in real terms; that is the consumption bundle that a farmer could purchase at the end of the loan period in nominal dollars was approximately equivalent to the same bundle that could have been purchased at the time the loan was made.

11.6   Border Currency and Regional Trade

By May 1940 the CPC began to expand its currency policy across the border regions where communists had political and military control. As they began to establish banks and other financial institutions these too started to circulate their own border currency as legal tender against the Japanese notes that were linked to gold as well as the CNC (Shanghai silver) which was linked to silver. The *Guanghua* Store, Beihai Bank, Shangdang Native Bank, and Southern Hebei Bank each issued notes that

Wei Hongyun(1990), Selected materials on finance and economy in Shanxi-Hebei-Shandong-Henan base area during Sino-Japanese war, China Financial Publishing House.

were to be used in the various base areas. Some were in conflict. For example the Shandang and Southern Hebei banks were issuing currency and notes within the same border region, causing an obvious conflict. The conflict brought about the Office for Joint Administration and ultimately the South Hebei notes became legal tender for the Shanxi-Hebei-Shandong-Henan border area.[22] These notes not only undermined the value of Japanese notes issued by the 'puppet' banks, but also the CNC. The Southern Hebei Bank, for example, issued $3 million in notes while the Central Hebei Frontier Bank issued $2.5 million. People in the regions were forced to use the newly issued notes and legal tender, CNC, notes were withdrawn from circulation in these areas within three months of issue.[23] Whether intentional or not (and most likely it was intentional) the various *luxi* notes issued by newly created banks had no means of exchange, and this, essentially eliminated trade across base areas.

To circulate currency, various methods were used including mobilizing the army and cadres to use the currency, encouraging the use of currency for the development of industry and agricultural products, encouraging and promoting the new currency through cooperative societies, encouraging and developing trade within the base areas, managing the trade of necessities between the base and outside areas, and holding reserve funds in cash, goods in stock, land taxes, and the confiscated property of 'traitors'. The communists did form credit societies for granting loans to people in different districts and regions of Hebei, for example, through which the circulation of notes issued by the Southern Hebei Bank was encouraged. Some $30 million of notes issued by the newly created *Beihai* Bank were similarly distributed. In Southeastern Shanxi the value of notes issued by the Southern Hebei Bank and *Shangdang* Native Banks was enhanced by communist propaganda that encouraged local governments (Hsien or district) to refuse legal tender CNC notes and provincial banknotes. Elsewhere, the communists purposefully devalued the CNC legal tender by artificially declaring that $1 CNC was worth only $0.70 of a *Shangdang* Native Bank note. In Hebei and Shansi, bonds were issued, the financial system readjusted, and additional taxes imposed on the rich for the sole purpose of absorbing legal tender CNC notes and to encourage the circulation of the Frontier Bank notes.

[22] Goodman *Op Cit.*
[23] Editorial "The Kuomintang Case Against the Communists (Part II): The China Weekly Review, May 11, 1940, page 366.

Banks could not print us much money as they wanted and needed approval of the Northern Bureau so there were some fiscal controls. The CPC would decide which, when, and how much each of the banks could print. However, the CPC did not in fact have a central bank of its own to coordinate financial activities in border and base areas. Each of the border region banks created would secure the notes based on local advantage. Some notes might be secured by cotton, some by cereals, and some by both. Others might be secured by agricultural commodities and cash and gold or silver deposits. A result of this was that currency issued by one bank in one region was non-exchangeable with currency issued by a different bank in a different region. Since the CPC required that all units of currency, whether Japanese or CNC, be converted to border currency, a medium of exchange was lost and each border region created its own closed microeconomy.[24] The CPC was well aware of this but instead of trying to develop a unified currency it used the non-exchangeability as a form of economic control. Farmers in the base areas were forced to convert CNC to respective border currencies, immediately impeding trade and the flow of goods and services not only between border regions but also between the border regions and free territories and Japanese-held territories. The Central Committee made several statements on this relating to self-sufficiency within the base areas and controlling goods and

[24] This is also a source of the hyperinflation recorded at the time. The CPC understood the basic elements of monetary control but found it difficult to contain inflation. By closing the flow of exchange and increasing the supply of money, price inflation was considerable and rapid. This was also the case in Nationalist areas of Free China as the Nationalists expanded the money supply to fund war operations. The transition from inflation to hyper-inflation is caused to some significant degree by a feedback loop when people come to the realization that prices will not stabilize. The impulse then is to hold as little cash as possible and start purchasing various goods and commodities whether needed or not. These commodities would hold value while the paper currency would not. As a consequence, the velocity of money in circulation would increase, which when combined with newly printed money would increase the amount of money in circulation. The communists attempted to control inflation at one point by stopping the increase in the money supply. This had the effect of reducing prices in the short run, but soon enough the various departments within the CPC asked for more money and banks asked for looser restrictions. With these actions, people realized that inflation was unlikely to be controlled and so began purchasing again on expectation. The CPC made several attempts at reducing the money supply, and these likely dampened inflation. But another key difference between the value of money inside Communist border regions and the free China regions was the reliance of the CPC on indexing to commodities, which preserved value through a natural hedge. See Campbell and Tullock *Op Cit.*

necessities from leaving or coming. The lack of medicine, for example, was to be alleviated by growing medicinal crops such as walnut.

In addition, to discourage the import of necessities into the base area the CPC established a trade bureau through which troops in North China would register the necessity and have the bureau purchase it from outside the base area, with a reduced tax. This suggests (but without explicit statement) that non-military individuals purchasing necessities from outside the base area were subject to numerous taxes at multiple checkpoints.

Closing base areas to trade, while providing some semblance of political control, had far-reaching economic impacts. The fact that local currency was linked to cotton or cereals rather than gold or silver meant that the currency itself would rise and fall depending upon the value and amount of crops grown. A drought affecting cotton and cereal output would, without trade, drive up the price of commodities far more than would otherwise occur. This would become particularly acute for foodstuffs that would face almost infinite inelasticity as starvation set in. Even if granaries were overflowing in neighboring border regions, without a means of exchange relief could only be achieved by the CPC.

11.7 Currency-induced Hoarding

An additional problem was one of hoarding. A likely scenario is that at the beginning of the war the demand price was more elastic in the neighborhood of supplies. But as more commodities were requisitioned for military use and supplies and distribution was disrupted in conflict zones, supply began to fall, increasing prices against a shifting wartime demand. This sudden rise in prices, combined with increased volatility, pushed demand to lower elasticity, exacerbating price increases, and with feedback exacerbated hoarding. Thus commodities replaced currency as a store of value and by holding commodities in place of assets one could preserve, at least partially, the real value of assets.[25] Particularly in communist areas where the currency was tied to commodity prices, hoarding provided a natural hedge, even though hoarding itself created price rises. For example, the communists at one point required all businesses to keep their accounts in terms of corn flour or some other commodity. The price of corn flour was published daily in the *Tianjin Daily News* so anyone could observe price changes in real time. All wages, debts, taxes, and other costs were then

[25] Campbell and Tullock, *Op Cit.*

paid in currency but according to the indexed value. For example, if the price of corn flour doubled between the time money was borrowed and due, the borrower would pay twice the amount borrowed.[26] But hoarding reduces available storage, bidding up the cost of storage. In addition, hoarders incorporated a convenience yield to offset having to acquire uncertain supply at a higher cost at a future date. If the convenience yield exceeded the costs of storage prices would still rise.[27]

Ironically, this would have been easier in nationalist territories or in the black market with the Japanese. Indeed, the CPC was often criticized for dealing with Japanese black marketeers. But in times of food and material shortage the only currencies held in large amounts would be Japanese or CNC since these notes were obtained in exchange for newly issued border notes. Food shortages would also encourage black market trading in non-border areas by black marketeers who had hoarded legal tender. Since demand inelasticity in a border region was dependent upon conditions in that border region, black marketeers could make handsome profits by purchasing goods in non-border areas at a relatively lower price and smuggling them into the affected border areas, then selling for a much higher price.

---

[26] Campbell and Tullock, page 242 *Op Cit*. Flour had a seasonal basis so over time several variants were attempted. In Shanghai the parity unit was the sum of 1.72 pounds of rice, 1 foot of 12 pound cloth, 1 ounce of peanut oil, and 1.33 pounds of coal briquettes. This index captured a weighting of prices covering food, clothing, and energy.

[27] The nature of commodity matters. Whether the hoarded commodity was gold, silver, or another storable precious metal versus grains, likely had an impact on this natural hedge argument. Metals such as copper, silver, and gold were essentially global commodities in the sense that there was no unique 'China' price, but rather a price determined in foreign exchanges based on global supply and demand by countries at war and at peace. With Japan controlling most of China's ports in the Northeast and Eastern seaboard there was unlikely to be a global effect on agricultural commodities, except perhaps in placing a ceiling on domestic prices. Instead local prices were likely determined by local conditions, including the cost of storage which would have been bidded up if the velocity of hoarding increased. Eventually the cash price would be so attractive that incentives to store, and incur the costs of storage, would diminish. As commodities were released from storage prices would fall, or at least rise at a lower rate, demand would increase, supplies would fall, and an anticipated rise would again encourage hoarding and storage. Even with restrictions on trade between free China, communist border regions, and Japanese occupied territories this cobweb effect would in most instances be determined by local conditions within, and between, conflict zones, and would have ultimately provided a stabilizing effect as Working suggests.

Working, H. (1949). "The Theory of Price of Storage" *American Economic Review*. 39(6):1254–1262.

Natural, political, or military risk would also play havoc on the border currencies. If there were conditions bad enough to affect, say, the cotton supply, then with a reasonably high probability those same conditions would also affect grain and cereal supplies as well. Thus, all prices in the base area might rise and this might artificially inflate the value of the currency. If farmers were able to retain some yield and sell at a higher price there are some scenarios, related to what in the modern era is referred to as a natural hedge, in which farmers would see a rise in income that might not otherwise come about in an open market. But this also meant that other foodstuffs affected by the covariate conditions were also rising so that the purchasing power of sales actually diminished in real terms. In the event of total loss of the crop, the price no longer mattered since the farmer had nothing to sell. Yet the rising prices of food set in motion a devastating set of conditions for famine. This happened in 1942 with drought conditions across base areas and unoccupied areas. Conditions were so bad that the CPC eliminated interest on debts so that farmers would not flee the areas.

11.8 Credit and Cooperation in the Shaanxi-Gansu-Ningxia Border Region

Building credit facilities and expanding cooperatives in the border regions was not always a simple task. Conditions across farming regions differed greatly so what might have been applicable in one region might not be applicable in another. An example of this was in the Shaanxi-Gansu-Ningxia border region established by agreement with the KMT in 1937 as part of the Second United Front because of its proximity to Yan'an where the CPC was headquartered.[28] Between 1935 and 1937 the communists had largely suppressed bandit groups by absorbing them into the CPC. With resistance diminished the CPC undertook land reforms and distribution, a task made much easier by the absenteeism of landlords. During the Sino-Japanese war, the Shaanxi-Gansu-Ningxia border region was unique among the border regions and base areas since neither Shaanxi Province nor Gansu Province was occupied by Japanese ground troops.

In the *Yanshu* area that surrounded Yan'an, the redistribution of land, plus additional efforts at reclaiming lands previously abandoned by conflict, was supported by the resettlement of some 170,000 famine, war and

---

[28] This section abstracted from Keating, *Op Cit.*

political refugees and reclamation of some 2 million mou of wasteland between 1937 and 1940. Farmers, once on the fringe, prospered. However, in the Northern counties of Shaanxi (the *Suide* district) the farmland tended to be more intensely cultivated with greater population density and a prosperous merchant-gentry. Land tenancy, however, was widespread, and competition for rental land was extreme. The vast majority of tenant farmers were poverty stricken. In 1943 the CPC made a push to increase agricultural output to meet the war effort, a unity call that was answered in the *Yanshu* area, but devolved into class struggle in the *Suide* area. Land redistribution did little to relieve the poverty burden since the population to land ratio was so high that the amount of land redistributed to former tenants did little to relieve the precarious burden of small farms. The only release valve for the population pressure in *Suide* was to reduce the population and this was accomplished by deploying laborers into non-farm production or to reclamation efforts in the hinterlands.

The abundance of land in *Yanshu* and the scarcity of land in *Suide* complicated strategies for agricultural cooperation and credit. Consequently, what were considered successful cooperatives differed in both areas. In *Yanshu*, the most prosperous cooperative was in transportation while in *Suide* it was cloth and garment manufacturing. Neither was a cooperative in the sense of bringing transporters or weavers into the cooperative, paying instead on a piecemeal basis.

At the same time cooperative models were being deployed, the CPC was engaged in a rent-reduction campaign which proved relatively successful. A derivative of these efforts was the emergence of numerous credit cooperative societies. These were initially local efforts with localized and decentralized management, but as they began to expand they were brought under a more centralized management losing their identity in the process and imposing restrictions, regulations, and oversight that might have done more harm than good. Centralized actions in 1944, for example, forced repayment of compulsory investments imposed on cooperative members, while also forcing dividends to be paid which bankrupted many, if not most, cooperatives. Efforts at collectivizing assets failed because what farmers really wanted were small cooperatives that organized production, marketing, and credit to solve problems at the local level rather than at the consolidated and aggregated county level.

Likewise, mutual aid societies, originally organized at the village level to share labor and tools, came under the same centrist pressures. Work gangs with specialization in tobacco cultivation and harvesting may not have the same skill set as cotton growers. Yet the CPC pushed towards aggregating the mutual aid societies so that the work gangs or brigades were deployed to areas and for production far from what was originally intended. In *Yanshu*, village-level brigades were treated as conscripts and sent to wastelands to reclaim land for agricultural production on a scale so large that the rate at which land was reclaimed exceeded population growth and with a labor intensity that caused farmers' own land to go to waste.

Two other initiatives, the coordination of farm household plans and agricultural credit, were not too affected by centralization.[29] Nonetheless, local conditions determined credit and credit policies. For example, in the poorer *Suide* region enough credit to make a real difference was inadequate because the required resources were beyond the capability of the local government. Loans were restricted to the purchase of livestock and tools, not other productive inputs. Likewise, so-called 'spring hunger' loans which allocated grain instead of money was more abundant in *Yanshu* than *Suide*.

11.9 Mutual-aid and Group Guarantees

Conventional loans in 1941 required a minimum number of households of five. This was reduced to three by 1943. Any borrower was required to find an agricultural loan group that was both willing to coordinate farming and work cooperatively as a mutual aid group, as well as guarantee the loan. Although most loans were for an individual householder borrowing on his or her own account, the loan could also be applied to the joint purchase of livestock or tools that would benefit the group as a whole. Loans were to be repaid one month after harvest. Perhaps the group that most benefited from the loans were poor farmers cultivating reclaimed land for the first time. A land grant and small-grain loan in the first year could be followed by a livestock or equipment loan in the second. It was a prudent thing for newcomer farmers in the same stage to form a mutual aid group and purchase livestock and tools collectively. A measureable

---

[29] The agricultural production plans were a precursor to centrally controlled agricultural production, but at a more local scale in 1940–43 than what followed. Farmers were instructed or encouraged to grow crops in relation to cropping targets, according to what neighbors were growing, and so on. The planning included cropping patterns, seed selection, fertilizer use, manpower and livestock deployment, farmland repair and improvement, sidelines planning, tax planning, and famine preparation. Keating, *Op Cit.*, page 1040.

outcome was that almost the entirety of reclaimed land in *Yanshu* was due to land grants, grain loans, and group loans.

11.10 Economic Warfare

As mentioned, the CPC had not been approved by the KMT to print notes. The CPC could have simply exchanged JCC notes for CNC notes to drive the soviet economies, and maintain trade with the KMT and unoccupied China. But for reasons of political-economy as well as military control over the region they chose not to do so. It is no wonder then that both the KMT and Japanese would attempt to destabilize the newly issued border currency, for that was the only mechanism outside of combat that could easily destabilize the stronghold the CPC had in the border regions.

To some extent the CPC set itself up for an economic trap with both the KMT and the Japanese going rogue with economic mischief and economic warfare. Between 1940 and 1941 the fabi legal tender was depreciated; but in 1942 the fabi was appreciated relative to *luxi*. This was mainly because in 1942 the KMT released counterfeit *luxi* into the base area. The KMT strategy was to pay troops in fake *luxi* and then send them into base areas to purchase goods. The economic consequence of simultaneously increasing the supply of notes, while increasing the demand and prices of goods in base areas, had an inflationary impact that drove down the value of the *luxi*.[30]

This appears to have been a short-lived success because with China at war the CNC in world markets was depreciating faster than the KMT could depreciate the *luxi*. Consequently, by late 1942 the *luxi* began to rise relative to the fabi. The other reason it was short lived was that the fabi was linked to gold while the CPC notes were linked to commodities or whatever was to the local advantage. Thus in times of war food was valuable, but in 1942 a great famine in Shandong drove up agricultural

---

[30] To visualize how this might have worked in a practical way consider that the CNC was linked to the price of gold, while *luxi* notes were linked to the value of a basket of agricultural commodities. If we assume in the short run that the quantities of gold and the quantities of commodity remained the same, then an increase in the price of commodities relative to gold would increase the value of the *luxi* relative to fabi. Under this scenario, introducing counterfeit *luxi* would mean that the quantity of commodity would be spread across more notes, decreasing the purchasing power accordingly. In this sense the KMT (and the Japanese) hoped that the *luxi* would depreciate so much that the entirety of the economy in the base areas would collapse and the *luxi* would become worthless.

commodity prices and the *luxi* note; CNC notes were linked to gold, but with war loans made to buy weapons from abroad, nobody had faith that the central bank actually had sufficient gold to secure notes, nor the economic wherewithal to support the currency by other means such as taxes.

In 1941, the Germans captured an American military cargo ship transporting billions of fabi notes to the United States. The Germans handed the notes over to the Japanese. To print fabi notes, the Chinese had processing centers in Tianjin and Shanghai run by British (De La Rue PLC) and American (American Bank Note Company) banknote companies.[31] But to complete the process they also had secret printing presses in Hong Kong and Burma. The split process would have incomplete notes drafted at one facility and shipped to the second or third for completion. In December 1941, after the Japanese consolidated control of Hong Kong, they acquired not only the printing presses but also billions of uncompleted fabi notes. When in 1942 the Japanese invaded Burma, they secured the last of the printing presses required to complete the fabi notes and were thus able to complete the process on unfinished notes, and print new notes.

Closing the borders of the base areas to trade also had a black market effect. To get essential medicines and other goods, farmers and others would breach the border to buy goods from the Japanese using JCC that they had not exchanged for *luxi*. In what in appearance was a good-hearted gesture the Japanese offered to exchange JCC (the Lian yin) for two *luxi* notes, a bargain at the time. The only problem was that the *luxi* notes were also counterfeit, and when placed into circulation increased the overall money supply in the base areas leading again to inflation. In addition, with so much counterfeit note in circulation from the KMT and the Japanese, the *luxi* note suffered a loss in confidence, creating an even greater wedge between the economies of the base areas and those of the warring KMT and Japanese.

11.11 Summary

Little is known about how agricultural credit was applied in the Japanese-occupied territories during the Sino-Japanese war, 1937–45. In Chap. 14 we have the benefit of a study by Buck on agricultural conditions and prices during wartime in free China. With a rapid rise in inflation,

---

[31] Sua Shou Yuan (2017). War between Border Currency and Puppet Currency in Qiindao *China Currency* Volume (1), pages 20–32.

some farmers benefited when the rise in commodity prices exceeded the rise of related production and consumption goods. As the beneficiaries of inflation, farm incomes and farm conditions were somewhat moderated. Even under these conditions, the KMT continued to progress on expanding cooperatives and related credit services, including the formation of policy banks dedicated to agricultural production credit. But as the number of cooperatives increased in unoccupied areas, they had virtually disappeared in the occupied areas. However, even within the occupied areas there were vast tracts of land that were ostensibly controlled by the Chinese Communist Party. These areas were required to be self-sufficient and self-reliant in order to sustain the war effort, so it is natural to ask how agricultural credit was applied in the border and base areas.

Ultimately credit was provided for agriculture but not until around 1940, three years into the war. Our discussion of the *Luxi* Bank in the Shandong base area illustrates how credit evolved. It was not by straightforward means. We identified two critical components to the emergence of credit. The first was the establishment of local currency in the base areas. This was accomplished by establishing banks like the *Luxi* Bank or Southern Hebei Bank, which were authorized by the CPC (but not the KMT) to print and circulate notes. These were first used for the military but ultimately transitioned to civilian control to establish credit for farmers. The second was a move away from a gold or silver standard to secure notes issued to what we refer to as a grain standard.

The CPC recognized that rapid or hyper-inflation was continually depreciating the value of currency, forcing more money to be circulated and in larger denominations. The inflation was most closely linked to commodities in general and agricultural commodities in particular. Millet, millet equivalents, corn flour, or synthetic baskets of commodities were used with varying purposes across base areas to secure the notes. The security was provided by the collection of taxes on farmland, so as grain prices increased the value of stocks and tax collected also increased. This did not eliminate inflation and border and base currencies still depreciated in consumptive value, but it did have a moderating effect that preserved base currencies more so than in free China or Japanese areas.

A unique aspect of this was that physical grain held a store of value, and in some cases—for example the issue of grain tickets or vouchers to soldiers—a medium of exchange. This worked to the farmer's benefit, especially when it came to the issuance of credit. In the base areas, loans were issued in currency for the acquisition of production inputs and other farm investments such as irrigation. The biggest concern was not so much farmers defaulting on these loans, a risk quite low given the appreciating value of commodities, but whether repayment in nominal terms was able to preserve value. Instead, repayment was made in real terms with the nominal loan value (plus accrued interest) indexed to grain or corn flour or other commodity prices. If the prices of the reference commodity doubled between loan origination and repayment, the farmer would pay twice the amount owed. It was an imperfect system since the reference commodity might not be perfectly correlated with farm revenues, but it worked fairly well under precarious and imperfect conditions. It also would have discouraged hoarding, in the sense that borrowing to buy physical commodity would provide no great gain in real terms. Hoarding, of course, was still an issue since holding the physical asset was far safer than holding or owing currency, but establishing a grain standard for loan repayment would have mitigated the borrow-and-hoard effect.

Finally, although we focused on the Sino-Japanese war era, the issuance of varied border and base currencies had a lasting effect on China's banking system. By 1948, with the CPC in firm control of large tracts of North and Northeast China, the flow of goods between base areas still hampered local trade and troop movements and various efforts were made to consolidate and unify currencies. But this was not a clean process. Some attempt was made after the war with Japan when the currencies issued by the New 4th Army in Huazhong were unified into a single Huazhong currency. Currency unification was stalled after the civil war broke out. But in October 1947 the liberated areas in Huabei (North China), Xibei (Northwest), and Dongbei (Northeast) under CPC control needed a unified currency to facilitate trade and troop movements. The Huabei Finance and Economics Agency of the CPC was formed to start this unification. The Southern Hebei Bank became the unified currency for the Northern provinces and all other banks stopped issuing currency. In the Northwest the Xibei Peasant Bank became the unified currency and all Northwest banks stopped issuing currency, and by November 1948 the currency of the Beihai Bank was the designated currency in Shandong and Huazhong liberated areas.

A further step to unify the currency was taken on December 1, 1948 when the Hubei Bank, Beihai Bank, and Xibei Peasant Bank were merged to form the People's Bank of China (PBoC) which issued one currency, the renminbi (RMB), for all areas. The first step was to remove base currencies from circulation by exchanging them for RMB. To accomplish this, decisions were made in terms of exchange. In December 1948 the PBoC exchange rate between *luxi* and RMB was set at 100:1, that is holders of *luxi*-issued currency could exchange 100 in the base currency for one RMB. Outstanding notes from the Southern Hebei Bank, Beihai Bank, Huazhong Bank, and Zhongzhou Peasant Bank were converted at the rate of 1 RMB per 100 border notes. The Shanxi-Chahar-Hebei Border Area, Dongbei, Rehe, and Great Wall banks were exchanged at 1:1000 and the notes of the Xibei Peasant Bank were exchanged at 1:2000.[32] The Chinese National Currency was basically worthless.

[32] Peoples Bank of China (1988). "Picture Album of the Renminbi" Compiled by Currency issuance department of the Peoples bank of China. China Financial Publishing House. Beijing, page 7–11.

CHAPTER 12

The Farmers Bank of China

12.1 Introduction

The formation of the Farmers Bank of China in 1935 was a pivotal point in the process of agricultural reconstruction during the Republican era. An offshoot of the blueprint for agriculture, as previously discussed, the Farmers Bank evolved more along the lines of a commercial bank than a cooperative lending institution as envisioned in the blueprint. But it was a start at financial sector development for agriculture and an integral component of rural reconstruction nonetheless. It represented part of a broad historical process which showed the efforts of the state to deepen and strengthen its command over rural society that distinguished the first half of the twentieth century from earlier times. For the first time, agriculture in China became central to China's economic strategy: "*In China, people residing in rural communities total 350,726,000 or 76.7 percent of the entire population of 457,611,858. Agriculture, being their oldest and principal industry, yields a total value amounting to 70 percent, constituting the largest source of revenue among the country's industries. It is evident from the preponderant proportion of farming population and the dominant importance of agricultural products that rural reconstruction must be regarded as the road to the progressive reconstruction of the Chinese Nation*".[1]

---

[1] Yieh Tsung-kao (1941). Rural reconstruction in free China, The Central Bank of China Bulletin, V.7 No.3, p. 361.

12.2 Rural Reconstruction and the Farmers Bank of Four Provinces

Rural reconstruction began with the inauguration of government agricultural institutions in the 1900s. Until then, there were very few, if any, well-organized institutions weighing in on agrarian reform. In 1903, a new Bureau of Commerce was created under the late Qing regime to develop agriculture and forestry. In 1906, this bureau was changed into the Bureau of Agriculture, Industry and Commerce, when a program was formulated to encourage agricultural production, forestry plantation, land reclamation, and livestock raising, as well as to improve spinning and weaving. In 1912, with the establishment of the Provisional Government[2] at Nanjing, an adjustment was decreed to fit the needs of the new era by establishing a Ministry of Industries in charge of agriculture, industry, and commerce. This led to several initiatives including the development of the Agricultural and Industrial Banks in 1915 and the Postal Savings Bank in 1918 as discussed in Chap. 5. After the removal of the Republican Administration to Peking in October 1913, the Ministry of Agriculture and Forestry was set to the development of agriculture, reforestation, sericulture, waste lands, irrigation system, weather observation, and the prevention of natural calamities. Not long after that it was reorganized into the Ministry of Agriculture and Commerce in 1914.

After the Northern Expedition in 1928, the authorities of the national government took more determined measures to rehabilitate the rural economy and its population through (a new) Ministry of Agriculture and Mining. In 1930, the two Ministries of Agriculture and Mining, and of Industry and Commerce, were combined into the Ministry of Industries to take charge of agricultural, industrial, fishery, and animal husbandry affairs. To meet the conditions arising from Communist suppression in Anhui,

---

[2] After the outbreak of the Xinhai Revolution on 10 October 1911, revolutionary leader Sun Yat-sen was elected Provisional President and founded the Provisional Government of the Republic of China in Nanjing. To preserve national unity, Sun ceded the presidency to military strongman Yuan Shikai, who established the Beiyang government in Peking. After a failed attempt to install himself as Emperor of China, Yuan died in 1916, leaving a power vacuum which resulted in China being divided into several warlord fiefdoms and rival governments. They were nominally reunified in 1928 by the Nanjing-based government led by Generalissimo Chiang Kai-shek, which after the Northern Expedition, governed the country as a one-party state under the Kuomintang, and was subsequently given international recognition as the legitimate representative of China.

Jiangxi, Hubei, and Henan provinces, the Rural Relief Commission was set up to aid farmers with capital, land, and labor. This was followed by a number of other organizations, including the National Economic Council, the Rural Rehabilitation Association, the National Reconstruction Commission, and the Central Agricultural Research Bureau. At the same time, Jiangxi and the Northwestern provinces, being in a state of the greatest poverty, were selected as experimental areas for rural reconstruction. For this work, the League of Nations created a Committee of Technical Collaboration with China and sent a number of technical advisors to the National Economic Council for active service.

As a start the Kuomintang (KMT) established four provincial banks known as Farmers Banks of Four Provinces (Anhui, Jiangxi, Hubei, and Henan) the purpose of which was to finance the program of constructive and reconstructive activities. It was probably no coincidence that these four provinces were infiltrated by communist forces with the formation of many soviets. The presence of the bank and the reconstruction efforts now offered political and economic competition with what the communists had to offer. It was not by coincidence that the KMT's efforts at cooperation were run through the military. The military problem was particularly acute in Jiangxi Province where between September 1933 and September 1934 there were at least four major military campaigns by the KMT to oust the communists. By October 1934 word reached Zhou Enlai that the KMT had amassed a force of nearly 500,000 soldiers for a final push to oust the communists. Rather than fight, the communists escaped on what is referred to as the Long March which ended in Shaanxi Province in September 1935.

From the beginning of the Long March in 1934 through September 1937 China had several years of tenuous stability. There were clashes between communist troops, KMT, and local warlords along the Long March but Mao Zedong and Zhou Enlai, with a largely depleted and demoralized force, went out of their way to avoid conflict. Consequently, with the exception of the Northeast which was still in control by the Japanese, China was at relative peace and faced no major calamities.

Divorced from war and catastrophe the relative calm of 1935 through August 1937 witnessed an unprecedented push in Chinese governance to getting its internal and external institutions right. Through the joint efforts of the national and provincial governments, rural schools, cooperative societies, medical centers, agricultural stations, and welfare houses were established for the rehabilitation of towns and villages. In December

1937, with the Japanese occupation of Nanjing, the government moved its primary services to Chongqing, but the core of government was removed only to Wuhan where a full government functioned until the Japanese broke through the Hubei defenses in the fall of 1938. Almost immediately the Wuhan government began to consolidate ministries. In order to maintain closer relations with other government departments and institutions for the furtherance of reconstruction work, the Ministry of Economic Affairs was created to take over the former Ministry of Industries as well as the Bureau of Hydraulic Engineering of the National Economic Council, the National Resources Commission, the National Reconstruction Commission, and the two Adjustment Commissions on Agriculture and on Industry and Mining. Under the Ministry of Economic Affairs were also the Central Agricultural Research Bureau and the Farm Credit Bureau (*Nong Ben Ju*). In July 1940, now in Chongqing, the Ministry of Agriculture and Forestry was organized to direct and supervise the highest administrative authorities of various provinces in the execution of agricultural and forestation policies.

While this was a natural outcome of rural reconstruction, by 1940 Japanese and Chinese forces were at a stalemate, and this lull provided an opportunity to focus on agriculture and forestry as a core element of the war effort in maintaining and feeding the standing armies and providing raw material for uniforms and munitions. After 1940, rural reconstruction pushed numerous critical development programs for agriculture including the reclamation of waste land, the redistribution of farm areas, the introduction of intensive cultivation, the experimentation of agricultural produce, the improvement of irrigation and drainage, and, as previously discussed, the successful management of cooperative banking institutions.

12.3 The Formation of the Farmers Bank of China

Of the institutions created throughout the reconstruction period, none was more important for the financial development of agriculture than the first regional farmers' bank called the Farmers Bank of Jiangsu which was established in Nanjing in July 1928 by the Jiangsu provincial government after the Northern Expedition. The new governor of Jiangsu made good use of the land surtaxes collected by the former governor, the warlord Chuan-fang Sun, to establish the Farmers Bank of Jiangsu using residual land surtaxes as capital. As part of its development, the Farmers Bank of Jiangsu invited Xue Xian-zhou, a well-known expert on cooperatives, to lead the preparatory committee, and this led to the first of the many alliances that would emerge between the policy banks and credit cooperatives. Meanwhile, as early as 1928 the Nanjing national government and its advisors urged the great need to develop a system of agricultural credit as a matter of basic importance. This was followed in 1929 by the Nanjing government's proposal to establish a nationwide farmers' bank.

1933 saw an amalgamation of the Farmers Bank of Four Provinces with a head office at Hankou. This new bank held the distinction in China, and amongst the commercial banks of the time, as being a policy bank. It then expanded into a nationwide bank and was renamed the Farmers Bank of China (FBC) on April 1, 1935, with the head office transferred to Shanghai from Hankou. In June 1935, its capital was augmented to $10 million, and beginning in January 1936 its bank notes were accepted as legal tender by government order.

As a financial institution, the FBC was entrusted with the special mission of assisting rural reconstruction, including the promotion of agriculture and handcrafts. It made certain advances to agricultural cooperatives and helped in the rehabilitation of areas taken over from the communists in Central China. It also handled certain army funds and was generally regarded as being especially important to Chiang Kai-shek. By 1937 the FBC was formally designated as a state-run bank which, among other privileges, permitted it to issue bonds and notes on behalf of the Chinese government. The amount of paid-up capital and reserves of the FBC is shown in Table 12.1.

In Table 12.1 we report on the growth in the number of FBC branches and offices from inception through to 1947. By 1936, three years after the amalgamation of the Farmers Bank of the Four Provinces, there were 14 FBC branches with local offices and branches numbering in total 75. This was 81 more than were in place in 1933. Following the beginning of the Sino-Japanese war the number of branches were reduced, and in unoccupied areas there were 87 offices by the end of 1937. As the war dragged on the number of branches reduced to eight and total offices fell to 70 by 1938. However in the 1940 reorganization, aided by the stalemate in the war, the KMT began again to introduce branches and offices in unoccupied territories with 13 branches and 114 offices by 1941. Also in 1939 the FBC expanded services into other financial institutions within the FBC umbrella including cooperative banks, farm-loan communication services, farm-loan offices, agricultural warehouses, public granaries, etc. By 1941 these provided an additional 263 outlets for agricultural credit. By 1947,

Table 12.1 Amounts of paid-up capital and reserves of the Farmers Bank of China, 1933–46

Year	Total paid-up capital and reserves (dollar)	Index 1932 = 100	Annual growth
1933	2,500,000.00	100.00	100.00
1934	3,028,000.00	121.12	121.12
1935	8,070,110.00	322.80	260.52
1936	8,447,610.00	337.90	104.68
1937	8,586,000.00	343.44	101.64
1938	8,726,000.00	349.04	101.63
1939	12,236,518.00	489.46	140.23
1940	14,311,492.06	572.46	116.96
1941	25,494,580.46	1019.78	170.14
1942	28,289,600.47	1131.58	110.96
1943	97,318,785.36	3892.75	344.01
1944	116,824,770.10	4672.99	120.04
1945	138,478,340.70	5530.13	118.54
1946	194,043,878.81	7761.76	140.12

Source: Archives of FBC,'FBC', p. 365

two years after the end of war with Japan, and in the midst of civil war between the nationalists and communists, there were 23 branches—with 278 offices and 466 related financial institutions making a total of 744.

In retrospect, was the FBC a success? In terms of loan dispersal, loans increased 1220 times in nominal terms between 1933 and 1947 from 3.144 million to 3834.24 million (see Table 12.3). From 1933 through the second half of 1934 no agricultural loans were made at all. All loans were commercial. Between the end of 1936 and the end of 1942, the highest percentage of loans to agriculture was 20.7% in 1938. By 1942 only 4% of loans made by the FBC went to farmers and agriculture with the vast majority of funds going to make commercial loans.

As previously discussed, the war years brought about debilitating inflation and hyper-inflation. While in many instances commodity prices increased at the same pace as input costs, the cost of consumer goods increased much further. In the absence of credit, farmers had little choice but to reduce economic efforts in the field in order to purchase household necessities such as food, clothing, and fuel. With an end to the war

Table 12.2 Growth in branches and offices of Farmers Bank of China, 1933–47

Year	FBC Branches	Sub-branches	Local branches	Local offices	Total	Agricultural credit institutions	Total
1933	2	2	2		6		6
1934	5	1	9	1	16		16
1935	11	2	23	1	37		37
1936	14	1	48	12	75		75
1937	12	4	48	23	87		87
1938	8	7	41	14	70		70
1939	8	6	51	10	75	85	160
1940	12	6	60	5	83	159	242
1941	13	6	77	18	114	263	377
1942	13	11	100	59	183	339	522
1943	13	12	96	103	224	526	750
1944	10	11	86	94	201	505	706
1945	24	13	119	76	232	458	690
1946	24	18	135	109	286	475	761
1947	23	21	123	111	278	466	744

Note: Agricultural Credit Institution includes cooperative banks, farm-loans communication services, farm-loans offices, agricultural warehouses, public granary, etc.
Source: Archives of FBC, 'FBC', p. 41

nowhere in sight Chiang Kai-shek and his political acolytes could foresee the impact of an agricultural liquidity trap on the provisions of food and raw materials for a nationalist standing army of 4.3 million as well as 750,000 to 1 million allied (at that time) communist troops. In 1942 the FBC was absorbed into the Joint Administration Office of the Four Policy Banks with the express purpose of making more direct loans to farmers, as well as providing loans to non-aligned credit cooperatives throughout unoccupied China, and to provide credit and capital towards a renewed push to expanding credit cooperatives.

As shown in Table 12.3 almost immediately, in the second half of 1942 loan volume increased from $242.864 million to $650.016 million, with the agricultural share of loans rising from 4.3% to 63.1%. By the end of the war in 1945 agricultural loans constituted between 53.3% and 67.2% of outstanding loans, and as the FBC continued to make loans even under the stress and strife of civil war, FBC loans increased to between 72.8% and 81.9% of loans.

Table 12.3 Loan dispersements by the Farmers' Bank of China, 1933–47 (unit: $1000)

Date (y/m)	Agricultural loans Balance	%	Land credit loans Balance	%	Commercial loans Balance	%	Loans by savings department Balance	%	Loans by trust department Balance	%	Total Balance	%
1933.06					3144	100.0					3144	100.0
1933.12					6036	100.0					6036	100.0
1934.06					8581	100.0					8581	100.0
1934.12	625	6.0			9732	94.0					10,357	100.0
1935.06	4262	26.1			12,079	73.9					16,341	100.0
1935.12	3515	14.4			20,895	85.6					24,410	100.0
1936.06	8058	15.6			43,651	84.4					51,709	100.0
1936.12	14,805	19.2			68,366	80.8					77,171	100.0
1937.06	20,253	18.8			86,922	80.7	556	0.5			107,737	100.0
1937.12	21,487	18.0			119,960	81.7	420	0.3			146,867	100.0
1938.06	31,529	20.7			120,493	79.0	530	0.3			152,552	100.0
1938.12	30,366	10.7			254,198	89.2	355	0.1			284,919	100.0
1939.06	35,975	9.6			339,117	90.3	330	0.1			375,422	100.0
1939.12	42,316	8.4			463,263	91.6	117				505,686	100.0
1940.06	68,576	9.6			647,277	90.4	219				716,063	100.0
1940.12	67,302	7.1			875,999	92.6	3116	0.3			946,417	100.0
1941.06	111,16	6.8			1522.631	92.5	12,247	0.7			1,646,094	100.0

1941.12	207,101	7.9			2,393,011	91.5	16,106	0.6		2,616,218	100.0
1942.06	242,864	4.3			5,398,816	95.3	20,958	0.4		5,662,693	100.0
1942.12	650,016	63.1			372,915	36.2	5277	0.5	35	1,030,776	100.0
1943.06	1,127,870	69.3	2533	0.2	478,374	29.4	7950	0.5	35	1,627,595	100.0
1943.12	1,512,117	68.7	13,366	0.8	521,719	23.7	93,013	4.2	35	2,201,666	100.0
1944.06	2,349,091	74.6	64,011	2.9	548,340	17.4	98,889	3.1	10,796	0.5	3,149,465	100.0
1944.12	2,712,111	70.7	134,679	4.3	849,859	22.2	97,009	2.5	18,466	0.6	3,834,240	100.0
1945.06	5,717,079	67.2	169,442	4.4	2,166,355	25.5	251,820	3.0	5819	0.2	8,503,840	100.0
1945.12	5,090,377	53.3	243,586	2.9	4,112,527	43.1	25,477	0.3	125,000	1.5	9,549,339	100.0
1946.06	24,647,319	56.8	316,757	3.3	16,056,085	37.0	42,015	0.1	4201		43,419,678	100.0
1946.12	90,279,261	66.7	2,674,259	6.2	36,836,014	27.2	376,658	0.3			135,343,673	100.0
1947.06	579,817,734	81.9	7,851,740	5.8	114,304,575	16.2	2,841,326	0.4			707,851,887	100.0
1947.12	880,021,516	72.8	10,888,252	1.5	269,127,737	22.2	2,555,794	0.2			1,209,360,860	100.0

Source: Archives of FBC, 'FBC', pp. 370–371

12.4 Joint Administration Office of the Four Policy Banks, Bank Specialization, and FBC's Monopoly and Banking Progress in War Time

We all know that there are two fronts in modern warfare: one is military and the other financial. Although armies, navies and air forces figure conspicuously in the public eye, yet the less spectacular weapons of warfare in the financial field are of equal importance in the conflict of nations under modern conditions. Indeed, especially is a long-drawn-out war which is a contest in the power of endurance, the prospects of ultimate victory depend on a nation's financial staying power perhaps even more than upon its military power.[3]

By the time the Sino-Japanese war broke out in 1937 there were a number of agricultural banks scattered throughout China that nominally made loans to agriculture. The major banks are listed in Table 12.4 as of 1937. The Nanjing government was greatly involved in banking, especially after taking control in 1935 of the Bank of China and the Bank of Communications. Personnel from the Finance Ministry and the National Economic Council were closely identified with the government banks and high officials acted as chief officers in the Bank of China, Bank of Communications, and the FBC. Viewing this situation, George E. Taylor observed in 1936 that *"'it would be difficult to say where the Government ends and the banks begin"*.[4] Moreover the banks, as large holders of government bonds, were deeply involved with government.

It is no wonder then that at the outbreak of war the nationalist government sought to gain greater control over the banking system, not only in terms of funding the expanding war efforts, but also through capital controls, interest rates, and maintaining credit supplies. In times of war the worst that can happen is capital flight, where banks send capital, particularly foreign currency reserves, outside the country. If this were allowed the reduction in credit supply would reduce liquidity and working capital stifling economic growth generally, but also depriving much needed enterprise, particularly in agriculture, agricultural inputs, and manufacturing. War with neither capital nor food is not winnable and knowing this the KMT took great strides from its Wuhan and Chongqing bases of govern-

---

[3] P.T. Chen. (1941). China's strong economic position, The Central Bank of China Bulletin, V7. No.3, p. 311.
[4] P.T. Chen. (1941). *Op Cit.*

Table 12.4   Major banks lending to agriculture, circa 1937

Name of banks	Provinces loans went to
Jiangsu Farmers Bank	Jiangsu
Farmers Bank of China	Henan, Hubei, Anhui, Jiangxi, Shaanxi, Fujian, Jiangsu, Zhejiang
China Agricultural and Industrial Bank	Zhejiang
Xian banks in Zhejiang	Zhejiang
Shanghai Bank	Jiangsu, Shaanxi, Anhui, Henan, Zhejiang, Hunan, Shanxi, Shandong, Hubei
Bank of China	Shandong, Shaanxi, Hebei, Henan, Anhui, Jiangsu, Hunan, Zhejiang
Jincheng Bank	Hebei, Shaanxi, Henan, Shanxi
Bank of communication	Shaanxi
Zhejiang Xingye Bank	Shaanxi
Continental Bank	Hebei
Reclamation Bank	Zhejiang

Sourced: Zhang, Youyi. (1957). Materials on Chinese Agriculture in Modern Era 1927–1937, Beijing: San Lian Press, p. 182

ment to ensure a steady flow of capital throughout the agricultural and industrial sectors.

Thus, the war brought many important changes to the Chinese banking system, the most conspicuous being the strengthening and consolidation of the central banking system, as evidenced by the great expansion of the government banks as well as provincial and municipal banks. The Nanjing government further tightened its supervision over the commercial banks through *Temporary Regulations of Banking Control in Wartime* which was promulgated by the Finance Ministry on August 7, 1940.[5] The new regulations required every bank to maintain a 20% reserve fund against its total deposits in any of the four government banks, to submit a 10-day report on the actual conditions of its deposits, loans, and remittances to the Ministry of Finance, to refrain from participation in hoarding any kind of commodities, and to confine its mortgage loans to legitimate business. Furthermore, the Ministry of Finance could send inspectors to examine the daily accounts, vault conditions, and other important documents of the bank at any time without previous notice.

[5] Lin Yi-chin (1941),Chinese commercial banks in war time, The Central Bank of China Bulletin, V7. No.3, p. 346.

The new regulations may be construed as wartime temporary measures, or they may be considered as setting the stage for incorporating all commercial banks within the framework of the central banking system.

In an effort to stabilize China's national currency and further strengthen its financial structure, the original plan of reorganizing the Central Bank of China into a Central Reserve Bank had been raised but postponed by the outbreak of the Sino-Japanese war. Instead, the Joint Administration Office of the Four Government Banks—namely, the Central Bank of China, Bank of China, Bank of Communications, and the Farmers Bank of China—was organized on September 8, 1939. The Joint Administration Office, with a Board of Directors headed by Chiang Kai-shek, was responsible for the conduct of the various activities of the four banks which were closely related to the financial policy of the Nanjing government. According to Hsu Kan, Vice Minister of Finance and concurrently Secretary-General of the Administration, the work of the Joint Administration of the Four Government Banks may be summarized as follows:[6]

1. Expansion of financial network in pursuance of the loan and discount policy, and investment in special wartime productive enterprises.
2. Stabilization of the Chinese dollar through careful examination of importer's applications for foreign exchange, open inspection of note reserves of the four banks, and collection of gold and silver.
3. Regulation of prices, facilitation of remittances to the interior and encouragement of exports.
4. Absorption of idle capital and promotion of special savings.

There were two committees in the Joint Administration Office (JAO), one for wartime finance and the other for wartime economy. The Wartime Economic Committee included the following divisions: special investment, material supply, and price stabilization. The Finance Committee maintained the following divisions: note issuance, loans and discount, domestic and foreign exchange, special savings deposits, collection and exchange of gold and silver, statistics and agricultural finance. The division of agricultural finance was charged with regulating farm loans across all of

---

[6] Hsu Kan, The Organization and Work of the Joint Administration of Chinese Government Banks, Economic Journal, Vol. 1, No 5–6, pp. 4–5.

(unoccupied) China including the drafting of regulations on rural credit and the formalizing of rural credit contracts. Bank specialization began with a mass transfer of all formal agricultural loans to the FBC from *Nong Ben Ju* in January 1941.

12.5 Debates and Conflicts on the Rural Finance System

12.5.1 Debates on Banks Specialization

As presented previously, the blueprint for agricultural finance outlined a dual track system comprised of two new entities, the Agricultural Bank of China and the Farmers Bank of China. The proposal held that the Agricultural Bank of China would be organized in a way to acquire funds for commercial purposes and provide capital to the FBC at the county level to be dispersed amongst the production, marketing, and credit cooperatives. For reasons that are not entirely clear only the FBC was formed in 1935. Perhaps the administrators felt that that the activities under *Nong Ben Ju* would be sufficient, but most likely the turmoil in the gold, silver, and currency markets and a decline in China's bond quality made the idea of issuing agricultural bonds untenable. Thus, although the FBC was supposed to provide financial services to farmers and farm sectors as directed on April 1, 1935, by 1942, less than 20% of the total loans each year were farm loans, while more than 80% were commercial loans.

This raised a question, and an ensuing debate, as to whether the FBC should run commercial operations as well as agricultural operations, especially between the experts of the China-USA Agricultural Mission. The China-USA Agricultural Mission was the first official cooperation plan advocated by the two governments. After World War II, to address the future direction of China's backward economy, the national government, inspired by the successful experience of the Nanjing University-Cornell University crop improvement plan in 1925,[7] presented a proposal for technical collaboration in agriculture and forestry to the United States and got approval. So in May, 1946 the governments convened a commission

---

[7] Love, H. H., and J.H. Reisner, (1963). The Cornell-Nanjing Story. the first international technical cooperation program in agriculture by Cornell University. Ithaca, N. Y., Dept. of Plant Breeding, New York State College of Agriculture, Cornell University.

comprised of 13 Chinese experts and 11 American experts.[8] The mission wrote the Report of the China-USA Agricultural Mission in 1947 after investigating 15 provinces and districts: Jiangsu, Zhejiang, Hebei, Northeast China, Shanxi, Gansu, Ningxia, Qintghai, Sichuan, Guangdong, Guangxi, Yunnan, Taiwan, etc.

As to the question on whether the FBC should run commercial operations as well as agricultural operations, most suggested not, especially the American members of the China-US Joint Commission on Agriculture. The Americans held the opinion that commercial operations of the FBC should be halted to make it a real farmers' bank. Some Chinese scholars argued further that the reason why the bank ran commercial operations was to offset the costs of its agricultural loans administration. The Chinese representatives pointed out that the key problem was the source of bank funds. In the United STates, agricultural bonds were issued by the Farm Credit Funding Corporation ostensibly secured by an implicit guarantee by the US government whereas in China funds for the FBC had to be collected by personal social networks. They argued that as the Chinese government could subsidize the costs of agricultural credit or promulgate policies to sponsor the bank it would not need to run commercial operations. It was also suggested that the FBC should be allowed to refinance and remortgage from the Central Bank of China.[9]

12.6 Single or Ternary Agricultural Financial Structure?

As with the discussions on the earlier blueprint, the 1940s reopened discussions as to whether a single institution should be responsible for providing all of short-term, medium-term, and long-term credit or whether issuance of these credits should be segregated according to different terms of credits. By 1943, the US experience with the Farm Credit System and the Farm Credit Administration was well-known and this brought up the idea that the Chinese system should follow suit. Under the US agricultural

---

[8] Participating in the commission were Claude b. Hutchison, Raymond T Moyer, J Lossing Buck, Robert H. Burns, Harley L. Crane, Charles Joseph Huber, H.C.M.Case, Charle E. Seita, B.L.Hummel, Robert A. Nesbit, Lucille Arras from USA and Zou Bingwen, Shen Zonghan, Ma Baozhi, Zhan Naifeng, Jia Weiliang, Ge Jingzhong, Luo Wansen, Shou Jingwei, Xu Kangzu, Wang Yikang, Wu Liuqing, Yang Maochun, Ye Qianji from China etc.

[9] Agricultural Finance Design Commission of Farmers' Bank of China, Issues on networks of agricultural finance, *Farmers' Bank of China Monthly*, Vol. 8(3), March 1947.

credit system a network of land banks (or Farm Credit Banks) issued bonds to cover the demand for farm mortgages and make intermediate term loans.[10] The government also provided capital to start Production Credit Associations, which were cooperatives for the production and marketing of agricultural products. In addition to government capital, loan funds were made up of farmers share subscriptions. These loans were almost exclusively used as short-term credit.

Along these lines the Chinese argued for a ternary (three-part) design for agricultural credit. The first was a Land Bank which could be expanded from the Land Finance Department of the FBC which was founded in 1942 to make long-term loans. Then a Cooperative Treasury (*Hezuo Jinku*) system would focus primarily on short-term loans. Third, the state-operated FBC would then lend primarily for medium-term purposes. This ternary agricultural financial structure would not only benefit from specialization, but would also relieve pressure on the FBC which at the time could hardly manage the demand for farm loans, land loans, and cooperative credits without adequate funds at its disposal.

A counter-argument was that a ternary structure was rather idealistic. It ignored the rising complexities from China's un-unified currency, political chaos, transportations blockages, and regional differences. The reality was that long-term land finance loans took up only 5% or less of FBC total loans in most years since 1942. Under this counter-argument a single agricultural financial structure would be more realistic and the FBC could manage land finance and short-term cooperative loans in addition to medium-term farm loans.

This view was agreed upon by members of the China-USA Agricultural Mission taking a survey on Chinese rural financial institutions in 1947. They suggested that the Farmers Bank of China the and Central Cooperative Treasury (*Zhongyang Hezuo Jinku*) should be merged into one institution named the Agricultural Bank of China (ABC) which would supply loans to all agricultural sectors.[11] Since the FBC had already played

---

[10] Bruce L. Ahrendsen, Charles B. Dodson, Bruce L. Dixon, Steven R. Koenig, (2005). "Research on USDA farm credit programs: past, present, and future", *Agricultural Finance Review*, Vol. 65 Issue: 2, pp. 165–181.
   Turvey, C. G., (2017). Historical developments in agricultural finance and the genesis of America's farm credit system. *Agricultural Finance Review*, 77(1), 4–21.
   Turvey, C. G. (2009). Liberty Hyde Bailey, the Country Life Commission and the formalization of farm credit in the USA. *Agricultural Finance Review*, 69(2), 133–148.
[11] Fu, Hong. (2009). *Op Cit.*

part of this role, the Agricultural Bank of China could take advantage of the qualified personnel from the FBC, its joint funds, and lower operating costs. On the organizational structure of the Agricultural Bank of China they recommended three departments. First was the Land Finance Department providing long-term loans to farmers for purchasing land, land improvement, and land reclamation to make Sun Yet-sen's vision that farmers obtain their own lands come true. Second, the Agricultural Production & Marketing Department would provide short-term loans to farmers and agri-businesses through farmers' organizations for supporting crop production and marketing. Including farmers' organizations—such as the Farmers' Union, Cooperative Society, Farmers' Storehouses—it would help individual farmers purchase seeds, fertilizers, agricultural equipment, forage, antidote to serum pests, etc., and would promote crop productivity, improve the transportation and sales of farm products, and build storehouses and other relevant businesses.

Third, was a Medium-term Credit Department which would be responsible for fund-raising to establish the Agricultural Bank of China. In addition, it would also provide loans to companies producing fertilizer, veterinary products, remedies for diseases and pests, facilities for reproduction, plants of seedlings, saplings, and livestock, and food processing factories, etc.

12.6.1 Conflicts Between Farmers' Bank of China and the Central Cooperative Treasury

Both the Farmers Bank of China and the Central Cooperative Treasury (CTT) lent to farmers through primary cooperative credit societies. So there were inevitably overlaps and conflicts. The Farmers' Bank of China made loans for: (a) agricultural production, agricultural extension, agricultural products, agricultural processing, and rural sidelines and farmland water conservancy; (b) managements or acceptances of agricultural reclamation, animal husbandry and debtor bonds and stocks; (c) investments of agricultural enterprises and organizations; (d) investments in rural credit cooperatives; (e) acceptance and discount of bills; (f) domestic exchange, the receipt of deposits the agency received, buying and selling securities, savings and trust business; (g) the operation of the warehouse and transportation; and (h) land.

The scope of business of the Central Cooperative Treasury was dominated by the lending and investment of industrial cooperatives, agricultural cooperatives, transportation and marketing cooperatives, insurance cooperatives, credit cooperatives and other cooperative undertakings, as well as special businesses entrusted by the government. Thus, the Central Cooperative Treasury was supposed to supply short-term loans to farmers and would be a self-owned, self-operated, self-help system for farmers, and operate as a separate entity from the FBC. Operating independently, it was pointed out by Chiang Kai-shek that the Central Cooperative Treasury might not be constrained by banking laws. In fact, however, it was founded by governments not farmers, ran by government not farmers, and operated much like the FBC.

In the blueprint, the national government divided the business focal points between the FBC and the CCT in advance: the FBC's business scope was mainly to manage agricultural credit lending and investment for agricultural machinery, fertilizer, seeds, manufacturing, transporting, disaster prevention, etc.; the CCT was given priority to support cooperative credit, namely to support cooperative undertakings of various kinds, such as industrial cooperation, agricultural cooperation, transportation, insurance, cooperation, and credit cooperation. However, in practice, both shared the same prospective borrowers, making loans to cooperatives.

Neither the CCT nor the FBC were able to abide by the division established by the government. Both found it inefficient to constrain the CCT to making loans only to cooperatives and the FBC only to other groups and agencies. The reality was that both found it feasible and economical to dispatch personnel to handle rural credit in the same areas in search of talent and funds. Moreover, since there were usually peasant unions and cooperative societies in the same areas, with many farmers having membership in both, some farmers might have received two loans and be puzzled by the different ways, amounts, and terms of the loans. Importantly, the CCT's mandate also included larger cooperative assemblages in industry and infrastructure development. Consequently, it could not cede any one district to the FBC. Likewise, the FBC's mandate included industry and other businesses so it could not cede any district to the CCT. To maintain profits and capital controls, they had little choice but to compete, despite the stipulated divisions of responsibility.

Scholars agreed that the imminent conflict between the CCT and the FBC was because of unsound cooperative organization. According to Qiao Qi-ming, it was fine that the FBC made loans to cooperatives and farmers' groups, and the CCT supplied cooperative loans. Nor was it a problem that both made loans in the same area. The key problem lay in the fact that farmers were not fully informed and were in a passive position. The FCB set up a farmers' union or cooperative society to make loans, while the CCT set up another farmers' union or cooperative society. Usually a farmer was asked to join both organizations, the same cooperatives had to borrow from the two organizations. Because certain obligations were involved, farmers were unable to choose optimally from the different organizations based on terms and conditions favorable to the borrower.

12.6.2 Conflicts Between County Banks and Other Rural Credit Institutions

In the early 1940s, the KMT introduced a new institution, the county bank, to carry out New County System policies and financial and economic policies during wartime, including charging and collecting taxes. The county bank was designed as a regional, government-owned, financial organization, supporting businesses within the boundary of a county, supporting local development, and promoting regional autonomy. Rural credit was not on its business list, but the county banks were closely related to rural financial institutions because the development of the rural economy was included in its goals. Although they were relatively small in number, only 559 by 1948 (see Table 12.5), the New County System was intended to empower local governance at the sub-county level. By doing so, the Nanjing national government attempted to promote a grassroots political organization, to strengthen local political power, and to intensify the competition for loyalty in rural areas with (and against) the Chinese Communist Party.

As might be expected, there were a number of conflicts which arose between the county banks and other rural financial institutions more directly involved in agriculture. It was believed by some that the county bank was an attempt to closely integrate the rural cooperatives with the old *Bao Jia* system, by means of which the gentry keep their stranglehold over the farmers.[12] Dr. Lewis S.C. Smythe says of this:[13] *"There has been a*

---

[12] Ten households make up a *Jia*; ten *Jias* make up a *Bao*. The basic work of *Bao Jia* was to implement "management, education, maintenance, and safeguard". "Management" included checking Hukou, checking guns, and carrying out joint guarantee, etc.; "Education" included handling schools, training of able-bodies man, etc.; "Maintenance" included the creation of a so-called cooperative, measuring land etc.; "Safeguard" included the establishment of civil corps, patrol, vigilance and so on.

[13] Lewis S. C. Smythe, Cooperatives and Christian Missions, *The Chinese Recorder*, August 1940.

Table 12.5 County banks established each year: 1940–1948

Year	1940	1941	1942	1943	1944	1945	1946	1947	1948	Total
Jiangsu	–	–	–	–	–	–	22	12	1	35
Zhejiang	–	–	–	–	–	–	6	21	2	29
Anhui	–	–	–	1	2	15	10	10	–	38
Jiangxi	–	–	1	1	2	1	14	7	2	28
Fujian	–	–	–	2	–	–	3	14	2	21
Hunan	–	–	–	–	1	–	3	10	–	14
Hubei	–	–	1	6	9	8	12	19	3	58
Henan	–	–	1	35	13	–	–	1	–	50
Hebei	–	–	–	–	–	–	–	3	1	4
Shandong	–	–	–	–	–	–	–	1	–	1
Shanxi	–	–	–	–	–	–	–	3	1	4
Gansu	–	–	–	1	–	–	3	3	2	9
Guangdong	–	1	–	1	–	1	–	7	–	10
Guangxi	–	–	–	–	–	–	1	1	–	2
Guizhou	–	–	–	1	1	2	3	5	–	12
Yunnan	–	–	–	1	2	2	19	21	1	46
Sichuang	2	15	42	38	18	11	5	1	–	132
Xikang	–	–	–	–	1	1	2	2	–	6
Shaanxi	–	–	4	17	25	11	3	–	–	60
Total	2	16	49	104	74	52	106	141	15	559

Source: Yanjin Wang (1979), Yearbook of County Bank in China, Tanbei: Wenhai Publisher

tendency during the past year for the Central Cooperative Administration to institute some form of 'compulsory' Pao (Bao) credit (cooperatives throughout the country in connection with the new Hsien system. In this, every family head in a Pao (Bao) would be required to join this credit cooperative. Such a system would be a parody on cooperation as we have described it here and should not be even called by the same name".[14]

A conference presentation of the Agricultural Finance Design Committee of the Farmers' Bank of China showed that there were more than 10 types of financial institutions running business at the county level by 1947.[15] These included sub-branches of the FBC, subsidiaries of the FBC like granaries, agri-management training centers, sub-branches of the

[14] Nym Wales. (1941). China builds for democracy: a story of cooperative industry, New York: Modern Age Book Inc.
[15] Agricultural Finance Design Committee of Farmers' Bank of China, Cooperation and communication among agricultural finance institutions, Farmers' Bank of China Monthly, Vol. 9(8), August 1947.

CCT, sub-branches of the Postal Remittance and Savings Bank, branches of provincial banks, county banks, branches of commercial banks, cooperative societies, other granaries, pawnshops, old-style Chinese native banks, and so on. The reality was that the Postal Remittance and Savings Bank only absorbed farmers' deposits and did not make agricultural loans; the provincial banks handled very few agricultural loans; commercial banks did not originate agrarian loans in county agencies; and cooperatives were only the grassroots of agricultural credit institutions' issuing agencies, not agricultural lending institutions; others were mostly traditional financial institutions. In fact the only types of rural financial institutions that made rural loans at the county level were branch offices of the FBC and their affiliated institutions, branches of the Central Cooperative Bank, and county banks. The county bank was established for the development of the county economy and later extended to the agricultural production business.

The main problems across these rural financial institutions were, first, that the pace of implementing national agricultural policies among various agencies were neither coordinated nor unified, and quite often the undertakings were either overlapping or contradictory; second, the sources and funds of different rural financial institutions were not under unified control, there was no overall plan of business; and third, the names of rural financial institutions were numerous, and the farmers were struggling to understand their business. And although there were many rural financial institutions, few actually established credit programs for the broad masses of farmers. Loans between rural financial institutions, loan interest rates, or deadlines were mostly inconsistent. There was even confusion on who handled and monitored loans. In some instances, loans were directly handled and managed by the banks, while others were handled by the local government, or by both.

12.7 Summary

Prior to 1935 China had made several attempts at extending credit to agriculture. Spurious attempts in the late Qing dynasty were followed by the promulgation of laws allowing for the Agricultural and Industrial Banks, with associated rights to support credit cooperatives and credit associations. The efforts of the International China Famine Relief Commission and the University of Jinling (Old spelling of Nanjing) started a push for rural cooperatives in the early 1920s. At the beginning of the period of agricultural reconstruction around 1930 the blueprint for agriculture laid out some foundations for supporting agricultural cooperation, including the beginnings of a Farmers Bank of China. The FBC that was formed in 1935 was more of a commercial type operation than a cooperative type, but ultimately supported credit cooperatives and an expanded portfolio of agricultural finance.

The role and importance of the FBC increased considerably during the war years. With the 1941 reforms the FBC became more than simply a lending institution to agricultural and related commercial enterprise, it also became an extension of the government itself in the delivery of policy. To this end the FBC was charged with the purchasing and marketing of most cash crop/agricultural products, like cotton, tea, tobacco, silk, sugar, and that were in wartime under the control of the Nanjing government. When the Farm Credit Bureau (*Nong Ben Ju*) was dissolved in 1942, its agricultural portfolio was absorbed by the FBC.

Most loans went to the following twelve provinces which were the main cotton-growing regions. The FBC had branches and offices across Henan, Hubei, Anhui, Jiangxi, Shaanxi, Fujian, Jiangsu, and Zhejiang so it did not itself have a national reach. Other banks such as the Farmers Bank of Jiangsu thus became an agent of policy in Jiangsu, the China Agricultural and Industrial Bank an agent of policy in Zhejiang, and so on. But even without an extended branch system, the FBC became central to the development of agricultural finance through its political clout and its policy role to support the development of agricultural cooperatives and cooperative societies.

CHAPTER 13

Nong Ben Ju, the Farm Credit Bureau, and the KMT's Agrarian Policy

13.1 Introduction

Under the 1930 blueprint discussed in Chap. 9 the plan was to establish a double-tier financial system with the Farmers Bank of China (FBC) driving the development of irrigation and production cooperatives as well as cooperative lending at the village level, and the proposed central agricultural bank—the Agricultural Bank of China (ABC)—to drive land credit, sales and supply cooperatives, and fund village Farmers Banks. Only half of this plan was set in motion with the expansion of the FBC in 1935. However, as discussed in Chap. 12 the FBC was not established on cooperative principles but rather as a continuation of the Farmers Banks developed in the 1920s (e.g. the 1928 Farmers Bank of Jiangsu in Nanjing).

By 1936 there was a sense of urgency to fully developing a nationwide structure and coordinating the organization of the provision of not only farm credit, but also credit for the development of agricultural infrastructure and related agricultural business interests. After credit cooperatives were established, different types of banks, national and local, commercial and/or agricultural, were encouraged to make loans to farmers. Loans provided by various commercial banks played some role in agricultural finance, but were utterly inadequate and preferred to lend, as most banks do, to lower-risk, higher-wealth classes of borrowers. Ignoring agriculture otherwise was a fairly easy task since those who controlled bank credit flowing through government channels had many common ties at the local

© The Author(s) 2018
H. Fu, C. G. Turvey, *The Evolution of Agricultural Credit during China's Republican Era, 1912–1949*,
https://doi.org/10.1007/978-3-319-76801-4_13

349

level with the landlord money lenders, who naturally opposed having to compete with the formal market. The tendency was to use rural bank credit for seasonal short-term needs, in the same way as the loans of old-style usurers, not for long-term productive investment. The push towards cooperative credit, while making some headway, was not progressing at a meaningful rate. Meanwhile the lack of storage and warehouse facilities in the agricultural producing regions, along railway lines, and at ocean ports were insufficient to even think that agricultural commodities and food products could meaningfully contribute to trade balances and foreign exchange. The sense was that the entirety of the agricultural economy was in disarray and a coordinated effort was required to streamline not only marketing channels but credit supply as well.

In April 1936, Wu Dingchang, the Minister of Industry, called a meeting with the leaders of China's major banks to discuss the issue. Included in the Shanghai meeting were representatives from the Central Bank, Bank of China, Bank of Communications, Bank of Shanghai, Jincheng Bank, South Bank, Zhejiang Industrial Bank, the Farmers Bank of China, and the Postal Remittances and Savings Bank among others. The topic under discussion was the coordination of a large number of agricultural activities, like rural credit, agricultural management, and technology, under an initiative administrative department called *Nong Ben Ju*.

13.2 *Nong Ben Ju* and the Farm Credit Bureau

In 1936 the Kuomintang (KMT) established a new initiative called *Nong Ben Ju* (*Nong*: farm, farmer, rural; *Ben*: root, center, source; *Ju*: Bureau) which included some sweeping initiatives in rural reform, rural reconstruction, and rural credit. Central to this initiative was the creation of the Farm Credit Bureau, which became an amalgam of public and private interests with the overarching goal of coordinating agricultural development and finance.

At this point we need to make a distinction between how we differentiate and use the term *Nong Ben Ju* in relation to the Farm Credit Bureau. The terms are often treated the same, that is *Nong Ben Ju* is often interchangeable with Farm Credit Bureau. However, we make a distinction between the two. When we refer to *Nong Ben Ju* we are making reference to the broader scope of the policy, including those policies and initiatives that are not directly related to credit. In comparison, we refer to the Farm Credit Bureau as a particular institution that deals specifically with agricultural finance and credit.

13.3 The Farm Credit Bureau

An important part of *Nong Ben Ju* was the formation of the Farm Credit Bureau. Importantly, the participating banks ceded agricultural lending institutions to the Farm Credit Bureau which allowed the banks to participate in the agricultural credit market without making any fixed capital investments. Instead, funding involved three tranches. First, fixed capital of $6 million/year would be made available for 1936–1940 by the Nationalist government in Nanjing which was issued common stock.

Second, was jointly invested capital by commercial banks. This would be matched by an equivalent amount of capital amounting to 1% of total bank deposits. From this funding source, the Farm Credit Bureau got $6.001 million capital in total from 30 participating banks. The top seven shareholders were the Joint Savings Society of the Yienyieh-Jincheng-Continental-China and South Sea Bank, Bank of China, Bank of Communication, Postal Remittances and Savings Bank, Jincheng Bank, Salt Industry Bank, and the Bank of Shanghai. Combined, these banks contributed 68.5% of total jointly invested capital (see Table 13.1). Participating banks would be issued transferable and securitizable interest-bearing notes with coupons no higher than 8%/annum. These notes were similar to cumulative preferred shares in the sense that coupons not paid in one year would be accumulated and paid in subsequent years. The capital provided by participating banks could be redeemed by installments following the expiry in 1940, or extended, depending upon the needs of the Farm Credit Bureau.

The third tranche would be working capital made available by an agricultural loan committee formed by participating banks and in conjunction with Farm Credit Bureau. If needed, the Farm Credit Bureau could also petition the Ministry of Economic affairs (i.e. the national government) to issue agricultural bonds up to the value of the Farm Credit Bureau's capital.[1]

There were several advantages to this setup. First, and perhaps most attractive to the banks, was an implied guarantee by the government's contribution. Since paper issued by the Farm Credit Bureau was deemed secured and interest bearing, then it could be assumed that underlying the bonds was an implied government guarantee.

---

[1] Jie Mu (1937). Banks investing Rural Areas under Policy of New Currency, *Statistics Monthly*, no.31.

Table 13.1 Amounts of jointly invested capital by participating banks (thousand dollars)

Participating Banks	Amount of capital invested in Farm Credit Bureau	Participating Banks	Amount of capital invested in Farm Credit Bureau
Joint Savings Society of the Yienyieh-Jincheng-Continental-China and South Sea Bank	–	Xinhua Bank	92
	–	Unio Commercial Bank	70
	840		65
Bank of China	701	Guohua Bank	55
Bank of Communication	651	National Industrial	46
Postal Remittances and Savings Bank	540	Bank of China	35
	518	Guohuo Bank	30
Jincheng Bank	497	Zhongfu Bank	26
Salt Industry Bank	366	Central Trust of China	21
Bank of Shanghai	250		21
Farmers Bank of Jiangsu	250	Cultivation Bank	20
Jiangsu Bank	220	Agricultural and Industrial Bank	20
Continental Bank	180		13
Zhejiang Industrial Bank	175	Zhongyi Trust Ltd.	11
Zhongnan Bank	150	Farmers Bank of China	10
Siming Bank	123		5
Zhejiang Bank		Bank of Agricultural and Commerce Quangong Bank Dong Lai Bank Central Savings Society Zhonghui Bank	

Source: Mu Jie, The new currency led the Banks to invest in the countryside, Statistics monthly, V.31, May, 1937

The second advantage, as mentioned, was that by virtue of their capital contributed, the participating banks could obtain the benefits of agricultural investment while not having to invest in bricks-and-mortar buildings and personnel.

Third, since agricultural investments were anticipated across provinces and agricultural regions, risks were spread amongst many participants providing a diversified hedge against covariate risks arising from floods, droughts, bandit activities, bandits, warlords, and other insurgencies of which there were many. By pooling capital for the Farm Credit Bureau risk too was pooled and shared amongst member banks.

13.3.1 Agricultural Products Department

Organizationally, the Farm Credit Bureau had two branches. The first branch was the Agricultural Products Department and this branch was set up to manage warehouse facilities for storage of agricultural commodities, negotiate with railway companies for the construction and leasing of warehouses at reasonable rates, handle the purchase and sale of commodities on behalf of the nationalist government, undertake the transportation and sale of agricultural products, and undertake improvements and adjustments of agricultural products. The aim was not only to develop a linked system of warehouses along major transportation routes but also to ensure that the transportation linkages and logistics had the overall effect of reducing transportation costs and accelerate product flow across an emerging value and supply chain. While many of the warehouses were anticipated to be owned, run, and managed by the state there would also be efforts to promote marketing cooperatives amongst farmers to reduce handling and negotiation costs and to allow farmers to consolidate crops for delivery at a fair and pre-negotiated price. In addition, *Nong Ben Ju* also included a research component with the aim of enhancing market transparency in agricultural products. These studies would include monitoring domestic and international trade patterns, shifts in demand and supply and market prices, as well as conducting research into rural finance development, the development, ways, and means of building rural cooperatives, identifying a regulatory platform for agricultural finance, and providing guidance for program implementation.

Under *Nong Ben Ju* the initial plan was to build a network of warehouses: First, to build Grade A warehouses with a capacity of more than 100,000 dan (1 dan = 50 kg) in big cities and terminal markets, specializing in selling products. Second, to build Grade B and C warehouses with a capacity of 10,000–100,000 dan in the second-tier cities, collection and distribution centers and markets along railways, and to run mortgage and agro-marketing businesses. Third, to help cooperatives to build Grade D warehouses with a capacity of 10,000 dan in places of crop production, specializing in mortgage businesses.

The main businesses of warehouses were storing, purchasing and selling, processing agricultural products and loaning to farmers. These are summarized in Table 13.2. Basically the loans provided by warehouses maintained by the Farm Credit Bureau were mortgage credit loans. From September 1936 through January 1938, with the aid of the Farm Credit

Table 13.2 Warehouses and cooperative banks maintained by the Farm Credit Bureau

Year	Warehouses			Cooperative Banks			
	Total numbers	Total capacity (dan)	Balance of loans (dollar)	Total numbers	Balance of deposits (dollar)	Balance of loans (dollar)	Balance of remittances (dollar)
1937	31	–	–	17	–	–	–
1938	57	373,630	246,206	76	147,197	3,555,944	191,747
1939	77	1,912,501	1,752,339	138	1,618,427	10,306,676	1,522,443
1940.10	69	3,317,368	665,271	175	2,896,135	23,780,438	1,375,420

Source: Farm Credit Bureau, Report on Businesses of Farm Credit Bureau in 1939, 1940, 1941, Library of Nankai University
Use of "–" denotes missing data.

Bureau, 31 warehouses were established in Jiangsu, Anhui, Shandong, Hubei, Hebei, Jiangxi, Hunan, Sichuan, Shanxi, and Guangxi; by the end of 1938, there were 57 warehouses in total; by 1939, 77 warehouses; by 1940, 69 warehouses with a capacity of 3,317,368 dan. The purpose for which the loans were utilized, can be divided into storage and mortgaging loans, marketing loans, warehouse-building loans, interbank loans and microcredit. Storing and mortgaging loans and marketing loans were loans made to farmers and cooperatives for the production and marketing of agricultural products. Warehouse-building loans were loans made to cooperatives to build the warehouses. Interbank loans were loans issued by the simple agricultural warehouse as operating funds. Microcredit was to help farmers buy farm tools and pay for the costs of production and living.

13.3.2 Agricultural Loans Department

The second branch was the Agricultural Loans Department. Through the Agricultural Loans Department the Farm Credit Bureau could appropriate funds to invest in and promote agricultural banks, agricultural cooperatives, and farmers' pawn shops. It could also make direct loans to agriculture or encourage participating banks to make direct loans to farmers. This could be achieved through direct involvement or by remortgaging on securities available. By remortgaging, county (Hsien) banks, rural agricultural banks, agricultural cooperatives, and pawn shops could issue bonds or commercial paper, secured by farmers' loans and other assets, to the Farm Credit Bureau, and in return replenish loanable funds. Since many of these credit sources resisted lending to farmers, the Agricultural Loans Department could also negotiate directly with them to increase credit to farmers.

Similar to the earlier blueprint initiatives, the primary credit objectives of the Farm Credit Bureau was to support the development of cooperative banks at the village level so that farmers could borrow money to purchase inputs and farm implements to improve cultivation. Table 13.3 provides a summary of loans made by cooperative banks maintained by the Farm Credit Bureau for the years 1939 and 1940 for various provinces. In 1939 the largest demand was for livestock at 41.8%, fertilizer at 16.8%, other uses at 16.2%, and production of food crops at 14.8%. This pattern was fairly consistent across China, with a notable difference in loan demand for sideline industries in Guizhou (18.4% and 13.6%) and Shaanxi in 1940

Table 13.3 % Uses of loans made by cooperative banks maintained by the Farm Credit Bureau

Province	Year	Seeds	Fertilizer	Livestock	Food crops	Farm tools	Sideline industries	Lands[a]	Other[b]
Total	1939	3.0	16.8	41.8	14.8	3.2	3.2	1.1	16.2
	1940	3.1	16.9	40.6	12.3	2.5	5.9	4.3	14.4
Sichuan	1939	2.2	18.5	61.5	1.1	2.2	0.0	0.0	14.5
	1940	2.8	26.5	44.9	7.5	2.2	3.9	2.8	9.3
Guizhou	1939	1.3	1.4	39.6	11.3	1.6	18.4	7.9	18.7
	1940	2.1	1.3	46.3	12.2	1.8	13.6	7.7	15.1
Guangxi	1939	1.7	23.5	28.8	30.4	1.9	0.0	1.8	12.0
	1940	2.8	22.2	33.8	22.2	1.0	0.0	3.6	14.5
Hunan	1939	5.6	21.7	24.2	20.2	5.6	1.2	0.0	21.6
	1940	2.9	21.5	25.6	12.5	4.2	4.2	2.0	27.2
Hubei	1939	9.2	12.9	35.8	17.2	9.5	0.0	1.4	14.2
	1940	10.3	12.8	38.0	12.4	8.1	0.0	2.4	15.9
Shaanxi	1939	5.5	6.5	55.3	12.6	8.4	1.1	0.0	10.5
	1940	1.8	3.9	45.2	7.6	3.1	16.3	9.3	12.8

Source: Guilin Office of Farm Credit Bureau, Statistics of cooperatives and housewares in Guangxi, 1939; NBJ, Report on Businesses of Farm Credit Bureau

Note: [a] Including for reclamation and land purchasing and redemption
[b] Including for weddings, funerals, clothing, education, medicine, houses, etc

(16.3%). The Shaanxi efforts at developing sideline industries might have been related to developing food and other related business in the communist-controlled base area.

The Farm Credit Bureau envisioned a system of cooperative banks across China with the Agricultural Loans Department providing seed capital as well as facilitating fund transfers between cooperative banks. Prior to 1936, the few cooperative banks had no direct linkages and although some cooperatives in close proximity might transfer funds this was very limited. With the Farm Credit Bureau, a remote cooperative in need of capital could request an inter-bank loan through the Farm Credit Bureau which would then tap the capital of cooperatives with excess funds. Thus the mobilization of capital would smooth liquidity and reduce credit constraints and credit rationing throughout the rural credit system. There would also be substantial effort towards cooperative extension, including instruction on how to be self-reliant in the organization and management of cooperatives and how to accept, record, and lend deposits.

13.4 Agricultural Loans of Commercial Banks and the Chinese Rural Credit Syndicate

Under *Nong Ben Ju* it was hoped that the Farm Credit Bureau could assist in the organization of the commercial banks to address the agricultural credit problem. This would actually be more of a complementary initiative since the commercial banks had already shown considerable interest in rural reconstruction and were willing to cooperate with the government's financial policy.[2] In this direction their activities may be conveniently grouped under two main headings: rural credit and loans for constructive enterprises. Quite independently of the blueprint, it was not uncommon for some commercial banks to channel bank credit into rural areas through credit cooperatives in the 1930s. In 1934, for example, the Bank of Communications, Jincheng Banking Corporation, Shanghai Commercial and Savings Bank, National Commercial Bank, and Farmers Bank of China organized a Chinese Rural Credit Syndicate for joint investment in the promotion of agricultural production in North China, particularly wheat and cotton. In the spring of 1935, another five institutions joined the Syndicate—China and South Sea Bank, Continental Bank, China State Bank, Xinhua Trust and Savings Bank, and Joint Savings Society (*Jincheng-Yanye*-Continental-China and South Sea). In addition to cotton and wheat in North China, rice in Anhui Province was added to the major items of investment. With the promotion of the Rural Credit Syndicate, agricultural loans increased year by year before the Sino-Japanese war.(Fig. 13.1).

---

[2] Before a more detailed survey of agricultural loans of commercial banks, it is perhaps necessary to define the exact meaning of commercial banks mentioned here. With the only exception of the Central Bank, all banks in Republican China may be included in the general term 'commercial', since their chief banking activities consisted of commercial credit, despite the fact that they took on misleading names such as 'industrial', 'agricultural', 'provincial', and even 'state'. Under such a broad definition two of the government 'Big Four' banks, the Bank of China and the Bank of Communications may also be included. It was also true that after the commencement of hostilities with Japan many Tianjin and Northeast banks had moved to, or been developed in, the interior provinces. Consequently, banking offices began to scatter throughout China rather than concentrating in major trading centers such as Shanghai and Tianjin. By April of 1936, however, the coming war with Japan was an unknown and so the meeting included the 12 big banks representing the Shanghai commercial banks. The Shanghai banks included the Bank of China, Bank of Communication, Jincheng Banking Corporation, Shanghai Commercial and Savings Bank, China and South Sea Bank, Continental Bank, Yianye Bank, National Commercial Bank, Zhejiang Industrial Bank, Ningbo Commercial and Savings Bank, Manufacturers Bank of China, and the China State Bank.

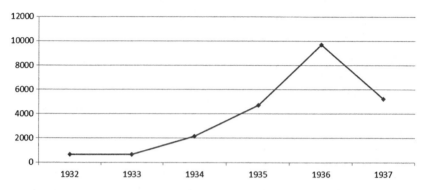

Fig. 13.1 Total amounts of agricultural loans in the 1930s ($10,000). (Source: Yueping Bai, Yong Yu (2002), Study on the amounts of rural financial relief in 1930s, Journal of Inner Mongolia University, V.1)

The original goal of $1 million of the Syndicate's investment was increased to $3 million in 1935 and to $5 million in 1936. In 1936, commercial banks in Shanghai extended more than 51 million to subsidize the production of silk, cotton, and Tong oil, to support the improvement of fisheries, and support the establishment of agricultural warehouses. All these loans, however, were short-term loans, ranging from 2 to 12 months. During the first seven months of 1937, about $57 million was invested by the commercial banks in Shanghai in important agricultural production, chiefly rice, cotton, silk, Tong oil, tea, and tobacco.[3] Of the Big 12 Commercial Banks, the Bank of China and Bank of Communications—semi-governmental in nature—were cooperating in a significant way with the financial policies of the government. The Farmers Bank of China was an energetic leader on reconstructing the rural economy and led all other banks, state-run banks as well as commercial ones. The loans made by the Big Four banks as well as the Farm Credit Bureau are provided in Table 13.4. In total, loans to agriculture from these banks alone increased from $34.715 million to $465.306 million with the largest shares coming from the Farmers Bank of China (56.5–47.3%) and the Bank of China (34.8–39.1%). The Farm Credit Bureau under *Nong Ben Ju* increased its share from 1.9% in 1937, peaking at 21.8% in 1938, and falling to 17.95% in 1940. By 1941 the Farm Credit Bureau was disbanded under wartime credit reforms.

[3] Lin Yijin(1941), Chinese Commercial Banks in War Time, *The central Bank of China Bulletin*,V.7 No.3, p. 359.

Table 13.4 Amount of agricultural loans from four government banks and the Farm Credit Bureau (Unit: $1000)

Bank		Year				
		1937	1938	1939	1940	1941
Farmers Bank of China	$	19,604	47,922	64,473	94,741	220,380
	%	56.5	71.7	56.6	45.8	47.3
Bank of China	$	12,095	12,665	17,365	51,350	181,830
	%	34.8	18.9	15.2	24.3	39.1
Bank of Communication	$	2344	1619	7341	14,483	36,240
	%	6.8	2.4	6.4	6.8	7.8
Farm Credit Bureau	$	672	4660	24,737	37,858	–
	%	1.9	7.6	21.8	17.9	–
Central Trust of China	$	–	–	–	10,995	26,856
	%	–	–	–	5.2	5.8
Total	$	34,715	66,366	113,966	211,408	465,306
	%	100	100	100	100	100

Source: Zhehe Hou (1942), Agricultural finance, Knowledge of Finance,V.1 N.6

13.5 Developing a Cooperative Financial System Under *Nong Ben Ju*

The development of a cooperative financial system in Modern China, started with the first provincial cooperative bank established in 1936. There were two distinct phases: before 1936, cooperative finance was dependent on the banking system when rural credit cooperatives were basically farmers' banks and other commercial banks. At the later phase, the Provincial Cooperative Treasuries (*Hezuo Jinku*), and a Central Cooperative Treasury had been established one by one. In this way, the national government began to purposefully build an independent cooperative financial system. Figure 13.2 illustrates the pattern of cooperative treasuries organized under *Nong Ben Ju* between April 1937 and November 1940. By 1947, the cooperative banking system under *Nong Ben Ju* had about 49 branches and was the fastest-growing segment of the rural financial system.

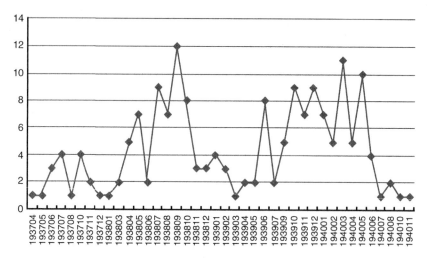

Fig. 13.2 Cooperative treasuries established by *Nong Ben Ju*, 1937–41. (Source: Hong Fu (2009) *Op Cit*)

13.6 *Nong Ben Ju*, the Farm Credit Bureau, and the War Years

By the middle of 1939 the full force of Japanese hostilities was being felt by the nationalist government in Chongqing. The nationalist government feared greatly that the financial system would collapse, especially those banks in the war zone or in its proximity. On March 6, 1939, Dr. H.H. Kung, President of the Executive Yuan and Minister of Finance urged local bankers to maintain as best as possible under difficult conditions normal banking procedures, leaving only when Chinese troops were ordered to withdraw.[4] This became policy for the four national banks including the Farmers Bank of China.

To the extent that farm credit was implemented after the Japanese conflict started, it nonetheless played an important role in wartime production policy. On May 15, 1939 Chiang Kai-shek outlined the role of government in wartime production.[5] In addition to stabilizing and main-

---

[4] Kung, H.H. (1939). War-Time Responsibilities of Local Financial Institutions. *Central Bank of China Bulletin*. 5(1):1–2.

[5] Chiang, Kai-shek, (1939). China's War-Time Production Policy. Central Bank of China Bulletin. 5(3):197–202.

taining a coherent banking system, China's challenge was balancing military resistance at the front while maintaining and promoting production in the rear. On this latter point was the recognition that China was materially weak and underdeveloped. On that day the General launched what he referred to as the 'National Spiritual Mobilization' in an effort to mobilize the material resources in unoccupied areas towards economic means with the purpose of improving the living conditions of the masses by keeping citizens fed and warm, and to heighten the power of national defenses by making every soldier properly equipped.

To achieve the goals of economic reconstruction in war time *Nong Ben Ju* was expanded to include the mobilization effort, including: (a) centralization of industrial capital, (b) an emphasis on national defense, (c) a study of scientific methods, (d) encouragement of personal thrift, and (e) encouragement of capital-labor cooperation. The centralization of industry was, in Chiang's Kai-Shek's view, core to meeting the military and non-military objectives in the sense that in wartime the economic signals that would ordinaryily encourage reallocation of scarce resources to the most profitable means were blurred and uncertain. Thrift, was an appeal to reduce selfish demands so that as many resources could be placed on military operations, and price stabilization. As Chiang stated in his speech:"*Figuratively speaking, one drop of oil represents our blood; one inch of iron resembles our life; and one minute of electric current is comparable to our breath. For one unit saved means one unit earned*".[6]

Chaotic, unpredictable, and largely increasing prices relative to wages were squeezing many citizens and the military. Prices were increasing for a number of reasons including the exodus of production and refugees from the coastal areas, the closing of ports or loss of ports to Japanese forces, the increased costs of transportation and freight charges, insurance, rents and wages, a devalued currency, as well as hoarding and profiteering. The procedure that various government agencies would use to implement controls was based on a crude balance between supply and demand or the production and consumption of the final good. To impose controls the Ministry of Economic Affairs adopted a strategy that would use prices and costs prevailing in the one to three years prior to the war to establish prices, or if those prices were not available then a value would be established by examining the total working capital plus a reasonable profit to establish the standard. Again, if volatility was a result of an inability to

---

[6] Kai-Shek, Chiang (1939). *Op Cit.* (page 201).

move commodities from production regions to consumer regions resulting in low wholesale prices at one end and high retail prices at another, the Ministry of Economic Affairs would (or could) take actions to purchase in the supply region at fair value and sell in the demand region at fair value to stabilize price expectations and reduce variability. An example of when this procedure was employed was in the early days of the war when the Japanese began bombing Nanjing.[7] Shop owners anxious to reduce inventory would self-liquidate by selling what was on hand without replenishing their stock. As local supply increased by fire-sales, prices would fall in the short-term—measured no doubt by days of inventory turnover—after which the lack of local supply would cause sharp increases in prices. The government then stepped into purchase 'daily necessities' from wholesale markets and deliver them to important retail markets in Nanjing. Thus the government, playing the role of interloper, dampened both the fall in wholesale prices in production regions and the rise in the price of necessities in retail regions. This would have been facilitated by the warehousing facilities brought into place by the Farm Credit Bureau.

The mobilization of resources towards increased production would thus involve open market operations by the government in purchasing agricultural goods and foodstuffs at fair or above market prices to be stored, distributed to the military, or sold to consumers in distant markets. On matters related to price regulation and stabilization the Farm Credit Bureau through the Ministry of Economic Affairs was to play a pivotal role. Commodity prices were swinging wildly as domestic supply from occupied regions were curtailed and imports and exports halted at Japanese occupied ports. For example, by November 1939 foodstuffs had increased by 249%, rent by 282%, clothing by 215%, fuel and light by 305%, relative to pre-war prices in 1936. The purchasing power of the silver dollar on all goods had fallen to 39.29% of its pre-war purchasing power.[8] In July of 1936, before the fall of Shanghai, imports were at $124.140 million, dropping to $55.5 million in August as hostilities commenced. It was not until March of 1939 that Southeast ports could again receive imports. Likewise, in July 1937 exports were $88.78 million dropping to $45.22

---

[7] Shaw, Kinn-Wei (1939). Government Policy on Price Regulations in War Time" Central Bank of China Bulletin. 5(4):318–322.

[8] Chinese Statistical Association (1939). Shanghai Workers' Cost of Living Index (1936=100). Central Bank of China Bulletin. 5(4):21 (appendix).

million as hostilities began in August 1937. It would not be until August 1939 that exports would return to pre-war values.[9]

13.6.1 Impact of War on the Cotton Spinning and Weaving Industry

To understand the disruption of the war and the challenges that China faced consider the cotton spinning and weaving industry.[10] Japan by 1937 had already taken a foothold in China's cotton-weaving industry through its annexation of mills in Manchuria and Tianjin, and had just started to expand production in China's South at Shanghai. Chinese manufacturers had about 2.5 million spindles and 24,000 looms. During the battle for Shanghai, 22 mills outside of the International and French Settlements were virtually destroyed, and even those within the settlements were damaged but ultimately taken over by the Japanese. Even those mills that could be reopened by the Japanese found raw materials, finished products, and machinery in short supply. Nonetheless, in Shanghai alone Chinese millers lost about 775,000 spindles or about 70% of their cotton-weaving capacity. As the war moved beyond Shanghai, cities such as Hangzhou, Wuhu, Suzhou, Taicang, Changshu, and Jiangyin had mills damaged by warfare to various degrees, but ultimately they were taken over by the Japanese. Likewise, in the North as far west as Shaanxi all mills not destroyed in battle fell into Japanese hands. In only a few localities were manufacturing facilities able to be moved to the rear before hostilities broke out. All told, through destruction, annexation, and sales to foreign entities and so on, estimates had Chinese manufacturing losses of 1,777,000 spindles and 17,800 looms or about 70% of pre-war capacity. Many more spindles and looms from smaller mills not included in the above were also lost. By 1939 it was estimated that only 200,000 spindles and less than 1000 looms were operating in the rear. Some of these were the result of moving entire factories from centers in Shandong and Wuhan and by 1939 increased capacity in free areas of Shaanxi, Hunan, Henan, and Yunnan led to a planned increase of spindles to 500,000 and looms to 5000.

---

[9] Chinese Statistical Association (1939). Value of Merchandise Imported and Exported. Central Bank of China Bulletin. 5(4):11 (appendix).

[10] CBCB (1939). China's Cotton Spinning and Weaving Industry in War Time. Central Bank of China Bulletin. 5(4):369–373.

Under these conditions, it is not surprising that clothing and apparel increased in price by so much. But even if cotton from the United States could be imported in adequate volume China did not have the wherewithal to procure it. Since the opening of hostilities certain Chinese bonds such as the 4½% 1898 or 1908 with 100 pound sterling face value were trading about par in July of 1936, but falling precipitously to between 50% and 57% of par by the end of 1939. Thus, only with extraordinary yields could China float bonds to procure imports on international markets. On top of this, the Chinese dollar was so devalued that exchange inflation also impacted prices significantly. In July of 1937 China had fixed her exchange rate with the US dollar at 0.2925 (1 Chinese dollar could purchase US$0.2925). By April of 1938 the Chinese dollar was forced to float against world currencies and as the Japanese advancements seemed not to be abating the exchange rate had fallen to 0.0825. Thus an article imported from the United States in July of 1936 for US$1 would cost the importer C$3.45 in 1939. But this also explained why Chiang Kai-shek also focused on increasing exports.

It is little wonder then that government would extend *Nong Ben Ju* in an attempt to coordinate certain aspects of the economy. The difficulties of making partial adjustments to move an equilibrium in one strategic part of the economy, while minimizing trickle-down and spillover effects to the general equilibrium was well recognized, but the government took the position that stability and procurement was more important.

By the Manifesto of the National Production Conference held at Chongqing on May 13, 1939 the necessities of war meant that the nationalist government was forced to face the harsh realities of its inferiority in industrial and agricultural production. Action was necessary under the Principle of the Peoples' Livelihood to adequately support the normal needs of compatriots while developing China's capital wealth, assisting private enterprise, and promoting the cooperative movement. The aim was to place whatever industrial and natural resources China had available to it, to ensure that the needs of soldiers and national defense were met, as well as the needs of civilians. It was decided that the government take initiatives, and indeed control, over certain aspects of the economy in order to meet its military and civilian objectives, and the proposed policy included the regulation of the quality, quantity, and variety of national products and the coordination of various production enterprises into an organic whole. Coordination in this context involved increasing agricultural production in the interior since coastal agriculture, largely under Japanese occupation, could not easily be transported to unoccupied areas. However, it was also felt that any policies, programs, and incentives for agricultural production should be coordinated with industrial and military demands. The push towards increased agricultural productivity was not only geared to farmlands in the unoccupied zones but also to the reclamation and cultivation of virgin soils in the underpopulated frontier regions using refugees. In addition, with the main financial sectors under Japanese occupation as well as a general collapse in bond values, agricultural production was also seen as a gateway to exports and much needed foreign exchange. The principal mechanism was to be price controls under the assumption that greatest incentive to increase production was to raise prices.

To accomplish these objectives the government employed the Farm Credit Bureau of the Ministry of Economic Affairs as the coordinating organization. Working with other governmental organizations such as the Foreign Trade Commission of the Ministry of Finance, the Farm Credit Bureau made purchases of rice, wheat, silk, tea, wool, Tung oil, pig's bristles, hide and skin, etc. at higher than prevailing market prices. To complement higher production of targeted commodities, the Farm Credit Bureau was tasked also with developing means of transit and transportation to increase the movement of goods to domestic and international markets as best as possible.

But the government also recognized that farmers rarely had access to scientific fertilizers or even scientific cultivation methods, because they did not have the capital required to invest in technologies. Thus the role of improved farm credit was seen as an important component to lifting cash constraints and improving agricultural productivity. More generally, the program of coordination would encourage all agricultural institutions to focus on improving silk-worm seeds and farm-plant seeds; preventing harmful insects and animal diseases; applying good fertilizer to improve production; increase self-sufficiency in farm implements; encourage the export of farm products; promote collective farming and organize farm cooperatives; protect farmers' properties in occupied areas; and strengthen the administrative machinery of agricultural production.

The Organic Law of the Farm Credit Bureau on June 18, 1938 provided the basic design for moving forwards. Its overall objectives were to rehabilitate agricultural production, circulate agricultural capital, and promote rural development throughout China. While the Farm Credit Bureau was to reside in the national capital at Chongqing, it could also petition for regional and even county offices as needed. The Farm Credit Bureau would divide China into five distinct regions with common agricultural characteristics and transportation linkages. Each region would be treated as its own agricultural economy with the different needs met by targeted policies. The regional policy frameworks would naturally be coordinated to meet the system as a whole.[11]

[11] Chiang-kai Shek drew his expertise from the learned class, many of whom were educated in the United States. There were three general managers of *Nong Ben Ju* while it existed from 1936 through 1942, Chen Zhenxian, He Lien (Franklin Ho), and Mu Ouchu. Chen Zhenxian (1877–1938) got his PhD in agronomy from the University of California in 1907 and gained extensive experience in improving farm implements and water conservatries, in breeding nurseries, and managing farmers' unions while serving as the Minister of the Ministry of Agriculture & Forestry, Beiyang government.

He Lian (1895–1975) obtained a PhD in economics from Yale University and was a professor of public finance and statistics at Nankai University. He had worked closely for three years with Irving Fisher, concentrating on index numbers. At Nankai, He was quick to establish a program for compiling and publishing index numbers on major economic magnitudes. He founded Nankai Institute of Economics (NIE) in 1931 which promised to teach economics in a manner relevant to Chinese conditions and to conduct research on China's economy in a way that would enrich teaching and provide textbook materials. NIE became one of China's leading centers of economics research during the Republican period and pioneered Nankai's systematic studies of economics of North China industries. Under the leadership of Ho, Nankai extended its graduate instruction and research to the problems of rural reconstruction and to establish close cooperation with the Mass Education Movement, which charted a new direction in the teaching of economics in China. In 1936, He presented fairly comprehensive visions of China's development problems and appropriate policies which affirmed the general merits of Sun Yat-sen's approach to development and emphasis on 'equalization of land ownership' and 'all land to the tillers'. While the KMT under the leadership of Chiang Kai-shek pledged itself to carry out the ideas of Sun Yat-sen, He, being reputedly Chiang Kai-shek's most trusted economic advisor, became head of the Political Department of the national government's Executive Yuan in Nanjing and became the general manager of *Nong Ben Ju* in August, 1937 and remained in high-level government service during most of the war. Mu Ouchu became the third general manager in February, 1941.

Ouchu Mu was a famous national industrialist and a forerunner of the scientific management of enterprises in modern China who actively introduced the advanced thought of enterprise management from the West. He established a set of effective systems of enterprise management and formed a distinctive theory of enterprise management. He sincerely believed in the principle of 'saving the nation by industry and commerce' all through his life and established many influential enterprises at that time, probing thoroughly and practically the methods that could develop industry and the Chinese economy vigorously and promote the sound development of enterprises. The main business of *Nong Ben Ju* was the produc-

13.7 Reform and Dissolution of the Farm Credit Bureau

The Farm Credit Bureau was neither a purely public authority nor a private joint-bank, but an amalgam of public and private interests. The Farm Credit Bureau, originally headquartered in Nanjing, had set up its branches in various provinces and cities, to improve local rural economy and financial institutions. It also had a five-year development plan for a number of regions based upon their respective industries and transport situations all over the country. It was authorized to issue agriculture bonds to finance the circulation of agricultural products. The Farm Credit Bureau was intended as the highest executive organization, with the hope it would act similarly to the US Federal Bureau of Agricultural Finance, to enforce the national agricultural policy, to manage rural finance, to promote cooperation projects, and to establish warehouses etc. The national government, the business community, and academia had high expectations, and these expectations might have been met had the war not intervened. But, even as the war expanded Westward through Nanjing to Wuhan, and the nationalist government retreated to Chongqing, the efforts continued.

Even without the war, however, the efforts at *Nong Ben Ju* faced internal conflicts and required sometimes contradictory policies. For example, acting both as a national rural finance management authority with the mission of achieving public policies, and also as a financial institution with commercial interests, it was difficult to marry the two conflicting objectives at the same time while balancing the interests of different parties. As a program, the Farm Credit Bureau faced criticism from government banks and commercial banks.

The proposal submitted by the Central Bank of China, Bank of China, and Bank of Communications states: "*The missions of Farm Credit Bureau were financing agricultural and adjusting agricultural products, of which one is the duty of financial institutions and the other is the duty of administrative bodies'. It's better for Farm Credit Bureau to divide these two businesses, keeping the administrative one, and giving up financial one to commercial banks...*".[12] Zhejiang Industry Bank pointed out the shortcoming of the

---

tion, purchase, and sale of cotton and cottonwool. Youci Zhu(1988), Helian's Memoirs, Beijing: Chinese Cultural and Historical Press,

[12] San Qiu (1936), The nature and future of Farm Credit Bureau, Collection of papers on Chinese economy, Shanghai Life Press.

Farm Credit Bureau's loans regulations more explicitly: "*the interests of farm loans, 0.8 % weekly interest rate, is too low to pay the costs; and terms of the loans are untold, maybe it's ok if commercial banks can recall those money from Farm Credit Bureau when needed*".[13] Therefore, the Farm Credit Bureau had to adjust its businesses several times, peeling off its credit business, and becoming a non-rural financial institution after 1941 solely in charge of managing the production, purchase, and sale of cotton and cotton-wool; and it was finally dissolved in 1942.

[13] San Qiu(1936), *Op Cit.*

CHAPTER 14

Successes and Failures of Agricultural Cooperatives and Credit Societies

14.1 Introduction

In the previous chapters, we examined the evolution of the cooperative movement in China starting with the initiatives of the China International Famine Relief Commission and the Kuomintang (KMT) reconstruction movement.[1] What we have not discussed in detail is the outcome of these efforts for China's agricultural economy and agricultural finance facilities. We will examine the progress of the cooperative movement, and make a determination as to its overall effectiveness. This includes the ideals of progress, and the complexities brought about by the Japanese war that took place just as the cooperative movement was at its maximum potential. These complexities not only impacted the distribution of cooperatives in occupied and unoccupied territories, but also the hyper-inflation that goes along with war. This inflation masks the true effects and, as reported in the statistics of the day, presents a mirage that disguises what was really occurring. We will examine these issues systematically. In this chapter we will outline the evolution and outcomes of credit cooperation. To this point we have only discussed the cooperative movement, but in fact the Chinese government made some extraordinarily progressive policies aimed

[1] Our focus has been on agricultural cooperatives. There were of course others. Also responding to the war effort were the Chinese Industrial Cooperatives, initiated in 1936 with the formation of a cooperative of blacksmiths. This story is told in Wales, N (1941). "China Builds for Democracy: A Story of Cooperative Industry" Modern Age Books, NY, NY.

© The Author(s) 2018
H. Fu, C. G. Turvey, *The Evolution of Agricultural Credit during China's Republican Era, 1912–1949*,
https://doi.org/10.1007/978-3-319-76801-4_14

at consolidating agricultural finance including developments in the Farmers Bank of China and the policy drivers behind *Nong Ben Ju* which, as discussed in Chaps. 12 and 13, complemented the cooperative movement. Here we provide a general overview of credit cooperative developments and then drill down into three separate time frames, 1924–36, 1937–45, and 1945–49. We need to segregate the three time periods because the conditions faced on the ground differed markedly between the time periods before and after the beginning of the Sino-Japanese war in September 1937, and the civil war period between 1945 and 1949.

14.2 Overview of Credit Cooperatives

Figure 14.1 illustrates the numerical growth in agricultural cooperatives and credit cooperatives from 1927 to 1949. The pattern of cooperative development over this period was calculated and deliberate. *Nong Ben Ju* was explicitly designed to increase capital for agriculture. This need progressed even further as the war years dragged on to ensure that farmers could survive in order to produce food for the military, households that had been displaced, and when possible for export to meet much needed foreign exchange. As previously discussed, we can break this down into three separate phases. The first phase between 1927 (and earlier) and 1932 was largely due to the push for cooperation by the China International

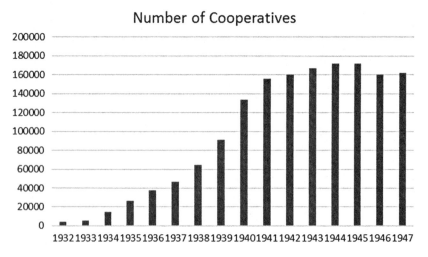

Fig. 14.1 Growth in number of cooperatives

Famine Relief Commission. Although Chiang Kai-shek had called for increased cooperation prior to 1932, it was not until then that he explicitly established clear objectives under military guidance as part of the program of reconstruction. The third phase was *Nong Ben Ju* which was established to consolidate agricultural credit institutions, including cooperatives under the influence of the army and those of the China International Famine Relief Commission. This occurred in 1936 with some sweeping reforms not only in terms of agricultural credit and cooperation, but infrastructure as well.

The growth in the three periods as captured in Fig. 14.2 shows a slow but respectable increase in cooperatives through 1932. During the construction period the number of cooperatives increased almost ten-fold from 3978 to 37,318. The reconstruction initiatives called for an expansion of not only credit cooperatives but also supply, marketing, and other cooperatives so the actual percentage of credit cooperatives declined from about 87% to about 55%. This still represented an absolute increase in the number of credit cooperatives from 3460 to 20,525.

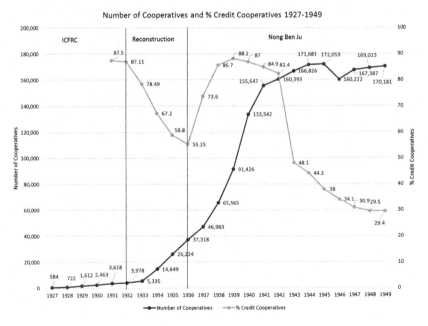

Fig. 14.2 Growth of agricultural and credit cooperatives

The growth in cooperatives was not evenly distributed around China. This was due to two forces. The first was the areas of influence in the Southern provinces below the Yangtze River prior to 1932 as developed by the China International Famine Relief Commission and the University of Nanjing. In the reconstruction era with the Kuomintang (KMT) having more influence on cooperative development, the focus was on those provinces that had been freed of communist influence. As previously discussed in Chap. 8 the KMT saw how mutual aid societies of one form or another were beneficial to the communist insurgencies and in the establishments of soviets. The KMT decided to build upon, rather than dismantle, these structures although this was more likely a dismantling of the communist societies with a rapid reconstitution of the same but under KMT authority, control, and guidance.

The final push of the 1930s was *Nong Ben Ju* (see Chap. 13) in 1936 which, as can be seen in Fig. 14.1, saw a rapid development in the number of cooperatives, through to about 1944. This was to be a national program of cooperative development but the Japanese invasion and subsequent occupation in the North of China and major ports in the South brought an abrupt stop to cooperative development in those areas. While Fig. 14.2 illustrates the growth in accumulated development of cooperatives throughout this period, Fig. 14.3 and Table 14.2 (later) provide the necessary granularity to observe more precisely how the war affected or arrested cooperative development.

But what we find so remarkable is how the cooperative movement continued to grow in unoccupied areas and even in provinces that were partially occupied. Beyond 1938, the Japanese consolidated power and occupation, mostly in urban areas, so that it would not be unusual for the KMT to organize and operate in a reasonably functional way within miles of the Japanese front lines. Even in these areas, the KMT sought expansion of cooperatives and maintained and/or developed further the financial institutions necessary to ensure that capital, extension, and governance would be provided. Because grain and other foodstuffs was militarily a necessity to feed a standing army of over 2 million men and women, it was also needed in the unoccupied Western provinces to feed and distribute to the millions of refugees from the North and East who had made their way to Sichuan and elsewhere. As important as increased agricultural production was, the need to ensure that farmers had access to credit in order to smooth consumption was great. With costs rising relative to commodity prices farmers found themselves in a perilous position with no cash to purchase food, clothes, or other staples. Credit was desperately needed to free up enough cash so that farmers could survive and be productive at

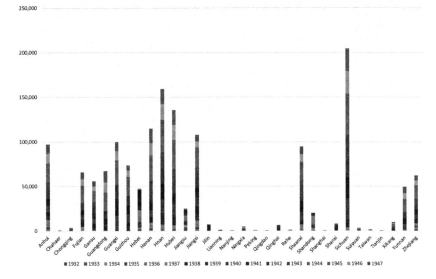

Fig. 14.3 Distribution and growth of cooperatives in the reconstruction era, 1932–46

even the most basic levels. Should farmers leave the land in search of food, this would provide the Japanese with an opportunity to cultivate for their own use, an encroachment on fertile lands that the KMT sought to prevent (Table 14.1).

14.3　Pre-War Impacts of Credit Cooperatives

The constructive use of credit cooperatives was more in line with the consumption-smoothing paradigm of modern-day development economics so that at times of crisis farmers did not have to sell fixed, mobile, or productive assets or forgo food, health, or education.[2] The cooperative

---

[2] Morduch, J. (1995). Income smoothing and consumption smoothing. *The journal of economic perspectives*, 9(3), 103–114.

Rosenzweig, M. R., and K.I. Wolpin, (1993). Credit market constraints, consumption smoothing, and the accumulation of durable production assets in low-income countries: Investments in bullocks in India. Journal of political economy, 101(2), 223–244.

Kumar, C. S., C.G. Turvey, and J.D. Kropp, J. D. (2013). The impact of credit constraints on farm households: Survey results from India and China. *Applied Economic Perspectives and Policy*, 35(3), 508–527.

Table 14.1 Geographical distribution of cooperatives

Year	1932	1933	1934	1935	1936	1937	1938	1939	1940	1941	1942	1943	1944	1945	1946	1947
Total	3978	5335	14,649	26,224	37,318	46,983	64,565	91,426	133,542	155,647	160,393	166,826	171,681	172,053	160,222	161,953
Credit cooperative %	87.11%	78.49%	67.20%	58.80%	55.25%	73.60%	85.70%	88.20%	87%	84.90%	82.40%	48.10%	44.20%	38%	34.10%	30%
Anhui	22	387	1463	2284	4125	4125	4098	4958	6742	7792	8900	9964	10,210	10,574	10,680	10,641
Chahaer	3	–	–	–	60	60	59	–	–	–	–	–	–	–	–	–
Chongqing	–	–	–	–	–	–	–	–	–	–	–	–	–	–	–	47
Fujian	4	–	14	–	1946	2615	3353	4681	5171	5782	7730	551	686	661	496	–
Gansu	3	–	–	33	244	437	2562	4407	5561	6659	6752	6197	9268	10,119	7522	7522
Guangdong	6	12	194	307	6	20	672	4025	1913	6639	8694	–	6105	5637	5637	5637
Guangxi	2	8	8	14	3	129	507	–	16,334	19,066	15,601	–	9994	10,722	11,291	12,427
Guizhou	4	–	–	–	–	–	4338	4532	9593	10,427	10,416	–	13,625	13,692	10,565	10,215
Hebei	999	956	1935	6240	6663	6663	6045	16,693	–	–	–	–	11,101	10,187	7174	5755
Henan	26	10	997	1761	3221	3484	4009	2597	7386	9747	9827	12,872	14,233	14,287	520	699
Hunan	17	14	558	963	1985	3674	6111	7077	14,947	17,755	17,530	17,809	18,139	18,139	14,355	15,791
Hubei	3	5	566	1228	1932	2717	5612	6607	11,062	11,926	13,440	14,340	16,071	16,522	17,513	16,849
Jiangsu	1798	1911	2937	4077	3305	3305	2415	4024	–	–	–	–	–	–	16,682	16,858
Jiangxi	15	489	1078	2038	3209	4614	7451	8390	10,387	10,853	11,033	11,361	11,382	11,041	333	805
Jilin	–	–	–	–	–	–	–	6694	–	–	–	–	–	–	7233	7221
Liaoning	–	–	–	–	–	–	–	838	–	–	–	–	–	–	–	10
Nanjing	8	5	–	50	15	–	–	–	–	–	–	–	–	–	–	59
Ningxia	–	–	20	–	78	–	–	–	189	359	395	653	728	788	9	31
Peking	6	–	85	7	–	–	–	1	–	–	–	–	–	–	804	780
Qingdao	–	–	–	–	–	1	–	–	–	–	–	–	–	–	249	332
Qinghai	1	–	–	312	–	–	–	5378	–	–	–	–	–	218	120	160
Rehe	–	–	–	–	290	290	5	–	–	–	–	–	–	–	281	288
	–	–	–	–	–	–	–	–	–	–	–	–	–	–	–	30

Year	1932	1933	1934	1935	1936	1937	1938	1939	1940	1941	1942	1943	1944	1945	1946	1947
Shaanxi	6	5	320	671	2066	4009	4659	44	9780	11,542	11,260	12,306	11,206	9345	8665	8529
Shandong	211	545	2472	3637	4985	4965	2597	360	—	—	—	—	—	—	103	304
Shanghai	2	37	16	123	19	—	—	—	—	—	—	—	—	—	40	94
Shanxi	19	7	190	453	69	69	44	6045	—	—	—	—	—	320	566	414
Sichuan	8	2	3	—	1322	2374	8236	166	24,146	23,599	23,586	24,349	22,663	23,400	24,981	25,473
Suiyuan	4	3	—	54	—	—	—	—	—	299	316	286	333	367	763	797
Taiwan	—	—	—	—	225	750	—	—	—	—	—	—	—	—	—	12
Tianjin	2	—	—	—	17	—	—	—	—	—	—	—	—	—	210	236
Xikang	—	—	—	—	—	—	—	360	629	1162	1297	1291	1277	1231	1272	1337
Yunnan	27	—	—	—	35	1487	234	725	4806	6450	7266	—	7424	7162	6654	7063
Zhejiang	782	1139	1793	1972	1518	1195	1558	3299	4766	5709	5970	6468	7236	7641	5504	5537

Table 14.2 Recognition of cooperative credit societies 1923–29

	1923	1924	1925	1926	1927	1928	1929
				Societies			
Recognized		9	44	97	129	169	246
Not recognized	8	2	56	220	432	435	572
Total	8	11	100	317	561	604	818
				Members			
Recognized		403	1270	3288	4354	5624	7862
Not recognized	256	47	1062	4744	8836	9677	14,072
Total	256	450	2332	8032	13,190	15,301	21,934
				Loans granted to societies			
China International Famine Relief Commission loans ($)		3290	10,450	32,440	60,795	89,374	122,414

Source: Mallory (1936)

societies banked savings from households that had no other mechanism to save, and lent those saving to farm households that had no mechanism other than usury to meet financial needs. Cooperation by design was intended to eliminate waste and make farmers more transactional and profitable, encouraging savings and the buildup of capital which could then be leveraged to promote further investment. Circulating money does not stagnate the rural economy like hoarding and usury do. Instead, circulating money is productive money in this environment and the China International Famine Relief Commission foresaw the economic benefits. It also saw the economic benefits of promoting cooperation in the selling of produce, purchasing commodities and inputs, shared ownership of implements, and so on.

Development, however, was slow-going and as with any new type of institution there was a steep learning curve, not only for the educated members of the China International Famine Relief Commission with knowledge gained from the United States and the Raiffeisen system in Germany, but with rank and file farmers from whom membership, management, and governance would be drawn. It is worth exploring these cooperatives in detail and fortunately the annual reports from Nanjing University were recorded in John Lossing Buck's recollections of agricultural economics at Nanjing.[3] By 1925 Nanjing University had sup-

---

[3] Buck, J. L. (1973). Development of Agricultural Economics at the University of Nanjing, Nanjing, China 1920–1946. Cornell Int Agric Dev Bull.

ported the formation of two cooperatives, but formed an additional 14 cooperatives in 1925–26, with an additional five slated for 1927. Membership in organized societies numbered 370 and of the 16 cooperatives, six made loans with the others engaged in marketing or production. One of the University of Nanjing sponsored cooperatives was the Cotton Marketing and Credit Cooperative at *Wujiang*. Cotton farmers encouraged to grow premium American cotton introduced by the College of Agriculture were refused a quality premium by the local mill. Buck suggested that the cooperative negotiate a forward price with a mill at *Wuxi* that was willing to pay the premium. The cooperative and *Wuxi* mill cooperated for many years, despite the willingness of the local mill to offer the premium the following year. The credit societies advanced $5530 bringing to a total of $7380 since the first cooperative society was formed. No loans were outstanding. A year later there were 20 cooperatives, with 473 members, $11,120 lent since inception, and again, no defaults. What Paul Hsu and Buck did in 1926/27 was to illustrate how agricultural extension activities could be combined with innovative cooperative societies to address significant problems facing farmers. To address problems of frequent drought in Jiangsu, Hsu sought a diversification remedy that would provide some profit protection to farmers in drought years and looked to sericulture and the raising of silk worms. Silkworms require mulberry and so Hsu, and a local church, organized seven separate societies, comprising 115 members, to work cooperatively to plant 70,000 mulberry trees.

In fact the cooperatives set up with unlimited liability appeared to work well. The rules of cooperation were stringent. Members had to be of good character, clean habits, engaged in a gainful occupation, and willing to assume unlimited liability for failure of other members' defaults. With a slogan of 'all for one, and one for all', farmers had to learn the meaning of democracy, equality of status and privilege, and group responsibility. They had to learn how to organize, elect officers who would manage and take responsibility for the business affairs, protect against the potential of illegal or illegitimate conduct of the controlling committee, and to elect a council of inspection—or board of directors—who would audit and if necessary veto actions, suspend functions, and protect the interests of members. Farmers had to learn to ignore the fungibility of money and ensure that loans were put to the production use originally stated in the loan application. Perhaps even more important in the early development of cooperatives promoted by the China International Famine Relief Commission was that loans made were not charitable, and required convincing suspicious (and superstitious) farmers that the motives behind the China International Famine Relief Commission initiatives were neither politically nor religiously motivated. Only when a group was properly organized was it finally recognized and counted as a cooperative, and only then would the China International Famine Relief Commission extend money at a low interest rate (Table 14.2).[4]

For its part the China International Famine Relief Commission had to refrain from overselling the idea of cooperatives and to not unduly pressurize farmers to join. It was true that cooperation was a 'movement' but the China International Famine Relief Commission did not propagandize it as such and did not seek 'converts'. Instead, the China International Famine Relief Commission moved slowly, or at least at the rate at which farmers could meet, digest, and discuss amongst themselves the promotional literature provided to them.[5] The China International Famine Relief Commission had to continually reinforce the ideas and ideals of cooperation by issuing monthly bulletins and other material provided at regular intervals, as well as annual training courses for officers. Initially (around 1924) the China International Famine Relief Commission used its own staff for training but also went out of its way to recruit trainers from villages and regions it sought to target. By 1931 this evolved into a train-the-trainers model in which local recruits would take over the training activities of the China International Famine Relief Commission . After recognizing a cooperative the China International Famine Relief Commission would continually monitor the society and subject it to a scorecard that was designed to discover defects and identify good and poor societies. From good societies, lessons learned were transmitted to poor societies, and defects were remedied in a timely fashion.

In 1931, Y.S. Djang, who was then the executive secretary of the China International Famine Relief Commission stated that: *"during the last decade, numerous plans have been proposed for rural development. But to my mind, none is more fundamental, more encouraging and more interesting*

---

[4] Mallory, W. H. (1931). Rural Cooperative Credit in China: A Record of Seven Years of Experimentation. *The Quarterly Journal of Economics*, 45(3), 484–498.

Trescott, P. B. (1993). John Bernard Tayler and the Development of Cooperatives in China, 1917–1945. *Annals of Public and Cooperative Economics*, 64(2), 209–226.

Lai, C. C. (1989). The Structure and Characteristics of the Chinese Co-operative System: 1928–49. *International Journal of Social Economics*, 16(2), 59–66.

[5] Djang 1931 ibid, page 164.

than the cooperative movement"[6] This he extended to some favorable and unintended consequences including a certain utility in self-help and cooperation that translated into altruism and benevolence. In 1928 the China International Famine Relief Commission provided some $36,000 at zero interest to a small group of cooperatives to distribute among farmers affected by drought. All but 2% of the funds were returned, and upon audit it was discovered that the money was not only distributed amongst the cooperative members, but by and large these members—upwards of 2,000 of them—gave up their budgeted allocation to ensure that the many non-members, equally affected by the drought, also received some of the funds.[7]

Djang reported on over 1000 cooperatives that had developed between 1924 and 1931, and thus provides an early glimpse at performance.[8] Capital invested in these cooperatives was about $65,000 across 26,000 members or about $2.5/member. But only 275 of these cooperatives had actually been certified or recognized by the China International Famine Relief Commission , and to these the China International Famine Relief Commission had advanced over $200,000 in 437 different loans, which in turn would be reloaned to farmers. Of these farmer loans 33% was used to cultivate crops including seeds, fodder, and labor, while 27% was used as capital outlay for implements and farm animals. A further 22% was used to help farmers pay-off high-interest usury debts and 16% was used to finance small trade, village industries, and enterprises, and for other personal needs. Because too few farmers could actually invest in permanent improvements, only 2% of loans was issued for that purpose.

A separate list was provided by Walter H. Mallory (in 1931) who was with the Council of Foreign Relations in New York. We believe that these are aggregated loans from 1924 to 1930. There are several differences in these numbers from those reported by Djang. First, by adding seed and fertilizer the total loan for crop production is only 10.07%, although it is possible that what is listed as 'food' is actually 'feed' which would add 12.97% to get 23.04%. Some 24.17% of loans went to the purchase of

[6] Djang 1931 ibid. page 168.
[7] Djang 1931 ibid, page 169.
[8] Djang ibid., page 167 states that there are 948 co-operatives in 'this' province and about two dozen in Shantung, but does not indicate to which province 'this' refers, so we have defaulted to 'over 1000'.

implements and animals. Meat as a food item was a luxury during this period so the animal purchases are most likely oxen for field work, although we cannot rule out that some of these loans went to the production of food for animals. The largest single item was in repaying old debts. The China International Famine Relief Commission understood that usury and high interest rates were a drag not only on improving agricultural productivity and efficiency, but also a key driver of poverty. Related to this is the reference to redeeming land (5.04%), which we believe refers to the paying off of a usufruct loan (*tien*) tied to a private mortgage. Land reclamation is most likely due to the recovery of land that had been damaged by militarism or flooding. If so, when combined with irrigation, the total land improvement loans accounted for only 6.52% of loans made (Table 14.3).

Working at Nanjing University with the China International Famine Relief Commission, Paul Hsu found that small and middle-class farmers did not borrow as much, if at all. In 1926–27 Hsu conducted a survey of 486 farmers in three rural districts in Anhui and Jiangsu to determine how these rates compared to alternative sources of credit and to get a sense of what credit was used for. He found that interest rates ranged from 18% to a high of 96.6% with an average of 34.8% or about 3%/month. With interest rates averaging 3%/month and returns so low in agriculture, the smaller farmers would not borrow because they simply could not afford

Table 14.3 Loan purposes, 1924–30

Purpose	Members borrowing	Total amount	Percent of total
Repaying old debts	1247	24,078	23.82
Animals	765	16,164	15.99
Food	729	13,116	12.97
Others	492	9623	9.52
Implements	425	8267	8.18
Seed	291	5143	5.09
Repairing houses	255	6812	6.74
Reclaiming land	229	4828	4.77
Fertilizer	221	5031	4.98
Redeeming land	198	5103	5.04
Marriages and funerals	64	1434	1.42
Irrigation	50	1503	1.48
Total	4966	101,102	100.00

Source: Mallory (1931, page 493)

the exorbitant rates on offer. The high rates were the result of a moneylender monopoly and an insufficient supply of credit. The China International Famine Relief Commission loans to the cooperatives averaged about 7% interest rate. The typical interest rate on a credit cooperative loan in 1926 China was about 18%/year, or about half of the 3%/month or 36%/year charged by money lenders and other informal lenders. Average loans at the Anhui location were $43 while those in Jiangsu ranged from $144 to $292. These loans, ranging in the short run at about 6.5 months and in the long run at 4.1 years, were put to mixed use with about 38% borrowing for productive purposes and 80% for personal consumption. Some 60–75% borrowed for the purpose of buying food and 11–41% for funerals, weddings, and celebrations. Production loans were for labor, fertilizer, and land improvements. Even at these rates, and as of 1931, the China International Famine Relief Commission reported that even with no security required (beyond unlimited group liability) "*of the $200,000 thus far advanced, not a cent is lost*".[9] It was encouraging for a movement that was also viewed as an experiment, that after six or seven years there were no bad debts and that farmers had the wherewithal to organize and establish cooperatives without outside pressure. Most important was the discovery that despite their poverty and economic backwardness the Chinese farmer paid his debts. For example the *Feng Rui* Society at Nanjing had 20 members each advancing $1 to cover amounts not repaid by other members at the time payment was required. In another instance, a credit society got caught up in a mini-war between two opposing societies called the Big Swords and Little Swords. These societies held certain occultist superstitious beliefs regarding magical abilities and impenetrability to bullets. Starting up as crop protection societies many of the factions became bandit groups, fighting over land claims and other matters. As the Big and Little Swords began fighting with each other it was unsafe to travel. Hence farmers did not repay loans for about three years, but when the warring subsided the farmers returned to the credit cooperative and paid their debts in full (Table 14.4).[10]

While this sounded promising, the other reality was that at the individual level none of the cooperatives produced a surplus. They went about their business receiving deposits, granting loans, and circulating credit within the community as intended. But the spread between interest earned

[9] Djang 1931 ibid, page 168.
[10] As told told by Buck to Colman (TRSC-2454-Colman) Cornell University Archives.

Table 14.4 Status of loans, December 1929

Status	Number of loans	Amount ($)
Repaid	160	83,245
Not due	59	24,901
Extended	23	9894
Due	13	4375
Total	255	122,414

Source: Mallory (1931, page 492)

and the costs of deposits (and China International Famine Relief Commission advances) was insufficient to cover expenses. By 1931 a union of credit cooperatives had been developed which could move funds between surplus and deficit societies, but the formal financial sector—and the discipline that goes with cooperative bank/credit society linkages—was not, as of 1931, involved in the cooperative movement so any deficits had to be made up with capital from alternative sources, including members. As indicated in Table 14.5, 13 of 255 recognized credit cooperatives asked for an extension of loan repayments. Keeping in mind that according to Djang, not a penny was lost, we can assume that extension is not synonymous with loan forgiveness. Table 14.5 ranks the reasons for extension requests and quite shockingly 45% were due to military disturbances and 6.73% to bandits. Loan extension due to natural calamities leading to famine conditions was the cause in only 7.46% of the cases. As previously discussed, the period between 1923 and 1927 was infected with warlords. The Northern Excursion in 1927 and 1928 moved Northwards from Canton to Henan to unify the country. The 1928–30 drought in the Northern provinces from Shaanxi to Shandong devastated agriculture, while the Japanese occupation of Manchuria in 1931, along with expanding Japanese influence in Shandong and the Shanghai incident were other factors.

In 1926–27 Hsu was able to assist in setting up four more cooperative societies, despite the increased militarism which affected transportation and communications and general banditry. This timeframe also included the Nanjing incident which saw the Vice-President of Nanjing University killed by government troops (still comprised of communist and nationalists) as they pushed Northwards from Canton as part of the Northern

Table 14.5 Reasons for loan extension

Causes	%
Military disturbances	45.06
Excessive remittance rates and interruption of remittance facilities	26.7
Non-productive employment of loans	9.69
Famine due to natural causes	7.46
Bandits	6.73
Combinations famine/military/bandits	4.33
Absence of society officers	0
Bad faith of members or irregular practices of officers	0
Other/unknown causes	0.03
Total %	100

Expedition. The direct threat to foreigners forced the exile of Buck (and his author wife Pearl Buck), John H. Reisner (then dean of the College of Agriculture), and other Western faculty to Shanghai, Japan, and elsewhere.[11] By 1942 Buck and his colleagues, led perhaps more by Paul Hsu, were responsible for organizing 253 cooperatives, most of which were credit cooperatives. In addition they had organized 22 farmers' associations for extension purposes comprised of 10,000 members. These were

---

[11] The Nanjing Incident refers to events starting March 24, 1927 when Nationalist forces entered Nanjing to rout the Northern warlord forces held up in the region. As the Nationalist troops entered Nanjing they began looting foreigners' homes, including the home of John Lossing Buck and his author wife Pearl S. Buck. Dr. John Williams, the vice-president of Nanjing University was murdered, as were Japanese and British consuls. Foreigners were herded to the University and it was not until the threat of bombardment from British and American gunships on the Yangtze River did the looting stop. The Bucks took exile in Japan, with John Lossing Buck returning to Nanjing eight months later.

"Buck Writes Parents of Riots at Nanjing" Poughkeepsie Eagle and News, Friday May 13, 1927 Page 1 and Page 11.

Buck, P. S. (2013). My several worlds: a personal record. Open Road Media.

Conn, P. J. (1998). Pearl S. Buck: A cultural biography. Cambridge University Press, Cambridge.

Stirling, N. B. (1983). Pearl Buck: A Woman in Conflict. New Win Pub., NY.

Spurling, H. (2010). "Pearl Buck in China: Journey to The Good Earth", Simon and Schuster, NY, NY.

self-supporting enterprises that employed an agriculturalist to provide technical support and advice on improved methods of farming.[12]

14.4 Cooperative Credit and the Sino-Japanese War

In Figs. 14.1 and 14.2 and Table 14.1 we have shown that the number of credit cooperatives increased dramatically over the period 1930 to 1947. We remarked above, and explain here, that this growth was all the more remarkable given that from mid–1937 through 1945 China was engaged in war with Japan. It is not enough to simply mention the war in passing, because the timing and places of occupation had profound effects on the expansion of credit cooperatives and related financial services under *Nong Ben Ju*, and to discuss this era in the absence of these details leaves incomplete a significant aspect of cooperative development in China.

The impact of war on agricultural productivity is not well understood, but war does bring about unforeseen forces that can impact the agricultural economy in many ways. In the following sections we first describe briefly the evolution of the war and map the expansion and timing of occupation forces to the changes in patterns of credit cooperative development. We then discuss the impacts of war on credit from two angles. The first deals with the macroeconomic impacts related to money supply, inflation, and market access. We then drill down to the farm level by reference to a study by John L. Buck and his colleague Chi'ang based on a survey of Sichuan farm households in 1941.

By treaty, the Japanese had agreed to notify the Chinese whenever they had a planned military training exercise. On July 7, 1937, however, the Japanese failed to notify and proceeded to move troops towards the Marco Polo Bridge in Beijing. Chinese troops stationed at the bridge, believing an attack underway, responded with small arms fire and mortar. By the end of the skirmish a Japanese soldier was reported missing and a formal protest was placed. With tensions rising another skirmish took place between Chinese and Japanese troops in the Battle of *Langfang*, a railroad city between Beijing and Tianjin. Two days later on July 27 a regiment of Chinese regulars was encamped outside the Japanese zone in *Tungchow*

---

[12] Yin, Lien-ken (1942). "Twenty-two years of agricultural economics: A review of the work of the Department of Agricultural Economics, College of Agriculture and Forestry, University of Nanjing (1920–42)". University of Nanjing, mimeo. December 1942. page 20.

(currently Tongzhou District, Beijing). Refusing to leave, the Japanese opened fire on the regiment and then ordered the Japanese-trained East-*Hopei* (Hebei) Army to attack. Instead, the East-*Hopei* Army mutinied and attacked the Japanese from within, killing hundreds of soldiers and civilians. The Tungchow mutiny placed increased pressure on the Japanese to engage the Chinese militarily to protect Japanese interests in Beijing.

The first response was to attack Tianjin using land and naval forces, including the destruction of Nankai University which we have previously identified as a major supporter of agricultural cooperation. To avoid the total destruction of Beijing, Chiang Kai-shek ordered all Chinese forces in Beijing to withdraw from the city to Southern Hebei, putting Beijing under Japanese control.

On August 13, 1937 the Japanese crossed from the International Zone in Shanghai into the *Zhabei* district, provoking again a small arms response by the Chinese Peace Preservation Corps. The Japanese responded with a naval bombardment of Chinese positions, triggering then a response by Chiang Kai-shek to retaliate by air and land. This was followed by a declaration of self-defense and the beginning of the war of resistance. The battle for Shanghai continued through October 26, 1937. Meanwhile Japanese troops were landing elsewhere on the East coast and started pressing Westward, including the first bombing of Nanjing in Jiangsu Province on September 21. On December 10, 1937 the Japanese ordered the taking of Nanjing by force, and Nanjing fell into Japanese control on December 13, 1937. In the North, the Taiyuan offensive ended in the almost complete occupation of Shanxi and parts of *Suiyuan* (currently part of Inner Mongolia) by November 9, 1937. Further expansion, was hindered by guerrilla tactics by communist forces including the 8th Route Army. The only other area in the North to be occupied by the Japanese was *Wuyuan* in Inner Mongolia but that was not until January 1940.

With the fall of Nanjing, Chiang Kai-shek ordered the government to move to Chongqing in Sichuan Province, while core government and military personnel moved to Wuhan in Hubei Province. In January 1938 the Japanese decided to press on towards Wuhan, occupying Anhui Province along the way, and further expanded the military theater by advancing troops through Jiangsu, Shandong, and Henan. By March 1938 Shandong, and later Henan, was fully controlled by the Japanese, but large parts of Jiangsu were being defended by a large number of Chinese divisions. It was not until October 1938 that Wuhan and Eastern parts of Hubei were finally occupied by the Japanese. On the Southern coast, the Japanese limited occupation to major coastal ports including Guangzhou (Canton city) in Guangdong in June 1939 and Nanning in Guangxi (Kwangsi) Province in November 1939. From Nanning, the Japanese launched a major offensive up to the *Kunlan* Pass in Guangxi about 60 km Northeast of Nanning, but large areas of Guangxi remained unoccupied.

Figure 14.4 illustrates the areas of occupation by 1940.[13] In the North *Chahar* (now part of Inner Mongolia), most of Suiyuan, Shaanxi, Southern Henan, North and West (of Wuhan) Hubei, all but East and central Hunan, most of Jiangxi except the border areas of Hubei and Nanchang, and the Southern tier of Zhejiang demarked the border area between unoccupied and occupied China. Along the Southern provinces the Japanese occupied only port areas including Xiamen in Fujian, and the inland areas around Guangzhou in Guangdong Province.

As of April 1941, the Japanese had not fully occupied Jiangxi and had made several failed attempts at controlling areas West to Changsha. But between May and September 1942 the Japanese launched the Zhejiang-Jiangxi campaign to rid the countryside of peasants supporting KMT resistance efforts. This campaign was instigated by the rage following the famed Doolittle raids on Tokyo, Nagoya, and Yokohama. The campaign was punitive, with 250,000 civilian casualties, and when done the Japanese returned to their original defensive positions.

It was not until late 1943 that the Japanese broke the stalemate to occupy further territory. This began on November 2, 1943 when the Japanese invaded the city of *Changde* in Northwest Hunan which was neither occupied nor defended. The battle for *Changde* lasted until December 20, 1943 after attack and counterattack that killed upwards of 300,000 civilians. On April 17, 1944 through May 25, 1944 Japanese troops moved from bases in Wuhan (Hubei) and Kaifeng (East central Henan) to central Henan and fully occupied Henan by the month's end. This was the first leg in the Japanese operation targeting Henan, Hunan, and Guangxi. The Japanese sought to open up a corridor between its armies and supplies in North China to Japanese occupation forces in French Indo-China following a route roughly along North-South railroad corridors. Changsha finally fell (after three previous attempts) on June 19,

[13] Source: https://upload.wikimedia.org/wikipedia/commons/9/9a/Second_Sino-Japanese_War_WW2.png.

SUCCESSES AND FAILURES OF AGRICULTURAL COOPERATIVES... 387

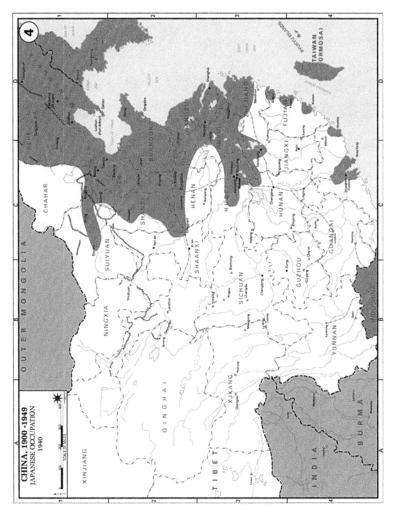

Fig. 14.4 Japanese occupation of China, circa 1940

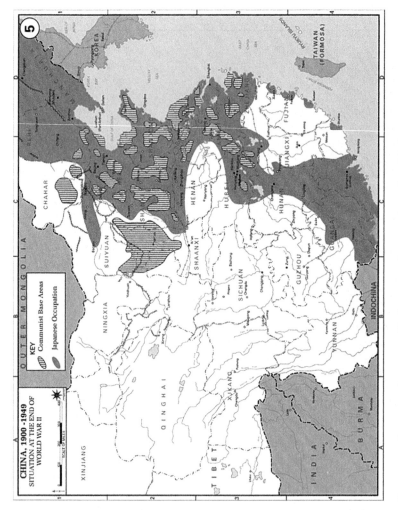

Fig. 14.5 Japanese and communist zones of influence and occupation, circa 1945

1944, and Hengyang, Hunan Province, where there was a large American air base housing the Flying Tigers, fell after 48 days of battle on August 8, 1944. Shortly after, the Japanese moved to occupying areas in Northeast Guangxi Province.

The areas of occupation are illustrated in Fig. 14.5. Between 1942 and 1945 the military map of China had been changed by two titanic forces. The first, as discussed above, was the observable push by the Japanese to open up the corridor from North China to French Indochina. This expanded the occupation zone from the border areas to the East and West of Hunan and Jiangxi, the Eastern half of Guangxi, and the Western half of Guangdong. Although encircled, vast areas of Zhejiang, Jiangxi, and Fujian remained unoccupied.

The second force was the infiltration strategy of the communist forces under Mao Zedong and Zhu De who had established a base in Yan'an in Northern Shaanxi. This followed the Long March from Jiangxi to Shaanxi by way of Sichuan to Yan'an in late 1935. By 1945, the communists had garnered political control in the areas of Shaanxi, *Suiyuan*, and parts of Gansu, and areas in *Chahar* outside of the occupation zone. In addition, they had also infiltrated vast areas within the occupied zones in Shanxi, Hepei, Shandong, Jiangsu, Anhui, Hubei, and Zhejiang from where they ostensibly conducted guerrilla warfare against the Japanese.

By late 1939 and into 1940 the war entered a sort of stalemate. As Theodore H. White and Annalee Jacoby note in *Thunder out of China*: "*China's front lines were secure by 1939; the government was reestablished; war had become the normal way of life. During the first few months after the migration the government hammered out some general routines of administration and built a complex administrative structure above them. There were very few mysteries about the way the Chinese ran their war*".[14] And, as White and Jacoby point out, central to the war strategy was the Chinese peasant farmer. Thus, it was imperative that farmers have the liquidity and economic wherewithal to continually produce sufficient food for the army as well as people involved in the manufacturing of military weapons and hardware, and consumer goods such as food and clothing.

Table 14.6 summarizes the timing of the Japanese occupation in China between 1937 and 1945 ranked by the number of new cooperatives added to the numbers closed. What is clear is that in regions that were unoccupied,

---

[14] T. H. White and A. Jacoby (1946). Thunder out of China, William Sloan Associates, NY, page 68.

Table 14.6 Changes in numbers of credit cooperatives 1937 to 1945 ranked by Japanese occupation

Year	War occupation status	1937	1945	Change
Total		46,983	172,053	125,070
Credit cooperative %		73.60%	38%	−0.356
Sichuan	Unoccupied. Chongqing established as national government	2374	23,400	21,026
Hunan	Occupied to East of Changsha October 6, 1939. Occupied areas to Northwest to Changde December 1943. A central corridor through Changsha occupied June 1944. Large areas East and West of the corridor unoccupied. Hengyang fell August 8, 1944	3674	18,139	14,465
Hubei	Occupied as far West as Wuhan, October 1938	2717	16,522	13,805
Guangxi	Occupied from coast to Nanning, November 1939. Advance to Kunlan Pass December 1939. North-South corridor from Changsha through Nanning to coast occupied May 1944	129	13,692	13,563
Henan	Partly occupied January 1938. Fully occupied April 1944	3484	14,287	10,803
Guangdong	Coastal ports occupied June 1937	20	10,722	10,702
Guizhou	Unoccupied	0	10,187	10,187
Fujian	Unoccupied except for port areas	2615	10,119	7504
Anhui	Japanese offensive May–September 1942 en route to Wuhan, but inlands not occupied	4125	10,574	6449
Zhejiang	Japanese offensive May–September 1942, but inlands not occupied	1195	7641	6446
Jiangxi	Unoccupied until 1944, partially occupied in 1944	4614	11,041	6427
Yunnan	Unoccupied	1487	7162	5675
Shannxi	Unoccupied, Northern Shaanxi controlled by CPC	4009	9345	5336
Gansu	Unoccupied	437	5637	5200
Xikang	Unoccupied	0	1231	1231
Ningxia	Unoccupied	0	788	788
Chongqing	Unoccupied, but suffered aerial bombardment	0	661	661

(*continued*)

Table 14.6 (continued)

Year	War occupation status	1937	1945	Change
Suiyuan	Partly occupied November, 9 1937. Largely controlled by CPC. Wuyuan in Inner Mongolia secured in January 1940	0	367	367
Shanxi	Mostly occupied November 9, 1937	69	320	251
Qinghai	Unoccupied	0	218	218
Liaoning	Occupied 1929/30	0	0	0
Jilin	Occupied 1929/30	0	0	0
Nanjing	Occupied December 13, 1937	0	0	0
Shanghai	Occupied October 26, 1937	0	0	0
Peking	Occupied August 8, 1937	0	0	0
Tianjin	Occupied July 30, 1937	0	0	0
Qingdao	Occupied Janurary 14,1938	1	0	−1
Chahar	Unoccupied	60	0	−60
Rehe	Unoccupied	290	0	−290
Taiwan	Not applicable	750	0	−750
Jiangsu	Occupied following fall on Nanjing, December 1937	3305	0	−3305
Shandong	Occupied January 1938	4965	0	−4965
Hebei	Occupied July 1937	6663	0	−6663

the Chinese government continued to push agricultural cooperation. Sichuan, which was not occupied, increased the number of cooperatives by 21,026. Other unoccupied provinces such as Gansu, Xikang (currently part of Tibet), and Ningxia which had no credit cooperatives in 1937 saw some modest efforts at cooperative development. But even in provinces that were partially occupied, the KMT continued to push cooperative development. Guangxi, partly occupied in 1939, saw an increase of 13,563 cooperatives from 129 to 13,692; Hunan from 3674 to 18,139 with an increase of 14,465.

In occupied areas, cooperatives all but disappeared. Chahar, which was not occupied, lost its credit cooperatives in 1939, two years into the war, and this was likely due to the fact that the areas were firmly controlled by the communists and outside the KMT's sphere of influence. But in Jiangsu, Shandong, and Hebei that were largely occupied early in the war, the cooperative movement all but ended, with virtually all credit cooperatives shut down.

Thus we see that between 1936 and 1942 the rapid rise in credit cooperatives relative to other cooperative types was dramatic, particularly in unoccupied areas of China. But even in provinces that were occupied the

KMT continued to develop cooperatives, which required that the administrative infrastructure remain in place.

The expansion of credit cooperatives continued until 1942 when policy makers decided that greater credit efficiencies could be obtained if credit cooperatives at the village level were consolidated at the township or county level (Hsien). This was called the 'Reform of Chinese County Governance' which was promulgated in 1939 and reformed township and county governance structures. The three-year window for implementation ended in 1942. Once this was accomplished, the last phase was to integrate credit cooperatives into the townships and counties to take advantage of the new governance structures. This applied only to credit cooperatives because most marketing or supply cooperatives were developed in relation to central markets already established.

Another driving force was the issue of local autonomy placing more control of credit cooperatives with officials at the county seat who had much greater political linkages with the KMT. The difference between credit cooperatives and other types of cooperatives was driven to a great extent by the reliance of the credit cooperatives on the formal banking system including the Farmers Bank as a source of capital and credit.

Another reason was the rising inflation that was found in China during the war years after 1937. The rate of inflation was favorable to cooperative prices, but not to costs and as Buck (1943) found from his 1942 study of Sichuan farm households during the war years the demand for credit more than doubled in 1941–42 relative to 1940–41.[15] While capital contributions were increasing in nominal terms the actual capital contributions in total, by cooperative and by members was diminishing greatly in real terms. Thus, in order to preserve capital and to maintain linkages between credit cooperatives and agricultural banks (e.g. Farmers Bank, see Chap. 12) it was imperative that the credit cooperatives achieve viable economies of scale and size in order to exploit any possible efficiency gains, and to decrease the transactional costs associated with raising capital and attracting borrowing funds from the cooperative banks. Thus from 1942 to 1945 we observe a rapid decline in the number of credit cooperatives. Again, this was not due to failures or Japanese encroachment, at least in unoccupied areas, but due to the consolidation effect. We note that the number of cooperatives in total stabilized at least within a narrow limit

---

[15] Buck, J. L., & Ch'iao, C. M. (1942). An Agricultural Survey of Szechwan Province, China. Farmers Bank of China, Chungking, China 1943.

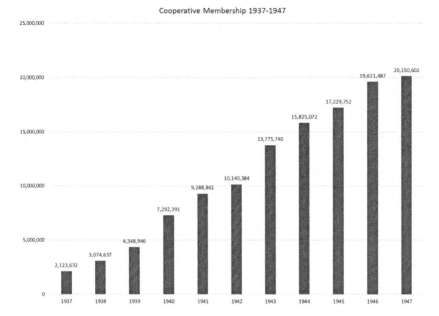

Fig. 14.6 Growth of cooperative membership 1937–47

around 170,000 with the decrease in the number of credit cooperatives being offset by a rise in the number of other-type cooperatives. This is also very clear in Fig. 14.6.

In the broader sense, the effect of the Japanese occupations was fourfold. First, since many credit cooperatives relied on cooperative banks for financial support and loans against capital, the KMT and the banking system found it impossible to maintain capital flows through the various financial institutions and many, if not all, cooperatives closed down or failed in quick succession. The second effect, particularly in townships and counties or villages that were physically occupied by Japanese troops, was an embargo on any type of public gathering of more than a few people. Thus it was impossible to either organize new cooperatives or meet the demands of cooperative meetings to make loan decisions. Third, the KMT both in reconstruction and *Nong Ben Ju* established clear strategies for cooperative development through extension, by-law development, membership drives, and so on. But this required a KMT presence as a governing authority at the local level. This became increasingly difficult as the KMT moved the government from Nanjing to Wuhan in December 1937, and then when Wuhan was occupied in December 1938 to Chongqing with all authorities and bankers asked to evacuate. It should be said, however, that Chiang Kai-shek ordered all high-level ministers and officials as well as all bank managers and executives to stay in place until the last possible moment before evacuation was called.

A fourth reason involves credit demand itself. In 1937, as Japanese troops moved towards Wuhan and elsewhere, Chiang Kai-shek ordered a scorched earth policy of total destruction of crops along the paths of the advancing Japanese armies. This was a deliberate order to deny the Japanese food from harvestable crops and stores held in granaries so that the Japanese advance would ultimately be constrained to the rate at which food could be shipped from ports along the East and Southern coastal regions. Chiang Kai-shek understood that without local food availability the Japanese would not be able to advance by land beyond Wuhan because of the treacherous Yangtze River and the three gorges beyond that. This is indeed what happened and after 1938 the war entered into a kind of stalemate. As for the farmers themselves, many suffered in the areas of Japanese influence, but since the Japanese preferred to remain in towns and cities, more remote counties could still cultivate and harvest a crop, storing grain in caverns, caves, and pits dug below houses, but always at the ready to destroy a crop when faced by a Japanese incursion. It seems quite reasonable that under such conditions there was unlikely to be a demand for credit.

In 1937, the first year after *Nong Ben Ju*, the reported cooperative membership was 2,123,632 persons (Fig. 14.6). Despite the war, membership grew considerably to over 10 million by 1941 when the United States entered the war against Japan, and over 17 million by the end of the war in 1945. Between 1937 and 1947 cooperative membership increased by 848% or by about 85% per year.[16] As membership grew, so too did the capital stock of cooperatives.

Figure 14.7 shows the percentage change in capital stock over this period. Between 1937 and 1938 the change in capital stock was 51% but between 1942 and 1943 it increased by 250%, and at the war's end between 1945 and 1946 by 311%. These numbers are of course a mirage. The war years brought on an extended period of high and hyper-inflation as China printed more and more money to support the war effort. By

---

[16] These are on a simple arithmetic basis. In log form the continuously compounded increase was 225% or 22.5%/year.

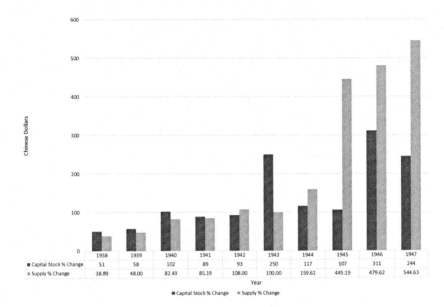

Fig. 14.7 Percentage change in money supply and capital contribution to cooperatives

1940 most sovereign and industrial bonds had been so heavily discounted, and risk premiums on yields were so high, that China found it near impossible to access foreign credit at reasonable rates. Figure 14.7 also shows the percentage increase in the money supply by about 39% between 1937 and 1938, 100% between 1942 and 1943, and 479.6% between 1945 and 1946. This increase in money supply continued as the war of Japanese resistance folded into a civil war between KMT and communist armies.

A consequence of the increased money supply was inflation and any understanding of the cooperatives during this timeframe would be in error if this factor was not fully considered. Figure 14.8 shows the nominal and real values of capital stock held by cooperatives between 1937 and 1947, while Fig. 14.9 shows the figures for capital stock per member. A myopic view suggests fantastic growth in both measures in nominal terms with capital stock rising from $5,309,079 in 1937 to $20,644,291,355 in 1947, an increase of 3888 times. The same myopia would show an impressive rise in member contributions from $113 to $127,471 an increase of 1128 times. But this is not the way to look at it. China faced

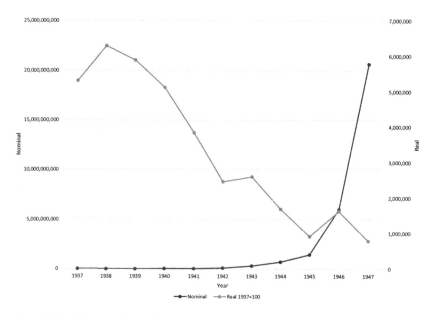

Fig. 14.8 Cooperative capital stock: nominal vs real 1937–47

hyper-inflation throughout this period, not only because of the rise in the supply of money as previously discussed but also in the imperfections of supply and demand in an economy which was virtually closed to any ports for trans-oceanic trade, and until the Burma Ledo road was completed in 1945 no land access to markets either. Inflation indexed to 1937 was 498 in 1940, 12,556 in 1943, 158,362 in 1945, and 2,617,781 in 1947. In other words, a bundle of goods that could be purchased for $100 in 1937 cost $2.618 million in 1947.

The adjusted real values in Figs. 14.8 and 14.9 show a completely different picture of cooperation. In real terms, cooperative capital declined significantly in value from $5,309,079 in 1937 to $922,622 in 1945 and $788,618 in 1947. Likewise, the capital per member also decreased from $2.50/member in 1937 to $0.05/member in 1945 and $0.04/member in 1947. Looked at another way, in 1937 there was sufficient capital stock within the cooperative system to make a loan of $2.50/member without exhausting the capital stock, while at the end of the war the most that could be lent based on capital stock was $0.04/member—a pittance.

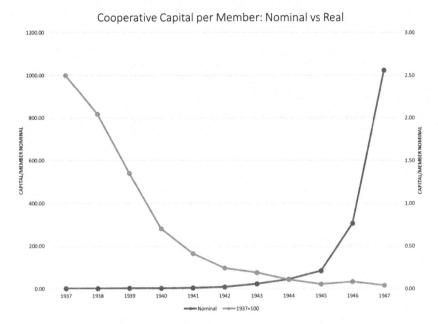

Fig. 14.9 Cooperative capital per member: nominal vs real 1937–47

This then begs the question of how effective the credit cooperatives really were, if at all. How was it possible that the member list included over 20 million members, when there was so little capital to lend in real terms. First, a simple reality check on the member numbers. If the population of China in 1947 was approximately 450 million, of which 80% were farm households, this suggests approximately 350 million farm households. Assuming about five members per household, this translates to something in the neighborhood of 72 million households. Assuming only one member per household, these very rough estimates suggest that something in the order of 28% or more than one in four households belonged to a cooperative and with about 80% of cooperative activity being related to credit this suggests that the cooperative movement provided credit access to some 22% or more than one in five farm households. Furthermore, even if cooperative, policy or government banks provided eight times the capital in loanable funds, the reality was that these banks would have to supply 25 times capital to make even a $1 loan on average to each farmer. While we have run roughshod over numerical accuracy here, the estimates will not be so far off the mark to bring the efficacy and equity of the credit cooperative movement into question.

A 1940/41 study of cooperative banks with deposit, savings, and remittance functions showed an average volume of business of 1,349,000 yuan ranging from 1788.000 yuan to 409,000 yuan yielding a range of profit from 6860 yuan to 169 yuan.[17] Surprisingly, the largest business unit was for remittances which accounted for 45% of business while deposits and credit accounted for 30% and 25% respectively. Between 1938 and 1940 loans more than doubled, while demand deposits increased by a factor of six. Cooperative banks also provided fixed deposits, presumably with higher interest rates, and these increased from 78 yuan in 1938 to 17,000 yuan in 1940—a substantial rate of increase for farmers wanting to reduce the inflationary impact on their savings, but a very small proportion of total business.

While the cooperative banks were managed by professional and career bankers, the same could not be said of the many (non-deposit) cooperative credit societies. These societies were plagued by a host of problems ranging from insufficient capital as the primary problem, to poor accounting, official restrictions, losses from heavy expenses, the encouragement of large loans by officers of the society, officers' personal use of capital funds, irresponsible officers, and difficulties in actually electing officers. The ordering of this list is more or less in importance, but even within the membership there were problems of insufficient attendance at meetings, lack of travel allowances, untimely meetings, and bad living conditions.[18]

Interestingly, we estimated above that the reported membership implied cooperative membership of about 80%. Buck and Ch'iao reported that across 562 cooperatives in 72 Sichuan counties, the participation rate was about 73% of all household heads. Of these cooperatives the average loan in 1938 was 812 yuan but by 1940 this had increased to 2612 yuan. Deposits on the other hand increased from only 15 yuan in 1938 to 69 yuan in 1940, suggesting a fall in loans to deposits from 54.133 in 1938 to 37.86 with the differences in loans to deposits having to be made up of capital.

The average loan in the credit societies was 52.50 yuan varying from between 40 and 68 yuan across the various regions.[19] The reality is that very few farmers were actually able to access credit. As before with *Nong*

---

[17] Buck, J.L., & Ch'iao, C. M. (1942), pages 20–24.
[18] Buck, J.L., & Ch'iao, C. M. (1942), pages 20–21.
[19] Buck, J.L., & Ch'iao, C. M. (1942), page 22.

Ben Ju, credit went primarily to the elites in the village, and with inflation so high it was most likely that elite borrowers would arbitrage inflation with negative real interest rates, and hoard borrowed capital for consumption purposes and an inflation hedge rather than it be put to use for productive purposes. Furthermore, given the power structure within a village at that time, the rapid rise in cooperative membership was more likely due to coercion than the groundswell of credit demand that the membership numbers suggest.

14.5 Impact of War on Farm Credit Demand

With high inflation over this period, combined with the natural calamities that so often hit China, identifying the impacts of the war on farm credit is very difficult. However, in 1941 a survey was conducted by Qi-Ming Qiao of the Farmers Bank of China and John L. Buck of Nanjing University to examine the consequences of the war on farmers over the crop year May 1940 to April 1941. By this time the war was in its fourth year and in a steady state with frequent clashes, but little territory changing hands. The survey conducted in Sichuan was safe from ground fighting and thus ideal to examine the economic consequences of the flow-through effects. Between May 1940 at the beginning of the crop year and April 1941 at the end of the crop year wholesale prices had increased by 153%. In other words, at the time of planting the first crop the breakeven receipts would have had to grow by more than 75% at the end of the first crop, and with the contemporaneously inflated cost of planting the second crop, the breakeven receipts would have to increase by another 75% to again break even in constant dollars at the end of the second harvest. For example, the cost of growing a mou of rice in 1940 across 333 farms growing 3688 mou was 90.49 yuan, which increased 3.873 times to 350.54 yuan/mou. In 1940–41 farm cash receipts for 408 farms averaged 1016 yuan with cash expenses of 969 yuan for a cash income of 46 yuan. A year later cash receipts had risen to 1945 yuan but cash costs rose to 1921 yuan, giving a profit of 24 yuan.[20] Taking inflation of 200.87% between 1941 and 1942 the consumption equivalent relative

---

[20] Source material, Buck, J. L., & Ch'iao, C. M. (1942). Table 7, page 45. In note (a) to this table Buck states that the 1941–42 prices were based on May 1941 prices and that actual prices in 1942 were higher. It is unclear as to whether prices referred to both receipts and expenses or just one or the other, so there may be some imprecision in these numbers.

to 1941 income was 300% less. Thus the 1942 receipts of 24 yuan had only 8 yuan in 1941 purchasing power. At a minimum the average farm household in 1942 required at least 38 yuan in credit just to keep consumption equal based on farm receipts. However, when all household receipts and expenses were considered, the financial condition of the household decreased from −37 yuan in 1937 to −337 in 1940–41 and −1002 in 1941–42. These are in nominal yuan actually received and expensed. The inflation-adjusted loss in 1941–42 was actually −334 yuan in 1941 equivalents which was only slightly lower than the observed −337 yuan recorded for 1941. The point is that with hyper-inflation the Sichuan farmer would have had to borrow 337 yuan in 1942 to balance household receipts and expenses, but to achieve the same breakeven in 1942 the household would have had to borrow 1002 yuan.

What they actually found across farms was a mix of credit supply and demand. Across 216 farms the average credit from all sources was 340 yuan per farmer. This differed by farm type. For example, farm owners borrowed 550 yuan, part-owners 333 yuan, and tenants 293 yuan. There is some evidence of credit rationing in that the actual demand for credit was 678 yuan, 591 yuan, and 466 yuan for each land tenure type respectively. This suggests that on average farmers' demand was unmet by 23.3%, 77.4%, and 59.0% for land owners, part-owners and tenants respectively.

The actual number of farmers surveyed was about 410, and although Buck did not state so explicitly we can reasonably assume that these numbers are only from those farmers who borrowed from one source or another. This suggests that about 53% of farmers had some form of credit. Of these, about 25% of the loan amount of 340 yuan, or about 85 yuan, was borrowed from credit cooperatives, with the remainder coming from other farmers (36%), merchants (24%), landlords (13%), and 2% from miscellaneous sources. In terms of the number of loans however, 48% came from cooperatives, 26% from friends, 21% from relatives, and 5% from other sources. It is difficult to discern cooperative loan amount per cooperative loan borrower because it is more than likely that a farmer would have borrowed from more than one source, and that source need not be a cooperative at all. The 216 households averaging 340 yuan suggests aggregate loans of 73,440 yuan of which 25% is from a cooperative, so then total cooperative borrowing was about 18,360 yuan. With dissatisfaction noted, if we allow proportionality, 48% or 104 households (at least) had one cooperative loan, so that the average loan under this calculation per cooperative borrower was about 176 yuan per cooperative bor-

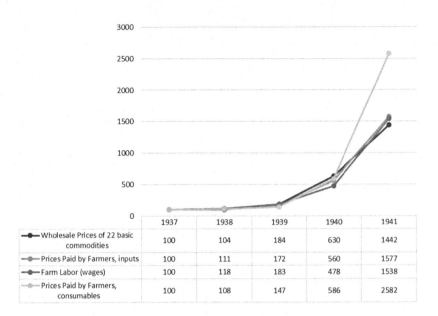

Fig. 14.10 Agricultural indices, 1937-May 1941, Sichuan Province, 1937 = 100

rower. This measure of cooperative credit per cooperative borrower is more than twice the average amount of cooperative credit per borrower. Taking this further, if there are only 104 actual cooperative borrowers then in proportion to the total number of farms surveyed, the proportion of cooperative borrowers is 25.4%. If 73% of households are members of a cooperative society then this suggests that about one in three cooperative members borrowed from the cooperative in 1940. These are very rough estimates and we have our doubts; but this being the best we can do we note the actual capital per member in 1940 across all cooperatives was 3.50 yuan per member, which compares favorably to per member capital found in Buck and Chi'ang's study of 3.40 yuan. Holding on to the one in three ratio this suggests that in 1940 there were 2,430,797 cooperative farm borrowers and by 1947 there would be 6,716,867 borrowers.

The pernicious nature of inflation can be viewed in Fig. 14.10.[21] For the most part wholesale prices of commodities kept pace with the cost of agricultural inputs (1442 yuan vs 1577 yuan in May 1941, an accumulated difference of about 10%). So too did real wages keep up with commodity

[21] Source: Buck and Chi'ang 1943, Table 2, pages 60–61.

prices and expenses (1538 yuan in 1941). But what is striking is the rate of inflation of household consumables which includes food, clothes, energy (mostly wood), and other miscellaneous items. This increased to 2582 yuan by May 1941. Thus not only did farm receipts not keep up with the cost of consumable items but neither did the wage rates paid for farm labor. On this latter point we can see the Ricardian wage effect of rising prices, but we can also see the beginnings of a poverty trap. Here is a situation in which both farmers and laborers faced real poverty, at least relative to the pre-war consumption bundle. And this was to persist, and even worsen, as the war continued.

14.6 Summary

With the efforts starting with the International China Famine Relief Commission, initiatives at the University of Nanjing, and the focus on rural cooperation under rural reconstruction, this chapter investigated how these efforts paid off through the end of the Republican era. What could not have been known at the time of rural reconstruction was the expansion of the Sino-Japanese war in 1937 that lasted until Japan's surrender in August 1945. Hostilities continued until 1948 with the civil War of Liberation between the CPC and the KMT.

What would have happened to cooperative credit had these events not taken place cannot be known. But what is surprising is that despite the war the KMT continued to promote agricultural cooperation. Part of this was to ensure that farmers had access to credit and inputs in order to provide food for the war effort. Between 1932 and 1937 the number of cooperatives increased from 3978 to 46,983 with 87% and 73.6% being credit cooperatives. Despite the war, and the loss of cooperatives in Japanese-held territory the number of cooperatives increased from 46,983 to 172,053 by 1945, with 38% being credit cooperatives. After the war the number of cooperatives decreased to 161,953 by 1947, with 30% being credit cooperatives.

Agricultural credit also increased dramatically during this period, but in nominal amounts. Because of hyper-inflation the real amount of credit extended was barely sufficient to keep up with the real costs of inputs and labor. Farmers saw rapid nominal increases in commodity prices but the costs also increased, and sometimes at a faster rate. To keep pace with the changing agricultural conditions and to ensure ready access to inputs and markets the expansion of cooperatives, credit and otherwise, was an economic necessity.

Index[1]

A

ABC, *see* Agricultural Bank of China
Adams, D.W., 14n23, 15n23
ADBC, *see* Agricultural Development Bank of China
Age distribution, male and female, 1921
  North China, 245
  South China, 246
Agricultural Adjustment Branch, 298
Agricultural and Industrial Bank, 11, 38, 161, 170–176, 173n27, 178, 233, 237n5, 275, 279, 285, 328, 337, 346, 347
  Changpin Agricultural and Industrial Bank, 173
  Tongxian Agricultural and Industrial Bank, 173
Agricultural and Industrial Cooperative Loan Association, 174
Agricultural Bank of China, 3, 5–7, 12, 14, 17–21, 24–26, 29, 38, 279–281, 283, 284, 339, 341, 342, 349
Agricultural Credit Act of 1923, 172
Agricultural Credit Administration, 238
Agricultural credit associations, 172–173
Agricultural and Cooperative Loan Associations, 172
Agricultural and Industrial Workers' Credit Association, 172, 173, 178
Agricultural Development Bank of China, 3, 17, 18
Agricultural financial structure, debates on single and ternary, 340–346
Agricultural intensification, 94
Agricultural loans in base areas, 313
Agricultural Production and Market Department, 342
Agricultural productivity, 2, 15, 32, 35, 55–61, 63–70, 199–202
  historical weather extremes and, 63–69
American Red Cross, 241

[1] Note: Page numbers followed by 'n' refer to notes.

© The Author(s) 2018
H. Fu, C. G. Turvey, *The Evolution of Agricultural Credit during China's Republican Era, 1912–1949,*
https://doi.org/10.1007/978-3-319-76801-4

404 INDEX

Anhui, 8, 8n14, 26n38, 41, 45, 52, 53, 78, 132, 135, 144, 186, 207, 242, 243, 251, 252, 261, 265, 269, 276, 287, 292, 294, 305, 328, 329, 337, 345, 347, 355, 357, 374, 381, 385, 389, 390
Anshi, Wang, reformer, 132
  Ten Thousand Word Memorial, 132
Anti-communist campaign, 264
Arnold, J., 150
Asset dynamics, 96, 96n34, 97, 97n36
Association of Chinese Industrial Cooperation, 298

B
Bailey, L.H., 250n29, 341n10
Baker, T.G., 128n7
Banditry, 55, 61, 157n63, 204n6, 235, 240n11, 258, 287, 287n3, 352, 382, 383
Banister, T.R, 163n4
Bank of China, 5, 22, 38, 145, 146n37, 149n47, 150n50, 175, 176n30, 237n4, 262n9, 267, 267n20, 284, 286n1, 298, 304, 308n15, 310n18, 324, 325n32, 327n1, 330–333, 336–343, 336n3, 337n5, 340n9, 345, 345n15, 347, 349–351, 357n2, 358–360, 358n3, 360n4, 360n5, 362n7, 362n8, 363n9, 363n10, 367, 392n15, 399
Bank of Communications, 298, 310n18, 336, 338, 350, 357, 357n2, 358, 367
Banks specialization, debates on, 339–340
Bao-jia system, 260, 344, 344n12
Barrett, C.B., 96, 96n32, 96n33, 97n36, 98, 98n38, 122
Base area, economic warfare, 321–322

Base area mutual-aid and group guarantees, 320–321
Beiyang army, 167
Beiyang government, 167n12, 178, 328n2
Besley, T., 14n23
Birth rate, 102, 103, 217, 221n8, 225n9, 226, 245
Blueprint
  Agricultural Finance System, 280
  Central Agricultural and Financial Commission, 280
  Central Agricultural Bank of China, 280
  Farmers Banks, 280, 282
  Rural Finance Discussing Committee, 280
Blueprint for credit under rural reconstruction, 277–279, 327, 346, 349
  outline of resolution on blueprint, 278
Bonds, 7, 29, 161, 168, 172, 176, 178, 266–268, 279–282, 314, 331, 336, 339–342, 351, 355, 364, 367, 395
Border currency, 322n31
  and regional trade, 313–316
Border regions and base areas, 304
Boserup, E., 93–95, 93n28
Boucher, S., 33, 33n42
Boulding, K., 57n14, 82n1, 99, 102n41
Bouman, F.J., 131n14
Boxer rebellion, 162, 162n2, 164, 164n5, 258
Brorsen, B.W, 128n7
Buck, J.L., 1n1, 52n2, 78, 78n40, 89, 89n18, 89n19, 89n20, 89n21, 90n22, 92, 92n26, 120, 120n45, 151n52, 152n53, 154n58, 154n59, 155, 155n60, 179–187,

INDEX   405

179n1, 180n2, 180n3, 189–191,
  193, 194, 196, 198, 199, 202,
  203n5, 204, 204n6, 207, 230,
  231, 235, 235n2, 238, 238n6,
  243, 249–252, 250n29, 252n31,
  254, 276, 276n1, 277, 277n2,
  277n3, 277n4, 285, 309n17,
  322, 340n8, 376, 376n3, 377,
  381n10, 383, 383n11, 384, 392,
  392n15, 398–401, 398n17,
  398n18, 398n19, 399n20,
  401n21
Buck, P.S., 383n11
Buck's data, digitizing, 183

C
Calamities
  and catastrophes, 108
  and conflicts, 51, 101, 102
Campbell, C., 304n2, 311n20,
  315n24, 316n25, 317n26
Cang-shui, X., journalist, 237
Cannibalism, 68
Canton, 258, 260n7, 261, 271,
  271n27, 272, 272n29, 382, 386
Canton rebellion, 271–272
Cao, Y., 7n9
Capacity to population ratio, 112–115
Capital investment, 89, 98
Carter, M., 33n42, 96, 96n32, 96n33
CBRC, *see* China Banking Regulatory
  Commission
Central Agricultural Research
  Bureau, 330
Central Cooperative Treasury, 286,
  298, 299, 341–343, 346, 359
  conflicts with Farmers Bank of
    China, 342–344
Central Trust Agency, 298
Chang, G.H., 150n50
Changchun Land Cultivation
  Company, 158

Change in money supply and capital
  contribution to cooperatives, 395
Chantarat, S., 97n36
Chen Du-xiu, 264
Chiang Kai-shek, 53, 53n6, 236, 257,
  258, 260–262, 264, 265, 269,
  271–273, 272n28, 276–278,
  328n2, 331, 333, 338, 343, 360,
  364, 366n11, 371, 385, 394
Ch'iao, C.M., 392n15, 398, 398n17,
  398n18, 398n19, 399n20
Chihli, 238, 239n7, 240, 242–245,
  247, 247n18, 249
Children, selling of, 247
China Banking Regulatory
  Commission (CBRC), 16,
  21–25, 37
China Development Bank, 17
China International Famine Relief
  Commission, 78, 233, 238–242,
  241n12, 242n13, 242n15, 247,
  250–252, 255, 257, 259, 275,
  277, 285, 369, 372, 376–382
China-USA Agricultural Mission,
  339, 341
Chinese Eastern Railway, 155
Chinese National Currency, 166,
  310–312, 310n18, 314, 315,
  317, 321, 321n30, 322, 325
Chinese National Meteorological
  Administration, 63n18
Chinese Nationalist Party, *see*
  Kuomintang
Chinese Postal Savings Bank, 176–177
Chongqing, 25, 25n35, 26n38, 270,
  290, 297, 299, 330, 336, 360,
  364, 366, 367, 374, 385,
  390, 394
Chongqing Rural Commercial Bank, 25
Chow, C.P., 145, 146n37
Christian General, *see* Feng Yu-xiang
Chuang-fang Sun, warlord and
  governor of Jiangsu, 330

Chun, Emperor, 73
Collateral, 7, 11, 12, 14, 22n33, 24, 34, 127, 160, 171, 172, 174, 178, 199, 267
Communist expansion, 260–264
Communist Party of China, 2, 11, 26n38, 37, 266, 276, 303–305, 307–313, 315–321, 315n24, 323, 324, 390, 391
Confucianism, 258
Confucius, 92
Conn, P.J., 383n11
Consumer societies, 237
Consumer surplus, 56
Cooperative capital per member: nominal vs real 1937-1947, 397
Cooperative capital stock: nominal vs real 1937-1947, 396
Cooperative credit
  administrative structures, 286–287
  associations, 291
  funding structure, 288–291
  rules and law, 287–288
  and Sino-Japanese War, 384–399
  system, structure of, 299
Cooperative credit society, 252, 255, 257, 301, 342, 398
  1923-1929, recognition of, 376
Cooperative financial system, 286, 288, 291, 292, 298, 299, 359
Cooperative Loan Association, 174–176, 178
Cooperatives
  distribution and growth of, 373
  geographical distribution of, 374–375
  growth in number of, 370
Cooperatives law, 287
  detailed rules of, 288
Cooperative treasuries, 298, 300
  established by Nong Ben Ju, 1937-1941, 360
  system, 298–300, 341

Copper, 142, 150, 154, 165, 266, 273, 317n27
Corn flour, 313, 316, 323, 324
Cornell University, 32n39, 234n1, 238n6, 250n29, 252, 339, 339n7, 381n10
Cornell-Nanjing story, 339n7
Cotton spinning and weaving, impact of war on, 363–366
County bank, 23, 344, 346
  established, 345
Covariate risk, 97, 97n35, 318, 352
Credit and cooperation, in Shaanxi-Gansu-Ningxia border region, 318–320
Credit conditions, 32–34
Credit constraints, 32, 97n37, 238, 280, 356, 373n2
Credit cooperatives
  associations of cooperatives 1938-1946, 293
  average subscribed capital per member, 289–290
  expansion of, 292–298
  overview of, 370–373
  pre-war impacts of, 373–384
Credit demand, 3, 5, 17, 22n32, 33–34, 34n45, 180, 199, 210, 211, 213, 213n7, 216n7, 217, 221n8, 225–226n9, 230, 230n10, 231, 235, 283, 394, 399
  agricultural productivity, 55, 59, 70, 75, 90, 180, 199, 202, 203, 207, 210, 211, 365, 380, 384
  consumption loans, 180, 190, 212, 221, 224, 226, 231
  crop yield risk, 180
  elasticity, 34, 107, 110, 112, 231
  farm size, 32, 33, 180, 182, 194, 198, 203, 221n8, 231
  impact of war on, 399–402
  percentage of farms obtaining credit, 189, 192

INDEX 407

perfectly inelastic demand, 181
production loans, 180, 190, 191,
  199, 212, 226, 229, 231
productive and market animals, 180
special expenditures, 180, 181, 187,
  194, 196, 211, 213, 217, 225,
  226, 229n10, 230, 231
who is borrowing?, 213–217
Credit rationing, 6n9, 14, 23n33, 34,
  283, 356, 400
Credit reforms, 1978-2016, 26–37
outcomes, 26–35
Credit relief and Yangtze River floods,
  252–254
Credit societies, in base areas and
  border regions, 314
Credit supply, 23, 180, 199, 204, 210,
  211, 216n7, 221n8, 226n9, 230,
  230n10, 267, 336, 350, 400
calamities, 205–206
friends and relatives, 181
sources of farm credit, 191–194
Credit unions, 2
Creditworthy, 30, 174
villages, 3
Crops
  corn, 74, 76, 89, 127, 316, 317,
    323, 324
  cotton, 89, 147, 267, 315, 316,
    318, 320, 347, 357, 358, 363,
    364, 367n11, 368, 377
  figs, 85
  fruit, 4, 68, 85, 199
  kaoliang, 156
  millet, 130, 132, 156, 308, 309, 323
  peanuts, 89, 147
  potatoes, 89
  rice, 54, 73, 74, 84–86, 84n7, 89,
    126, 127, 129, 155, 158,
    158n64, 158n65, 159, 198,
    199, 253, 254, 269, 270,
    317n26, 357, 358, 365, 399
  soybean, 156, 157n63

sweet potatoes, 89
vegetables, 199
wheat, 8, 54, 84, 89, 110, 132,
  147, 155, 191, 198, 199, 253,
  254, 258, 270, 308, 357, 365
Crop yield risks, 202, 205–206,
  208–209
Currency and monetary control, in
  CPC base regions, 310–312
Currency chaos, 164–166

D
Da Wan Agricultural and Industrial
  Bank, 275
Darity, W.A., 93, 93n28, 94
Death rate, 95, 102
Demand for credit, *see* Credit demand
Deng Xiaopeng, 5
Djang, Y.S., 257n2, 378
Doolittle raids, 386
Dorward, A, 15n26
Dowager, Empress, 164n5, 166
Drought, 52–54, 61, 63, 63n18, 64,
  68, 77, 78, 96, 97n35, 97n36,
  101, 116, 120, 121, 125, 138,
  158, 164n5, 191, 204, 204n6,
  207, 212, 238, 247, 248, 316,
  318, 377, 379, 382
  frequency distribution for extreme
    drought, 66
Duara, P., 151n51
DuHalde, P., 71, 71n22, 72n23,
  72n24, 73n25, 73n26, 73n27,
  74n28, 74n29, 74n30, 74n31,
  74n32, 74n33, 75, 75n34,
  76n35, 76n36, 76n37, 76n38,
  77, 78, 85–87, 85n10, 85n11,
  126n6, 133n23
The General History of China,
  71n22
Dujun system, 169
Dynastic rule, agriculture and, 71

E
Earthquake, 52
Egalitarianism, 306
Eighth Route Army, 305, 312, 385
Elvin, Mark, 82n3, 84, 85n8, 85n9, 87, 90–95, 90n23, 99, 110, 121
Engel coefficient, 36

F
Fair burden tax system, 307, 308
  base areas, 305
Familial loans, 8, 15, 26, 29–31
  friends and relatives, 8, 9, 12n17, 15, 15n25, 26, 30, 31, 33, 142, 146, 181, 193, 211
Famine, 52–54, 62, 68, 69, 74, 76, 77, 86, 88, 97n36, 103, 110, 120, 127, 129, 191, 204, 204n6, 233, 234, 236, 238–242, 239n9, 240–241n11, 244, 246–251, 248n21, 258, 259, 268–271, 313, 318, 320n29, 321, 382, 383
  and household economy, 243
  and population, 243–248
Fang Zhi-min, Communist commander, 264
Farm Credit Administration, 173n26, 250n29, 340
Farm Credit Associations, 7
Farm Credit Bureau, 284, 298, 330, 347, 350–367, 367n12
  Agricultural Loans Department, 355–356
  Agricultural Products Department, 353–355
  amount of agricultural loans from four government banks, 359
  amounts of jointly invested capital by participating banks, 352
  reform and dissolution of, 367–368
  uses of loans made by cooperative banks maintained by, 356

Farm Credit System, 7
Farmers Bank of China, 147n41, 265, 265n16, 274, 284, 286, 298, 300, 327, 331–343, 340n9, 345, 345n15, 347, 349, 357, 358
  growth in branches and offices, 333
  loan dispersements by, 334–335
Farmers Bank of Four Provinces, 331
Farmers Bank of Jiangsu, 252, 330, 347, 349
Farmers National Salvation Association, 305
Farmers Storehouses, 342
Farmers Union, Cooperative Society, 342
Federal Farm Loan Act, 1916, 171
Fei, Hsiao-Tung, 131n15, 138n27
Feng Yu-xiang, 53, 261, 271
  Christian general, 271
Field Headquarters of Suppressing Bandits, 287
Financial deepening, 3, 15, 23, 37
Financial inclusion, 37
Financial liberalization, 16
First cooperative savings bank in China, 237
First independent agricultural cooperative, 237
Flooding, 52, 61, 64, 78, 120, 121, 138, 146, 158n65, 204, 207, 241, 248, 252, 253, 269–271
  frequency distribution for extreme flooding, 66
Fo Hi, Emperor, 71
Foreign investment, 25–26
Formal credit, 9–11
Fractal poverty trap, 98–99, 98n38
Fractional, 75, 100, 101, 108, 116, 119, 120, 122
Fractional poverty trap, 108, 113–115, 121, 122
  excursion and, 112, 115, 119, 121
France, 162, 163, 167

Frost, 52
Fu, Hong, 126n5, 148n45, 341n11
Fu Xi, Emperor, 71
Fujian, 26n38, 39, 43, 53, 186, 207, 261, 294, 297, 299, 307n11, 337, 345, 347, 374, 386, 389, 390
Futan University, 237

G
Gamble, S.D., 131n18, 141n29
Gansu, 8, 9, 26n38, 32, 34, 34n45, 42, 46, 52, 102, 186, 191, 206, 207, 214–216, 216n7, 218–220, 221n8, 222–224, 226n9, 227–229, 230n10, 268, 269, 292, 294, 297, 299, 303n1, 318, 340, 345, 374, 389–391
Gardner, B.L., 128n7
Geometric Brownian motion (gBm), 101, 102, 104, 108–111, 116–118
Germany, 163, 167, 171, 233–235, 376
Gold, 148, 165, 166, 266–268, 273, 310n19, 313, 315, 316, 317n27, 321–323, 321n30, 338, 339
Gong, W., 63n18
Gonzales-Vega, C., 15n23
Goodman, D.S.G., 303n1, 304n3, 305n4, 314n22
Government sponsored enterprise, 282
Graham, D.H., 14n23
Grain standard, currency, 308–310, 323, 324
Grameen Bank, 22n32
Granaries, 74, 124–130, 128n7, 133n23, 160, 241, 260, 265, 308, 316, 345, 346, 394
 borrowing against stored grain, 127
 Chang Ping Cang (ever-normal granary), 126–128
 charity granary, 126, 128–132
 commonalities with Commodity Credit Corporation (CCC), 128n7
 community granary, 128–131, 130n11, 130n12
 and demand for credit, 127
 grain shortages and famines, 127
 She Cang (community/local granary), 126
 storage, 54, 124–128, 125n2, 270, 300, 317, 317n27, 350, 353, 355
 Yi Cang (charity granary), 126, 128–131
Great Britain, 82n1, 162, 322, 383n11
Green Sprouts Policy, 132–133, 160
 Green Sprout money, 132
 mutual guarantee, 133
Gresham's Law, 165
Group guarantees, 11–12, 12n17, 14, 22–23n33, 178, 234
Group lending, 22, 22n32
Guangdong, 26n38, 39, 43, 53, 144, 186, 205, 207, 264, 271, 272, 294, 340, 345, 374, 386, 389, 390
Guangxi, 3, 26n38, 39, 43, 186, 205, 207, 213n7, 214–216, 218–220, 222–224, 225–226n9, 227–229, 230n10, 261, 264, 271, 272, 292, 294, 297, 299, 340, 345, 355, 356, 374, 386, 389–391
Guarantee companies, 17
Guirkinger, C., 33n42
Guizhou, 26n38, 42, 46, 52, 186, 205, 207, 214–216, 217n7, 218–220, 221n8, 222–224, 225–226n9, 227–229, 230n10, 292, 295, 297, 345, 355, 356, 374, 390
Guo, P., 17n29
Guo-fu, C., 262

H

Hagen, E.E., 57n14, 88, 88n17, 95, 95n30, 95n31
Hail, 52
Hainan, 26n38
Han dynasty, 126
Han Wu Di, Emperor, 126
Hao, Z, 63n18
Harbin Commercial Bank, 17
Harbin dollars, 156
Harbin notes, 157n63, 269
He, G., 7n9, 33n44
Hebei, 26n38, 39, 43, 52, 81, 109, 131n13, 132, 147n44, 153, 185, 205, 207, 214–216, 218–220, 221n8, 222–224, 225–226n9, 227–229, 230n10, 287, 292, 294, 303n1, 304, 305, 308–310, 310n19, 313, 313n21, 314, 323–325, 337, 340, 345, 355, 374, 385, 391
Heilongjiang, 8, 8n12, 9, 26n38, 43, 157n63, 269
Henan, 26n38, 32, 41, 45, 52, 53, 76, 77, 132, 168, 186, 207, 238, 247, 259, 261, 265, 276, 287, 294, 297, 303n1, 306, 310, 310n19, 313n21, 314, 329, 337, 345, 347, 363, 374, 382, 385, 386, 390
Hezuo Jinku, *see* Cooperative treasuries, system
Hezuoshe Lianshe, see Cooperative credit associations
High-level equilibrium trap, 90–93, 90n23
  compared to low-level equilibrium trap, 90
Hired labor and subsidiary labor, 202–204
Hoarding, 239, 317
Hoarding currency, 316–318
Hong Kong, 25, 267, 272, 312, 322
Hoover, President Herbert, 270
Household income, 2, 8, 9, 32, 33, 243, 244
Household responsibility system, 2, 6
Howard, H.P., 235, 235n3
HSBC, 24, 25, 26n37
Hsu, Chi-Lien, 131n17, 154n57, 171n21, 171n22, 172n24, 172n25, 173n27, 173n28, 176n29, 176n31, 176n32
Hsu, L., 257n1
Hsu, P., 249–252, 377, 380, 383
  Shanghai Commercial and Savings Bank, 252, 357, 357n2
Hu, H., 180n2, 180n3
Huang, J., 4n5
Huang, P., 72, 84, 84n6, 92, 92n27, 99, 99n39, 103, 109, 109n44, 149n46, 261
Huang Di, Emperor, 72
Hubei, 2n2, 24n34, 26, 26n38, 41, 45, 53, 156, 168, 261, 264, 265, 269, 272, 276, 287, 292, 294, 297, 303n1, 306, 324, 329, 330, 337, 345, 347, 355, 356, 374, 385, 386, 389, 390
Hui, 273
Human capital, 84, 103, 106–108, 110, 112, 121
Hunan, 2n2, 26n38, 41, 45, 52, 53, 147, 148, 237, 241, 261, 264, 265, 269, 272, 292, 294, 297, 337, 345, 355, 356, 363, 374, 386, 389–391
115th Division, 305, 312
Hungman society, 262
Hurst coefficient, 117–119, 121, 122
Hyperinflation, 166, 301, 315n24, 323, 332, 396, 402

I

India, 32n39, 84n7, 90n23, 94, 97n37, 373n2
Industrial Development Bank of China, 172
Informal loans, 8, 26, 29, 33
Inner Mongolia, 17n30, 26n38, 41, 45, 303n1, 358, 385, 386, 391
Interest rates, 3, 8, 17, 23, 34, 128, 133n23, 142, 146, 171, 179, 180, 190, 191, 194, 196, 211, 212, 217, 224–226, 229–232, 249, 265, 313, 336, 346, 380, 398, 399
and credit demand, 190
International China Famine Relief Commission, 69, 255, 346, 402
Involution, 84, 91, 92, 103
Ironsides, 261, 271
Ito's Lemma, 101, 104–106, 109

J

Jacoby, A., 389, 389n14
Japan, 11, 38, 52, 53n5, 156, 156n61, 157, 158n64, 158n65, 159, 163, 166, 167, 170, 204, 204n6, 205, 252, 258, 263, 263n10, 266–268, 270, 291n5, 292, 300, 301, 303–308, 303n1, 310–312, 310–311n19, 312–313n21, 314, 315, 317, 317n27, 318, 321–324, 321n30, 329, 330, 332, 357, 357n2, 360, 362–365, 369, 372, 373, 382–386, 383n11, 389–391, 393–395, 402
Japanese and communist zones of influence and occupation, circa 1945, 388
Japanese Controlled Currency, 310–314, 321, 322
Japanese occupation
changes in numbers of credit cooperatives 1937 to 1945, 390–391
of China, circa 1940, 387
effects of, 393
Japanese puppet government, 306
Jia, X., 17n29
Jiangsu, 5n6, 13, 26n38, 39, 43, 52, 102, 135, 145, 154, 168, 180n2, 186, 207, 237, 242–245, 248, 270, 286, 287, 292, 303n1, 305, 337, 340, 347, 352, 355, 374, 377, 380, 385, 389, 391
Jiangxi, 2n2, 3, 26n38, 41, 45, 52, 53, 85, 260–262, 264, 265, 269, 271, 276, 287, 292, 294, 299, 307n11, 329, 337, 345, 347, 355, 374, 386, 389, 390
Jiaqing, Emperor, 148
Joint Administration Office of Four Policy Banks, 333, 336–339
Joint Administration of the Four Government Banks, 338
Joint liability, 11–12, 14, 24, 173, 279
Joseph effect, 62, 247, 247n18

K

Kaldor, N., 124, 125, 125n2
Kang Wang, Emperor, 74
Keating, P., 306n7, 306n9, 306n10, 307n11, 318n28, 320n29
Khantachavana, V.S., 33n43
Kirin provincial notes, 157n63
Kong, R., 7n9, 12n17, 15n25, 32n40, 33n41, 33n44, 34n45
Korea, 158, 158n65, 159
Kropp, J.D., 97n37, 373n2
Kumar, C.S., 32, 32n39, 97n37, 373n2
Kung, H.H., President of the Executive Yuan and Minister of Finance, 360

INDEX

Kuomintang, 2, 166, 167, 167n12, 236, 238, 257, 258, 261–265, 271, 276–279, 281, 283, 285, 292, 298, 300, 304–307, 304n3, 307n11, 310–312, 311n19, 314n23, 318, 321–323, 321n30, 328n2, 329, 331, 336, 344, 350, 366n11, 369, 372, 373, 386, 391–393, 395, 402
Kuribayashi, S, 179n2
Kydd, J., 15n26

L

Labor, man-equivalent, 89
Lai, Jian-cheng, 287n4, 292n7
Land
  and agricultural productivity, 58
  elasticity, 84, 103, 112
  farm holdings in local mou, 245
  land per capita, 89, 91, 112
  land tenancy, 154, 319
  lease contracts, 154–160
  mortgaging land, 151–154
  parceling, 116
  size of farm business, 198–199
  subdivision of, 86, 247
  usufruct rights, 151–154
Land Finance Department, 341, 342
Land redistribution under Communists, 264
Land tenancy
  cash-crop system, 154
  cropper system, 154
  share system, 154
Land to labor ratio, 63, 84
Land to population ratio, 119, 122
Land use
  livestock and fertility maintenance, 197
  rights, 2, 7, 37
Lease contracts
  Changchun lease, 158
  Manchurian lease, 155–157

Lee, F.E., 164n7, 178n35
Lei, L., merchant, 148
Lending companies, 16, 18
Li, S., 170
Li, X., 63n18
Liang, Y, 63n18
Liang piao (grain tickets or vouchers), 308
Liaoning, 10, 11, 26n38, 39, 43, 185, 205, 207, 221n8, 295, 374, 391
Likin, 53, 162–164, 168, 169, 177
Lin, J.Y., 16, 16n28, 82n1, 82n2, 82n3, 84, 92, 93, 106, 106n43, 239n9
Lin, Y., 286n1
Lindsay, M., 305n4, 305n5, 306n6, 307n12
Liping Bai, 130n12
Liu, Q., 144n35, 147n40
Livestock
  cattle, 68, 171, 196, 234
  chickens, 198
  donkeys, 196
  hogs, 86, 198
  labor animals, 196, 212, 213
  oxen, 73, 89, 196, 198, 240, 380
  productive animals, 196, 198
  sheep, 198
Loan
  amounts, 189
  purposes, 1924-1930, 380
  status, December 1929, 382
Local mou, as tax base, 73, 199, 309, 309n17
Locusts, 52, 61, 76, 78, 270
Long March, 306–307, 307n11, 329, 389
Low-level equilibrium trap, 79, 87–90, 87n16, 98, 99
  escaping from, 88
Lu, G., 147n41
Luxi Bank, 312–313, 312n21
Luxi currency, 312

INDEX   413

M
Ma, J., 7n9, 33n44
Mckinnon, R.I., 3n3
Major banks lending to agriculture, circa 1937, 337
Mallory, W.H., 239, 240, 240n11, 291n6, 376, 378n4, 379, 380, 382
Malone, C.B., 241, 241–242n13, 242, 242n14, 242n16, 249
Malthus, T.R., 56–61, 56n10, 56n11, 56n12, 57n13, 58n15, 59n16, 59n17, 63, 69, 70, 75, 76, 86, 86n12, 86n13, 86n14, 94, 95, 99, 101, 102, 121
  vice, virtue, and population growth, 60
Malthusian trap, 57, 57n14, 61–63, 75, 88, 95, 107
Manchu dynasty, 166
Manchuria, 53, 155, 158n64, 158n65, 205, 263, 263n10, 266, 269, 270, 311, 363, 382
Manchurian bank notes, 311
Manifesto of the National Production Conference, 364
Mao Zhedong, 5, 13n21, 53, 264, 272, 329, 389
Markov process, 117
Meagher, P., 33n44, 34n45
Mexican dollar, 165
Mexico, 33n43
Mi, G., 144n34
Microcredit, 13, 15n25, 17, 30
  companies, 17
Microfinance institutions, 22
Microloan companies, 16
Migration, 95, 101, 102, 389
Ming dynasty, 69, 74, 76, 77, 128n8, 130, 144, 150, 269, 399
Ministry of Agriculture and Mining, evolution of, 328
Missionary, 71, 85n9, 131, 239, 241, 250, 251, 276

Money lenders, 9, 26, 350, 381
  See also Traditional credit
Money lending society, 144–147
  Dian Dang (pawn shops), *see* Traditional credit, pawn shops
Money loan society, 131–151
  Biao Hui (bidding society), 135, 141–144
  Duiji Hui (Amounts increasing society), 135–138
  IRR (Internal rate of return), 136–138, 140, 141
  Lun Hui (rotating society), 135, 139–141
  Suojin Hui (Subscription decreasing society), 138–139
  Yao Hui (dice throwing society), 134, 135
Monte Carlo, 81, 109, 111–116
Morduch, J., 373n2
Morrison, J., 15n26
Mortgages, 7, 37, 151n52, 172, 176, 253, 279, 282, 341, 355
Mortgaging land, Tien, 151
Mude, A.G., 97n36
Mukden provincial notes, 157n63
Mutual-aid societies, 259, 265, 266, 319, 320, 372
Mutual-help associations, 24
Myers, R.H., 131n13, 146n39, 147n44, 151n52, 153, 153n54, 153n55, 153n56
Myers, W.I., 250n29

N
Nanjing Agricultural University, 179, 180n2
Nanjing College of Agriculture and Forestry, 250, 251
Nanjing incident, 382
Nanjing University, 249, 250, 254, 255, 257, 285

Nankai University, 257
Nathan, A.J., 241n12
National Flood Relief Commission, 52, 52n2, 259
National Rural Social-Economic Survey, 26
National Spiritual Mobilization, 361
Native banks, 147–151, 313, 314
 Shanxi native banks, 148, 149
Nayak, G.N, 7n9
Needham, Joseph, 82, 82n1
Needham puzzle, 82–87, 82n1, 89, 91–94
Nelson, R.R., 87, 87n16, 88, 90, 98, 99, 108, 111, 121
New Countryside Campaign, 16–24
1931 Flood, 52n2
Ningshu Agricultural Relief Association, 253
Ningxia, 26n38, 42, 46, 186, 207, 214–216, 216n7, 218–220, 222–224, 226n9, 227–229, 230n10, 295, 303n1, 318, 340, 374, 390, 391
Nong Ben Ju, 238, 274, 284, 298, 300, 330, 339, 347, 350, 351, 353, 357–367, 370, 372, 384, 393, 394, 398–399
 mobilization effort under, 361
North, D.C., 124n1
Northern Bureau of the Central Committee of the CPC, 311
Northern expedition, 170, 236, 238, 258, 261, 285, 328, 328n2, 330, 382–383
Nurkse, R., 87, 87n15, 121

O
Opium, 53, 54, 162, 258, 281n5
Opium Wars, 162
Organic Law of the Farm Credit Bureau, 365

Outline for County-level Cooperatives, 287
Output dynamics, 104–108, 119
Output per capita, 88, 90, 91, 95, 111, 116
Output to land ratio, 112

P
Patriocracy, 86
Pawn shop, *see* Traditional credit, pawn shops
PBC, *see* Peoples Bank of China
Peking National University, 237
Peking United International Famine Relief Committee, 239n8, 247n18, 248n20, 248n22, 249n23, 249n24
Peking United International Relief Committee, 241
Peng, Y., 12n17
Peoples Bank of China, 4, 5, 12, 24
Perkins, D., 82, 83, 83n4, 83n5, 93, 100, 100n40, 104, 104n42, 109n44
Perry, E., 164n5, 262n8, 265n15
Policy rationing, 34
Political economy and dynastic rule, 70–77
Population growth, 55–61, 77, 86–88, 91, 92, 93n28, 94, 94n29, 99, 101, 102, 104, 107–109, 115, 120, 320
Population to capacity ratio, 102
Postal Remittance and Savings Bank, 346
Postal Savings Banks, 18, 20–22, 25, 176, 281, 328
Poverty, 2, 15, 16, 20, 21, 23, 35–38, 53, 54n8, 55, 57, 60, 61, 78, 86–88, 93–103, 96n32, 96n33, 96n34, 97n36, 108, 112–114, 116–122, 132, 194, 243, 251, 313, 319, 329, 380, 381, 402

Poverty line, 243
Poverty reduction, 35–37
Poverty trap, 55, 60, 79, 86, 88, 93, 95–103, 96n32, 96n33, 96n34, 97n36, 108, 112–114, 116–122, 402
Production Credit Associations, 173, 173n26, 282, 341
Provisional Cooperative Legislation for Rural Cooperatives, 252
Provisional Regulations of Cooperatives, 287
Pugh, J., 276n1, 277n2, 277n3, 277n4
Puppet banks, 314
Puyi, child Emperor, 166

Q

Qianlong, Emperor, 148
Qi-ming, Q., 343
Qing dynasty, 71, 74, 76, 99, 128n8, 130, 144, 148–150, 152–154, 160–164, 164n5, 166, 167, 167n12, 169, 170, 177, 234, 235, 258, 275, 328, 346
Qinghai, 9, 10, 26n38, 42, 46, 186, 205–207, 214–216, 216n7, 218–220, 221n8, 222–224, 226n9, 227–229, 230n10, 294, 374, 391
Qing Hua University, 241
Qinxian, 243, 244, 249

R

Raiffeisen model, 7, 171, 234–237, 242n15, 283, 376
  Agricultural Central Loan Bank for Germany, 235
Raiffeisen, F.W., 234
Rainfall, frequency distributions of, 65
Ravallion, M., 239n9

RCCs, *see* Rural Credit Cooperatives
RCCU, Rural Credit Cooperative Union
Red Spears Society, 262
Red Swastika Society, Shanghai, 53, 53n7
Reisner, J., 238, 252, 339n7, 383
Renminbi, 166, 308n15, 325n32
Renzong, Emperor, 132
Responsibility system, 4, 5, 6n9
Ricardian rents, 55, 58, 77, 94, 402
Ricardo, D., 56, 56n11, 58, 59, 61, 63, 69, 121
Risk rationing, 33n42, 33n43, 34
ROSCA, *see* Rotating Savings and Credit Associations
Rotating Savings and Credit Associations (ROSCA), 124, 131, 137–139, 141, 160, 273
Rozelle, S., 4n5
Rural Commercial Banks, 22
Rural construction vs reconstruction, 257
Rural Cooperative Banks, 1, 22, 25
Rural Cooperative Committee, 287
Rural Cooperative Credit Societies, 238
Rural Credit Banks, 1, 13, 13n21, 22, 25
Rural Credit Cooperatives (RCCs), 1–6, 2n2, 6n9, 8, 12–14, 13n19, 13n21, 18n31, 19–30, 22n33, 32–34, 38–50, 248–249, 287
Rural Credit Cooperative Union (RCCU), 6, 13, 18n31, 22n33
Rural credit societies, 2
Rural Credit Syndicate, 357
Rural Financial Institutions, 17
Rural Mutual Credit Cooperatives, 18
Rural reconstruction, 2, 38, 82, 255, 257, 257n1, 259, 260, 264, 264n11, 273, 277, 278, 285, 327–331, 350, 357, 366n11, 402

Rural *conti.*
  and Chinese Communist Party, 264–266
  and lack of currency control within China, 268–269
  and price volatility in copper, silver and gold, 266
Russia, 148, 155, 156n61, 162, 163, 167, 262

S
Salisbury, H.E., 307n11
Selden, M., 306n8
Self-help, 257, 276
Sen, A., 239, 239n9, 258
7 Cs of rural credit, 33n44
Shaanxi, 26n38, 32, 34, 34n45, 42, 46, 52–54, 77, 207, 238, 247, 269, 271, 292, 303n1, 307n11, 311, 318, 319, 329, 337, 347, 355, 356, 363, 375, 382, 386, 389, 390
Shan, Q., 138n26
Shandong, 3, 6n9, 12, 26n38, 39, 43, 52, 76, 81, 102, 109, 116, 131n13, 147n44, 148, 151, 153, 156, 168, 186, 205–207, 238, 241, 242, 247, 261, 269, 287, 292, 294, 303n1, 305, 306, 310, 310n19, 312, 312–313n21, 314, 321, 323, 324, 337, 345, 355, 363, 375, 382, 385, 389, 391
Shang dynasty, 76
Shanghai, 53, 53n7, 78, 144n34, 144n35, 145, 146n37, 147n40, 149, 165, 175, 237, 258, 263, 263n10, 265, 267, 268, 295, 312, 317n26, 322, 331, 337, 350, 351, 357, 357n2, 358, 362, 362n8, 363, 367n12, 375, 382, 383, 385, 391
Shanghai incident, 263n10
Shanxi, 26n38, 41, 45, 144, 148, 149, 149n46, 154, 168, 185, 207, 213n7, 214–216, 218–220, 221n8, 222–224, 225–226n9, 227–229, 230n10, 241, 247, 269, 271, 292, 294, 303n1, 305–309, 310n19, 313n21, 314, 325, 337, 345, 355, 375, 385, 389, 391
Shao Shi-ping, Communist commander, 264
Shaw, E.S., 3n3
Shen, C, 63n18
Shen, H.Y., 52n2
Shen, M., 4n5
Shen Nong, Emperor, 72
Shenzong, Emperor, 132
Shi Zong, Emperor, 76
Sichuan, 17n30, 26n38, 42, 46, 53, 77, 142, 148, 186, 207, 252, 261, 270, 292, 294, 297, 298, 340, 355, 356, 372, 375, 385, 389–392, 398, 399, 401
Silk Road, 160
Silk worms, 73, 171, 377
Silver, 52, 142, 147, 148, 150, 154, 162, 165, 166, 263, 266, 268–270, 273, 312, 312n21, 313, 315, 316, 317n27, 323, 338, 339
Simon, J., 82n1, 94, 94n29, 383n11
Sinha, R.P., 85n8, 90, 90n23, 91n24
Sino-Japanese war, 11, 38, 166, 258, 304, 306, 318, 322, 324, 331, 336, 338, 370, 402
Skinner, J.W., 95, 273, 273n30, 274
Small and medium enterprises, 17
Small Sword Society, 262
Smith, A., 133n23
Smith, A.H., 131, 131n16, 131n19, 135n25
  Chinese characteristics, 131, 165, 194

Smith, J.F.H., 128n8
Smythe, L.S.C., 52n2, 344, 344n13
Snow, E., 51, 51n1, 64, 68n19
Song dynasty, 84n7, 92, 129, 132, 144, 160, 273
South Manchurian Railway, 155
Special expenditures
  birthdays, 180, 213, 217
  birth of sons, 180
  dowry, 180, 211, 213, 217
  funerals, 180, 194, 196, 211, 217, 220, 221, 221n8, 225n9, 231, 249, 380, 381
  weddings, 8, 180, 187, 194, 196, 211, 217, 220, 221, 221n8, 225n9, 231, 249, 381
Spurling, H., 383n11
State-run bank, 331
Stiglitz, J.E., 16, 16n28
Stirling, N.B., 383n11
Stochastic differential equation, 101, 108, 109
Stokes, W.N., 173n26
Stross, R.E., 250n28, 251n30
Su, Q., 180n3
Sua Shou Yuan, 322n31
Subsistence, 51, 55–57, 59–61, 63, 70, 74, 75, 77, 84, 86, 88, 95, 101, 102n41, 110, 113–115, 120, 122, 124, 126
Sui dynasty, 74, 92, 126, 129
Sui Wen Di, Emperor, 74
Sun Yat-sen, 166, 167, 237, 261, 275, 276, 278, 286n2, 328n2, 366n11
Surplus, economic drivers of, 58
Suzhou, 175, 243, 244, 363
Swallow, B.M., 98, 98n38, 122

T
Tael, 150, 163, 165
Tai Kan, Emperor, 74
Taiping rebellion, 100, 130, 163, 177

Taiwan, 26n38, 287n4, 292n7, 294, 295, 340, 375, 391
Tai Zong, Emperor, 75, 76, 129
Tan, C.C., 162n2, 164n5
Tang, A.M., 92, 92n25, 93
Tang dynasty, 75, 76, 129, 164
Tariff, 162, 164, 168, 169, 177
Tariff autonomy, 162–164
Tartars, 74, 76
Taxation and dues, 53, 54, 75, 76, 129, 131, 147, 152, 153, 155, 157n63, 158, 162, 164, 168, 169, 172, 177, 236, 261, 262, 272, 277, 281n5, 304, 307, 310, 314, 316, 322, 323, 344
  bandit-suppression duties, 53
  land registration fees, 53
  land tax, 53, 54
  military dues, 53
  opium land duty, 54
  poll tax, 53
Tayler, J.B., 77, 78, 78n39, 134n24, 238, 241, 242n13, 242n15, 243, 243n17, 244, 246, 249–252, 249n26, 250n28, 250n29, 254, 259n3, 264n12, 336, 378n4
Tcheou dynasty, 133n23
Technology adoption, 35
Temple, R., 69n21
Temporary Regulations of Banking Control in Wartime, 337
13th Five-Year Plan (2016-20), 37
Thomson, J.C. Jr, 250n28
Three People's Principles, 275, 286n2
3SLS, *see* Three-stage least squares
Three-stage least squares (3SLS), 180, 210, 212–214, 213n7, 216–217n7, 217, 218, 221, 221n8, 222, 224–227, 225–226n9, 230, 230n10, 232
Town and village enterprises, 6
Township and village enterprises (TVEs), 4, 5, 9, 11, 12

Traditional credit
  money lenders, 124
  pawn shops, 26, 29, 54, 124, 144, 146, 147, 249, 264, 355
  Piao Hao (old-style native private banks), 124, 147–151
  Qian Hui (money-loan society), 124, 131–151, 160
  Qian Zhuang (money shop), 124, 147–151
  ROSCA-rotating saving & credit association, 124
  See also Granaries
Treaty of Nanjing, 162
Treaty of Tianjin, 162, 163
Trescott, P.B., 242n15, 250n28, 250n29, 254, 378n4
Ts'ai, K'O-Hsuan, 164n6
Tullock, G.C., 304n2, 311n20, 315n24, 316n25, 317n26
Tungchow mutiny, 385
Turvey, C.G., 3n4, 6–7n9, 7n11, 12n17, 15n25, 15n27, 32, 32n39, 32n40, 33n41, 33n43, 33n44, 34n45, 96n34, 97n36, 97n37, 128n7, 173n26, 234n1, 341n10, 373n2
TVEs, *see* Township and village enterprises

U

Unification vs egalitarianism in base areas, 306
United States of America, 7, 16, 64, 88, 89, 92n26, 128n7, 162, 163, 164n7, 165, 166, 171, 171n23, 172, 266, 267, 270, 274, 282, 283, 310n19, 312, 322, 340, 340n8, 341n10, 364, 366n11, 394
University of Liverpool, 250

University of Nanjing, 238, 238n6, 251–253
Urban Commercial Banks, 17, 25
Usufruct rights, Chih-ti chieh-chien, 151

V

Verteramo Chiu, L., 33n43
Vietnam, 84, 84n7
Village and Township Banks (VTBs), 16, 18n31, 25
Village Banks, 18, 23–24
Von Pischke, J.D., 14n23
VTBs, *see* Village and Township Banks

W

Wagel, S.R., 165
Wakeman, F.E. Jr., 69n21
Wales, N, 369n1
Wang, W.C, 63n18
Wang Mang, Emperor, 76
Wanpaoshan Incident, 158n64
Warehouses, 331, 333, 353–355, 358, 367
Warlord era, 162, 167–169, 177, 241
Warren, G.F., 250n29
Warren, S., 52n2
Washington Consensus, 15, 15n24, 16
Water control projects, 83
Weather insurance, 97n36
Wei, H., 313n21
Wen Di, Emperor, 126, 129
White, T.H., 389n14
Wiener process, 104, 106
Williams, J., 383n11
Winchester, S., 82n1
Wind, 52
Working, H., 124, 125, 125n2, 317n27

Wu Dingchang, Minister of Industry, 350
Wuhan, 269, 270, 330, 336, 363, 367, 385, 386, 390, 394

X
Xia dynasty, 73
Xian-zhou, X., economist and expert on cooperatives, 237, 330
Xiao, Z., 143n32
Xiao Ming Di, Emperor, 74
Xiaozong, Emperor, 129
Xinjiang, 26n38, 42, 46
Xizang, 26n38
Xi Zhu, philosopher, 129
Xi Zong, Emperor, 76
Xu Liu, 129n10

Y
Yan, J., 7n9
Yan'an, 303n1, 306n7, 307n11, 311, 318, 389
Yang, H.K., 237n4, 262n9, 265, 265n16, 266n17
Yangtze River, 76, 131n15, 138n26, 138n27, 207, 258, 259, 263, 269–272, 292, 298, 372, 383n11, 394
Yangtze River floods, 207, 252, 263, 269–271
Yanjing University, 241, 250, 254
Yan Xi-shan, warlord and governor, 261, 271
Yao, Emperor, 73
Yellow River, 52, 52n3, 52n4, 68, 74, 76, 77, 248, 271

Yenching University, 257
Yieh, Tsung-kao, 327n1
Yieh, Y.C., 52n2
Yuan dynasty, 130
Yuan Shikai, 165–167, 178, 328n2
Yunnan, 26n38, 42, 46, 186, 205–207, 213n7, 214–216, 218–220, 221n8, 222–224, 226n9, 227–229, 230n10, 292, 295, 297, 299, 340, 345, 363, 375, 390

Z
Zarrow, P, 167n11, 167n12, 168n14
Zhang, D., 63n18
Zhang, L., 4n5
Zhang, Y., 281n5
Zhang Yin-wu, General, 305
Zhejiang, 5n6, 26n38, 39, 43, 52, 135, 144, 149, 175, 186, 206, 207, 237, 242, 243, 261, 264, 287, 292, 297, 299, 337, 340, 345, 347, 350, 352, 357n2, 367, 375, 386, 389, 390
Zheng, W., 180n2
Zhiping Chen, 130n11
Zhong, F., 180n2, 180n3
Zhong Ding, Emperor, 76
Zhongyang Hezuo Jinku, see Central Cooperative Treasury
Zhou, L., 96n34
Zhou dynasty, 74
Zhu De, 53, 264, 272, 389
Zung, W.T., 77, 78, 78n39

CPSIA information can be obtained
at www.ICGtesting.com
Printed in the USA
LVOW13*0821030618
579368LV00008B/99/P